Baltimore Sports

SPORT, CULTURE & SOCIETY

DAVID K. WIGGINS, SERIES EDITOR

Other Titles in This Series

Baltimore Sports

Stories from Charm City

Edited by Daniel A. Nathan

Hope you enjoy the book, Jack.

Best wishes,

Daniel Nathan

The University of Arkansas Press
Fayetteville
2016

To Baltimore and Baltimoreans, everywhere
And SBZ, who mean so much

Contents

Series Editor's Preface

Sport is an extraordinarily important phenomenon that pervades the lives of many people and has enormous impact on society in an assortment of different ways. At its most fundamental level, sport has the power to bring people great joy and satisfy their competitive urges while at once allowing them to form bonds and a sense of community with others from diverse backgrounds and interests and various walks of life. Sport also makes clear, especially at the highest levels of competition, the lengths that people will go to achieve victory as well as how closely connected it is to business, education, politics, economics, religion, law, family, and other societal institutions. Sport is, moreover, partly about identity development and how individuals and groups, irrespective of race, gender, ethnicity, or socioeconomic class, have sought to elevate their status and realize material success and social mobility.

Sport, Culture, and Society seeks to promote a greater understanding of the aforementioned issues and many others. Recognizing sport's powerful influence and ability to change people's lives in significant and important ways, the series focuses on topics ranging from urbanization and community development to biographies and intercollegiate athletics. It includes both monographs and anthologies that are characterized by excellent scholarship, accessible to a wide audience, and interesting and thoughtful in design and interpretations. Singular features of the series are authors and editors representing a variety of disciplinary areas and who adopt different methodological approaches. The series also includes works by individuals at various stages of their careers, both sport studies scholars of outstanding talent just beginning to make their mark on the field and more experienced scholars of sport with established reputations.

Baltimore Sports: Stories from Charm City provides a fascinating look at the pattern and meaning of sport in a city that has experienced its share of problems and heartache as well as successes and triumphs. Edited by noted historian Daniel A. Nathan, who was born in and maintains a close connection to the city, the book is the latest in the series on sport in major American cities. It includes twenty essays written by established academicians with long publication records, sportswriters and journalists, and younger scholars just starting their careers. Although similar to other anthologies in that space did not allow for the coverage of every conceivable topic, much insight is provided on Baltimore sports at all levels of competition and among men and women athletes at different moments in the city's history. The book comprises essays on topics ranging from an examination of the Preakness Stakes and the career of boxer Joe Gans to an analysis of the Baltimore Bullets championship season of 1947–1948 and the history of physical education at The Bryn Mawr School for Girls. Taken collectively, the essays, as made clear by Nathan in the introduction to the volume, demonstrate how sport both divided and brought people together in the "city of neighborhoods," home of such luminaries as Edgar Allan Poe and H. L. Mencken, and the site of Francis Scott Key's writing of "The Star-Spangled Banner."

David K. Wiggins

Acknowledgments

This book began thanks to a phone call from David Wiggins, a prolific historian and longtime friend, and Larry Malley, a publishing trailblazer who was then director of the University of Arkansas Press. They had an idea. They were thinking about publishing a series of anthologies about sports and different cities. A few of these books were already in the works, including one on Washington, DC. Great idea, I said. Then they asked me about editing one about Baltimore, a city they knew I had written about and love. It was not a tough sell. Several years later, I'm still grateful for the opportunity. I have learned a lot working on this book.

All manner of friends (old and new), colleagues, acquaintances, and even some strangers helped this book come to fruition. First and foremost, though, I need and want to express my gratitude to the book's twenty-one contributors. Without their ideas and knowledge, hard work, and patience, this book would not exist. Thank you all for being part of this project.

In Baltimore, librarian Tom Warner and the many men and women who staff the Periodicals Department and the Maryland Department of the Enoch Pratt Free Library were uncommonly helpful and gracious. At the Babe Ruth Birthplace Museum & Sports Legend Museum, deputy director John Ziemann and curator Amanda Peacock were generous with their time and expertise. Perusing the holdings of the John F. Steadman Research Center was a useful treat. At Morgan State University's Beulah M. Davis Special Collections Department, Edith Murungi went above and beyond to help me. Other Baltimoreans, past and present, contributed to this book: Kenneth Brown, Roberta Crawley, Tyrone Crawley, Dennis Deslippe, Jessica Elfenbein, Norman Johnson, Ronald Johnson, Alison Kibler, Harvey Polston, Jerome Powell, Joseph Sims, John Smith, Lil and Nates Straus, and Willard Wright. Thank you all.

As I have said many times over the years, the North American Society for Sport History (NASSH) and its members have been very supportive of my work. NASSH provides people from all over the world with a venue to discuss and debate ideas and methods—at its annual conference, in the pages of the *Journal of Sport History*, and online—and to share a sense of fellowship. It is no accident that I first met some of this book's contributors at NASSH and that some of the chapters in this book began as papers presented at NASSH meetings. In addition to the NASSHers who are in this volume, Sarah Fields, Allen Guttmann, Murray Phillips, and Maureen Smith have been especially encouraging.

Skidmore College contributed to this book in many ways. I'm grateful for the collegiality, support, and friendship of Erica Bastress-Dukehart, Beau Breslin, John Brueggemann, Matt Hockenos, Beck Krefting, Susan Matrazzo, Jacquelyn Micieli-Voutsinas, Pat Oles, Greg Pfitzer (who read many of these pages in draft form), Jeff Segrave, Amber Wiley, and Megan Williams. They are all superb colleagues and people. I am also proud to acknowledge that former Skidmore students Hannah Doban and Nevon Kipperman made this a better book. My gratitude is also extended to Sandie Brown of Skidmore's Inter-Library Loan Department and her student workers for tolerating my many requests and for helping me track down all manner of sources and loose ends. Skidmore also supported this work in the form of Faculty Development grants and Dean of the Faculty ad hoc grants. Thank you, Faculty Development Committee and its former chairs Alice Dean and Shirley Smith and associate deans of the faculty Paty Rubio and Crystal Moore, and Susan Blair, senior administrative assistant extraordinaire.

At the University of Arkansas Press, Larry Malley deftly passed the directorship baton to Mike Bieker, who has nurtured this project from his first day on the job. David Scott Cunningham, Deena Owens, Sam Ridge, Brian King, Charlie Shields, and Debbie Upton were all dedicated, conscientious, and patient professionals throughout the process.

In ways large and small, my family contributed to this book. Thanks to the Burr, Farah, and Kelley clans for the good times in Michigan; Marg Taylor for the enthusiasm and the impressive stamina on the long drives to Saratoga Springs; Marilyn Nathan and Wes Porter for the e-mails and newspaper clippings; Scott and Suz Kashnow for their love of and dedication to Sowebo; my late great-aunt Irene Forshlager and the rest of the Forshlagers, Kramers, and Hurwitzes for their kindness and generosity; my grandparents Sol and Irene Nathan, who would have loved this book, are always in my thoughts. My two sets of loving, supportive parents—Jerry and Ron Matthews, and Irvin Nathan and Judy Walter—have enriched this book and me in countless ways. Finally, thank you, Susan Taylor, Ben and Zoë Nathan, and Sam the wonder dog for keeping me on my toes. You make every day brighter, better, and more interesting.

Introduction

Located on the Patapsco River, which flows into the Chesapeake Bay, Baltimore, Maryland, is the birthplace of Francis Scott Key's "The Star-Spangled Banner," the incomparable Babe Ruth, and three generations of Nathans. Most people, I realize, probably do not associate these things with one another. (Well, no one does, except for me.) That I do says something about how the past and place sometimes commingle in interesting, idiosyncratic ways, about how history and heritage are linked. So let me be clear: Baltimore looms large in my memories and imagination.

Like all cities, Baltimore is complicated. It has a rich cultural history and contemporary social landscape, with diverse and distinct neighborhoods, some of which are obviously in crisis—as was dramatically illustrated on April 27, 2015, when the city experienced its worst civil unrest and violence since the calamitous 1968 riots following the murder of Dr. Martin Luther King Jr.[1] Clearly Baltimore has serious, seemingly intractable problems (poverty, under- and unemployment caused by de-industrialization, disturbing violent crime rates, a failing public education system, etc.). It also provides many residents with a sense of belonging and joy. Sports have contributed a great deal to that sense of community and pleasure.

This book chronicles and sometimes celebrates many different ways that sports have been and are an integral part of Baltimore, its history, and its identity. It is predicated on the idea that sports are an important strand in the cultural fabric that makes Baltimore unique, interesting, and, for some of us, lovable. Just as Randy Roberts's *Pittsburgh Sports: Stories from the Steel City* (2000) does not provide "a laundry list of victories won and opportunities squandered," neither does this book.[2] Rather, like Roberts's anthology, this one "is a collection of essays, all grounded firmly in history, several anchored in personal experience."[3] It strives to give readers a sense of what specific athletes and teams (scholastic, collegiate, and professional), games, and places tell us about Baltimoreans, their hometown, values, and numerous meaningful relationships.

My interest in this project is personal and has deep roots. It is the result of having been born in Baltimore—like my father and grandfather, both of whom were raised and educated in the city—and having spent a great deal of time there, often visiting my paternal grandparents and going to Orioles games with family and friends. Eerily similar to my own experience, Daniel Rosensweig, the author of *Retro Ball Parks: Instant History, Baseball, and the New American City* (2005), writes: "Even though I grew up in an upper-middle-class suburban Washington neighborhood, I believed myself to be spiritually linked to both the Orioles and the blue-collar town they represented."[4] In my case, after moving away from an upper-middle-class suburban Washington neighborhood and having lived many places over the years, that spiritual link has endured. The city has always captivated me, which is partly why my stepmother once called Baltimore the center of my universe.

So yes, I love Baltimore, just not blindly or uncritically. There is considerable human frustration, indifference, and desperation all over town. These are some of the sad facts of life that journalist-turned-television-producer David Simon has reported and dramatized for over thirty years. There is of course much more to Baltimore than what is represented in Simon's articles, books, and *The Wire* (2002–2008), his brilliant HBO show that depicts "Baltimore as a multifaceted city of interlocking [and failing] institutions" and Baltimoreans "as beholden to the forces created by the microprocedures of bureaucracies, politics, and individual players."[5]

But *The Wire* has received local pushback, and not just from politicians and high-ranking police administrators. A few years ago *Baltimore* magazine, a glossy monthly periodical with lots of ads for fancy restaurants and expensive real estate and boutiques, asked a few locals, "What's the Biggest Misconception about Our City?" One woman replied: "That the whole city is exactly like *The Wire*."[6] It's not—and it's hard to imagine that many Baltimoreans suffer from this misconception. Yet while perusing the magazine in which this response was printed, I couldn't help thinking that it represented Baltimore in ways that were extremely selective and perhaps more fictional than *The Wire*.

Most of Baltimore is not glamorous or cool. As one local millennial puts it, "We're not Manhattan with its Broadway shows and billionaires. We're not Los Angeles with its sunshine and celebrities. Heck, we're not even D.C. with shiny politicians, international flair and national monuments."[7] Fair enough. But Baltimore is not bereft of beauty.

For me, the huge neon Domino Sugars sign atop the company's refinery lit up at night, its multihued reflection shimmering on the water near the Inner Harbor, is a lovely sight.[8] During the day, up close, the Sugar House is less enchanting. Perhaps this kind of duality helps explain why the iconoclastic filmmaker and writer John Waters calls Baltimore a "gloriously decrepit, inexplicably charming city."[9]

Sadly, much of it *is* decrepit. This has been true for a long time. Despite and sometimes because of urban renewal efforts, large sections of the city are greatly diminished versions of their former selves. Marion E. Warren and Mame Warren's enchanting pictorial history *Baltimore: When She Was*

What She Used to Be, 1850–1930 (1983) represents an especially poignant example of this sentimental theme.

Nonetheless, much of Baltimore *is* charming, amiable, and authentic. This is why I, unlike some snarky people I know, have never thought that the popular Charm City sobriquet was wholly ironic. For many of us, parts of Baltimore and myriad Baltimoreans are truly charming. It's a place rife with character and characters. Baltimore is "a salty old broad with harsh edges and ridiculous hairdos," muses hometown boy Rafael Alvarez.[10] A bit hyperbolic, but the point is well made and taken. Baltimore is an unpretentious place, unafraid to embrace its quirky side.

There are in fact "multiple Baltimores, real and imagined."[11] They are all multifaceted. Baltimore encompasses the gritty Pigtown and the upscale Roland Park, the Pagoda in Patterson Park and the pink flamingo in Hampden, historic Fort McHenry and the equally historic cluster of buildings formerly known as the Maryland Penitentiary. "From funky Fells Point to classic Mount Vernon," writes local historian Frank R. Shivers Jr., "Baltimore is nothing if not a city of contrasts."[12]

That's one way to describe Baltimore. Another is to call it "a city of contradictions," asserts Joanna Crosby of Morgan State University:

> Located on the Mid-Atlantic rust belt, once home to Bethlehem Steel's largest plants, Bal'mer now sprouts more condos than sheet metal. Technically below the Mason-Dixon line, Charm City was one of the first cities where freed Blacks could remain free. The bus stops' benches say it's The City That Reads, but thirty-eight percent of adults in the city can't. Johns Hopkins University and Medical Center is the largest employer, but the high school drop-out rate is fifty percent.[13]

These are sobering, important facts, and they give us a sense of the city, yet perhaps rather than thinking of them as contradictions, these realities bespeak some of Baltimore's complexity and heterogeneity.

Even the imagined versions of the city are remarkably disparate. John Waters's Baltimore is campy, quirky, and irreverent. David Simon's Baltimore is dark and dysfunctional, if not dystopian. Crime novelist Laura Lippmann's Baltimore is a much different place than fellow fiction writer Anne Tyler's Baltimore, which "has an idyllic feel, with winding, tree-shaded streets and a mix of beautiful old houses."[14]

Mark Cottman's vibrant painting *This is Baltimore!* (2011) is also notable. A former architectural engineer, Cottman is a poet and self-taught artist with a gallery in the Federal Hill neighborhood. His *This is Baltimore!* is an engaging visual medley, a catalog of some of the places, things, and imagery that makes Baltimore Baltimore. It includes the heart of downtown

Mark Cottman, *This is Baltimore!*, 2011. *Courtesy of the artist.*

at Baltimore and Charles Streets, Penn Station and the Pagoda in Patterson Park, Fort McHenry and the Washington Monument, the Shot Tower and the Bromo Seltzer Tower. A portrait of Baltimore would be incomplete without rowhouses or a Chesapeake Bay blue crab, both of which are prominent. Perched on top of the rowhouses is a raven, made famous by Edgar Allan Poe, author of macabre tales and poetry such as "The Raven" (1845), who died in Baltimore in 1849 when he was forty years old. There is of course a double meaning to this raven, for it is also represents the city's purple-and-black-clad NFL team, the two-time Super Bowl champion Ravens. The same kind of double meaning applies to the painting's Baltimore Oriole. It is the Maryland state bird and the name of the city's cherished Major League Baseball team. There are many other images in Cottman's lively portrait (Lexington Market, a horse-drawn arabber cart, black-eyed Susans, etc.). In keeping with Cottman's sense of the city, his understanding that sports are part of its history and culture, the three thoroughbreds racing in the lower-left-hand corner, a reference to Pimlico Race Course, home of the Preakness Stakes, are significant.

And of course there is Barry Levinson's Baltimore: *Diner* (1982), *Tin Men* (1987), *Avalon* (1990), the NBC TV series *Homicide: Life on the Street*

(1993–1999), *Liberty Heights* (1999), and the ESPN documentary *The Band That Wouldn't Die* (2009). Collectively, Levinson's films constitute an appealing mix of social realism and sentimentality. In some ways, the essays in this book do likewise.

Beyond my affection for and connections to Baltimore, this project is driven by an ongoing interest in the nexus of sport, community, and identity. In my anthology *Rooting for the Home Team* (2013), I worked with a team of terrific scholars and writers who examined "the ways different American communities (big cities, small rural towns, suburbs, college towns, and so forth) used or use sport to create and maintain a sense of their collective identity."[15] Some of the same issues and ideas can be found in these pages. I remain intrigued by the complex process of people coming together and being divided by sports, and how "sports appear to be (or are constructed as) a kind of social glue that holds together heterogeneous and contentious communities."[16] Baltimore is a good example of this.

For many Baltimoreans, playing and watching sports are important means and expressions of communal belonging. Think of the people all over the city who proudly wear Ravens gear, especially when the team is winning, and the roar of the crowd at Camden Yards when, say, Delmon Young's pinch-hit bases-loaded double scored three runs and gave the Orioles the lead against the Detroit Tigers in game two of the 2014 American League Division Series. The noise was deafening. These and other sporting phenomena and moments provide shared touchstones, moments and contexts in which people can be together. At the same time, sports in Baltimore have and can provide wedges between people: men and women, whites and blacks, neighborhood versus neighborhood. Consider the City-Poly and the Calvert Hall-Loyola high school rivalries and the ways in which they pit students and alums from the different schools against one another.

The romance of sport is often overdone, taken too far. After all, the games we play and cheer, no matter how much we care about them, are not a magical elixir that solves serious problems. Moreover, the sense of belonging that sports sometimes produce is often fleeting. It is here and gone, faster than Boog Powell could get down the first-base line. "Sports offer us grand illusion," writer Michael Olesker argues:

> We enter the ballpark for a few hours, and it almost seems like childhood. It's [Cal] Ripken going into the hole, but it's a vision of our formerly youthful selves turning the base hit into a double play. It was [John] Unitas throwing to [Raymond] Berry and [Lenny] Moore across all those autumns, but it was our wanna-be selves hearing the crowd calling our own name.[17]

Perhaps for some Walter Mittys among us. For others, including the producers of the enjoyable Maryland Public Television documentary *Gone But Not Forgotten II* (1994), sport is an escapist and community-building institution and practice: "Sports always took us away from the daily world of work and home," *Baltimore Sun* columnist Dan Rodricks narrates, "it took us to public arenas where we could all share the moment and form a happy bond. That's what this show is about, revisiting the bright fields of memory and savoring all that happened."[18] Many of the chapters in this book have similar intentions. A few have a critical edge and push us to think about how Baltimore sports reflected or exemplify local challenges and tensions, many of them race related.

The essays in this book are certainly eclectic—appealingly so, to my taste. They discuss popular professional and amateur sports (e.g., intercollegiate and interscholastic) and less familiar subjects (such as the "physical culture" program at a local girls prep school), from the nineteenth century to the present. They examine famous athletes and teams and some that have been ignored or forgotten. Many of the stories told here are triumphant. Others are about struggles and failures. Still others are bittersweet, such as David Zang's intrepid sojourn among the final resting places of some of Baltimore's athletes and other sportsmen. For the most part, the chapters are organized chronologically, although in a few instances (like Zang's and Lee Lowenfish's) they are not about a single time period. One need not read these chapters in the order they are presented to appreciate them. Taken together, though, there are fascinating connections to be made among them. Ultimately, the collective portrait of Baltimore sports that emerges here is kaleidoscopic.

Although it covers wide-ranging subjects, this book is not intended to be comprehensive. Unfortunately and yet inevitably, it leaves out a great deal. Readers looking for well-worn stories about or fresh insights on Orioles Jim Palmer, Boog Powell, Paul Blair, Mark Belanger, Mike Flanagan, Eddie Murray, and other Birds will be disappointed. They are not here. Neither are tales of great Colts Alan Ameche, Raymond Berry, Jim Parker, Gene "Big Daddy" Lipscomb, and coaches Weeb Ewbank and Don Shula. The great, nearly mythic John Unitas merits his own chapter; then again, so much has already been written about him that one cannot argue that historians and biographers have neglected him.[19] Other sports superstars with Baltimore roots are also absent, such as Baseball Hall of Famer Al Kaline and NBA All-Star Carmelo Anthony. There is no golf or Grand Prix auto racing here, no Baltimore Blast or Chesapeake Bayhawks. Someone suggested that we should include a chapter on Chuck Thompson and Vince Bagli, Baltimore sports broadcasting favorites. "Where is Mary Dobkin?" and "How about

Wild Bill Hagy?" a few people asked me when we were talking about the book. These are good suggestions and questions. I wish these subjects could have been included. Likewise, I wish there were chapters on long-gone Negro league teams such as the Baltimore Black Sox and the Elite Giants. The same goes for the International League Baltimore Orioles, which won seven straight pennants (1919–1925). I mention all of these subjects in the hope that some energetic, knowledgeable people will produce their own essays about them.

If some of us are occasionally sentimental or nostalgic about Baltimore, the city always reminds us to resist these impulses. That is my experience, at least. The devastating April 2015 riots were an especially intense example of this.

The riots were sparked (but not caused) by the tragic death of Freddie Gray, a twenty-five-year-old African American man, who was arrested for the alleged possession of a switchblade on April 12. He died a week later due to severe spinal cord injuries he sustained while in police custody. The justifiable outrage and anger that many African Americans (and others) experienced—which had been simmering for years due to persistent acts of police brutality, oppression, and racism—erupted on April 27, not long after Gray's funeral. As the *Baltimore Sun* put it, "Baltimore descended into chaos."[20] There was looting, millions of dollars in property damage, arson, and assaults on police and civilians—mostly caused by teens and young adults, all televised by the local and national news media.

It is hard to be sentimental or nostalgic about Baltimore when it is on fire and people are enraged.

In this context, it is surprising that the April 29 "fanless" baseball game at Camden Yards between the Orioles and the Chicago White Sox received so much attention.[21] *Time* magazine reported, "Because of security concerns amid city unrest, the game was closed to fans for what was believed to be the first time in Major League Baseball history."[22] Then again, unique and anomalous events are newsworthy.

But the game was not exactly "fanless." There were some Orioles fans outside the locked gates at the ballpark's Eutaw Street entrance, rooting for the home team, albeit from a distance.[23] It was a footnote to a much larger and more important story. "That anyone would spend 24 hours fretting over the plight of a baseball team that had to play a game in an empty stadium while a major American city struggled to maintain order in its streets seemed comical to me at first," wrote Kevin Van Valkenburg of ESPN.

> Camden Yards is a majestic ballpark—the perfect place to take the family for a lazy Sunday afternoon game, if you can afford it. If you

can't, OPACY [Oriole Park at Camden Yards] looks like just another playground for the wealthy. It's an easy symbol for the economic and cultural divide that exists here. The divide that's fueling a lot of that anger you're seeing on the news. State lottery tickets funded a huge chunk of its construction. A majority of those tickets, some studies have shown, were purchased by Baltimore's have-nots, people longing for a financial Hail Mary and, in turn, a better life.[24]

There it was: sports once again finding a way to say something meaningful and revealing about Baltimore, its people, history, and identity.

Spending time in Baltimore's disparate neighborhoods and talking to all manner of local people drive home that the city is "complex, ever changing, often gritty and dangerous, [and] always interesting."[25] The rich amalgam of sports that have been and continue to be played and cheered in Baltimore contributes to the city's distinctiveness and culture; it helps make Baltimore much more than just streets, buildings, and people, most of whom do not know one another. In other words, sports are a big part of what gives Baltimore its identity, nourishes its "municipal soul," and puts the charm in Charm City.[26]

1

Till Death Do Us Part

The Grand Tour of Baltimore's Graveyard Greats

DAVID ZANG

A city is a collection of disparate families who agree to a fiction:
They agree to live as if they were as close in blood or ties of
kinship as in fact they are in physical proximity.
—A. Bartlett Giamatti, *Take Time for Paradise* (1989)

Walk the promenade at Harborplace, stop in at the B&O Railroad turn-table, crack a few crabs at Captain James's Landing before drinking yourself blind at Fell's Point, absorb a few "What'll ya have, hons" from big-haired local waitresses, and it is easy to start putting some stock in the fiction of a city. Yes, you are assuredly in Baltimore, pronounced by many of its provincial natives as "Bawlmer." It is a schizophrenic place. There is no downtown shopping district, no theater district, and no longer a newspaper worthy of the name. American connoisseurs of pop culture identify Baltimore with two television paeans to the area's unremitting, and apparently unfixable, drug problem: *Homicide* (1993–1999) and *The Wire* (2002–2008). Tiny homesteads like the Poe House, the H. L. Mencken House, and Babe Ruth's Birthplace masquerade as museums.[1]

The city is home, however, to the original Washington Monument, the internationally acclaimed though locally undervisited Walters Art Gallery, and a first-class public library that does a quarter of the business it deserves. In an apparent effort to both praise and raise the latter's profile, a mayor in the 1980s declared our urban motto to be "The City That Reads," an unfortunate claim that critics quickly transmuted to "The City That Bleeds." Soon thereafter, a new mayor with national political ambitions declared us to be "The Greatest City in America," a slogan still mocking us from the backs of fading park benches. In another unfortunate bit of labeling, a quite recent mayor, deposed after allegations that she took gift cards for her own use that had been contributed to the city for distribution to the poor, came up with the jaunty, and, in her case, literal, slogan: "Get In On It." Even before race riots charred areas of the city in the 1960s, issues of color loomed like a dreaded plague. Although part of the Union, Maryland had divided loyalties, and so its state song featured, until the 1940s, the lyrics: "Huzzah, huzzah, she scorns the Northern scum."[2] In short, the city is southern without the hospitality or charm. This has not kept the populace from calling it "Charm City."

Still, the city continues to press its case on me, and sports have sometimes been the primary reminder of the good things it holds. In Baltimore, it was the Orioles, Colts, and NBA Bullets, for example, who presented the hope of integration at a time when there was still a public "colored" swimming pool and African American women were still prohibited from trying on dresses in downtown department stores. But trying to stretch the fiction of a city across sports is difficult inasmuch as most of the athletes representing us weren't born or raised here. I decided, then, that the heart of Baltimore sport was less likely to be found in the present than in the past. That is, I decided to visit the city's graveyards in search of the sportsmen who finished their lives here, on the entirely unscientific grounds that something about Baltimore made it feel like home.

These onetime stars may lie in the graveyard as indistinguishable from the common dead as one M & M is from another, but from "Buttercup" Dickerson to "Cupid" Childs, some of the liveliest characters in Baltimore were players, broadcasters, writers, owners, and icons. They played not only for the Orioles and Colts, but for the Quicksteps, Orphans, Beaneaters, Black Sox, and the Federal League Terrapins. They rest alongside Lincoln assassin conspirators, gifted jazz musicians, and members of the Little Rascals. Where we buried them and where we now find them reveals a society's character across time, leaking light from the earthy depths onto issues of power, class, gender, race, religion, and—most important of all—onto what we made of sport, that most vital engine of all human existence.

Not to be contrary, but I'm actually going to begin the tour outside the city; and, again, not to be contrary—really—I'm going to begin it with a horse; and if you don't believe a horse can be an athlete, I refer you to William Nack's *Secretariat: The Making of a Champion* (1975), which will settle the question for you. Despite the utter absence of charm at the downtrodden Pimlico Racetrack in the northwest part of the city, Maryland and Baltimore can trace their colonial sporting interests to horse racing, and the rolling hills north of the city are as lovely as any "horse country" locale anywhere in the nation. White-painted fences that stretch out to forever signal that you have found Sagamore Farm in Reisterstown. Owner Kevin Plank, the now-billionaire founder of Under Armour, bought the farm in 2007—not out of corporate chutzpah, but because he thinks this onetime staple of the state's sporting industry deserves better. Originally built by Alfred Gwynne Vanderbilt, Sagamore was home for thirteen years to Native Dancer, racing's "Grey Ghost." According to biographer John Eisenberg, the horse's twenty-one wins in twenty-two races were amplified by the grey coat that made him easily distinguishable on black-and-white television sets in the early 1950s, a time when people were "still awestruck by the ability to see what they previously had only been able to hear."[3] When Native Dancer won the Preakness and Belmont Stakes in 1953, he had already lost his shot at the Triple Crown by a nose in a race in which he'd been controversially bumped and cut off. His loss came in the first Kentucky Derby that millions had watched on TV. During his racing days, at least 700,000 Americans spent a day at one of the nation's tracks. Horse racing now exists on the outskirts of our sports world, and Sagamore's quaint patch of pasture houses the plots and engraved stone slabs that mark the graves of Native Dancer and a dozen or so other horses, including Hall of Famers Discovery and Bed O'Roses (plus the first famed horse to run under Plank's name, Millionreasonswhy, who died as a three-year-old after crashing through the barriers at the farm's track) track the remove at which Baltimore and the country now view the sport.

While we're on horse farms, let me mention Jim McKay. First a newspaper writer for the *Baltimore Sun*, and then the voice that famously announced during the 1972 Olympic massacre of the Israeli team, "they're all gone," McKay won thirteen Emmys, some as the voice of ABC's seminal *Wide World of Sports*. He lived on a horse farm in nearby Monckton. After he died in 2008, he was interred there. He was an advocate for Maryland racing, especially during its decline, for which he deserves some applause, though Baltimoreans tended to think of McKay as more of a national figure than one of their own.

If you head a few miles east of Sagamore Farm, where the folks embrace a different type of equine love—the kind that favors foxhunts and equestrianism—you will find the improbable resting place of someone the city did consider its own. A large shopping center—the "Hunt Valley Towne Centre"—occupies a huge tract of ground, and right there in the middle of a walkway that connects Dick's Sporting Goods and Coldwater Creek to

Wegman's supermarket is the Chuck Thompson Memorial Plaza. It is essentially a large stone fireplace piled with fake cordwood. Somewhere within its beautiful stonework lie the ashes of Baltimore's TV and radio icon, Chuck Thompson, the voice of the Orioles. When I arrived in Baltimore in 1980, I had no choice in matters of television and radio reception and found myself unhappily assaulted nightly by the pairing of Thompson and Brooks Robinson, the former Orioles great. To my ear, the two were cloying, provincial, and cheesy. They were, I discovered, an acquired taste, and sure enough I acquired it after a few years. Robinson's spot was eventually taken over by the former pitcher Jim Palmer, but Thompson chugged along, beloved by O's fans. He was a good fit for some good times: the wildly successful early 1980s and mid-1990s, when Wild Bill Hagy led cheers in Section 33 of Memorial Stadium, and then when the magic of Camden Yards brought busloads of fans to the ballpark as well as good cheer to the radio booth. Thompson was an especially nice man; he began his mornings at the Wagon Wheel, a few miles north of Hunt Valley, mixing congenially with other regulars. He became known for opaque sayings like "Go to war, Miss Agnes" and "ain't the beer cold." I always assumed he was a local, but, in fact, he began with the Phillies in 1946; he just came to love Baltimore like a local.

One of Thompson's more interesting gigs was acting as the host from 1962 to 1974 of a weekly program called *Duckpins and Dollars*, giving him a thin but interesting connection to some of the most famous Baltimoreans of all time. Duckpin bowling—a version of the real thing with squat pins, small wooden balls, and shortened alleys—is so familiar to old-time residents that many have come to believe the inaccurate tale that it was created in the city at the turn of the twentieth century in a Howard Street saloon too small to allow for full-sized lanes. The owners of the saloon were the baseball stars Wilbert Robinson and John J. McGraw, Orioles who lay across a great divide from the modern O's of Chuck Thompson's times. Playing in the 1890s for championship Orioles teams (a franchise that would eventually leave town and become the New York Yankees), the pair would go on to baseball fame elsewhere, McGraw as the winningest manager in National League history with the New York Giants, Robinson as manager of the Brooklyn Dodgers. Robinson later became McGraw's pitching coach before they had a falling out in 1913.[4] Unbeknown to most city denizens, when they died in 1934, they were reunited in the city's New Cathedral Cemetery, just a short distance from what was once St. Mary's School, the adolescent stomping grounds of another Baltimorean who became renowned elsewhere for ruining McGraw's brand of small ball (McGraw is credited with perfecting the "Baltimore chop"). Babe Ruth's home runs eclipsed McGraw on the diamond, but the Babe could not outdo the Little Napoleon's burial splendor. While Robinson has a small stone marking his grave, McGraw rests eternally in a magnificent crypt as outsized as his feisty reputation. New Cathedral's reputation was once grand as well. There are other early Orioles there, and also Robert T. Mathews, a native Baltimorean who in 1871, while with the Fort Wayne Kekiongas of the National Association, became the first pitcher to start, win, and throw a shutout in a professional game. Despite the renown within, New Cathedral now sits framed by some of west Baltimore's more inhospitable streets.

This is the fate, in fact, of many of Baltimore's cemeteries. Leaving New Cathedral's southwest location, we head south to Mount Auburn, a black burial grounds located in an even rougher area just beyond the city's downtown. Mount Auburn has suffered greater neglect than most. Over the last few decades it has launched numerous campaigns begging for help in cleanup, restoration, and maintenance. The appeals are usually justified because, along with runaway slaves, early black legislators, and Methodist bishops, Mount Auburn also houses the grave of Joe Gans. His fame now as neglected as the cemetery, Gans has been resurrected recently through an excellent biography by William Gildea. Acclaimed as one of the greatest fighters of all time in the early twentieth century, among Gans's 196 career fights was his 1902 lightweight championship bout that made him the first black world champion in any sport, and his forty-two-round title defense against Oscar "Battling" Nelson. The payday from the latter allowed Gans to open what may have been the nation's first integrated "black-and-tan" club; among its employees was pianist Eubie Blake.[5]

One of the more fascinating aspects of Gans's life was his death. Having contracted tuberculosis, Gans had gone to live in the more accommodating aridity of the Arizona desert. When it became apparent in 1910 that the disease was going to claim him in short time, he decided to make a desperate run for home and family. As the train headed east, local newspapers picked up the tale of Joe Gans's "race with death." Gans arrived in Baltimore in August and died shortly after at age thirty-five. The city, still very much an outpost of southern sympathy, and one largely segregated, turned out in huge numbers as friends and fans, black and white, followed the fighter's hearse through the streets and out to Mount Auburn. The *Baltimore Sun* ran an article on the one-hundred-year anniversary of his death in 2010, and Mount Auburn, surrounded by bent and busted cyclone fencing, finally succeeded in recent years in cleaning and adding more engraving to Gans's headstone, which means it now stands out among the many ruined and toppled stones.

Quarantined from whites in death just as in life, Benjamin Taylor and Leon Day, baseball stars of the Negro leagues in the 1930s and 1940s, nonetheless were dealt a better hand than Gans when they were interred in Arbutus Memorial Park. Southwest of the city, like Mount Auburn, the park is well kept, the office building is relatively new, and dignified bronze plaques mark the graves of Taylor and Day. First baseman Taylor hit over .300 in all but one of his sixteen years, some with the Baltimore Black Sox. He was inducted into the Hall of Fame in 2006. Day, a star pitcher from the Negro National League did not live to see his induction, dying just six days after learning of his election.[6]

From Arbutus, let us make our way into the heart of the city proper. Most graveyard aficionados are drawn to the Westminster Burying Grounds, a small lot at Fayette and Greene Streets, because Edgar Allan Poe (who would provide all three names for the mascots of the Baltimore Ravens) has a prominent tomb here. Alas, there are no athletes here unless you count the spirit of Frank the Body Snatcher, whose ability to dig up bodies at Westminster in the nineteenth century caused eastern medical schools to laud him as "the best man to ever lift a spade."[7] Pulling corpses from the ground with meat hooks, he could be in and out of a grave in thirty minutes flat, about the time it takes to get from Westminster to the city's largest and most famous burial ground.

Green Mount Cemetery, once a bucolic location at Greenmount Avenue and Oliver Street, is now one more former oasis swallowed by the squalor and danger of surrounding low-income neighborhoods and isolated from them by a chain-link fence topped with barbed wire. In its heyday it was the final resting place favored by many of the city's wealthy, prominent, and respectable citizens, prestigious enough to have enticed some of the city's old money to dig up their kin from crowded downtown plots and transplant them here. Find-A-Grave lists eighty famous names: governors, senators, mayors, generals, and the most famous of all, Lincoln assassin John Wilkes Booth. Strange, then, that I had such a difficult time confirming that it also held the remains of a man whose notoriety should be a match for any of them: Robert Garrett. No, not the tall guy from television's *Everybody Loves Raymond*. The Olympic-gold-medal-winning Robert Garrett. That Robert Garrett. Still not ringing any bells? Let me fill you in.

Robert Garrett was born into the wealth of the family that owned the Baltimore & Ohio Railroad. Raised in a mansion, Garrett had private tutors as a child before enrolling in a school in Tours, France. He was at Princeton in the 1890s when the French aristocrat Pierre de Coubertin resurrected the Olympic Games. As a 6'2", two-hundred-pound athlete, Garrett became part of a contingent that Princeton permitted to travel to Athens for the inaugural contest in 1896. Garrett also had a twenty-five-pound discus crafted in case he decided to enter the first-ever discus contest. As might be expected, he found he couldn't throw it very far. He won gold in both the shot put and long jump in Athens; when he discovered that the official Olympic discus weighed just 4.5 pounds, he entered and won gold there, too, modifying the classical arm swing of the ancient Greeks with a crouch-and-spin technique that anticipated the modern form used today.

His Princeton classmates had dubbed Garrett "a safe man to follow," and upon his return to Baltimore, he became a leader in the style expected of both a "muscular Christian" and a man whose sense of *noblesse oblige* placed him on the board of many civic institutions, including the Boy Scouts, which he had a hand in planting in the city, and the YMCA.[8] He represented both the best and worst of old Baltimore, "a man of good will," one 1961 obituary stated, "and rigid principles."[9] Both traits were on display in his role as the head of the city's Parks and Recreation for over three decades. While he financed construction of four outdoor gymnasia in the parks, he also oversaw a system that reinforced Baltimore's southern sympathies and ways. During his tenure, the parks were not only segregated, they clearly provided inferior facilities for the African American population. The "colored golf course" at Carroll Park did not even bother to plant grass, opting instead for sand greens that were oiled and rolled daily. In the city's crown jewel park, Druid Hill, blacks swam in a segregated "colored" pool tucked far out of sight in a remote corner of the park. Reflecting white reservations about black hygiene, the pool was equipped with an advanced filtration system to insure its cleanliness. The pool has now been filled in—a kind of graveyard in its own right—but the ladders and lifeguard chair remain, part of a public memorial to those days of separation. Lest you think Garrett's leanings in this matter were just a product of the times, I offer this politically tinged contribution to consider. When Garrett's sister died, she left money for the construction of a statue of Robert E. Lee. Garrett used the money instead to buy an enormous park north of the city. He left the name intact, however, so I now walk my dog in Robert E. Lee Park, both a lovely spot and a reminder of the city's stance on race.[10]

Garrett is buried in a prominent spot near the cemetery's chapel, about thirty yards from the philanthropist Johns Hopkins, and close to the tombs of his forebears. In front are small crosses that mark the resting places of a son who died at age one and a daughter who died at age three, a reminder that even the wealthiest could do little to hasten the closing of the gap between disease and the cures that modern medicine would one day discover.

Just a few miles away, on Belair Avenue, is the Baltimore Hebrew Cemetery, home to what may be the most obscure grave of any baseball player in the Hall of Fame. I know, because after forty-five minutes of wandering its dense rows with a map in hand, I could not find the damn stone. Except in the small, "newer" section, set apart from the main yard, there have been only a handful of dead buried here in the past twenty years. Apparently the cemetery is full, so the office was shut down for good, and the caretakers now housed in its former spot, while they keep the grass mowed, have no interest in helping out visitors. Wayward golf shots from the adjacent metropolitan course at Clifton Park dot the grounds here and there, raised letters have begun dropping from headstones, and large marble pieces have begun to topple from their pedestals. It is as if the cemetery has seceded from the city in imitation of the exodus staged by a huge part of the Baltimore Jewish community in the 1960s, when its members built a pipeline from the city's core to its northwest suburbs in their flight from urban blight.

All of which may be fitting in this case, because Bill James, the man acknowledged as the creator of the game's moneyball mindset, dubbed the man I was looking for—lefthander Richard "Rube" Marquard—"probably the worst starting pitcher" inducted to Cooperstown.[11] Still, Marquard won 201 games, mostly for John McGraw's New York Giants. His connection to Baltimore is tough to determine. It is my guess that this native of Cleveland wound up here after he began an affair in the 1920s with a married woman he'd met on Broadway, eventually stealing Blossom Seeley for his own. The two became a vaudeville song-dance-and-comic act, which may have put them on the boards in the burlesque houses that constituted the city's (in)famous "Block." Now a tawdry strip of peep shows, in its glory days the Block made a case for the respectability of the Two O'Clock Club's Blaze Starr and other ecdysiasts of renown. Marquard was later in life a pari-mutuel clerk, a job that allowed him the winter months in Florida, so it may have been the presence of Pimlico Racetrack that kept him here. For whatever reason, Marquard stayed in town, eventually marrying his third wife, Jane Hecht Guggenheim, a pairing that brought him, after his death at age ninety-three, to this Jewish cemetery.[12]

Feeling a need for both fresh air and a bit of uplift, I depart for the cemetery at the All Hallows Episcopal Church in Davidsonville, Maryland, a town closer to Annapolis and DC than Baltimore, but the resting place of one of the city's truly heroic and important sportsmen, John "Jack" Iglehart Turnbull. There is no caretaker here, either, but no need for one. The cemetery is small and pleasant to navigate, and I found Turnbull's stone amid a slew of Igleharts. Born in 1890, Turnbull attended Johns Hopkins, where he played lacrosse, football, and ice hockey. Particularly skilled in lacrosse, Turnbull won Olympic bronze and silver medals with America's 1928 and 1932 teams (lacrosse was a demonstration event in both Games), an achievement that brought him the sobriquet of "The Babe Ruth of

Lacrosse," an acclamation that probably does not sit well with the game's Native American originators. College lacrosse still annually awards its best attackman the Jack Turnbull Award.[13]

In 1936, Turnbull also played field hockey in the "Nazi" Olympics held in Berlin, where he met Adolf Hitler. Though most people in the city shake their heads at the idea of a men's field hockey team, I must confess that I feel the same way about their beloved lacrosse. I've tried to like it; I simply don't, and I am particularly repulsed by its prominence in the private schools, hotbeds of upper-crust privilege that leech most whites out of the public schools, which are left to the inadequate resources of the city and its lower classes.

This is not to denigrate Turnbull. There is obviously something compelling about the sport to many. Further, Turnbull did what I have never done. He joined the Maryland National Guard at the outset of World War II. In 1944, now a lieutenant colonel, the B-34 he was flying in collided in midair over Belgium following a bombing run of Hitler's fatherland. Originally buried in Belgium, his mother brought his body home to Davidsonville.

Head back to the city for a final run, one that will feature two of the most prominent men in National Football League (NFL) history: one with a legacy assured for generations, one with a career pockmarked by controversy.

Actually, Baltimore has had two of the most controversial team owners in sport history. Jack Dunn (buried in the city's St. Mary Catholic Cemetery) will forever be the man who sold a young Oriole named Babe Ruth out of his hometown and into national acclaim as one of the greatest athletes who ever breathed. But it is the recently deceased Art Modell who so enraged his hometown of Cleveland when he relocated the NFL Browns franchise to Baltimore that his entry on the Find-A-Grave website hosts a running commentary on his worth as a human being. The most recent posting I read said, "Browns fans are still glad you're gone."[14] Art Modell's reputation was built from greed, bad luck, lack of business acumen, or a combination of them all. He is beloved, of course, in Baltimore, owing, I think, to the city's enduring sense of inferiority—fed by the sudden departure of the Colts in 1984—that has made fans here defensive about how they were able to reconnect to sport's biggest treasure chest. Modell, a salesman at heart, left Cleveland after decades of sold-out crowds failed to give him the financial stability he desired. He blamed the decrepit stadium. So, Baltimore built him a brand-new one, filled it every week on their way to a Super Bowl title, allowed him to charge and keep millions in personal seat licensing fees, and made him the toast of the city. Alas, Modell failed again to turn all of that into financial solvency and had to sell most of his interest in the team in 2008 to Steve Bisciotti.[15]

More egregious, at least to me, was his uncompromising support of linebacker Ray Lewis in the wake of a murder following the Super Bowl in 2000, a twin killing for which no one ever spent a day in jail, and for which Lewis pled only to obstruction charges despite having disposed of material evidence: his bloody suit, which was never found.[16] Well, that is all terribly uncharitable of me. Modell had, no doubt, some qualities that were admirable, and this is what I am thinking until I pull up next to his gravesite in Druid Ridge Cemetery in nearby Pikesville (also home to the remains of William Jones "Boileryard" Clarke, catcher of the pennant-winning Orioles teams in the mid-1890s). Modell's mausoleum is an outsized white affair that smacks of self-promotion, not the modesty often claimed for him. A 150-foot flagstone walkway runs from the road to this hilltop monument alone. It is an echo of the empty self-aggrandizement that plagues modern sport. Indeed, many Baltimoreans continue to lobby for Modell's induction into the NFL Hall of Fame on the grounds that he was instrumental in fostering the marriage between television and pro football. Unfortunately, it is that very pairing that has helped move all American entertainment in the direction of the Roman Colosseum's bread-and-circuses mentality. Modell, of course, is no more to blame for this than the fans. He was, after all, only using the well-worn rationale of the snake oil salesman (and the drug dealer), that is, simply giving the people what they say they want. Well, that really is uncharitable, but such are the consequences of failing to follow the golden rule.

All of which leads me, finally, to the man with the Golden Arm. I put both this name and this trip off until last because there is no better way to leave someone with a favorable impression of Baltimore than to mention the name of Johnny Unitas. Although he would, at the end of his career, be eclipsed by Joe Namath and the flamboyant style of behavior that TV demanded, Unitas remained the quarterback that all others sought to emulate for four decades. Ironically, it was Unitas's performance that helped usher in the age that regards sport as entertainment first and sport second when he led the Colts to the 1958 championship in overtime against the New York Giants in the first championship game that many Americans watched on television.[17]

What made Johnny Unitas such a beloved figure in Baltimore, however, was his embrace of the city—and his character. I once found myself sitting next to him at a high school football game in the early 1990s. I recognized him, of course, but decided not to speak to him—to give him a rest from what I imagined must have been relentless public attention. Within minutes, however, I saw that many others were not thinking the same thing; one after another, they approached Unitas as if he were an old friend, and whether he knew them or not, that is how he received them. It was an impressive display of unforced cordiality.

Some years later, two of his children, Chad and Paige, ended up as students in my classroom at Towson University. Unpretentious, humorous, and level headed, they'd clearly grown up without a sense of entitlement. Because Unitas knew one of my colleagues, I occasionally got to sit in as he matter-of-factly told old Colts stories. When the Ravens dropped the ball in deciding how to honor him, Towson swooped in and named its stadium for him. Eventually the Ravens erected a large bronze statue of Unitas outside their stadium (note to Art Modell, Joe Paterno, and Mike Kryzewski: when you are truly great others will build monuments to you after you're gone). The last time I saw Unitas was on a lovely fall Saturday as he sat watching a game in the stadium that would one day bear his name. Chad sat next to him; he had just had his hair cut into his dad's signature flattop. A few days later, Johnny died of a heart attack. A large and loving crowd appeared for his funeral.

He was laid to rest in the Dulaney Valley Memorial grounds just north of Towson. His grave is one of a modest group of identical "bench" stones set beside a small manmade lake that hosts swans and Canada geese. It had been cleared the day I visited, but visitors frequently leave horseshoes—the

The John Unitas gravesite, Dulaney Valley Memorial Gardens, Timonium, Maryland. *Photograph by James G. Howes, 2009.*

symbol of the Colts—atop it. The back is inscribed with loving messages from his family and this observation: "A common man of uncommon talent and even more uncommon grace . . ."

After thirty-five years of living in what I've always considered a grace-less city caught in a graceless age, I am thinking of Unitas and his legacy. So, maybe before I die it's time I throw in with Johnny Unitas and try to find the grace to start calling this city my home.

2

Jockeying for Position

The Preakness Stakes, Pimlico, and Baltimore

ARI DE WILDE

Promoters first held the Preakness Stakes at the Pimlico Racetrack in 1873. There have been 140 Preakness Stakes since, not all of which have been held at the famous Maryland track. The second race of the famed "Triple Crown," the Preakness attracts the sports world's attention each May. Other than important games with the "bird" teams—the Orioles and Ravens—and Baltimore's lacrosse culture, the Preakness is the most prestigious and popular sporting event in Baltimore and the one with by far the longest tradition.

The race continues to symbolize Baltimore's quest for status as one of the most important trading ports and largest cities on the East Coast; the quest to maintain this status is a struggle that has continued for over two hundred years. The race, the track—Pimlico, which is northwest of downtown—and the culture are largely outgrowths of the Maryland Jockey Club. The club was formed in 1743—that is, well before the American Revolution—and its members have included George Washington and other prominent political figures. As historians such as Kenneth Cohen have shown, the racing and political posturing around horse racing was an important forum in which many of the power-driven networks that defined the United States were established. Though horse racing's popularity has ebbed and flowed, the sport continues to be a site of power, status, and prestige in and for Baltimore.[1]

This chapter examines the Preakness Stakes, Pimlico, and horse racing more generally in Charm City. It considers how horse racing became culturally and economically important and its meaning over time in Baltimore.

13

To accomplish this, I focus on the entrepreneurs who created the Preakness Stakes and explore how and what the Preakness Stakes has meant.

Origins: Mid-Atlantic Horse Racing from Colonial Times to the Early Republic

Almost from the time European explorers first arrived on this continent, when horses were reintroduced in America, people have wanted to race them. Initially, racing in the seventeenth century was not formal. What would become known as the "quarter" horse or the American horse, named for the quarter-mile stretches they raced, were similar to common horses of mixed lineages. Until the 1750s, it was conceivable that a horse belonging to someone of lower-class origin might run and beat the horse of someone of upper-class status. Horse racing largely evolved in the United States as a tavern amusement, for which the short distance was ideal. As Kenneth Cohen has shown, though, by the mid-eighteenth century wealthy people turned the sport back toward "the Sport of Kings" by beginning to import thoroughbred horses that had more endurance and were taller than quarter horses. The wealthy also began to copy older European and British models of having tracks with longer loops of up to four miles on which to race horses. Maryland, with the growing ports and communities in Baltimore and Annapolis, developed a culture of racing, as did New York and parts of the South. While the American Revolution resulted in the outlawing of horse racing in places like New York until the 1820s, the culture of thoroughbred racing was well established in antebellum Baltimore.[2]

Beginnings: The Preakness Colt and the Dinner Stakes

During the antebellum period, Baltimore had tracks and races in various locations around the city, including in the east and north. The racing, like the city, was seriously altered by the Civil War, which threw the city and its social order into turmoil. Located south of the Mason-Dixon Line and one of America's main train hubs, Baltimore was in a paradoxical situation; many of its citizens were pro-south, but, for all practical purposes, they resided in a northern city. Many of the elite saw Baltimore as an occupied city during the Civil War, one stripped of their idea of its identity. One way to restore some traditional values for the aristocracy was to restore the antebellum horse racing culture. The biggest advocate for a renewed racing scene was Maryland governor Oden Bowie, a descendant of the old Maryland upper class. He was an ardent racing fan, making trips north to racing tracks almost as soon as the Civil War ended. He also helped to restart the once famous Maryland Jockey Club as president of the organization.[3]

On one trip to the track at Saratoga Springs, New York, in 1868, Bowie was invited to a party hosted by Milford H. Sanford, a successful New York–area businessman, owner and breeder of several thoroughbreds and stables in the New York area and in Kentucky. At the meal, John W. Hunter, an elite former New York congressman and prominent "turfman,"[4] proposed a race in two years. Sanford added, "by horses that were yearlings at the time." He supported an entry of $5,000 for each horse, but this was reduced to a $1,000 ante. Despite many offers to host the race in other states, Bowie convinced the others at the dinner party to hold the event in Maryland.[5] Thus, all the men involved signed an agreement:

> We the subscribers, agree to run a sweepstakes in the fall of 1870 for colts and fillies then three years old; dash of two miles: entrance one thousand dollars, half forfeit; to be called the Dinner Party Stakes; the race to be run over a course to be built at Baltimore, Maryland; to be governed by the rules of the American Jockey Club.[6]

Having secured the race, Bowie needed a racetrack. The Maryland Jockey Club found the former grounds of the Maryland Agricultural and Mechanical Society for the state fair. There was some controversy over the racetrack's proposed site due to the area's reputation for poor weather conditions, to which the *Sun* noted that weather events at two previous fairs contributed.[7] But ultimately the fair ground location, a plateau overlooking Falls Road, was deemed acceptable. Beginning on October 16, 1870, a day with relatively good weather, there were several races. The biggest was the "Dinner Party Stakes," for which organizers raised a purse of close to $19,000. There was heavy betting throughout Baltimore with hundreds of people interested. Yet when it came time for the race, only six of the original thirty horses were left, one of which was Milton H. Sanford's horse, Preakness. The horse received its name (an "Indian word meaning Quail Woods") from Sanford's farm located in the village of Preakness in New Jersey.[8]

The race and track turned out to be a success. With his political position as governor of Maryland and as a descendant of an aristocratic family, Oden Bowie marshaled significant public investment in the track and racing—$35,000 from the state, $25,000 from the City of Baltimore, and another $55,000, which was raised privately. The result was a track with a grandstand for 4,000 spectators and an indoor room located below in which parties could be held. In the big race, the Dinner Party Stakes, to the surprise of many, the Preakness colt won. Some writers had written the horse off as a "cart horse," but it was victorious and 12,000 spectators became fans. The horse, the later namesake of the race, went on to have strong races in other events and raced well in Saratoga.[9]

Another factor that helped Pimlico, and professional horse racing in general, was the rise of pari-mutuel betting. From its early existence in North America as a transported pastime of old-world patricians, horse racing grew to appeal to a much-wider audience due to its long tradition of gambling. Horse racing's popularity at Pimlico and the Preakness Stakes was also a clear example of gambling's importance. After the original "Dinner Party Stakes," Baltimoreans were eager to gamble for pleasure and potential profit. In the late nineteenth century, the rise of the "French Mutuel" betting process and device in the early 1870s revolutionized and streamlined the experience. A machine produced $5 tickets and, unlike human bookies who set the odds, it functioned by paying a portion of the money that had been bet. Pari-mutuel betting made the gambling process more transparent and helped horse racing significantly. The essential process is still used at Pimlico and many other tracks and is critical to their success.[10]

In 1873, the Maryland Jockey Club voted to have a meet in the spring. To garner recognition for the spring race and to compete with a fall meeting and other races, club members decided to use the name of Milton Sanford's horse, "The Preakness." This was sensible, as Sanford was involved in founding the race and was a fan favorite in Baltimore. Therefore, in 1873, the first official "Preakness Stakes" was held. It was advertised "for three-year-olds, one-and-a-half miles, $50 entrance, pay or play, club to add $1,000 of which $200 goes to the second horse." The spring race established itself as a mid-major race; the club renewed the race in 1874 and successfully held it at the Pimlico track in Maryland until 1889.[11]

Governor Bowie's entrants, such as his horse Catesby, which drew much interest in the late 1870s, highlighted these years. From 1878 to 1882, however, one name dominated the Preakness Stakes: George L. Lorillard. He was a medical doctor trained at Yale, but went into the tobacco business with his brother. Due to his financial success, Lorillard built a breeding farm in Oakdale, Long Island, where he had horses such as the Duke of Magenta, Harold, Grenada, Vanguard, and Tom Ochiltree. With his own stable, Lorillard and his horses dominated the Preakness Stakes from 1878 to 1882. As evidence of the race's stature, some of his horses, like the Duke, won other premier races such as the Belmont Stakes and the Breckenridge. Lorillard's horses won the races for five years, capturing the nation's attention.[12]

By 1883, George Lorillard was dying and selling his horses. The loss of Lorillard was a major blow to the Pimlico-based Preakness Stakes. In addition, during the 1880s most of the major stables were in the New York area. Symbolic of the different economic fates of Baltimore and New York, the Maryland Jockey Club, from 1838 to 1889, was unable to sustain strong interest in the Preakness Stakes at Pimlico and unable to maintain the races financially. On August 7, 1889, the Jockey Club—despite continued support of Governor Bowie—voted to disband and end its lease on the Pimlico track.[13]

Nonetheless, the name "Preakness Stakes" did reappear in the newspapers. It became a June race in Old Morris Park, New York, in 1890. And then, in May 1894, the Brooklyn Jockey Club at the Gravesend, also in New York, ran one race. The Preakness Stakes ebbed and flowed as a middle-of-the-road race in the New York area until 1908.[14]

While the relative fortunes of New York as the country's major financial center and the beacon of East Coast racing continued to rise in the 1890s, the world of national racing governance and thoroughbred breeding formalized and centralized. Twenty-seven prominent breeders and racers, some of whom had surnames such as Vanderbilt and Sturgis, formed the National Jockey Club in 1894 as a national governing body of thoroughbred racing. By the end of 1897, the organization owned the rights to the *American Stud Book*. The annually updated book published the bloodlines of American and imported thoroughbreds and has since been the main national organizer of breeding rights. The organization was formed at a time of increasing and intense Jim Crow racial segregation, laws and customs that ranged from banning African Americans from voting to outlawing equal seating on public transportation, among many other forms of racist discrimination. Influenced by this trend, the club was instrumental in pushing black jockeys out of the sport in the 1890s.[15]

Even in northern areas, few black jockeys prospered after the nineteenth century. This is a racial legacy that remains to this day, as there still are very few black jockeys on the professional circuit. Yet in the nineteenth century, black jockeys dominated horse racing. The jockey of the colt "Preakness" was the only white jockey in the original 1870 "Dinner Party Stakes."[16] The most famous black jockey, Isaac Murphy, won almost at will at the Kentucky Derby. The Preakness, however, had fewer black winners than the other races in what would become the Triple Crown. Only two black jockeys have won the Preakness. In 1889, jockey George "Spider" Anderson won at Pimlico. Then, Willie Sims rode Sly Fox to a win in 1898—when the Preakness was held in New York.

The Preakness at Pimlico Comes of Age

Meanwhile, things in Baltimore improved in the new century. The Maryland Jockey Club restarted in 1904. While the club had disbanded and stopped leasing the track, the Pimlico track remained, barely. There was a fire in

1894 and, in the same year, the track's greatest patron, former Maryland governor Bowie, died. With the club gone and the track's most famous race, the Preakness, in New York, the track's fate was far from certain. The Maryland Agricultural Society maintained ownership of the track, and various organizations used the facility in the 1890s. For example, the Pimlico Country Club and the Pimlico Drivers Club hosted events and there were smaller races, but not always on a regular basis. But, ultimately, the track and its hosting of smaller races was a catalyst for restarting the Maryland Jockey Club and a Pimlico-located Preakness Stakes.[17]

More interest in holding larger races grew in the new century. In particular, the Maryland Steeplechase Association hosted a series of races at Pimlico in 1903. Though some had mentioned restarting the club in the late 1890s, there was so much interest in holding major races again in 1903 at Pimlico that resurrecting the Maryland Jockey Club became a plausible scenario. Finally, in September 1904, several prominent men announced the reorganization of the club before a series of fall races at Pimlico. To grow membership, the club initially asked for a fee of $15 to join. By October of 1904, there were many potential members, and prominent members fought to add an initiation fee of $50. The squabble was a moot point in the growth of the club. It was a success and became a power in horse racing again.[18]

The Preakness's rebirth in Baltimore was largely due to the New York governor and legislature, which passed the Hart-Agnew law in 1908. The law banned betting in New York and effectively stopped horse racing in the state. The ban meant that New York stable and horse owners were willing to race their horses in Maryland. Taking the opportunity, the club was able to restart the Preakness in May 1909. To be sure, the Preakness restarted in the 1910s as a relatively minor race and it still only had a $1,500 purse in 1914. The race struggled into the late 1910s. It had tradition but was by no means a classic—even within Maryland. It continued despite the resumption of betting in New York and the resurrection of New York racing in the late 1910s.[19]

The Maryland Jockey Club made the Preakness into a national classic, a spectacle, by increasing the race purse. In 1918, the club raised the purse to $15,000.[20] Moreover, to build brand recognition, the Maryland Jockey Club moved the race to five days after the Kentucky Derby. With a matched prize purse and a new date, the Preakness's popularity quickly rose. Further, the increased purse brought some of the greatest horses in American thoroughbred history in the years following, which certainly contributed to the significance of Baltimore's Preakness Stakes.

One of the greatest horses of the twentieth century, Sir Barton, demolished the field at the Derby, Preakness, and Belmont in 1919. The horse was not a great favorite in the Derby and the *Baltimore Sun* noted that the horse had a "12 pound maid allowance," which allowed it to win too easily.[21] In contrast, at the Preakness, the *Baltimore Sun* emphasized that the horse had trained in the winter in Maryland and described the race saying, "It was Sir Barton at the quarter, Sir Barton at the half, Sir Barton at every post—Sir Barton all the way—and he won . . . 15,000 and 20,000 persons— . . . [were] astonished at the ease with which the victory was scored."[22] Sir Barton also went on to win the Belmont Stakes. Historians would later classify him as the first unofficial "Triple Crown" winner, a term that did not exist in America's thoroughbred racing at the time.[23]

The same year, the Maryland Jockey Club furthered interest in the Preakness with a purse of $30,000. In 1920, the legendary Man O' War further sealed the Preakness's reputation as a classic. The horse won the most money among two-year-old thoroughbreds in 1919 and won nine of ten starts.[24] But the owner, Samuel J. Riddle, still thought he had over-raced the horse in 1919, and, controversially, decided to skip the Kentucky Derby and race only in the Preakness. So he had the horse winter in Maryland and limited his racing. The press hyped the horse's grand potential throughout the winter, even noting that Maryland was "Becoming Recognized as Home for the Thoroughbred" because Riddle had decided to winter and train Man O' War on Maryland's Eastern Shore.[25] Man O' War dominated the Preakness. The *Baltimore Sun* noted cheekily, "There were the horses, headed in the beginning by one Man O' War—and headed in the end by the same horse, himself a king among his kind, looking like it and behaving like it."[26] At this point, the Preakness had finally established itself as a preeminent race in the eyes of horse racing aficionados.

The 1920s was a good decade for the Preakness. In 1921, the Maryland Jockey Club once again increased the race's purse, this time to $40,000. That year, the *New York Times* noted that the prize purse was "$5,000 more than the Kentucky Derby prize, thus making the Maryland event the richest of the three-year-old tests of the year."[27] And in 1922, the *New York Times* noted that the "Preakness May Be Richest Turf Classic" when the Maryland Jockey Club announced that it was increasing the purse to $50,000.[28] This was almost fifty times the amount that the Maryland Jockey Club had offered in the early 1910s. The Preakness remained a popular event throughout the decade with huge purses, large enthusiastic crowds, and premier thoroughbreds competing.[29]

More broadly, the 1920s was a so-called Golden Age of sport in the United States. Sports were buoyed by a booming economy and new consumer-friendly media technology such as radio broadcasts and newsreels, which brought immediate access to race results and the first moving pictures of races. The newsreel technology made the races seem faster than they would have in person, as the technology could not capture enough frames per second to portray reality, so when the reel was played the movement sped up. The era of a larger-than-life Babe Ruth living the high life—driving fast cars, eating to excess—symbolized the growing consumer ethos. While the American professional sports scene was evolving into one filled with celebrities and more team sports, horse racing became more popular and its purses grew. The Preakness's entrants and purses captured attention—with the *New York Times*, for example, using headlines such as "Horses, Jockeys and Odds in $50,000 Preakness Today." Similar to other sporting events in the 1920s, the Preakness Stakes gained an aura of being spectacular.[30]

The 1930s brought economic turmoil to the nation. The Depression's impact was not missed on horse racing tracks. Horse racing revenue, prize purses, salaries, and staff all declined. The Maryland Jockey Club decreased the Preakness Stakes prize purse from $50,000 to $25,000 during the early 1930s. Still, the Preakness remained of great interest to fans and a prominent race. Those interested included Alfred G. Vanderbilt of the famous railroad baron family, who bought into the Maryland Jockey Club in the mid-1930s. And as the Depression wore on, horse racing continued and, with Vanderbilt onboard in 1937, the Jockey Club increased the Preakness purse back to $50,000.[31]

Horse racing in the 1930s was anything but depressed. The horses and their jockeys captured the nation's attention and in some cases served as an important distraction. In 1930, the "Fox of Belair" was especially interesting to Marylanders. Though Gallant Fox was bred in Kentucky, he spent most of his racing life based on a farm in Collington, Maryland.[32] Gallant Fox lived up to his hype: he won the Preakness, the Derby, and then the Belmont Stakes. As *New York Times* writer Bryan Field exclaimed, "Another horse has joined the ranks of the great racers. Within ninety days, William Woodward's Gallant Fox has won the Wood Memorial, Preakness, Kentucky Derby, Belmont Stakes and Arlington Classic, obtaining for his owner purses of more than a quarter of a million dollars."[33] Field also noted, "There was one race especially of Gallant Fox's this season where Sande [the jockey] has no breath to sing, for the horse ran and won on his brains and courage, on his thoroughbred heart, which would not give up when things seemed most hopeless. This was the Preakness." Although these races were still not recognized as an official series, Field used the term "Triple Crown" while reporting on Gallant Fox. By the 1940s, the idea and phrase had caught on.[34]

Five years after Gallant Fox, Omaha was the next colt to be victorious in the three races. Omaha also captured Marylanders' hearts, as he was from the same owner, William Woodward, and farm as the Gallant Fox. With much less fanfare, Omaha dispatched his rivals and again Bryan Field used the term Triple Crown to describe the racing.[35] In 1937, the Triple was again captured. A descendant of Man O' War (the horse that captured the nation's attention in 1920), War Admiral continued his ancestor's legacy by winning the three races.

Popular interest in the race remained high throughout the decade and another World War was a boom time for horse racing. The term Triple Crown came into common vernacular in the 1940s and the Preakness became part of the most famous trio of races. While war-rationing requirements almost

Pimlico Race Course, from the grandstand, 1943.
Arthur S. Siegel, Library of Congress, Prints & Photographs Division, FSA/OWI Collection (LC-USW3-026512-E).

stopped the Preakness from occurring in 1945, the race and horse racing in general were at or near their zenith in the 1940s.[36]

A now popular tradition solidified at the Preakness Stakes in the 1940s: the Black-Eyed Susan Blanket given to the winner. The black-eyed Susan was made Maryland's official state flower in 1918, as it incorporates black and yellow, the official state colors, and in 1940 the Preakness adopted the black-eyed Susan as its flower. The flower's status is not without controversy; critics say it is not really native to Maryland. Moreover, it is a strange choice as a winner's award for a May race in Maryland since the flower does not usually bloom until June. As a result, over the years race organizers have used a variety of flowers and methods to fake the appearance of the black-eyed Susan. Nonetheless, the tradition is so well known that spectators sometimes refer to the Preakness Stakes as "The Run For the Black-Eyed Susans," and there have been many Preakness-themed, black-eyed-Susan-inspired cocktails created and served for spectators.[37]

The Preakness attracted all the champions of the 1940s. There were a record four horses that won the Triple Crown in this period—more than at any time before or after the decade. The first horse, Whirlaway, won in 1941. He was a product of the famed Calumet farm in Kentucky and swept the series, including the Preakness. Only two years later, Count Fleet, another Kentucky-bred horse, followed suit. Three years later, a rare Texas-bred horse, Assault, was not a favorite, but became the third Triple Crown winner of the 1940s. The final horse, Citation, again came from the Calumet farm in Kentucky and dominated the 1948 season, taking the Triple Crown. Unlike many other horses, he successfully continued racing until 1951, when he became the first horse to win $1 million in prize money.[38]

The 1950s were not as positive for horse racing as they were for the American economy as a whole. The decade marked the beginning of a decline in overall interest in horse racing in the United States and Baltimore. Not coincidentally, this decline correlated with the steady rise of the "Big Four" professional team sports of baseball, football, basketball, and ice hockey. One of the main reasons for the success of these sports was their sports administrators' proactive use of the new medium of television, which brought games to thousands of households. Horse racing was also on television but was less prominent and was losing ground to other American sports that had more regular schedules, such as baseball and football. The steady development of off-track betting in horse racing also meant that spectators no longer had to attend the race to easily follow the action, so fewer people came to the races.

By 1952, the Maryland Jockey Club and Pimlico were once again on shaky financial ground. The club, which still had traditional figures such as Alfred G. Vanderbilt on its executive board, was perhaps outdated. Two businessmen, brothers Herman and Ben Cohen, with a few other investors, would change the club and track. The Cohens were successful entrepreneurs, but were known primarily for being the Baltimore television owners who operated Baltimore's WAAM station. Already by 1952, there were rumors of a hostile takeover of Pimlico by investors who threatened to buy a controlling share of stock on the track. In addition, the Maryland Jockey Club seriously considered shutting the track down and moving the Preakness Stakes to a track in Laurel, though the effort ultimately failed. There was fear, too, that the new investors would not be from or interested in the Baltimore area. While there were rumors of interest from several parties, by the end of 1952 a syndicate that included the Cohens bought a controlling interest. The Maryland Jockey Club had a four-person voting trust comprised of Alfred G. Vanderbilt and three other prominent members. According to the *Baltimore Sun*, they approved the Pimlico sale in November when the Cohens and Cary Boshamer, a South Carolina textile manufacturer and horse breeder, purchased 78,000 shares (of the 90,800 available) for $1.95 million. This was 86 percent of the available shares. They announced, "we have discussed the present low standing of the Preakness . . . we have agreed that it should be built into its most glamorous . . . possibilities . . . Pimlico is the second oldest race track now in operation. It was founded 82 years ago."[39]

Initially, the syndicate made Cary Boshamer president. He only lasted one year as president and quit the position in 1953. In his stead, Baltimorean Herman Cohen became president, while his brother Ben became the secretary-treasurer. The *Baltimore Sun* noted that the Cohens promoted an all-Baltimore staff. This was notable, as Boshamer had been an outsider to the community.[40] The Cohens would run Pimlico and the Preakness until the 1980s and guided the track successfully through several challenges.

Despite the general decline and new ownership, Pimlico and the Preakness remained a steadfast part of the Triple Crown. However, one of the most tragic events to occur happened in 1966. Around 11:30 p.m. on June 17, a fire began in the old historic clubhouse at Pimlico. The clubhouse was home to the Maryland Jockey Club's records and memorabilia. While the fire was quickly noticed and the fire department was fighting the blaze by midnight, the fire burned largely out of control until 1:00 a.m. According to the *Baltimore Sun*, it "was a spectacular fire. Spectators jammed Park Heights and Belvedere Avenues near the fire, which shot up high above the roof and could be seen a mile away in Northwest Baltimore." The newspaper also reported on the front page, "Damage Appears to Be Total; Weathervane Stands Amid Ruins." Thus, in 1966 the old clubhouse at Pimlico burned down, along with most of the old records of the Maryland Jockey Club. Ultimately, Pimlico persevered and the fire did not spread beyond the clubhouse, thankfully.[41] Still, much was lost. "You can't put a price on tradition, history and art," said Charles "Chick" Lang, then the track's racing director.[42]

Before the fire, the Cohens hired Lang to manage racing at Pimlico in 1962 and in 1969 named him general manager of the track. Lang led the track and the Preakness through one of the most culturally turbulent decades since the Civil War.[43] In addition to the clubhouse burning down, several race-related riots in Baltimore, and in the neighborhood that surrounded Pimlico, challenged the track's very existence. Nonetheless, the Preakness remained at Pimlico and, during Lang's tenure from 1969 to 1989, attendance at the event tripled to 90,000.[44] In 1973, Secretariat, now the subject of a Hollywood movie, shocked a nation. First, the horse's owner was a woman, Helen Bates "Penny" Chenery, which was an anomaly in a normally white male-dominated position; second, there had been no Triple Crown winner since Citation in 1948.

Overcoming the odds, Secretariat dominated all horses and silenced many critics.[45] He set track records at all of his events except, controversially, the Preakness—due to a timing error. Nearly forty years later, the Maryland Racing Commission used film to reverse engineer a still-record time of 1:53 flat, to give Secretariat the Preakness record in 2012, which still stands.[46] Subsequently, two horses won the Triple Crown. Seattle Slew, a Kentucky-bred horse, without much initial fanfare, remained undefeated in 1977 and took the Crown. The horse would have the shortest reign of any Triple Crown winner, as Affirmed raced to the Crown the next year.[47]

The Cohens successfully ran Pimlico through the 1980s. Herman Cohen remained president of the Pimlico Race Course from 1953 until he retired in 1986. During that time, he also served as president of the Maryland Jockey Club and acted as a trustee for the prestigious Thoroughbred Racing Association from 1964 until the year before he retired from Pimlico. The Cohens were also active and successful horse breeders and handicappers.

By the mid-1980s, Pimlico was in need of renovation and modernization. The same was true of much of Baltimore at the time; there was a rundown feeling to the track and there was some fear that the Preakness might be moved to a more updated track. Additionally, some people in surrounding communities were unhappy with Pimlico's parking and event management and particularly unhappy with the Preakness.[48] In this context, Frank De Francis came on the scene. De Francis was a politically connected lawyer from Washington, DC, who had also served as the state economic development secretary for Maryland. He was involved with harness racing, and made a big splash in 1980 when he gained the controlling interest in the Laurel Race Course, where he increased the number of races and the track's revenue.[49] By the mid-1980s, it became no secret that he wanted to control Pimlico. De Francis was a powerful ally of William Donald Schaefer, the Baltimore mayor who had largely engineered the Inner Harbor of Baltimore and brought the National Aquarium to the city. In 1986, Schaefer was elected governor of Maryland and De Francis bought the Pimlico track from the Cohens. The governor planned for his inaugural ball to be held at De Francis's Laurel Race Course.[50]

Almost immediately, De Francis began the process of modernizing the track, its betting system, and other features when he purchased Pimlico in the mid-1980s. To increase interest among a new generation of horse racing fans, Francis installed large video screens in many locations in the track, including a twelve-foot screen. This innovation allowed fans to watch multiple sporting events while waiting for races. While not all Baltimore residents were excited about the increased traffic that an updated Pimlico track would bring, the politically powerful De Francis threatened to move the Preakness from Baltimore if he did not gain the support he needed. In the end, De Francis increased the popularity of the Preakness at Pimlico.[51]

When De Francis died in 1994, his son Joe took over the family horse racing business. Joe De Francis continued to run the track until 2002. Horse racing, however, slumped further as increased competition with slot machine gambling in Pennsylvania and New Jersey decimated the income potential at Pimlico. In 2002, De Francis sold Pimlico and Laurel to Magna Entertainment Corporation, a Canadian-based entertainment company.[52]

Pimlico and the Preakness Stakes remained a premiere event in horse racing. By 2002, the purse at the Preakness had grown to $1 million.[53] However, with an economic recession in 2008 and a declining revenue base, Magna Entertainment Corporation filed for bankruptcy protection in 2009. A further consolidation of American racetrack ownership occurred when the Stronach Group, the parent company of Magna, purchased a controlling percentage in both Pimlico and Laurel Park. The Stronach group also owns the Santa Anita Park in California; Gulfstream Park in Hallandale Beach, Florida; Golden Gate Fields in California; and Portland Meadows in Oregon.[54] Pimlico, nonetheless, has prospered under the new ownership.

Conclusion: A Race and a City for the Ages

Much like the Preakness, Baltimore's fortunes have ebbed and flowed. From being one of the three largest cities in the country and an early center of the railroad industry, the city declined in relative population and industry compared to New York City, Washington, DC, and Philadelphia. As centers of politics and commerce, Washington and Philadelphia surpassed Baltimore. But with Pimlico and the Preakness, Baltimore does have a horse racing tradition that those cities could be envious of, and still symbolizes the area's colonial-era power and prestige.

Similar to the political economy of Baltimore, the race has been subject to changing power dynamics of race and gender during the nineteenth, twentieth, and twenty-first centuries. Although the participants, or owners and managers of them, have almost uniformly been white, upper-class men, there seems to be change in the air. Politically, Baltimore, despite having a clear majority of women and minorities, was long dominated by white men. While the trend continues to a degree, it is notable that women and minorities have moved into many positions of power, including the city's mayoral office. The trend, too, seems to be reflected at the Preakness. In 2013, Kevin Krigger became the first African American jockey to race in the Preakness since the Sims victory in 1898.[55] Also in 2013, jockey Rosie Napravnik challenged the male dominance by entering and racing in the Preakness; she was only the third woman to ride in the Preakness.[56]

The Preakness has reflected and heightened Baltimore's image as a city with a rich, if sometimes troubled, history. It is raced in a city that is imbued with the change and continuity of the Mid-Atlantic region. For many, the race is experienced as a background to a big party, traffic annoyance, or news channel fodder. At the same time, it is a steadfast ritual on Baltimore's cultural calendar and important to the city's identity. It has been used alternatively as evidence of the city's renaissance and decline. To be sure, the Preakness Stakes is a signature event in Baltimore and reflects the city's long and distinguished pedigree as a great American metropolis.[57]

3

Black Knights and Engineers

The City-Poly Football Rivalry

DEAN BARTOLI SMITH AND TED PATTERSON

Two weeks after John F. Kennedy's presidential election in 1960, on Thanksgiving Day in Baltimore, tens of thousands flocked to Memorial Stadium on Thirty-Third Street to watch a high school football game. All over the city, families gathered around their TVs to watch the nation's second-oldest public high school football rivalry, Baltimore City College vs. Baltimore Polytechnic Institute, better known as City and Poly. Poly hadn't lost to City in ten years and had only two losses that year. City didn't have a chance, with only two wins all season.

Poly led by four points with a little more than twenty seconds left in the half. City running back Tom Duley stood on his ten-yard line to take the Poly kickoff, when a referee told him, "Keep your head up, son." Duley responded, "I will."[1] Duley lived in fear of his coach George Young, a large and imposing presence who would go on to coaching positions with the Baltimore Colts, the Miami Dolphins, and eventually became the general manager of the New York Giants. Earlier that season, as City was driving down field for a game-winning touchdown against Frederick Douglass High School in the rain, Duley could hear his coach screaming at him. The running back finally understood. "Tuck your shirt in!" Young was yelling. The drive fizzled.

Now he was waiting for a kickoff with his underdog team only down by four points.[2] The ball bounced twice, and four Poly guys hit him as he reached the 25. They lifted him up and there was no place for him to fall, so he ran 75 more yards for a game-changing, rivalry-altering touchdown.

"Duley, Duley, Duley," they yelled. City beat Poly for the first time in ten years, 30–26.[3]

A young reporter for the City College newspaper, the *Collegian*, who would go on to work for the *Baltimore Sun*, Michael Olesker asked Duley what he was thinking when he crossed the goal line. Duley replied that he was worried about his coach George Young. He didn't want to be yelled at for showboating, so he just laid the ball on the end zone turf.

Duley took an MTA bus home after the game. At his stop on Harford Road, he discovered the day's final edition of the *Evening Sun*, and a front-page headline: "City Upsets Poly; Duley Electrifies Crowd of 18,000." His mother was impressed as the family sat around the dinner table for its Thanksgiving Day feast. "It took my son to knock John Kennedy off the front page," she said.[4]

The memory of Duley's eighty-five-yard run remained lodged in the city's football consciousness for decades, in part because it exemplified the intensity of the rivalry and defined an era. City won eight of the next ten contests in the series. "The game was a very big deal," said Olesker. "It was broadcast on two local television stations. I was a spotter for Jim West on Channel 11. Colt Buddy Young was doing the color. That's how big it was."[5]

Today, in its 127th year, the City vs. Poly game is still a meaningful contest between two of the city's largest high schools. It's a rivalry that has been defined by legendary coaches. City's football prowess has owed much to Harry Lawrence, George Young, and George Petrides. Bob Lumsden and Augie Waibel combined to lead Poly for fifty years. Except for the early years and a tough stretch in the 1930s and early 1940s, Poly has more than held its own against City. Poly has an edge in the series with sixty-two wins. City has won fifty-five games and there have been six ties.[6]

The two schools have long, rich histories and distinct cultures rooted in part to their different academic emphases. A college preparatory school, Baltimore City College first opened its doors in 1839 and is one of the nation's oldest public schools. Its curriculum has always emphasized the study of classics, humanities, and the liberal arts. Now located at Thirty-Third Street and the Alameda, students refer to the "Gothic stone castle on Collegian hill" as the "Castle on the Hill." Among its distinguished alumni are scientists who have won the Nobel Prize and many of Maryland's city and state leaders. The list includes US congressman Elijah Cummings, Senator Ben Cardin, Baltimore mayors William Donald Schaefer and Kurt Schmoke, *New York Times* columnist Russell Baker, and the poet Karl Shapiro.[7]

With a focus on math, science, and engineering, the Baltimore Polytechnic Institute began in 1883 as an all-male trade school for "engineers"—hence, its nickname. "Poly" was located for many years on North Avenue and Calvert Street before moving northwest to its current location at the intersection of Cold Spring Avenue and Falls Road. The school went coed in 1974 and has graduated numerous political and civic leaders, along with writers Dashiell Hammett and H. L. Mencken. The sciences are also well represented by Robert H. Roy, dean of engineering at Johns Hopkins University, and physicist Dr. Carl Oliver Clark, the first African American to graduate from the University of South Carolina with a degree in physics. Jacqueline Williams, a 1981 graduate, became the school's first African American principal in 2012.[8]

The Early Years

The City-Poly football rivalry dates to 1889, but poor recordkeeping makes it hard to trace the exact scores. All that is known of the first game in 1889 is that the City JV team played Poly at Clifton Park and won the first of six unreported games. City fielded a competitive team long before that, playing the Naval Academy as early as 1894. In fact, game programs indicate that before 1903, when scores began to be officially recorded, City won all the games. This is because City was playing several college teams and considered Poly contests mere exhibitions.[9] City College, nicknamed the Black Knights, has competed in more than 1,200 football games, winning more than twenty Maryland Scholastic Associations and Baltimore city championships.

Located close to Courtland Street and the nearby, imposing City College, the Baltimore Polytechnic Institute started fielding a football team in 1889. The first recorded score between City and Poly was from the 1901 game, won by City 5–0 at Union Park. Poly's first win over City didn't come until an 11–0 shutout in 1908, with 2,000 fans in attendance at Oriole Park. The win gave the Engineers of Poly the Interscholastic championship of the East.[10]

In 1906, City College had its thirteen-member team pictured in *Spalding's Official Football Guide*, a first for a local high school. That year, City College was playing an eleven-game schedule against college teams such as the Maryland Agricultural College in College Park, as well as local high school rivals such as Poly, Mount St. Joseph, and Sparrows Point. Poly, then known as the Baltimore Manual Training School, began fielding an official team, against the wishes of faculty and administration. The team was not allowed to use the school name, for fear it would discredit the institution.[11]

By 1916, the intensity of the City-Poly game was palpable. On the night before he was to play, Poly's Ernie Hill dreamed he booted the game-winning extra point. Hill awoke in agony, having kicked a bedpost and broken two toes.[12]

One of the most famous City-Poly games was played on November 20, 1926 at the Baltimore Stadium on Thirty-Third Street. With over 20,000 fans in the stands, the game was scoreless heading into the fourth quarter. Poly's Harry Lawrence, who had already missed two drop kicks, tried a third from the thirty-yard line and split the uprights for a 3–0 win. Later, after a stellar playing career at Bucknell College, Lawrence became a legendary coach at City College. One of Lawrence's protégés at Bucknell was George Young. By 1929, the Knights had a new $3 million, forty-acre home in northeast Baltimore. The "Castle on the Hill" had spacious practice fields and a separate "game day field."[13]

Under coach Harry Lawrence, the Knights dominated local teams, including Poly, whom they beat consecutively from 1934 to 1942. By 1940, Lawrence's teams were unbeaten in thirty-eight straight games and won three consecutive state titles. In 1947, Lawrence parlayed his success into becoming the head coach at Bucknell.[14]

On the occasion of the sixtieth anniversary of the City-Poly game on November 25, 1948, at Babe Ruth Stadium, an unidentified booster summed up the contest in the game program:

> Reflect for a moment what is wrapped in that simple statement. Two male high schools of Baltimore have been meeting in annual football competition for well over half a century. Through two World Wars, through a great depression and some minor ones; through a concerted attack upon the game of football from the office of the Chief Executive of the United States (Theodore Roosevelt); two high schools of Baltimore have kept their annual date.
>
> Perhaps, somewhere in Ohio or on the plains of Texas, high school teams play better football. Maybe they draw greater crowds. But they can't conjure up the tradition which has grown around one of the longest rivalries in the country, exceeded in the collegiate ranks, as far as is known, by only Yale's annual series with Harvard and Princeton.
>
> Best then, old grad and friends, stand no longer between you and the precious experience of being a boy again. Somewhere in the game and between the halves today, that rare privilege awaits you.[15]

This commentary by an anonymous fan reveals the power of this intense rivalry and foreshadows its impact on generations of Baltimore football fans for more than a century.

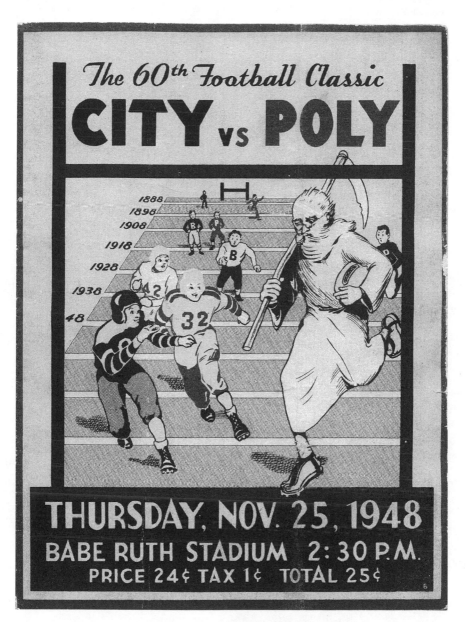

The 1948 City-Poly football game program.
From the personal collection of Ted Patterson.

They Called Him "Mister Poly"

An assistant coach at City in the late 1940s, Bob Lumsden left the Knights to take over the head coaching duties at Poly and dominated City and Maryland football during the 1950s. City was unable to win any of the rivalry games during that decade. Lumsden led his football teams from 1949 to 1966 to a 139-24-6 record.[16]

Lumsden played tailback for Poly from 1938 to 1940, walked the sidelines as the Engineers coach, or sat in the stands for over sixty City-Poly games, beginning in 1932. He was eighty-one when he retired and fifty of those years were spent at Poly. Lumsden coached several sports, including football and baseball, retiring as Poly athletic director in 1980. "In my years as coach we used to draw over 30,000 fans at Memorial Stadium for City-Poly," remembered Lumsden. "There were only eight public high schools and most kids went to either Poly, City, Forest Park or Southern. There were 3,000 boys at Poly and 3,000 boys at City and the fervor for the schools was community wide, not just East Baltimore or in the county," recalled the man dubbed "Mister Poly."[17]

The rivalry game became a Thanksgiving Day tradition in 1944. That game ended in a 7–7 tie with a crowd estimate anywhere from 27,000 to 35,000.[18] It was a tradition that Lumsden said began by accident. "We had to move the game from a Saturday because the Naval Academy wanted to play the Army-Navy game in 1944 on the same date in Baltimore. Loyola and Calvert Hall, the other great rivalry who played on Thanksgiving, were kind enough to let us follow them on Thanksgiving afternoon and it stayed that way for the next 50 years."

Both rivalry games on Thanksgiving Day stayed heated until 1992. During the twelve years the city endured without a professional football team (1984–1996), these two rivalry games filled the void and gave football fans something to look forward to on Thanksgiving Day. "In the 30s and 40s, City vs. Poly was a much bigger game than Loyola vs. Calvert Hall," explains legendary Baltimore sportscaster Vince Bagli. "But that changed in the 1950s and 60s and the games were of equal importance. Loyola and Calvert Hall became the marquee match-up as time wore on."[19]

The Loyola Dons and Calvert Hall Cardinals, two Catholic schools, started playing each other in 1920 and their rivalry is in its ninety-sixth year. The teams play at 10:00 on Thanksgiving morning in M&T Bank Stadium, where the NFL's Ravens play. Like City-Poly, these schools also have a colorful rivalry filled with tradition and mayhem. In 1978, after upsetting the No. 1-ranked Calvert Hall, 30–12, the Loyola players returned to campus and jumped into the swimming pool with their uniforms on. For many years,

Joe Brune, a former assistant to George Young, coached Loyola. "George Young influenced everything I did," said Brune, who coached Loyola with integrity and grace for thirty-five years.[20]

Brune battled Calvert Hall's coach Augie Miceli in the 1960s and 1970s. Miceli once ruined Loyola's championship season by executing a perfect reverse on a kickoff late in the game. "We practiced it on special teams, but we'd never run it before," said Miceli. Both schools sent scouts to every game to prepare for the "Turkey Bowl." The fate of entire seasons hinged on winning the Thanksgiving Day game. Records were thrown out the window.

The rivalry has had its ebbs and flows in recent years. Calvert Hall has won five out of the last six contests. In 2013, Loyola broke a four-game losing streak by blocking an extra point in overtime to win 21–20. The Dons hold the series lead 48-37-8.[21]

High school football was at its zenith in Baltimore in the years immediately after World War II and into the 1950s. "We'd play night games at Memorial Stadium against Loyola, Calvert Hall and others and draw 15,000 or more," remembered Bob Lumsden, who died in 2002 at the age of eighty-one. "It was a town thing, a family thing, and a community thing because the schools were all closely associated. The kids knew the kids on the other teams, the families knew the families and they were just big, fun events."[22]

Lumsden lost his first game to City as head coach at Poly 26–12 in 1949, but starting in 1950 he won five straight and nine of ten. His overall record against City was 11-7. "Coaches create their own pressure but when you're attached to a school as much as I've been attached to Poly, it was like life or death when we played City," he said. His list of top City-Poly moments: "The 1950 win, 12–0, which broke a four-game losing streak, was great and so was the 1959 win, also 12–0 because that team was one of the greatest in Poly history," recalled Lumsden. "When you look at speed, size, and ability."[23] The 1962 team, which later that year played a team from Miami in the Orange Bowl, was also one of his favorites. Lumsden, though, cringed at any reminder of the aforementioned Tom Duley, the stocky fifteen-year-old running back at City who took the second half kickoff, burst through a pile of would-be tacklers and ran eighty yards for a touchdown.[24]

Lumsden had a profound effect on many of the young men he coached. For every great player, there were eight or ten who had limited ability but were made better players and human beings because of their association with "Mister Poly." Those that come to mind include Roland Savage; Ernie Torain; Ed Stuckrath; the Spangler brothers, Bill and John; Jack Scarbath, a converted center who won All-American honors as starting quarterback at the University of Maryland; and Harry Olszewski. Before he stepped down as coach, Lumsden picked an able assistant named Augie Waibel to replace him on the Poly sideline.

George Young Restores Knights to Prominence

The bespectacled George Young took over at City for Frank Lee in 1959. He beat Poly six times and won as many championships.[25] Young, a history teacher, assembled a great young staff led by Joe Brune, Mel Filler, Ed Novak, and Bob Patzwall. His summer practices were brutal affairs, which focused on running and conditioning—and not blocking and tackling. He was also a disciplinarian who focused on his players getting good grades. The owner of the Ivy Bookstore, Ed Berlin, recalls his first class with Young at City. "He told us that he hated everyone. But I found the opposite to be true."[26]

Michael Olesker recalls being summoned to Young's classroom to defend his comments about the football team in the school paper. The young reporter stood in the front of the class as Young questioned his loyalty to the team.

An especially memorable City-Poly game during Young's tenure occurred on Thanksgiving Day 1965, at Memorial Stadium, with approximately 25,000 fans and alumni in the stands. City thrashed Poly, 52–6, and completed an undefeated 10-0 season. Additionally, the team was ranked eighth in the nation according to one poll. The 52 points scored by City are the most points scored by either team during the rivalry. Two Knights from that game, Sykes and Ara Person, later played in the National Football League. Future Baltimore mayor Kurt Schmoke was the quarterback.[27]

When Bob Lumsden moved on to become the athletic director at Poly in 1967, Augie Waibel replaced him. A teammate of Jack Scarbath's at the University of Maryland, Waibel coached Poly football for thirty-one years, winning 280 games and 14 MSA A Conference championships before retiring in 1997. Only four of his teams finished the season without a winning record. He beat Poly twenty-one times and coached wide receiver Antonio Freeman, who later started at Virginia Tech and with the Green Bay Packers.[28] In 1990, in the snow and freezing cold at Memorial Stadium, Freeman hauled in two long touchdown passes from quarterback Chris Lafferman as the Engineers won, 27–0.[29] When Waibel died in 2001, the *Baltimore Sun* reported that he was eulogized "as a man who influenced many lives with his dedication, humility and honesty."[30]

Petrides Weathers the Storm and Shines

When George Young left to coach the Colts in 1967, his assistant Bob Patzwall took over as head coach at City College. Bob Terpening and Ron Chartrand followed Patzwall before former City lineman George Petrides became head coach in 1975. Petrides would eventually lead City to a twenty-nine-game winning streak during the 1990s, the longest in the history of Maryland high school football. During the 1960s, Petrides played on City College teams that never lost a game, but at the beginning of his coaching career, he was faced with almost impossible circumstances.[31]

The City College building was being renovated, which caused enrollment to plummet and the student body to take courses at the old Poly building on North Avenue in midtown Baltimore. The athletic practice field was two miles away, and in 1979 Petrides was forced to use his junior varsity team to play Poly's varsity because of the dwindling enrollment. The "Castle on the Hill" reopened in 1978 but the Knights did not beat Poly again until 1987. They dropped seventeen straight games to Poly from 1970 to 1986, and were outscored 464–71, before George Petrides brought the Knights back to prominence.[32] A quiet leader, Petrides used an old-school approach based on the fundamentals he learned from playing center for George Young's teams in the 1960s, and he continued to ride that formula to success until he retired in 2015.

One of Petrides's most memorable games at City came against Poly in 1987, a 34–22 win on Thanksgiving. The Knights had not beat Poly since two years after Petrides graduated in 1967. He was coach of the year in 1987, beating Poly and earning an 11-0 record. The Knights won that ninety-ninth game because of "The Play." Quarterback Chris Smith, the *Baltimore Sun*'s All-Metro Player of the Year in 1987, handed the ball off to fullback Paul Williams, who tried to sweep left but was chased down by Poly's defense.[33]

Petrides has won several city championships, including one in 2006 that was punctuated with a 44–8 pasting of Poly to finish the season 11-1. City lost in the state championship game, 7–6. In 1988, the game's one hundredth anniversary, Petrides led the Knights out of the first base dugout at Memorial Stadium, and Waibel did the same with his Engineers from the third base side. City won the game, 27–0.[34]

In 1992, the tradition of the City-Poly game being played on Thanksgiving Day ended when Baltimore City public schools sports programs moved to the Maryland Public Secondary Schools Athletic Association (MPSSAA). MPSSAA football playoffs start in November and so the City-Poly game has been moved to the first week of November. To keep some of the luster on the rivalry, the game is still played at Ravens Stadium.

Unfortunately, the City-Poly rivalry has lost some of its intensity since moving from Thanksgiving Day. There are still pranks and the occasional postgame mêlée, but no crowds rushing the field as they did in 1936 to tear down the goal posts, leaving the police to hold up the crossbar as time ran out. In its heyday, the rivalry was so intense that not even a peace pact could prevent one thousand boys in 1948 from charging through city streets, cheering their teams, setting off firecrackers, and overturning trash cans and bursting "into movie theaters and hotel lobbies."[35]

Since 1993, City has won eleven of twenty games against Poly. For George Petrides, the rivalry is no longer especially significant. In 2013 he said, "To me, it's the next game."[36] Former Ravens defensive tackle and University of Maryland standout Larry Webster now coaches Poly, and the game still has meaning to the students of both schools.[37] "It's an exciting game," said Astrid Kamali, at the time a rising junior at City College. "There is a lot of school spirit, more school pride than anti-opponent angst—our band performed better than theirs did. It's fun to be in the big stadium."[38]

For myriad reasons, the City-Poly football game lacks the neighborhood dynamic that made it such a fierce rivalry in the past, when city blocks included students attending both schools and emotions ran high. More schools were opened and that helped water down the rivalry. But it still brings generations of families together, fathers and sons, and ardent supporters of both schools. The rivalry was cemented into Baltimore's sports mythology and lore during the 1950s, 1960s, 1970s, and 1980s. After the Colts left Baltimore for Indianapolis in 1984, the Thanksgiving Day games were the only storied football games the city had. During that time, City-Poly was the marquee matchup, not Loyola vs. Calvert Hall.

For 1985 Poly graduate and Baltimore writer Gregg Wilhelm, the City-Poly game will always remain a football rite of passage: "It was the first time I was allowed to go out and be with my friends on a holiday. There was a real sense of freedom. We always beat City in those days."[39]

The rivalry entered its 127th year in 2015. It remains an important game for both schools: for the students, the players, and their families. It is also a major part of the city's rich football history. The "rare privilege" identified by the anonymous fan in 1948 is still there for the taking—the chance to venture into the heart of Baltimore and watch two schools make one more entry into their distinguished football legacy allows us to stoke the embers of our own gridiron memories.

4

"For a White Boy's Chance in the World"

Joe Gans, Baltimore's Forgotten Fighter

WILLIAM GILDEA

Often I'm asked, "Why Joe Gans? Why did you write a book about him?"

The answer is easy: He came from Baltimore and so did I.

At least that's what got me interested. The result: *The Longest Fight: In the Ring with Joe Gans, Boxing's First African American Champion* was published in 2012.[1] Gans fought from 1891 to 1909. He was lightweight champion from 1902 to 1908. I had never heard of Joe Gans until 1966, a long time ago but pretty far along in my lifetime. Having been born in 1939, I'm not happy to admit that it took me so long to become aware of Joe Gans. Even when I first saw the name, it was mentioned only in passing in a magazine article.

I was raised in a corner of Baltimore, near Gwynn Oak Junction, a white community then. No one that I knew, my family included, spoke of black people, or spoke of black people respectfully. I went to an all-white grade school and an all-white high school, then went away to college and it, too, was all white except for one black, who was a day student. I cared about sports, which I learned from my father, but I never knew anything about the Baltimore Elite Giants or where they played, and it wasn't until much later that I learned that Roy Campanella and Jim Gilliam played for them—and I suspected that the black team was probably better than the minor-league Orioles, whom I followed.

From that bleak start, in terms of race, my thinking expanded readily because fellow students in college came from around the country and had fruitful experiences with African Americans that I never had. I also met a number of African Americans in graduate school and the army. I wrote about blacks during my twenty-two months on the *Baltimore Sun* and, for years, at the *Washington Post*.

In 1966, a year after I was lucky enough to be hired by the *Post*, I saw Gans's name in an article by Mark Kram in *Sports Illustrated*, a story about Baltimore leading up to the World Series that year.[2] He mentioned that the city was where boxing champions were raised. I, in turn, mentioned Joe Gans a couple of times in articles. He stuck in my mind. But I had no idea then that I would write a book about him.

When I retired from the *Post* in 2005, I pursued Gans, gingerly at first, because little was written about him. He was a significant figure, I knew. Jack Johnson, Joe Louis, the young Muhammad Ali, and the young Mike Tyson copied parts of his repertoire. But I didn't want to write a book strictly about boxing. I was interested more in what it was like to be black in America a century ago, and it was obvious that Gans faced discrimination as an African American man. As David Remnick, editor of the *New Yorker,* has written, boxing's subtext has always been America's subtext—race.[3]

I began work on Gans at the Library of Congress with a one-evening class on the vastness and complexities of the place. A bit of advice from that class was memorable: If returning, bring patience. I did. I worked in the newspaper reading room for at least six months before gathering up enough courage to go to the main building. During that time, I found enough on Gans to drop all thoughts of doing anything else. I had left the *Post* and slipped almost immediately into writing a book. The only problem continued to be a lack of information. I hoped for an onslaught of facts that would make me feel a little more comfortable, that would make writing a book easy. I guess nothing worth calling a book is easy. I heard about one man who started a book on Gans and gave up. His philosophy might have been: Who would want to hear about Gans anyway?

But that was what spurred me on. Most people were like I was, they had never heard of Gans, or only faintly. Baltimoreans, I thought, should have heard of him and celebrated him. He wasn't a president, but he was a first. In answer to the question, Who was the first African American boxing champion? most would say Jack Johnson. But, of course, he was the first heavyweight African American champion.

Researching Gans was a departure for me, being more familiar with press boxes than libraries. I took a decade out from the *Post*'s sports department and went to the Style section, where I was, first, a reporter, then an assignment editor. Then, I went back to Sports. I wrote a couple of books, taking a leave of five months for one. But one thing I always knew about

Gans: If I were to write a book about him, he would take my full attention and it would take more than a few months.

Gans deserves to be recognized. He was a gentleman who picked up opponents he had felled. He invented certain practices in the ring, mostly defensive ones, that boxers copied. He had to do what white people at the time thought a black boxer should—lose, even if he had to throw a fight. Above all, he could not win too handily. His manager took most of his money. He was clubbed by a policeman. His life was threatened. Those were enough obstacles, and yet the book took on a still deeper meaning for me when the host of a party, celebrating the book's publication, read a segment near the end, which I had written without much thought. In it, Gans is conversing with his manager, Al Herford:

> As our train neared Baltimore, Joe and I were seated opposite each other in a parlor car. Joe was wrapped in deep silence, his sad expression even more doleful than usual.
> "Isn't it wonderful, Joe," I asked, "being champion and all that it means? To have all of those folks enthused about you, and all of the money you are going to make? I'll bet your mother is proud of you."
> Joe didn't say anything for a long moment. Then he said wistfully, "Yes, Mr. Herford, it sure is wonderful. But do you know what I'm thinking?"
> "What?" I asked.
> "That I'd give it all up—the money, the fuss, the championship, everything—for just one thing."
> "What's that?" I asked.
> "For a white boy's chance in the world."[4]

Thinking more about this portion of the book, I realized that I had written about Joe Gans for everyone, like myself in the beginning, who hadn't heard of him or knew of him only slightly. More than that, idealistic but true, I thought that race should never disqualify anyone from happiness or the same chance to succeed as anyone else, and that maybe this book would contribute something, maybe just a small something, toward that end.

The Library of Congress, on Capitol Hill, is made up of the Jefferson Building, the main one, and two other buildings, the Madison and the Adams. One day, quite by accident, I wandered down a narrow carpeted hallway in the Jefferson Building, and sitting behind a mahogany divider was Dave Kelly, a research librarian. We began to chat. At one point in our conversation he casually said, "Well, there is some film of Joe Gans." He believed it was of a fight with Battling Nelson and told me to go across the street and try the Motion Picture and Television Reading Room, in the Madison Building, on the second floor. And so I went back to where I started. There

I found two bulky gray canisters with the film inside, the record of Gans's fight to the finish with Nelson in that time-stilled eternity under the blistering sun of the Nevada desert—the twentieth century's longest championship fight, forty-two rounds. It took almost three hours to watch the film, just about the time it took for the fighters to fight. It was the high point of Gans's boxing life, and of my quest to better understand and appreciate Gans.

I compared the Associated Press's account with the film, and everything coincided. Here for one of the first times you could see what was happening: the men in the ring's corners holding up umbrellas to shield the fighters from the afternoon's sun, most spectators in shirtsleeves, the two fighters' suffering. I watched the fight twice, on different days. I don't know how many times I visited the newspaper reading room on the Madison's first floor, but as many times as I did, and we're talking about dozens, I can't tell you definitively everything about Gans. I wish I could. I searched.

I can't say for certain that Gans was born in Baltimore. I can't tell you like the film documents the fight in black and white; nowhere that I could find is it written that Gans was born in Baltimore. But in all likelihood, he was. Without question, Baltimore was his home for most, if not all, of his thirty-five years. The problem is this: The year of his birth, 1874, and there's no reason to believe he was born in a different year, was one year before births in Baltimore were recorded. It's possible he was born in Pennsylvania or Virginia and brought to Baltimore at a young age. But in the end I doubted it. My research turned up nothing.

Baltimore, in Gans's time, was a southern city. Almost a hundred thousand blacks lived in the city, one-fifth of the population, but they were confined to one-tenth of the area. Gans opened the Goldfield Hotel and Saloon in east Baltimore, where blacks and whites mingled. George M. Cohan and Eddie Foy stopped in. Congressmen rode the train over from Washington. Eubie Blake played the piano in the Goldfield, getting his start there. Gans owned a Matheson, the first black man in Baltimore to own a car.

His name originally was not Gans, and it was not Gant, even though he told the *Baltimore Sun* it was. It was Joseph Butts. His mother is unknown. At the age of four, he was given by his father, Joseph Butts, to Maria Gant. (His name became Gans early in his boxing career, when a reporter spelled it that way). She raised him and he respected her, always consulting with her about what he was going to do next. His adoptive father James worked in a fish market, and Joe quit school after just a few grades to work in the market, too. One of the things he did was shuck oysters. It wasn't easy; he worked in the almost unbearable heat of August and the frigid months of winter. But Gans caught a lucky break, for a change.

Joe Gans of Baltimore, 1898, from the Police Gazette.
Library of Congress.

His boss in the market, Caleb Bond, was an amateur boxing coach. What odds could be had on that? Together they bought Gans's first pair of boxing gloves. Bond arranged for Gans to box two boys at a time to improve Gans's defense, which was why Gans grew up to be virtually unhittable when he was feeling well. (Not every boxer goes into every fight feeling tip-top.) Gans perfected the art of self-defense. He picked off punches with his gloves, forearms, and elbows. He sensed what was coming next. Almost overlooked was his natural ability to knock out anyone his size with one punch. He told his adoptive mother that he wanted to be a boxer, but she was against it. She had envisioned for him a lifetime shucking oysters. Reluctantly, she granted permission.

Soon he was being written up in the *Sun* as Baltimore's best boxer, and he added to the newspaper's glowing reports by watching heavyweight champion Bob Fitzsimmons, in training in the city. Gans received many tips from him—not only the fine points of boxing, but how to behave in the ring. I could only find one mention of Gans losing his temper in a fight, and that was when Nelson repeatedly hit him low during their forty-two rounder. Otherwise, and even in that fight, Gans helped his opponent up after he had knocked him down; he ministered to opponents when he flattened them for longer than ten seconds. Most of these opponents were white, because Gans's trainer, the previously mentioned Al Herford, knew that two black boxers in the main event usually meant that white patrons would stay away. When whites saw Gans tending to his beaten opponents, they were impressed. Anytime he scored a knockout, they were more impressed. Gans became the first black athlete to successfully cross the gaping racial divide. When he became champion in 1902, he knocked out Frank Erne with one punch in the first round.

Gans had to win over whites twice. In 1900, he fixed a fight in Chicago against Terry McGovern. Gans could have knocked out the smaller McGovern, but all he proved that night was that he wasn't very good at fixing: He kept falling but kept getting up. His manager had wanted to make a financial killing, and maybe he did, but Gans received only $4,500 when he thought he would receive $45,000. After that, he managed his own affairs, and he vowed never to commit such a despicable act again. He won back his fans with his boxing skills and his well-mannered ways. No amount of money, however large, was worth impinging on his good name. In 1906 at Goldfield, Nevada, most white fans rooted for him, not Battling Nelson.

Gans was no saint. He was married four times. With his first wife he probably had the two children who are mentioned in some stories. His second wife died of tuberculosis, rampant at the time. He ignored his third wife, living what he thought was a good life on the road. His fourth wife seemed to be his true love; but, by then, it was almost too late.

It probably won't ever be known how badly tuberculosis infected his body during the forty-two-rounder, but it was in his body nevertheless. The best that my research showed was that, likely, it was in his system—and that the illness flared as a result of the dehydration he must have suffered during the long fight in the desert. It's hard to say how he caught tuberculosis, or consumption, as it was called then: It could have been in a gym or from a crowded city like Baltimore. In any event, fighting with full-blown tuberculosis he was knocked out twice by Nelson, in the seventeenth and twenty-first rounds. (If a twelve-round championship limit was in force then as it is now, Gans might have won one or both fights. BoxRec.com lists Gans's record as 145-10 with 16 draws, plus decisions rendered by newspapermen as 14-2 with 4 draws, plus 5 fights ruled no contest, a total of 196 bouts.)[5] Gans gave one poor performance in New York in 1909, took to Arizona in 1910 in hope of curtailing the tuberculosis, then, realizing his trip was futile, doubled back home to Baltimore where he wanted to die. People stood in mourning at whistle stops along the way as his train passed. He died on August 10, 1910.

At his funeral, the crowd was so thick outside the church that the horse-drawn hearse could not get through and pallbearers carried the coffin through the city streets to a place where the hearse was parked. It was the largest funeral procession for a black person in the city's history: one hundred and four horse-drawn carriages and three large wagons carrying flowers. Gans is buried at Mount Auburn Cemetery, on the south edge of the city. The white press, with the exception of the Baltimore papers, gave only modest space to Gans's death and funeral, whereas the black press covered both in greater detail.

I wrote about one-third of the book before I showed it around. Tony Reid, who had been an editor on the Post, was with me from the start and suggested that I begin in Goldfield. Yet there was a problem: My literary agent, whom I had entrusted with my two previous books, told me that few publishers were interested in boxing books, and gave me a list of the places she tried. We parted, amicably. Andrew Blauner took me on and ushered me around to three houses, selling the book to two, including Farrar, Straus and Giroux.

Hank Kaplan, whom I visited at his home in Miami in 2006, had the most extensive boxing library I'd ever seen, or could hope for. In his garage, which was taken up entirely by boxing memorabilia, was a folder on every boxer who ever gained slight prominence; I found myself photocopying the

Gans folder late at night near his house. After Hank died in 2007, his collection went to Brooklyn College, which established the Hank Kaplan Boxing Archive. Tony Cucchiara, head of the archives, let me continue searching the Kaplan material before it was available to the public. I did research at more than a dozen places from New York City to the West Coast. I went to Baltimore many times. I interviewed several of Gans's descendants, and others.

The Library of Congress proved to be the most fruitful place, partly because of its historic newspapers digital collection. I consulted with more than fifty newspapers and read Sally Zanjani's books on early Nevada.

Why was Gans forgotten? There are at least two reasons: He died at thirty-five from tuberculosis, so he wasn't around as a reminder of what he had accomplished. Secondly, whites' obsession with having Jack Johnson punished—he was convicted of violating the Mann Act, that is, for transporting a (white) woman across state lines "for immoral purposes" and served almost a year in prison.[6] Gans, I have become convinced, is the most forgotten person in Baltimore who reached his goal; there are no memorials to him. He was a champion, yes, but other traits make him special: He was honest, although sometimes misled, and he was persistent despite being disadvantaged from birth.

5

On the Courts of Druid Hill

Lucy Diggs Slowe and the Rise of Organized Black Tennis

AMIRA ROSE DAVIS

Lucy Diggs Slowe stood near the net on a decaying tennis court. She wore a white tennis skirt and short-sleeved white shirt and had her short hair pulled back with a few wayward strands sticking out. Around her, Baltimore's Druid Hill Park was bustling with black Americans who had traveled from near and far to watch the newly founded American Tennis Association's first annual national tennis tournament. It was 1917. A newspaper photographer snapped her picture as she stood there firmly, confidently gripping her tennis racket: she was a national champion, the first black woman to ever hold that title.[1] The photograph captures an early twentieth-century black woman who was modern, respectable, and athletic.

Slowe is mainly known as a tremendous educator and one of the founders of Alpha Kappa Alpha, the first black sorority, but her illustrious, albeit brief, tennis career is also worthy of consideration. The story of Slowe and the rise of organized black tennis reveals a little known history of sports in Baltimore during a time of intense segregation. Legally barred from white schools, colleges, public buildings and athletic organizations, African Americans formed their own institutions and organizations to meet the needs of a population newly freed from bondage. Out of this "nation within a nation" emerged an aspiring black middle class, which settled in major cities in both the North and South. Although many studies have been done on the black elites in Washington, DC, and Philadelphia, Baltimore's aspiring-class blacks are mostly overlooked. Examining the rise of organized black tennis in Baltimore highlights the attempts of aspiring-class blacks to tie

Lucy Diggs Slowe, winner of the American Tennis Association's first tournament in 1917, which made her the first African American woman to win a national championship. *Courtesy of the Moorland-Spingarn Research Center, Howard University Archives, Howard University, Washington, DC.*

athletics and recreation to ideas about racial uplift while also insisting upon their right to live and play in a rapidly changing city.[2] Furthermore, centering this examination on Slowe highlights the long history of black women in sports and illuminates the ways in which athletics were central—not antithetical—to the construction of modern black womanhood.[3]

After situating the segregation of the Druid Hill tennis courts alongside the rise of the Jim Crow era, this chapter will trace Slowe's brief tennis career alongside her assertions of a modern middle-class identity and the development of organized black tennis. Weaving these threads together, this chapter not only reveals an important and largely ignored piece of Baltimore sports history, when the color line created two distinct yet overlapping cities, but it also highlights the long history of black women's athletic participation.

"Jim-Crowin at Druid Hill": Racial Segregation in Early Twentieth-Century Baltimore

Born July 4, 1883, in Berryville, Virginia, Lucy Diggs Slowe was the youngest of six children. Following her parents' early deaths, when she was six years old, Slowe and her sister Charlotte were placed under the care of their father's sister, whom the girls called "Aunt Martha." The girls relocated to Lexington, Virginia, where their aunt lived. Martha was strict with the girls and took great care to stress the importance of education. When Lucy was thirteen, Martha decided to move to Baltimore, noting that "city schools" offered more educational opportunities for the Slowe sisters.[4] Slowe was excited about the move and remembered "living in a dream" from the time Martha broke the news. "I shook the dust of Lexington from my feet," Slowe recalled, "and faced the mysteries of the city."[5]

Slowe's two-hundred-mile journey from Berryville to Baltimore reflected the growing migration of black Americans from rural to urban spaces in the years following the Civil War.[6] An industrious port city, Baltimore saw tremendous growth of its foreign-born citizenry, primarily immigrants from Russia, Italy, Poland, and Ireland. By 1900 the city's black population, which had been a little over 67,000 in 1890, had grown to around 77,000, or 14 percent of the population.[7] Baltimore's immigrant and general population continued to rise as well.[8] In this fast-expanding modern city, Baltimoreans moved to make forceful claims on residential and recreational spaces.

Upon moving to Baltimore, Slowe, along with her aunt and sister, settled into a small house on 1116 Division Street.[9] Martha's daughter, Louise Stuart, whom Slowe called "Cousin Lou," lived in the house, along with her husband and two daughters.[10] Slowe's multigenerational and multifamily household is indicative of typical housing arrangements for poor and working-class urban dwellers. Yet Slowe's family was also part of a growing aspiring-class black population forming in west Baltimore. Unlike the black neighborhoods in east Baltimore, Slowe's neighborhood was located in close proximity to many city resources and amenities, in particular, Druid Hill Park.

Built in the 1880s, the "grassy slopes" and "shady groves" of Druid Hill Park were the largest and most popular in Baltimore.[11] The park lay on the northwest periphery of the city and was not easily accessible to all Baltimoreans. "Poor people can not be forced to spend their hard-earned money and scanty hours of recreation in travelling out . . . to Druid Hill Park," noted famed architect and city planner Frederick Law Olmsted Jr.[12] While the poor and working-class citizens in the eastern part of the city found it hard to travel to Druid Hill, black citizens like Slowe, who were ideally located to access the park, visited it frequently. One *Baltimore Sun* reporter wrote, "about 30,000 persons visited the park . . . of that number 8,000–10,000 were negroes."[13] As historian David Zang notes, there was a "certain fluid dimension" to race relations in late nineteenth-century Baltimore. There was no written policy that barred blacks from Baltimore's public parks. In fact, the first rule in the park's rules and regulations stated that Druid Hill was to be "open to all persons upon absolutely equal terms."[14] A columnist from the *Baltimore Afro-American*, a leading black newspaper, wrote that at Druid Hill "colored people enjoyed every right that white people enjoyed," adding that black Baltimoreans "felt like there was at least one place in Baltimore where they were free."[15] This "freedom" would soon be tested.

The same year Slowe moved to Baltimore, the US Supreme Court declared racial segregation to be constitutional under the doctrine of "separate but equal" and ushered in a period of legalized segregation, known as "Jim Crow."[16] Baltimore, as well as the state of Maryland, began to introduce restrictive legislation that hardened the social and legal boundaries between the races and served to reestablish and reinforce a second-class black citizenry.[17] The segregation laws did not just target public places, and by 1910 Baltimore had become the first city in the nation to pass residential segregation ordinances.[18] As black Baltimoreans fought for inclusion in well-resourced, high-valued neighborhoods, a parallel battle was being waged over the right to maintain access to the city's public recreational space, namely, the tennis courts at Druid Hill Park.[19]

There were many things to do in Druid Hill, and the tennis courts fast became the biggest attraction. By 1900, Druid Hill boasted ten grass courts and ten clay courts. In 1902 the popularity of the courts led the Park Boards to begin issuing permits for their use.[20] By all accounts, black players were able to get permits, yet this practice soon drew the ire of some white citizens who looked to the Park Board to address the problem of "the color line in Druid Hill Park."[21]

Letters from white Baltimoreans to the *Baltimore Sun* and the Park Board reveal a growing concern about the presence of black people in Druid Hill. Arguing that blacks were "encroaching on the tennis courts," white citizens urged the Park Board to "vote them off."[22] "I don't know who is responsible for the use of the ball ground at Druid Hill Park," wrote a concerned citizen in 1903, "but it seems that the Negro element is too frequently in possession of it."[23] The letters argued that the presence of blacks on the tennis courts and in Druid Hill would bring a "strong probability of serious trouble," create "disorder," intimidate "young [white] girls," and increase the spread of disease.[24] These concerns echoed the commonly cited arguments for racial segregation. Tropes of black lawlessness and sexual and cultural degeneracy were epitomized by the brutish black men who lusted after white women and the loose black women who spread diseases through numerous sexual encounters and who failed to keep a clean home and raise hygienic children.

In 1905, the Park Board officially "voted off" blacks from the tennis courts.[25] The city made plans to build "negro courts" in a less desirable part of Druid Hill known as the "sheepfold."[26] Until the courts were built, blacks were allowed to use only "certain groves set aside for colored use." The board argued that the "negro groves" were "in every way as desirable" as the rest of the tennis courts. Yet many black Baltimoreans disputed this notion. J. H. Murphy, the editor of the *Afro-American Ledger,* argued that there was only one "plausible explanation" for the new ruling:

> The superintendent felt that colored people ought to be discriminated against in some way and as there was no reasonable excuse for keeping them out of the Park, there must be some way found to let them feel that this great people's play ground was not to be as free for them as for other people.[27]

Murphy also critiqued the arguments about black disorder. However, instead of dismissing the correlation between black bodies and inherent lawlessness, he ascribed that behavior to "lower class" blacks and drew distinction between them. "It has been the policy of the better class of colored people to frown down on anything which looked like rowdyism on the part of colored people in this park," Murphy asserted, adding that he and other upper-class blacks were "willing and did all they could to keep good feeling on the part of all."[28] For aspiring-class blacks such as Slowe, an essential part of claiming an upper-class status within the black community was by distinguishing one's self from the "black underclass."

As Jim Crow crept into the fabric of the city, an emerging black middle class created parallel black institutions in response to their exclusion from white-only schools, social organizations, and sports leagues. Black middle-class arguments against discrimination, from residential segregation to the separate tennis courts in Druid Hill, reflected this burgeoning class ideology. Slowe made her way through elite black schools, joining tennis clubs and other social organizations. She reflected a growing group of blacks who, through their morals, their education, and their recreation, asserted a middle-class identity upon the backdrop of legalized racial segregation.

"What We Do with Our Leisure": Sports, Urban Reform, and the Black Middle Class

As Aunt Martha had predicted, the educational opportunities for Slowe in Baltimore exceeded those available in rural Virginia. Baltimore, like many other urban centers, had developed schools for black youth that differed from the primary and secondary schools in the rural South. Northern philanthropists, most notably Julius Rosenwald, poured money into rural southern schools for blacks.[29] These philanthropists overwhelmingly embraced the idea of industrial and "normal" education for blacks, which emphasized practical, skill-based education in agriculture, mechanics, and home economics.[30] However, schools in cities like Nashville, Philadelphia, and Baltimore adapted a classical liberal arts curriculum. The year Slowe began high school, Baltimore's Colored High School merged with the Colored Polytechnic Institute to become the Colored High School of Baltimore (CHSB). The merger resulted in an expanded curriculum that featured both classical education as well as professional training.

Just prior to the merger there was some local effort to try to shut down the Baltimore's Colored High School completely and simply have a training school. Dismayed by a growing black middle class that was "learned in arts and letters," one school examiner argued that it was the school's responsibility to promote "useful citizenship" through manual labor and domestic service and it was failing to do so. "This labor has become unreliable and inefficient," the examiner bemoaned, "the old class of Eastern Shore cooks, trained by their mistresses in slavery days, has about passed away and but very few have been trained since to take their places."[31] Despite the protests, the merger was completed and the CHSB was formed.

Given the tremendous effect of education on black social mobility it is not surprising that schools like CHSB held a vital position within the community. Like the black church, schools were thought to shape and guide the next generation of "race men" and "race women" and united "the most respectable and well-to-do colored people in the city."[32] It was here, at the CHSB, that Slowe's progressive education would allow her to join a growing number of aspiring-class black women who, instead of going into domestic service, would attend college and pursue professional careers as teachers, social workers, or nurses. In addition to differences in curriculum, city schools offered many extracurricular opportunities. Student government, clubs, organizations, and athletic teams were common features of urban black high schools. The CHSB was no exception, and it would be the place where Slowe first picked up a tennis racket.

Slowe had always been an active child. When she lived in Virginia she enjoyed racing against neighborhood kids, playing in the mud, and climbing trees. Despite Martha's disapproval at her niece's "ruggedness," Slowe recalls "some joyous times" at her "dignified aunt's house."[33] Though she loved playing outdoors, recreation for Slowe was largely informal prior to arriving in Baltimore. Moreover, Aunt Martha, who had frowned upon Slowe's leisure activities in Virginia, encouraged them in Baltimore. When Slowe entered the CHSB she immediately joined the tennis club, basketball team, student government, and a group for young women. These school groups were well organized. The sports teams played against other elite black schools in neighboring cities and enjoyed considerable attention in the Negro press.[34]

The girl's tennis club at the CHSB highlights the emergence of organized athletics opportunities for black girls in the city. For middle- and upper-class white women, organized physical education and athletic programs had begun to emerge in the 1870s. These women, who had previously played sports as a "liberating pastime" and to "strengthen elite social ties," now began to play in competitive tournaments and join school leagues. The national sporting organizations for golf, tennis, and archery started to include women's championships as well.[35] By the turn of the century, middle- and upper-class blacks pushed for the subsequent development of comparable programs for black women. A 1908 newspaper column from the *Indianapolis Freeman* illustrated such sentiment, arguing:

> Our neighbors' wives and daughters (white) take interest in athletics, and why not those of our race? Athletics are not copyrighted: they are at the disposal of everyone . . . why not our girls? Why wait until the white girls have worn all the "new" off?[36]

Applauding the "efforts . . . being made to get the fairer sex interested in athletics," the writer urges black women to "take up athletics, girls."[37] Slowe, like many other black girls, readily answered that call.

Aunt Martha's new interest in Slowe's extracurricular activity, as well as the school's commitment to them, illustrates a moment when leisure and recreation were becoming a central element in philosophies of Progressive-era reform.[38] Organizations such as the Public Athletic League (PAL) and the Children's Playground Association (CPA) argued that the "play life of a people indicates its . . . vitality, morals, intelligence and fitness."[39] These groups worked to build playgrounds, establish sports leagues, and promote exercise for urban children. While the PAL and CPA argued that play was necessary for *all* children, the playgrounds and sports leagues often excluded black children from participation. In Druid Hill Park, for instance, the single, rundown playground for "colored youth" stood in stark contrast to the ten large play areas for white kids.[40] Black leaders such as W. E. B. Du Bois and Emmett Scott echoed similar philosophies of leisure, arguing that "community recreational facilities" worked to deter crime, improve health, and develop a "right-thinking citizenry."[41] Advocating for the development of recreational facilities as a way to uplift the black underclass and steer its members away from idleness and vice echoed mainstream philosophies of "Muscular Christianity." However, the formation of organized athletic clubs and leagues also contributed to the development of black institutions that asserted the respectability of middle-class blacks and indicated that they were "fit" for national inclusion.[42]

In 1904, Slowe prepared remarks for her high school graduation. During her time at the CHSB, Slowe had become fairly outspoken and well known in Baltimore's black community. In a speech entitled "A True Education," Slowe applauded the well-rounded nature of her schooling, including her extracurricular education.[43] Upon graduation, Slowe was offered admission at Howard University. Located in Washington, DC, Howard was widely considered the "capstone of Negro education" and was the largest and arguably the best university for black Americans at the time.[44] At Howard, Slowe would find similar opportunities for a "true education." Howard was marketed as a place where "young [black] women who came from the best homes in the country" could receive a respectable, Christian education. Moreover, the school prided itself on being a place where students could experience the "larger benefits of university life in the capital of the nation where the highest facilities of culture and improvement exist[ed]."[45]

At Howard, Slowe majored in English and joined numerous student groups, including university choir and the debate club. In her senior year, Slowe and eight other women founded Alpha Kappa Alpha, the nation's first black sorority. Slowe was elected its first president. College presented Slowe with numerous opportunities to try new activities, yet there was one extracurricular that remained constant in her life: tennis. Based on her ability, Slowe was named president of the Women's Tennis Club at Howard and played for the duration of her college career.

When Slowe graduated from Howard in 1908, she moved back to Baltimore and accepted a position as a teacher at her old high school. Cementing herself as a prominent member of Baltimore's black middle class, Slowe joined many local organizations, including a literary society called the Browning Club, the Baltimore Chapter of the National Association for the Advancement of Colored People (NAACP), and the Du Bois Circle, a women's group that met to discuss the writing and philosophy of the brilliant and controversial leader. Coupled with her desire to remain active, Slowe's love for tennis led her to join Baltimore's Monumental Tennis Club (MTC).

While baseball and football were more accessible and popular sports for urban black communities, a small group of aspiring-class and elite blacks were very interested in tennis. When the United States Lawn Tennis Association (USLTA) was founded in 1881 it immediately banned black players from participating, so blacks began to form citywide tennis clubs such as MTC. The fact that tennis was associated with an upper-class status made it an attractive sport for many blacks who sought to assert their own class status while also distancing themselves from "lower-class" sports like boxing. From the moment tennis was introduced in the United States, it was a game for the "upper classes." Like golf, the exclusivity of the facility in which it was played added to the game's allure. That cities constructed lavish clubhouses, golf courses, and tennis courts and bragged about their "modern conveniences" seems to highlight Elizabeth C. Barney's assessment that the enjoyment of the game revolved around "social intercourse" at the clubhouse or grounds. As Slowe returned to Baltimore, tennis was gaining in popularity and the city's black elite was pushing for new facilities on which to play.

The desire to build new tennis courts derived from two concerns. First, the Druid Hill restrictions from 1905 left blacks with only two tennis courts on which to play. The black "doctors, lawyers, high school teachers and society ladies and gentlemen" dominated use of the courts and "the ordinary citizen with nothing in front or behind his name" was reportedly told to "stay out of the fray."[46] Members of the black middle class of Baltimore sought to distance themselves from the "ordinary citizen," while also endeavoring to connect with the middle-class populations of surrounding cities. In this vein, the desire to build tennis grounds and "modern clubhouses" was fueled by friendly competition between clubs in Richmond, Washington, DC, and New York. Improved tennis grounds would allow the MTC to host tournaments, and match the already established tennis facilities for black people in other East Coast cities.

Attracting middle- and upper-class blacks from Richmond up to Boston, the local tennis tournaments drew "large and enthusiastic crowds" and functioned as large social events. As historian David K. Wiggins notes in his work on black college football "classics," these sporting events worked to unite upper-class blacks while simultaneously promoting distinct city pride.[47] The competitions between cities also served as a measuring stick by which each city could assess itself. The push for athletic fields in Baltimore was bolstered by the constant losses to tennis clubs in Washington and Philadelphia. An *Afro-American* reporter lamented the fact that Baltimore had been "somewhat behind the other cities" in ensuring the "physical welfare of its race."[48] Baltimoreans pointed out that while black Philadelphians could use the tennis courts on the roof of the John Wanamaker building, black Baltimoreans had "no such roof space."[49] Similarly, reporters also claimed that the Association Tennis Club of Washington (ACTW) produced the "largest number of excellent players" and owed its "proficiency" to the proximity of its courts to white progressive organizations such as the YMCA. By 1915, however, the MTC had started to make up ground on its rival clubs. An "Athletics in Baltimore" spotlight noted that Baltimore could now boast "successful athletics clubs" in the city. The only woman singled out for recognition was Lucy Slowe, "a tennis talent."[50]

"Best and Noblest Self": Cultivating Modern Black Womanhood

In the summer of 1916, Slowe and her fellow members of the MTC met with the ATCW to discuss the formation of a national tennis association. The tennis clubs from Baltimore and Washington decided to form a temporary organization and sent out letters to black tennis organizations throughout the United States. In November, representatives of black tennis clubs from Richmond to Chicago arrived in Washington to discuss the matter. After a vote, a permanent national organization, the American Tennis Association (ATA), was founded. The ATA, with cosponsorship from the MTC, planned to hold its first national tennis championship in Baltimore's Druid Hill Park the following year. Hoping to attract the top black tennis talent from local and regional tournaments across the country, the ATA sent out flyers advertising the highly competitive stakes that the national tournament would bring. Headlining the ATA flyers were the players who had dominated the last few regional tournaments: Talley Holmes, Dr. John Wilkerson, and Lucy Slowe.[51]

Slowe had risen to prominence on the tennis circuit as both a women's player and in the mixed-doubles category with Dr. John Wilkerson. Yet her tennis career was just part of her growing reputation. In Baltimore, Slowe had become well known as a prominent "race woman" who was active in the community and social organizations. Slowe understood her visibility as a race woman and embraced and advocated for a "modern negro womanhood." Slowe stated, "regardless of the wish of many parents that their daughters become the adjuncts of 'man,' modern life forces them to be individuals." For Slowe, individual modern black womanhood was, at its essence, well rounded. Her athletic career was supplemented by community work and education. While teaching in Baltimore, Slowe simultaneously earned her master of the arts in English at Columbia University, one of the few black students enrolled at the time. Slowe became a vocal member of the Baltimore NAACP chapter, especially on the matter of suffrage. She delivered a speech entitled "The Relation of the NAACP to the Suffrage Movement" in which she argued that the NAACP must support universal suffrage because a "voteless group in any republic is a helpless one."[52] By 1915, however, Slowe began to feel limited in Baltimore. Washington, DC, offered more professional and social opportunities for modern black women.[53]

Much to the dismay of black Baltimoreans, Slowe resigned her position at the CHSB and accepted a job at Washington's Armstrong Manuel Training High School.[54] Within a year Slowe became "lady principal" of the school. Slowe also helped found Washington's first black junior high school, Shaw, where she also served as principal. At Shaw, Slowe encouraged her pupils to excel in their studies and in leisure activities. Slowe especially advocated athletics to her female students, imploring them to "choose a wholesome sport and become the very best player you can."[55] At Shaw, girls had several options for organized sports, including a track team, a schlagball team, and a girls tennis club.[56] In addition to becoming a prominent educator and school administrator, Slowe began to establish herself in the Washington social scene. Slowe was named president of Washington's chapter of the College Alumni Club, a prestigious organization for college-educated black women. Upon her appointment, women from Baltimore transferred their membership to the Washington chapter. While Slowe relocated her professional and social life to Washington, tennis kept her tied to Baltimore. Despite the success of the ATCW, Slowe continued to play with the MTC and represented Baltimore on the tennis circuit.

Slowe's continued dominance of black women's tennis was a point of pride for Baltimore's aspiring-class blacks. Under a headline that read "Miss Lucy Slowe Again Champion" the *Afro-American* celebrated her ATA win and lauded her for "representing the city well."[57] After winning successive championships, Slowe lost in the championships two years in a row to Miss Rae, who was from Jamaica. In 1921, Slowe regained her crown and won back-to-back titles again. Despite the "strong competition" evident in the women's tennis championships, the event remained a footnote to the men's tournament. The women did not receive trophies or winnings for their accomplishments.[58] Although the black press applauded female athletes, the focus of women's athletics remained less about competition and more about the development of respectable women. "All the recreation our girls have are the dirty, low indecent places of amusement," lamented one paper, "the girls should have tennis clubs, basketball teams . . . gymnastic classes."[59] Tennis remained a means to a moral and respectable modern womanhood. "The modern women simply refuses to stay in the background," wrote another columnist, "she looks just right when she comes running down the steps to greet you. She is ready to play tennis, golf, out to boating, swimming, fishing—a good healthy woman."[60]

Slowe enjoyed tennis. She was fiercely competitive and relished winning each match she played. However more than anything, Slowe prided herself on being a "good healthy women." As she accomplished more professionally, tennis had less of a role in her life. Slowe found herself questioning if she could sustain involvement in her many interests. Confiding to a friend, she wrote, "there are too many of me for me to know each one; and yet I feel each clamoring for a hearing from the depths within me. Which shall I listen too, above all others?"[61] Slowe juxtaposed her "vigorous self" that loved the "great outdoors, tennis, golfing and hikes" with her "demure self" and her "motherly self." While she viewed these selves as parts of a whole, Slowe felt as if one had to move to the foreground, writing, "All of these are me; pray tell me which shall become articulate? Which shall lift its voice above all others? Which shall be the voice triumphant guiding me on to full expression of the best and noblest self?"[62]

Slowe continued to encourage her students to be active. She continued to assert that there was "not a more pressing problem than what we do with our leisure."[63] Slowe helped organize and oversee multiple athletic clubs for girls. Yet Slowe also began to warn of "modern problems" that women face, noting that that "women cannot do two things well" and encouraging women to focus on a single facet of themselves.[64] Perhaps her introspection had led her to abandon tennis. Perhaps Slowe simply disagreed with her tennis rankings and refused to compete, as some papers asserted.[65] Whatever the reason, after nearly two decades of playing tennis, and four national championships singles titles and multiple doubles titles in six years of ATA tournament play, Slowe hung up her tennis racquet for good. Tennis was an essential component of developing a healthy and active life as a modern woman, but Slowe ultimately saw herself as an educator and an administrator. The same year she stopped playing tennis, quit the MTC, and severed her last prominent connection to Baltimore, Slowe was named dean of women at her alma mater, Howard University, further entrenching herself in Washington, DC. Yet Baltimore was never completely out of her mind. Toward the end of her life Slowe reflected on her success and concluded that she owed a "great deal of it" to "that high school in Baltimore" and her early years in "charm city."[66]

Epilogue

Lucy Slowe's years in Baltimore and the rise of tennis occurred during a moment of transition. Over the next decade, thousands of rural and southern blacks would migrate, like Slowe's family. The First World War created industry jobs, especially in port cities such as Baltimore. Moreover, the increased violence toward black Americans in the aftermath of the war, a period of time nicknamed "Red Summer," also motivated families to flee the Deep South. Jim Crow was hardening across the South, but it was still being challenged. In 1917, the Maryland Court of Appeals struck down the residential racial segregation ordinances. Two years later, in Druid Hill Park, a tennis court was finally installed in the park's muddy back corner. Blacks were now relegated to this court only. Separate swimming pools soon popped up next to it. Druid Hill Park would remain segregated for another twenty-five years.

Slowe worked at Howard for many years. She became one of the foremost women college administrators, black or white, in the country. Slowe advocated tirelessly for the rights of blacks and of women; she endeavored to set an example of what modern black womanhood should look like. In October 1937, in her fourteenth year as dean of women at Howard, Slowe died of heart failure. She was fifty-four years old.[67]

Ten years after her death, Althea Gibson would win her first of ten ATA national titles. A year later, the ATA would stage an interracial tennis match on the clay courts of Druid Hill Park, demanding integration. Within six years, Gibson would become a poster child for muscular integration, becoming the first black athlete to break the international color line in tennis, and Druid Hill would finally desegregate its tennis courts and pools. When we remember black women or black tennis, we usually remember these events, understandably so. But both Gibson's success and the ATA protest speak more of integration and efforts toward establishing legal racial equality. Unfortunately, integration hobbled the ATA, as it did many black institutions, such as the Negro baseball leagues. While the ATA still exists, like many black institutions its importance and its most vibrant years are mostly forgotten. As Slowe illustrates, the significance of black tennis, and black women in tennis, exists beyond its push for integration. It was a central part of a burgeoning black community. The ATA and the other organized tennis clubs Slowe played for and against were vital parallel institutions that sustained a growing urban black populace that, like Slowe, was navigating life on one side of the color line.

In 2011, three years after Alpha Kappa Alpha, now boasting a membership of over 265,000 women worldwide, celebrated its centennial and a year before Serena Williams would win the US Open and Wimbledon for the fourth and fifth time, respectively, Slowe was elected to Maryland Women's Hall of Fame. Her induction underscores her long-lasting connection to Baltimore. At her posthumous induction, Slowe was honored as a person who worked tirelessly for black women and was the "mother of black tennis."[68] In the wake of her death, similar sentiments were echoed, as eulogies were given and condolences rolled in. Perhaps the most stirring remembrance of Slowe came a few months after her death. At the ATA championship of 1937, the players as well as the over 2,000 spectators in attendance stood for a moment of silence for Slowe. Edmund Burke, the chairman of the tournament, read an official resolution from the ATA: "Lucy Slowe will long be remembered as one of the great educators of her time. Her life and work will ever live in the memory of those who knew her and our young women will do well to emulate the sterling qualities of this champion of women."[69] A fitting title for Lucy Slowe, who, no matter what title she assumed—tennis star, educator, social leader—was always a champion of women, on and off the court.

6

Sweat Equity

Physical Education at The Bryn Mawr School for Girls

ELIZABETH M. NIX

In the post–Title IX world, it is hard to imagine a time when women's physical education was controversial. Nationwide, girls' sports thrive in high schools and colleges. First Lady Michelle Obama invites all American schoolchildren to get out from behind their desks with her "Let's Move!" initiative.[1] Scientific studies confirm what educators have known for decades—exercise is essential for healthy and attentive students, and encouraging all children to do some physical activity that they enjoy builds healthy adults, whether or not they consider themselves athletes.

It is not widely known, but Baltimore women played an important role in establishing the expectations around fitness that we now see as self-evident. In 1885, five young women instituted a "physical culture" program at the independent school they founded. The progressive curriculum of The Bryn Mawr School for Girls (BMS) promoted physical activity for all students and grew to encompass interscholastic competitive sports by the turn of the century. In the 1920s the BMS physical education program established what is today the longest-running women's lacrosse team in the United States. The five female founders intended that the physical education curriculum at the school would be a model for other secondary schools and colleges around the nation, and it could be argued that their success in demonstrating that girls should have equal access to "the life of the intellect and the spirit"[2] was an important predicate to the philosophy behind Title IX.[3]

The young women who created The Bryn Mawr School for Girls were not athletes; they functioned as a "team" but adopted the more sedentary name of "The Committee."[4] However, the founders appreciated the benefits that an intentional physical education program could bring to their individual students and to their overall enterprise. At the outset, the most controversial aspect of the plan was not athletics but academics. The Committee insisted that girls should study "the grand fields of literature and science and conjecture"—the same subjects that boys took, offered with the same intensity.[5] Thanks to the founders, students at Baltimore's Bryn Mawr School for Girls could graduate only after passing the entrance exam for Philadelphia's Bryn Mawr College. This ambitious goal faced fierce cultural opposition. Educational theorists at the time were convinced that rigorous academic pursuits would physically weaken female students. BMS founder M. Carey Thomas, who graduated Phi Beta Kappa from Cornell University in two years and then received a doctorate summa cum laude from the University of Zurich, was "terror-struck" by this notion, suggesting that if it were true then she and every other educated woman "were doomed to live as pathological invalids."[6] In 1873, Dr. Edward Clarke of Harvard University provided a summary of this theory in his *Sex in Education: Or, A Fair Chance for the Girls*. In this treatise, which went through seventeen editions in fifteen years, Clarke ceded that a girl was capable of studying any subject that she wanted, but warned that she could not engage in intensive studies "and retain uninjured health and a future secure from neuralgia, uterine disease, hysteria, and other derangements of the nervous system, if she follows the same method that boys are trained in. Boys must study and work in a boy's way, and girls in a girl's way."[7] M. Carey Thomas remembered years later, "We were haunted in those early days by the clanging chains of that gloomy little specter, Dr. Edward H. Clarke's *Sex in education*."[8]

Clarke's declarations grew out of the Victorian notion of "vitalism," the idea that the human body harbored a limited amount of energy. It was reasoned that exercise depleted some energy, and that thinking drew on additional reserves, but the theory asserted that reproduction demanded the most energy of all. It is logical that a growing fetus places additional needs on the female body; however Victorians theorized that the female reproductive organs (as Clarke deemed them "a source of strength and power") needed substantial energy to develop properly.[9] Any exertion in girls, mental or physical, directed energy away from the essential organs at the core of the body to the brain and limbs, imperiling the future of their wombs and ovaries and, by extension, the future of the species. Clarke warned, "Force must be allowed to flow thither in an ample stream, and not diverted to the brain by the school, or to the arms by the factory, or to the feet by dancing."[10]

The founders of The Bryn Mawr School embarked on a plan to harness that flowing force in ways that they believed would be most beneficial to their students. Instead of accepting the vitalist notion of a finite amount of energy within the body, The Committee thought that physical exercise would counteract the potentially draining effects of demanding intellectual activities.[11] However, they wanted to assure the families of potential students that they were looking out for the whole child and future generations of children as they safeguarded the wombs that would one day nurture the scions of Baltimore's elite. To that end they created the full-time position of medical director at the school and recruited Dr. Kate Campbell Hurd from Boston to fill it. Mary Garrett, a member of The Committee and the daughter of the president of the B&O Railroad, provided funds the year before the school opened to send Dr. Hurd to Sweden, Germany, England, and select American cities to observe the most progressive exercise programs of the day.[12] In Cambridge, Massachusetts, Dr. Hurd took classes at Dr. Dudley Allen Sargent's School of Physical Culture where Dr. Sargent, the director of Harvard's Hemenway Gymnasium, demonstrated his system of assessment and adjustable apparatus designed to promote "harmony in function and symmetry in development."[13] In Europe, Dr. Hurd enjoyed therapeutic baths and observed Dr. Gustav Zander's facilities, in which a variety of specialized machines exercised particular muscle groups in order "to restore the disturbed equilibrium of the organs, to direct the development into normal channels and in this way prevent the excitement of the nerves."[14] Dr. Zander claimed that his system of medico-mechanical gymnastics successfully treated hysteria and neurasthenia, precisely the nervous diseases Dr. Clarke had predicted female scholars would experience. In the promotional literature for the Zander System, with its references to the normal development of organs and equilibrium as opposed to excited nerves, Dr. Hurd found a counterargument to parents who might cling to the vitalist theory.

When she returned to Baltimore, Dr. Hurd worked closely with Mary Garrett and M. Carey Thomas to craft their own physical culture curriculum that would combine the equipment of both Drs. Sargent and Zander with daily calisthenics, baths, and drills.[15] Once the students arrived, Dr. Hurd assessed their physical condition according to the Sargent system and developed an individual daily exercise program for each girl.[16] Dr. Lillian Welsh, who came to town later to institute a similar program at the Women's College of Baltimore, remarked on Bryn Mawr's commitment to the health and fitness of its students: "This was pioneer work in medical inspection, and so far as I know was the first time a secondary school either for boys or for girls had made adequate provision for such work."[17] When the school completed a massive new building in 1889 at the corner of Cathedral and Preston Streets,[18] The Committee was able to realize its vision of a fitness program by carefully designing areas devoted to physical activity. The building's lower level housed a gymnasium and a mezzanine running track. The space was filled with rings and ropes and exercise machines designed by both Dr. Zander and Dr. Sargent. Designers included an indoor swimming pool, one of the earliest in any school in America, and "needle baths" or showers. Outside, a tall brick wall kept curious onlookers from observing basketball games and tennis matches in the broad spaces adjacent to the classrooms.[19] The allocation of resources to a full-time physician, state-of-the-art athletic facilities, and an individualized physical culture curriculum established The Bryn Mawr School as a leader in the movement for women's fitness. Since Bryn Mawr was one of the first academically rigorous independent girls' schools in the country, and since it attracted the daughters of doctors, lawyers, prominent businessmen, and Johns Hopkins faculty, it set a high bar for physical culture for young girls in the world of independent schools.

The physical culture curriculum grew stronger under the guidance of Bryn Mawr's most celebrated head mistress, Edith Hamilton, a classics scholar who led the school from 1896 to 1922.[20] During her tenure, every student was required to take gymnasium,[21] which included German drills, basketball, and genteel individual pastimes like archery, tennis, and fencing. Girls also used the exercise machines and participated in track and field and swimming activities.[22] Under Hamilton, the school instituted the first Bryn Mawr uniform, which was intended to allow girls "a perfectly free and easy movement" at all times.[23] She organized outdoor classrooms, which exposed children to healthful air and sunshine on the roof of the school, even in frigid temperatures.[24]

Hamilton's efforts attempted to respond to the rapidly changing trends in athletic education. By the turn of the twentieth century, exercise machines were passé and needle baths no longer a novelty. During World War I, the gymnastic drills of the "Hun model" fell out of favor, and by the 1920s schools were emphasizing competitive team sports as the basis of physical education.[25] Dr. Hurd had conducted her research tour just before the sporting revolution in which Victorians "taught the world to play" by inventing an astounding number of new team games.[26] When Dr. Hurd had toured Europe, boys' schools were playing only two organized sports with established rules: cricket and golf.[27] In the next decades they added football (the game Americans call soccer), field hockey, lawn tennis, table tennis, badminton, and squash.[28] As these sports crossed the Atlantic, modern American parents thought their children would learn best playing them at a "country school," surrounded by bucolic athletic fields where hearty and hale young scholars could breathe fresh air far away from the smoke and filth of the city. Gilman, which would eventually enroll the sons of many Bryn Mawr families, was one of the first country day schools in America, founded as the Country School for Boys of Baltimore City on the Homewood estate in 1897.[29] Having invested hundreds of thousands of dollars in their specialized urban campus only a few decades before, the leaders of Bryn Mawr hoped to stay put, but they knew they needed more extensive athletic facilities. Available lots of land were scarce around the Cathedral Street property, and although they temporarily established sports facilities in an annex east of town,[30] it became clear that The Bryn Mawr School would have to move,[31] in large part to build athletic facilities that would compete with those of the newer independent schools. Although The Bryn Mawr School had been on the forefront of the physical culture movement in the 1880s, it had been surpassed by the 1920s. Some of the most desirable students were picking other schools solely on the basis of athletic programs.[32]

The trend away from individual exercises and drills and toward organized team sports and the "country school" model was easy enough for the boys' programs. They could incorporate football and baseball into their physical culture curriculum, but girls' schools increasingly asked what team sports were appropriate for their female students. Basketball had been integral to The Bryn Mawr School since its beginnings. The girls had enjoyed the sport so much that when they established the Bryn Mawr School League in south Baltimore in 1915 to educate working-class and poor girls, they made sure that all participants would have the opportunity to join a basketball team.[33] A new era in Bryn Mawr basketball had begun in 1901 when a BMS team faced a squad from St. Timothy's School in a contest for the St. Timothy's Cup.[34] The initial interscholastic match attracted one hundred spectators (all female except for the umpire) and engendered a new spirit of competition in the Bryn Mawr girls. Years later Millicent Carey McIntosh recalled, "I think the greatest excitement that I have ever had in my life was the St. Timothy's Game."[35] McIntosh's sentiment would have sounded an alarm for most leaders in the world of physical culture. It had been acceptable for girls to challenge themselves within individualized plans designed to make them healthier and fitter. It was something else entirely for young girls to find the ultimate in excitement and personal fulfillment through athletic competition. Senda Berenson, who had developed the first rules for women's basketball during her tenure as instructor of physical culture at Smith College, warned in 1903 that "unless a game as exciting as basket ball [sic] is carefully guided by such rules as will eliminate roughness, the great desire to win and the excitement of the game will make our women do sadly unwomanly things."[36] In 1912, Dr. Hurd's former mentor Dr. Dudley Allen Sargent published an article in Ladies Home Journal entitled, "Are Athletics Making Girls Masculine? A Practical Answer to a Question Every

Girl Asks." Sargent assured every girl that "while there is some danger that women who try to excel in men's sports may take on more marked masculine characteristics . . . this danger is greatly lessened if the sports are modified so as to meet their peculiar qualifications."[37] To adapt the nineteenth-century sentiments of Dr. Edward T. Clarke, "Boys must play in a boy's way, and girls in a girl's way." But where The Committee had challenged Dr. Clarke's view of girls' education and insisted that girls could learn the same things boys could learn and be educated in the same way, the twentieth-century leaders of Bryn Mawr did not challenge the idea that girls' athletics had to be different from boys'. They followed the advice of Berenson and Sargent, deciding that competitive sports for women would be acceptable only if women played modified versions of the games that men played.

Despite their willingness to modify boys' games for girls, physical culture directors embarked in the 1920s on what one sports historian has termed "the first wave of athletic feminism,"[38] in which girls and women could take a prominent role on a public stage. This trend was felt keenly at all levels of Baltimore society. In 1921, after becoming restless in their required rounds of social events, some Bryn Mawr school graduates organized an all-debutante basketball team intent on challenging their younger counterparts still in school. The *Baltimore Sun* reported that "the project, like many another deep-laid feminine wile, was formed last week at the meeting of the Debutante Bridge Club." The article suggested that these young women did not want "their hours of glory" to end as quickly as "those of the butterfly," but instead were eager to push the limits of propriety to get back into the competitive arena.[39] Women of other classes in Baltimore were watching their example. In 1922, Miss Edna May Frances, the supervisor of girls' work of Baltimore's Public Athletic League, told the *Baltimore Sun* that the chance to play basketball, volleyball, and hockey in the city's recreational centers was "attracting girls away from the jangle of the dance parlors and giving them a taste of more satisfying and wholesome recreation." Miss Frances reported that for the winter season, 5,113 girls were registered with the athletic league, an increase of 2,000 members from the year before.

In addition to organizing athletic schoolgirls, the league sponsored bowling teams made up of women workers from the B&O Railroad, the Western Maryland Railroad, the Gas and Electric Company, and the Maryland Casualty Company. Miss Frances underlined the opportunity for these working-class Baltimore women and girls to use sports as a means of social uplift: "Girls coming out over weekends learn to swim, run, play ball and do almost anything."[40] Noting that the 1922 season marked the first time that her female teams had insisted on competitive matches, the reporter cited the influence of the Bryn Mawr model: "A few years ago the few young women interested in athletics were quite content to play among themselves without seeking 'outside games,' in fact it wasn't considered quite the thing. This year the society girls led the way and hundreds of others have followed them."[41]

Nationally, officials at the highest levels sensed that even when girls were engaged in less intense versions of boys' sports, they were not just playing games. The US Department of Education issued an official report in 1924 that opened with the warning, "Girls have taken whole-heartedly to the athletic field . . . but we should be deeply concerned as to how far [they] should go."[42] Girls felt it, too. The same Bryn Mawr student, Millicent Carey McIntosh, who had remembered the excitement of the St. Timothy's Cup, used a telling simile when she described her team's uniforms during those contests: "We were dressed in white flannel blouses with a yellow BMS, and distinguished brown serge bloomers (what a change from our red flannel gym suits). When we acquired this blouse and these bloomers, it was really like receiving a knighthood from the queen."[43] In this memory, McIntosh puts herself in the place of a male warrior who is celebrated for his accomplishments through public recognition and at the same time is elevated to a position where he can embark on future quests. When McIntosh found herself dressed in her team's colors, fighting to win, she had to reach for an analogy that historically had been available only to men.

It is probably no accident that McIntosh used a British reference to express her sentiments; British women had been leading the women's physical culture movement for decades. In the late 1880s, girls at English colleges, day schools, and boarding schools were playing badminton, fives, rounders, ninepins, squash, and netball. Field hockey was all the rage in the 1890s.[44] The girls who had been student athletes during those years graduated and went on to become the first generation of female physical educators to spread competitive female sport in England and the United States. In its characteristic way, Bryn Mawr chose one of these pioneering English women as its athletic director in 1925, just as it was making the commitment to a new campus, accessible playing fields, and interscholastic sports. Rosabelle Sinclair was enmeshed in the network of enthusiastic English women who ran sports camps, published articles in *The Sportswoman*, and developed the rules for women's versions of men's sports that made them acceptable as activities for elite girls. Sinclair remained at The Bryn Mawr School for twenty-five years, and introduced women's lacrosse to Baltimore.

Rosabelle Sinclair was a graduate of St. Leonards School in St. Andrews, Scotland. Founded in 1877 as the St. Andrews School for Girls, St. Leonards was the Scottish boarding version of The Bryn Mawr School. The first school for girls that took its curriculum from English boys' public schools, St.

The Bryn Mawr School for Girls students, playing lacrosse, circa early 1930s.
Courtesy of The Bryn Mawr School for Girls.

Leonards instituted a rigorous academic program; physical culture played an integral role in it. Administrators had transformed a barn into a gymnasium and equipped it with machines designed by the feminist Madame Bergman-Osterberg; they set aside three hours every afternoon for physical activities, including cricket.[45] Like Edith Hamilton, the St. Leonards headmistresses required every girl to take gymnastics, swim, and spend time outdoors.[46] They also conducted regular medical inspection and kept detailed records on each student.[47] The school inserted competition into its physical culture curriculum when it instituted interhouse competitions in gymnastics, cricket, and a sport called goals. These contests were held three times a year until 1890 when St. Leonards, frustrated by the difficulties of judging girls on gymnastics skills, found a competitive sport that was easier to score: women's lacrosse.[48]

"Originated by Iroquois Indians, modernized by Canadian gentlemen, adopted by English sportsmen, feminized for British schoolgirls, women's lacrosse in Britain and then America was as much a product of Victorian sporting culture as it was of Native Americans," writes historian Donald Fisher.[49] Indians in the eastern part of North America developed many different stick ball games over the centuries; native men would play for days on fields that stretched for miles. In 1860, a Canadian teenager named William George Beers domesticated a Mohawk form of the game by producing a pamphlet of rules and instructions and then promoting it as the "National Game of Canada," just in time for the creation of the Dominion of Canada in 1867.[50] Canadian migrants brought the game to America, where it thrived for a period through rowdy, working-class clubs, including the Baltimore Druids.[51] In most American cities these clubs had disappeared by the 1890s, but in England the game was popular with gentlemen, and in elite colleges in America's northeast it continued as a spring alternative to the more democratic baseball.[52] Although Beers harbored hopes of teaching lacrosse skills to "the future mothers of a manly race," women's lacrosse did not develop in Canada or the United States in the nineteenth century.[53] It did, however, take hold in Scotland at St. Leonards. The school's head-mistress, Louisa Lumsden, had witnessed a lacrosse match when she visited New Hampshire in 1884.[54] She waited until she saw a need for a new con-test in the interhouse competitions in 1890 to introduce the game to her students. In that year, St. Leonards became the first school in Britain to play women's lacrosse.[55] By 1910, the Ladies Lacrosse Association had formed in England, and in 1913 Scotland's first international team, including a young Rosabelle Sinclair, defeated Wales, 7–2.[56]

English sportswomen including Sinclair transplanted their passion for women's adaptations of men's games to the United States early in the twen-tieth century, and their tight networks encouraged the development of new and acceptable athletic pursuits for girls. The British woman Constance Applebee brought women's field hockey to the United States in 1901, and M. Carey Thomas, always on the lookout for the next trend in physical culture, recruited her as the athletic director for Bryn Mawr College in 1904.[57] Applebee wrote that in 1908 an attempt was made to establish a women's lacrosse team at Bryn Mawr College, but there were not enough female athletes to form complete teams for both field hockey and lacrosse, so lacrosse faltered.[58] In 1923, Applebee founded Camp Tegawitha Field Hockey Camp for Girls in Mount Pocono, Pennsylvania, where girls would come to perfect their technique for three weeks in the fall. The Bryn Mawr School sent its athletic director Carmen Santos to the camp, where lacrosse joined girls' field hockey in the sporting line-up during that first season.[59] Sinclair, who had tried unsuccessfully to introduce lacrosse at Rosemary Hall in Connecticut, met Santos at the camp, and two years later Sinclair became the "Director of Out-Door Sports" at The Bryn Mawr School for Girls.[60]

In the months before she came to Baltimore, Sinclair codified women's lacrosse in the pages of *The Sportswoman*. Sinclair's language reflects the desire of this group of physical educators to portray lacrosse as "An Ideal Game for Women and Girls."[61] Some of Sinclair's adaptations were physical. She recommended using the Lally Ladies' College Stick, asserting that the "men's stick is much too heavy and inappropriate for women." In terms of the field dimensions, Sinclair stated that boundaries should be agreed upon by the two teams but advised readers, "for women it is best to have 100 yards between goals rather than the full 110."[62] Other notes suggest that the overall tenor of the women's game was completely different from that of the rough men's contest. Sinclair wrote: "A player shall not: Deliberately charge or shoulder an opponent . . . Note, There can be absolutely no 'charging' or 'shouldering' an opponent of the ball at any time. 'Charging' or 'shouldering' implies motion and unnecessary force and is forbidden."[63] She clarified, "The distinction between 'shoulder an opponent' and push the opponent with the shoulder, etc. is a fine one and roughly amounts to this: One may come into personal contact and gently 'insinuate' one's body but one may not 'displace' one's opponent." It is doubtful that the fathers and brothers of these female lacrosse players were encouraged to "gently 'insinuate'" anything during their matches, but restraint was expected of girls. Joyce Cran and Joyce Riley wrote in *The Sportswoman* in 1931, "It should be clearly understood that the rules of women's Lacrosse do not allow the methods of tackling and checking used by the men. This avoids any chance of rough or reckless play."[64] Sinclair also asserted that it was beyond the realm of possibility that female athletes would cross a gender line into raw physical competition. When discussing the rules surrounding fouls and suspension during a game, she wrote, "The 'suspension' of a player very rarely, if ever, occurs, as the 'foul' causing 'injury' in Lacrosse can hardly occur without deliberate intent, and such a case need hardly be considered."[65]

Paradoxically, female physical educators of this period promoted the rewards of team play while they de-emphasized the competitive motive.[66] Cran and Riley claimed that women's lacrosse "is definitely a team and not an individual game, as it must be realized that passing the ball through the air from player to player is far quicker than carrying the ball in the crosse. Speed and quick passing make every player an essential unit of the team."[67] Two paragraphs later, they touted the joys of individual accomplishment rather than competition: "It is a fascinating feeling just to be able to catch and control the ball, and it is even more thrilling to find one's self able to throw and catch while running at top speed."[68] The excitement comes not from scoring a goal and certainly not from blocking an opponent but rather from the realization that girls and women have enough coordination to simultaneously run and pass.

Most women's lacrosse enthusiasts were quick to point out the myriad ways the game helped young women physically. Constance Applebee wrote in *The Sportswoman* in 1931, the year the US Women's Lacrosse Association was founded, "As a game for women it has no equal. The deftness and skill required for manipulating the crosse, the training of the eye, balance and quick body movements necessary in dodging and above all the freedom from tenseness, all help to make it one of the most enjoyable and beneficial forms of sport."[69] As the 1930s progressed, the rhetoric surrounding women's lacrosse focused more explicitly on its promotion of traditionally female physical qualities, including claims that it was the most feminine of the emerging women's sports. As historian Susan Cahn has noted, physical educators in the 1930s "embraced an activist approach toward heterosexuality. Coursework emphasized beauty and social charm over rigorous health and fitness."[70] Cahn cites a perfume advertisement from the period that reminded consumers "The first duty of a woman is to attract," and quotes Alice Sefton, who asserted that by playing sports during the day, a girl might "be more beautiful on the dance floor that evening."[71] Sinclair echoed this tendency in a *Baltimore Sun* interview conducted seven years after her retirement; Sinclair called women's lacrosse "an exhibition of coordination and grace."[72]

These two major trends in women's physical education in the twentieth century—the de-emphasis of competition and the hyperemphasis on displays of feminine coordination and grace—were combined in a Bryn Mawr tradition that is still practiced today. Gym Drill started in the early years of the school, and Sinclair's stamp can still be seen on the twenty-first-century proceedings. In the 1890s, students invited visitors to their gymnasium to see them swim, exercise with their various apparatus, and then play basketball. Drills and marches, folk dancing by each class, and German exercises were added in the early decades of the twentieth century. In the 1920s Sinclair made some changes to the Gym Drill agenda by eliminating the demonstrations that did not fit in with prevailing ideas of female physical culture. "The old German exercises," she explained to the *Baltimore Sun* in 1948, "place emphasis on muscular strength rather than balance and poise, and are apt to build you up to a point that would be most unstylish today."[73] The article explained that Sinclair had instituted "a vigorous coordinated program of folk dancing, Scandinavian gymnastics and athletics." In the Sinclair years, Bryn Mawr girls spent two hours each week preparing for the folk dances. As early May approached, rehearsals moved out to the playing fields. One alumna remembered, "During Gym Drill rehearsals, it never failed to startle and amuse me when Miss Sinclair would shout over the megaphone, 'Get on your blobs!' Where else in life have we ever had to get on a blob?"[74] On the day of Gym Drill alumnae, friends and relatives lined the low hills that surrounded the fields. They cheered as the various grades moved through the dances that many of them once danced themselves, and everyone held their breath as the girls entwined their wooden swords and, if they had practiced enough, held their sword stars proudly aloft.

In 1948, the *Baltimore Sun* reporter Martha Millspaugh remarked that the Bryn Mawr girls

> may not have been aware at the time of the overall aims and scope of the program; they may not even now attribute ease of motion, a straight back, prowess in golf, or agility in dancing to the arduous hours spent in the gymnasium or on the hockey field, under the supervision of eagle eyes that missed not a movement of a muscle.[75]

The memories of Sinclair's students indicate otherwise. In 1978, when the school marked Sinclair's death at the age of eighty-seven with an athletic fund in her name, dozens of alumnae included memories with their donations. Kathryn Forsythe Barrow, Class of 1932, wrote: "I am indebted to Miss Sinclair for many things—my sustaining interest in women's sports and my participation, even at 64, in Scottish dances . . . my interest in taking care of my physical self and most of all for my determination to 'sit and stand up straight.'" Georgia Sherwood Dunbar, Class of 1936, recalled, "Throughout my years at Bryn Mawr, I lived in terror and admiration of her quick wit and impeccable standards." Kay Barnes, Class of 1955, reminisced, "I shall never, never forget the beautiful and stately and exciting Gym Drills and banner marches. What a treasure it was to have been lucky enough to have gone to BMS."[76]

The five original founders might have been surprised to discover that some Bryn Mawr graduates went on to devote their lives to sport. Judy Devlin '53 and her sister Sue Devlin '49, whose Irish father had been an international badminton champion, won the US Open Women's Doubles Badminton title in 1953. Judy claimed the world's singles title in 1954 and continued winning international championships for the next twenty years.[77] Frances Turner, who graduated in 1934, became a professional sportswriter, and included articles about Bryn Mawr athletics in her weekly section on women's sports in the *Baltimore Sun*. Other Bryn Mawr girls who were not immersed in sports full time continued to include exercise in their daily routine, just as The Committee, Edith Hamilton, and Rosabelle Sinclair would have wanted. Janet C. Brown supplemented her contribution to the Rosabelle Sinclair fund with a sentiment that would have made Miss Sinclair proud: "I can clearly hear, thirty and more years later, your field command, 'move.' To me, 'move,' as you used it and in the way you meant it, has always been the most expressive word, conveying the soundest advice, in the language."[78]

The influence of the Bryn Mawr physical education program extends beyond individual graduates. The school is the home to the longest-running girls' lacrosse team in the nation. Lacrosse for both girls and boys is currently the fastest-growing team sport in US high schools. In 2011, over a quarter of a million players participated in women's lacrosse. In that year, girls' lacrosse had the tenth highest number of participants of all high school sports, after a 48.2 percent growth rate in the preceding five years.[79] Rosabelle Sinclair's name gained national prominence when posthumously she became the first woman inducted into the Lacrosse Hall of Fame in 1992. But the legacy of the Bryn Mawr approach to academics and athletics goes further than the success of one particular sport. "The Committee" believed that every student should engage in athletic pursuits, and increasingly institutions are adopting that philosophy in the early decades of the twenty-first century. Spelman College, the historically black women's college in Atlanta, left the NCAA in 2013 after realizing that out of its 2,100 students, only 80 were playing varsity sports. The college divided the $900,000 it had been spending annually on competitive athletics and used it to establish a "wellness program" in which all of the students use the gymnasium, courts, and playing fields to maintain their personal fitness. The college president intends to establish a "culture of movement" on campus,[80] echoing the physical culture movement that found a home in Baltimore in the 1880s. Educators no longer worry that a rigorous education will threaten the reproductive systems of their female scholars, but they still recognize the essential importance of Rosabelle Sinclair's field command to all of her students: "Move!"

7

"More Than a Century of Champions"

Johns Hopkins University Lacrosse

NEIL A. GRAUER

A humdrum meteorological occurrence such as the advent of the vernal equinox does not herald the arrival of spring in Baltimore. Citizens of the city know that spring is here when lacrosse sticks start to sprout—which is as early as mid-January. That's when public and private school teams, as well as the region's renowned collegiate squads, start practicing for a forthcoming season of fast-paced, balletically graceful yet bone-crunching games that begin as early as February and culminate in championship playoffs come the Memorial Day weekend in May.

It remains debatable why Baltimore became the epicenter of enthusiasm for an ancient, Native American sport first reported by seventeenth-century European settlers in the wilds of what is now upstate New York and Canada. Some theorists speculate that lacrosse's popularity in Baltimore was due to the absence of any major league teams in the city when the sport was beginning to take hold on college campuses and in prep schools early in the twentieth century.[1] The original Major League Orioles left town in 1904 (moving to New York to become, of all teams, the Yankees); the Baltimore Colts weren't founded until 1947; and the modern Orioles (formerly the St. Louis Browns) arrived in 1954.[2]

Hence many Baltimoreans took lacrosse—the quintessential amateur sport—to their hearts. They continue to support it with unusual fervor. The city's press provides greater coverage for lacrosse than it receives anywhere else. The University of Denver and former Princeton University head lacrosse coach Bill Tierney told a reporter in 1998: "I grew up on Long Island, went to college in upstate New York and first coached there. It meant a lot to be in Baltimore [as an assistant coach at Hopkins] and see lacrosse be that important in an area. Nowhere else will lacrosse ever have that history of that importance or carry the weight it does in Baltimore."[3]

Almost from the start of collegiate lacrosse in the United States, Johns Hopkins University has fielded one of the sport's premiere programs. This is not hyperbole; it is a fact. Exceptional lacrosse programs exist elsewhere—and some have impressive records—yet over the span of collegiate lacrosse history, no school's name has been more synonymous with lacrosse or done more to advance it nationally and internationally than Johns Hopkins.[4]

Consistency is the reason for the program's success. For more than 130 years, Hopkins lacrosse has been a major force. It always has competed with the best teams and come out well—44 national championships, either won outright or shared; 101 winning seasons and eight all-even ones for a total of 109 out of 126.[5] Hopkins players constitute 64 out of the 382 members of the National Lacrosse Hall of Fame—far more than from any other program. The nearest rival is the University of Maryland, with 35 members. Other notable programs—such as Syracuse (23 members), Cornell (17 members), Navy (14 members), Virginia (12 members), North Carolina (four members), Duke (three members), and Loyola University of Maryland, the 2012 NCAA champions (no members)—are unlikely ever to match Hopkins' roster of all-time greats. (The Hall of Fame itself, once housed in the Hopkins athletic center, now sits adjacent to Hopkins' Homewood Field on land the university provided.)[6]

In addition, Hopkins has had 183 first-team All-Americans since the selections first were made in 1922, another all-time high. Overall, Hopkins has had 549 players named to All-America teams. Hopkins also represented the United States in the two Olympic Games at which lacrosse was played, 1928 and 1932. The Blue Jays were invited to participate in the NCAA championship tournament for forty-one years in a row. No other school has such a record—either in lacrosse or any other NCAA Division I sport.[7]

Hopkins' influence on the development and spread of lacrosse, both nationally and internationally, has been profound. Blue Jay coaches literally have written the book on the sport—four times. William Schmeisser (1905–1909; 1923–1925); W. Kelso Morrill (1935–1946; 1950); and Bob Scott (1955–1974) wrote books about lacrosse that influenced generations of coaches and players during their eras. Scott's 1976 book *Lacrosse: Technique and Tradition* became the acknowledged "bible" of the sport, selling more than 40,000 copies. It even was translated into Japanese. Dave Pietramala, the current Hopkins coach, completely revised Scott's book in 2006, and this update has sold more than 10,000 copies so far.[8]

Indeed, ever since the late nineteenth century, Hopkins players also have had an enduring impact on the way lacrosse is played. In 1898, Hopkins attackman Ronald Abercrombie, a short man, decided to cut down his long, wooden lacrosse stick to make it lighter and easier to maneuver. By 1899, other Hopkins players had ordered special, less heavy and shorter sticks, which led coach/captain William Maddren to develop the short, passing offense that perhaps became Hopkins' biggest contribution to lacrosse tactics. Seventy years later, in 1970, former Hopkins All-American Dick Tucker led the design team that created and patented the first plastic lacrosse stick head—which revolutionized the game. By 1971, every goal in the NCAA's first national championship game was scored with one of Tucker's new sticks.[9]

Howard "Howdy" Myers Jr., the Blue Jays' head coach from 1947 to 1949, arguably did more than anyone else to introduce lacrosse on Long Island in the 1950s, helping to make it the important center of the sport that it is today. Willie Scroggs, who played for three national championship teams at Hopkins in the 1960s and served as an assistant Blue Jay coach on two more title teams, went to the University of North Carolina in 1979 and transformed the Tar Heels into a lacrosse powerhouse during his twelve years as North Carolina's coach. Similarly, Bill Tierney, an assistant coach at Hopkins from 1985 to 1987, brought Princeton back to prominence in lacrosse after nearly forty years in the shadows, helped spark the still-growing popularity of lacrosse in New Jersey, and now is doing the same at the University of Denver, which won the 2015 NCAA championship.[10]

Hopkins coaches and players also introduced lacrosse to Japan and China. In April 1986, Bob Scott and Ross Jones, the then vice president and secretary of Johns Hopkins University, paid a goodwill visit to Keio University in Japan at the request of a university alumnus who lived there. Scott and Jones donated ten lacrosse sticks—possibly the first ever seen at a university in that nation—to Keio's athletic department.

Soon those sticks multiplied rapidly. By June 1987, the Japan Lacrosse Association was founded. That same month, Don Zimmerman, then the Hopkins lacrosse coach, held the first lacrosse camp in Japan, assisted by Hopkins' then goalie and future television sportscaster and lacrosse exponent, Quint Kessenich. The following month, Keio University played the first recorded lacrosse game in Japan against a club team located on the Yokota Air Force Base. Seven Japanese universities formed the Japan Lacrosse Student League in April 1988; Hopkins and the Australian national team played against Japanese teams in the first International Lacrosse Friendship Games at the Komazawa Olympic Stadium in 1989; and in 1990, the Japan Lacrosse Club Team Association was founded. Japan's men's team competed for the first time in the International Lacrosse Association's World Games in 1994.

It now is estimated that tens of thousands of Japanese high school and collegiate athletes play lacrosse—all as a result of Hopkins' gift of ten sticks in 1986 and the continued support from Hopkins coaches and players. (Don Zimmerman alone has made more than a half dozen trips to Japan to promote the sport.)

Similarly, Larry Quinn, a national Lacrosse Hall of Fame goalie from Hopkins, was among the leaders of a delegation from US Lacrosse, the sport's national governing body, who made a 1992 goodwill visit to Beijing University in China and held clinics there to demonstrate the basics of the game to Chinese youngsters—whose enthusiasm for the sport has also been fostered by efforts of the Hopkins-inspired Japanese lacrosse community.[11]

With many former Hopkins players serving as high school and collegiate coaches, founders of lacrosse camps, and role models, the Blue Jays' impact on lacrosse's explosion in popularity throughout the United States is unquestioned. Such former Blue Jay stars as Kyle Harrison, winner of the 2005 Tewaaraton Trophy as the nation's finest player, and Paul Rabil, named the nation's finest midfielder while at Hopkins in 2007, the top offensive player in both the indoor and outdoor professional lacrosse leagues in 2009, 2011, and 2012, and Most Valuable Player in the 2010 World Games, have immense influence. For example, Rabil has been proclaimed "Lacrosse's First Million-Dollar Man" by Bloomberg's *Businessweek*, in recognition of his endorsement deals and untiring efforts to enhance the sport's profile.[12]

The Hopkins Lacrosse Tradition Begins

The Johns Hopkins University was founded in 1876 with a then-mammoth, $7 million bequest—estimated to be worth up to $11 billion in today's money—from the city's wealthiest entrepreneur and philanthropist, a Quaker merchant and banker, Johns Hopkins (1795–1873). Hopkins's unusual first name, *Johns*, was the maiden name of his great-grandmother, Margaret Johns. Always relatively small in size, Johns Hopkins University was the nation's first research university, offering the sort of advanced education and degrees that previously had been available to Americans only by going abroad to study.[13]

For nearly a century, Hopkins' undergraduate school was a somewhat insular, close-to-home institution—largely comprised of white students and faculty. It was an all-male university favored by the graduates of Baltimore's prep schools and elite public schools, as well as top high schools nationwide and abroad. (By contrast, Hopkins' medical school, which opened in 1893, accepted women from the outset—fifty-two years before the Harvard Medical School admitted females.) Hopkins' exceptional academics, renowned faculty, and successful alumni brought it worldwide fame. (Woodrow Wilson, the twenty-eighth president of the United States, was a Hopkins graduate—and the only US president to earn a PhD.)[14]

When change came to Hopkins' undergraduate school, it did so rapidly. Women were admitted as undergraduates in 1970 (and a women's lacrosse team was established in 1976) and outreach efforts to attract minority students grew exponentially. JHU now has a far more diverse faculty and student body, as well as an even greater international reach, having established scholarly institutes and medical affiliates in Europe, Latin America, and Asia. Despite the many changes over the years, the school's devotion to lacrosse has remained steadfast.

In 1878, just two years after the university's founding, Baltimore's first recorded lacrosse game was played. Although Hopkins had no connection with that first contest, four years later, on October 10, 1882, the Johns Hopkins Lacrosse Club was organized. Its initial game was not auspicious. On May 11, 1883, the Hopkins team was defeated by the local Druid Lacrosse Club, 4–0.[15]

Hopkins did not field a team again until April 19, 1888. Once more, the results were disappointing. Hopkins' first official season began with a 4–1 loss to the Druids. Hopkins' first victory, however, was in the only other game it played that season, a 6–2 triumph over the Patterson Lacrosse Club of Baltimore. Since then, Hopkins has fielded a team every year, with the exception of 1944 when World War II curtailed intercollegiate athletics.[16]

In 1890, Hopkins joined the Intercollegiate Lacrosse Association, and in 1891 it won its first national championship, defeating the University of Pennsylvania twice, as well as Lehigh and the Stevens Institute of Technology.[17]

Seven years later, in 1898, the intercollegiate championship returned to Hopkins. JHU won championships in 1899 and 1900 as well. The 1902 team, which also won the intercollegiate championship, was captained and coached by William C. Schmeisser, later affectionately known to generations of Hopkins players as "Father Bill." He coached the Blue Jays to championships in 1903, '06, '07, '08, '09, '23, and '24 and remained a valued advisor to the team until he died in 1941. Two years later, the United States Intercollegiate Lacrosse Association (USILA) named its national award for the finest defenseman in the game in his honor. It still is known as the Schmeisser Award. He was in the inaugural class of players and coaches elected to the Lacrosse Hall of Fame when it was founded in 1957.[18]

Johns Hopkins' championship lacrosse team of 1908 was the first to play on Homewood Field, which opened in October 1907. Homewood has served as the site not only for all Hopkins home games, but many North-South all-star lacrosse games, national club lacrosse championship matches, numerous high school title games, and two International Lacrosse Federal World Championships (1982 and 1998), featuring teams from around the globe. Some have called Homewood Field "The Yankee Stadium of Lacrosse," but, in 1982, a player from Australia simply called it the world's lacrosse players' "Mecca."[19]

The first All-American lacrosse teams were selected in 1922, and Hopkins' representative on the first-ranked team was Douglas C. Turnbull Jr. He would go on to be named to the first All-American team four straight years, a feat unequaled for the next fifty-four years.[20] Turnbull led Hopkins to championships in 1923 and 1924. His younger brother, Jack, was a three-time All-American in 1930, 1931, and 1932 and is considered one of the game's greatest players. A star at Baltimore Polytechnic Institute high school before attending Hopkins, Jack Turnbull was killed in combat during World War II. In 1947, the national honor for the top attackman in lacrosse—the Turnbull Award—was created by the USILA in his memory.[21]

Ray Van Orman was head coach from 1926 through 1934, a period during which Hopkins won three championships, was the leading team in the country for three years when the USILA did not name a champion, and twice represented the United States in the Olympics—giving lacrosse its most extensive international exposure up until that time.[22]

To decide which lacrosse team would don the U.S.A. jersey at the 1928 Olympic Games in Amsterdam, a playoff of the country's top six teams was arranged. The Mount Washington Club of Baltimore was the decided favorite, and Johns Hopkins was ranked sixth. Hopkins' first-round game was with Mount Washington, the only unbeaten team to enter the Olympic playoff series. The club team had a 3–2 halftime lead, but Hopkins came back to win 6–4. In the semifinal round, Hopkins beat Army 4–2. The finals were played in Baltimore Stadium (then the city's equivalent of today's Oriole Park at Camden Yards), and Hopkins defeated Maryland 6–3.[23]

At the Olympics, the Americans defeated Canada, 6–3, but the next day lost to Great Britain 7–6. When Canada beat Britain 9–5, it looked like a three-way tie. The United States offered to play another series; Canada agreed, but Britain declined.[24]

Four years later, Hopkins won all nine of its regular-season games in 1932, but a playoff system was again used to determine the American representative at the Olympic Games. Eight teams competed and Hopkins won its first two games against St. John's and the Crescents Club. In the final game with the University of Maryland, the Terps led 3–2 at halftime, and Hopkins did not take the lead until the last three minutes of play. The final score was 7–5.[25]

The 1932 Olympic Games were played in Los Angeles, and Canada was the only other participating nation. The teams met on August 7, 9, and 12, and the total attendance was an impressive 145,000 people. The United States won the opening game 5–3, Canada the second 5–4, and the Americans the deciding match 7–4, thus showing the 20,000 spectators, the *New York Times* wrote, "that they know something about this Canadian game."[26]

Dr. W. Kelso Morrill, a Hopkins mathematics professor who had been a superb Blue Jay player in the 1920s, succeeded Van Orman as head coach in 1935.[27] Under Morrill, the 1941 Hopkins team was one of the school's greatest. It allowed its opponents only thirteen goals during the eleven-game regular season, which ended with a 10–3 victory over Maryland. The Mount Washington Wolfpack was also undefeated and had a string of twenty-four consecutive victories when it challenged Hopkins to play a postseason game for the benefit of the British War Relief Society. The Blue Jays weren't sure if they wanted to take on the always-formidable Wolfpack, which was stacked with former Hopkins stars. Father Bill Schmeisser then spoke to the team for what would be the last time. He assured them that this was the year they could beat the Wolfpack. The challenge was accepted, and the Blue Jays justified Father Bill's confidence in them with a 7–6 victory. (Hopkins would not beat Mount Washington again until 1967.)[28]

Because so many athletes were in the military during World War II, Hopkins did not field an official team in 1944. Athletic director and dean of students G. Wilson Shaffer nevertheless kept the sport alive in the Baltimore area, arranging for players from Hopkins, Mount Washington, and other local teams to form the Johns Hopkins Lacrosse Club, with Kelso Morrill and Gardner Mallonee, a member of the 1928 Hopkins Olympic team, as coaches. The service academies were the only teams played. An informal Hopkins student team was organized in 1945, and it split a two-game schedule.[29]

The postwar period began slowly for Hopkins lacrosse, but when Howdy Myers became head coach in 1947, a new championship era was born. His teams of 1947, 1948, and 1949 did not lose a single collegiate game, notching twenty-four consecutive victories.[30]

Before the 1950 season, Myers left Hopkins to become the director of athletics, as well as football and lacrosse coach, at Hofstra University in Long Island, New York. He would become something of the Johnny Appleseed of lacrosse in the Northeast, working tirelessly to popularize the sport in the New York metropolitan area. Eventually, it would rival Maryland as a producer of outstanding lacrosse players.[31]

Following Myers's departure, Kelso Morrill returned to coach the Blue Jays. The 1950 team also defeated all its college opponents—giving Hopkins an astounding four consecutive years of undefeated collegiate lacrosse teams—but lost a 6–5 heartbreaker to the powerful Mount Washington Club in the last game of the season.[32] Still, the 1950 team, along with the '47, '48, and '49 teams, belongs with the best in Hopkins' history. An amazing eleven of its players made an All-American team at least once during their playing careers.[33]

With many top players graduating, Hopkins did not figure in the championship picture for the next six years under head coaches Fred Smith and Wilson Fewster. Smith, a 1950 team member, later served as a volunteer assistant coach and would become one of the most beloved of Hopkins lacrosse mentors. He had a profound impact on Hopkins players—and on the game of lacrosse itself—for more than thirty years.[34]

A master of defensive strategy, Smith had among his protégés future Princeton and University of Denver head coach Bill Tierney, who spent three years as an assistant coach at Hopkins, learning from Smith; and future Hopkins head coach Dave Pietramala, who is considered perhaps the greatest defenseman in the game's history. Collectively, Tierney and Pietramala coached teams that have won a combined nine national championships (so far). Smith died in 1987 and whenever Tierney comes to Baltimore he always tries to drive by Fred Smith's former home to pay his respects.[35]

The next to assume the Hopkins lacrosse coaching mantel was Robert H. Scott—"Scotty" to almost everyone—whose remarkable two decades as head coach began with the 1955 season and ended in 1974. During that period, the Blue Jays won seven national championships and almost always were in the thick of the competition for the lacrosse crown.[36]

Among the outstanding players on Scott's early teams were Bill Morrill—the son of Kelso Morrill—and Mickey Webster. During what would later be dubbed the "Morrill/Webster" era of 1957–1959, both players were first-team All-Americans for three years and led one of Hopkins' most potent attack units.[37]

The 1959 graduation of fourteen seniors, eight of whom had received All-American recognition during their careers, affected the 1960–1961 teams, but Hopkins' offense still sparkled with the likes of Henry Ciccarone, a future Hall of Fame coach, and Jerry Schmidt—who in 1962 became the only lacrosse player ever featured exclusively on a *Sports Illustrated* cover.

(Another Hopkins player, Jake Byrne of the 2005 national championship team, also appeared on a *Sports Illustrated* cover, but in a thumbnail-size photo beneath a picture of NBA basketball greats Shaquille O'Neal and Amar'e Stoudemire.)[38]

The careers of several future Hopkins lacrosse legends began on the field and the sidelines during the 1960s. Ciccarone's Hopkins coaching career was launched in 1963 as an assistant varsity coach, and leading players of that era included future Hall of Famers Joseph Cowan, Benjamin H. (Hank) Kaestner III (who would follow his father, Benjamin H. "Bud" Kaestner Jr., Class of 1941, into the Lacrosse Hall of Fame), Willie Scroggs, later the founder of the University of North Carolina's lacrosse program, and Jerome Schnydman, who became the admissions director at Hopkins, then head of the alumni office, and finally an executive assistant to the president of The Johns Hopkins University.[39]

In 1971, the USILA ceded the awarding of the national lacrosse championship to the NCAA, which established the playoff system that is still in place. As a relatively small school that had some excellent athletic teams but only one—lacrosse—of long-standing, national renown, Hopkins lacrosse was allowed to compete in the NCAA's Division I, while all its other teams played Division III. A similar arrangement was made for seven other schools, all of which had either been traditional powers in ice hockey, soccer, or volleyball. A move to eliminate that waiver in 2004 was fought vigorously by Hopkins—led by university president William Brody and his executive assistant, Jerry Schnydman, a former Hopkins face-off star—and representatives from the other affected schools. It was overwhelmingly defeated, 296–106, at the NCAA's national convention, and the waiver continuation was approved 304–89.[40]

Once the NCAA playoff system began, Hopkins sustained heartbreaking losses to the University of Virginia and the University of Maryland in the '72 and '73 national championship games, respectively, before offensive aces Jack Thomas and Rick Kowalchuk led the Blue Jays to their first NCAA title in 1974, beating Maryland 17–12.[41] The victory had special meaning for Bob Scott, who previously had announced plans to retire from coaching to become the Hopkins athletic director. It was, needless to say, a lot easier to bow out of the coaching ranks with a championship rather than a third second-place finish.

The Modern Era: 1975–2000

Henry "Chic" Ciccarone was one of the finest coaches in the history of lacrosse. From 1975 to 1983, he led Hopkins through a phenomenal era of championship competitions and victories. Under Chic, the Blue Jays appeared in an unprecedented and still unequaled seven consecutive NCAA title games and were the first to win three championships in a row, defeating Cornell, 13–8 in 1978; Maryland, 15–9 in '79; and Virginia, 9–8 in double overtime in '80.

Ciccarone's championship teams included outstanding players such as future Hall of Famers Jeff Cook, Del Dressel, Mike O'Neill, Dave Huntley, Mike Federico, Mark Greenberg, and Brendan Schneck.[42] Along with Fred Smith, assistant coaches collaborating with Ciccarone on the sidelines was a remarkable group of former Hopkins players—some destined, like Ciccarone and Smith, to become members of the National Lacrosse Hall of Fame. These included Willie Scroggs, Joe Cowan, and Jerry Schnydman, along with their former teammates, Dennis Townsend and Jerry Pfeifer.[43]

Ciccarone was an explosive, charismatic, immensely engaging person with a raucous sense of humor, astounding ability to get the most out of his players, and an unquenchable desire to win. As a tribute to him in the National Lacrosse Hall of Fame observes, he

> was demanding, hard-driven, fiercely determined to bring out the best in his athletes, and to make them better individuals by virtue of their experiences on the field. . . . A player's coach, Chic was an incomparable motivator. . . . He made his players want to outperform their expectations, and he could convince them that whatever they lacked in firepower would be overcome by sheer force of will—and following his game plan.[44]

Ciccarone retired from coaching after the 1983 season. He was inducted into the National Lacrosse Hall of Fame in 1987 but died, tragically, just a year later at the age of fifty from a heart attack. Today, the Henry Ciccarone Center for the Prevention of Heart Disease at the Johns Hopkins Hospital—which was founded and directed by cardiologist Roger Blumenthal, who as a Hopkins undergraduate had been an assistant sports information director for Chic—is dedicated to the assessment of all the factors that contribute to heart disease. The name "Ciccarone" now is not only legendary in lacrosse, but also associated with heart research around the world.[45]

Don Zimmerman, a former Hopkins player who had been an assistant to Willie Scroggs at North Carolina and to Chic at Hopkins, took over as the Blue Jays' head coach in 1984. Known as "Zim," he became the first (and so far only) rookie coach to lead his team through an undefeated 14-0 season, capped with a 13–10 NCAA championship victory over Syracuse. Hopkins would repeat as champion in 1985 and again in 1987.[46]

With a stifling defense featuring future Hall of Famers such as Larry Quinn, twice named player of the year, goalie of the year, and most valuable player of the championship game; defensemen John DeTommaso and Dave Pietramala, both winners of the Schmeisser Award as best defenseman of the year (with Pietramala winning it twice in a row); and defensive, long-stick midfielder Steve Mitchell, the first in that position ever named a first-team All-American; along with a potent offense spearheaded by such future Hall of Famers as four-time first-team All-American midfielder Del Dressel and attackman Brian Wood, these teams regularly locked down and out-gunned their competition.[47]

Numerous lacrosse writers—and amateur commentators on the Internet —made much of the fact that, after 1987, it took Hopkins another eighteen years to win an NCAA championship, although it did appear in the title games of 1989 and 2003. That eighteen-year lapse in championships was the longest in the history of Hopkins lacrosse. Of course, the Blue Jays worked hard to end it. If one really studies lacrosse history, however, that eighteen-year hiatus hardly sets a record for gaps between winning the title. Syracuse went *fifty-four years* between championships (1929 to 1983, including twelve years of the NCAA tournament). Princeton went almost forty years between titles (1953 to 1992, including twenty-one years of the NCAA playoffs). Maryland has not won a championship since 1975 (forty-one years); Virginia was title-less for twenty-seven years (1972 to 1999); Cornell hasn't won a championship since 1977; North Carolina hasn't won one since 1991. And Navy—like all these others, an exceptionally fine program—has *never* won an NCAA lacrosse championship.[48]

Put in this perspective, the Hopkins championship drought does not seem so daunting. The Blue Jays were in the running every one of those eighteen years, making every NCAA playoff series, appearing in the Final Four nine times, contesting in the championship game three times. You can't win them all.

Each of Hopkins' title-winning coaches over the past half century has had a distinct personality. It could be said that Bob Scott was an "old school" coach—never swearing, philosophically patient (his standard expression was, "It'll all come out in the wash"), showing his frustration only by breaking clipboards over his knee. He became almost a surrogate father figure to many of his players. Henry Ciccarone was a fiery older brother, quick to anger but equally quick to tell a joke (sometimes off-color), match wits at cards with players, and make sure the team had a case of beer on the bus when returning from away games. Don Zimmerman was more reserved but recognized by his players as a brilliant X-and-O man. Dave Pietramala is as fiery as Ciccarone and as concerned about his players' personal well-being as Bob Scott. For all of these coaches and their teams, however, the goal has always been the same: be the best.

Former Hopkins goalie and subsequent radio commentator for Hopkins games, Larry Quinn once dubbed the 1990s an "Orange" decade—with the team color of Princeton and Syracuse dominating the championship game playing field—but the Blue Jays nevertheless had impressive teams featuring many outstanding, All-American players.[49]

Following the 1990 season, in which the Blue Jays went a disappointing 6-5, Don Zimmerman left the lacrosse coaching ranks for a short while. He eventually became the head coach at the University of Maryland at Baltimore County. Tony Seaman, a rare, non-Hopkins-associated choice, who was the veteran coach at the University of Pennsylvania, succeeded Zimmerman at Hopkins.

Led by Seaman, the 1995 Hopkins team went undefeated in the regular season. Among its top players were Terry Riordan, winner of the USILA's Enners Award as the nation's finest player and the Turnbull Award as the country's top attackman, and his partners on offense, Brian Piccola and David Marr.

Riordan and Piccola were the 1990s version of the legendary 1950s duo, Morrill and Webster—only possibly better. Riordan still holds the Hopkins record for career points (247) and goals scored (184), with Piccola just behind him at 245 points and 154 goals. David Marr, who would become Hopkins' all-time leader in assists, with 134, joined them on the field.[50]

Despite these remarkable accomplishments, the 1995 Hopkins team came up short in the NCAA semifinal game against Maryland, 16–8, as the Terps' goalie, Brian Dougherty, made an incredible twenty-three saves before a then-record crowd of 30,327 at Maryland's Byrd Stadium, the NCAA's first lacrosse playoff game sellout.[51]

Although Hopkins missed the 1995 championship, Blue Jays were well represented at a half-time ceremony at that game. The twenty-fifth anniversary of the Division I finals was marked by the naming of a twenty-five-member Silver Anniversary Team. Nearly half of the team—ten players—were from Hopkins, and between them they had won a combined seventeen NCAA championships (in a couple of cases, three apiece). Among them were Mike O'Neill ('78), Jack Thomas ('74), Del Dressel ('86), Rick Kowalchuk ('74), Brendan Schneck ('81), John DeTommaso ('86), Mark Greenberg ('80), Mike Federico ('80), Larry Quinn ('85), and Dave Pietramala ('90).[52]

The Tradition Continues: The Twenty-First Century

After Tony Seaman left Hopkins in 1998 (and soon thereafter became the coach at Towson University), he was succeeded by John Haus, a former North Carolina All-American defenseman who had been an assistant coach at Hopkins under Don Zimmerman. After two moderately successful seasons (his teams went 11-3 and 9-4), Haus left Hopkins in 2000 to return to his alma mater as head coach. His departure enabled Hopkins to bring back one of its own great players, Dave Pietramala, already a Coach of the Year award winner at Cornell.[53]

Under Pietramala—nicknamed "Petro"—Hopkins returned to the NCAA Final Four. By the end of the 2002 season, the Blue Jays were ranked No. 1 but lost the semifinal game to Princeton, 11–9. Nevertheless, the Jays' outstanding record that season earned Pietramala his second Coach of the Year award—making him the only person in history to get that honor at two different Division I programs.[54]

The Blue Jays were greatly motivated in 2003 and achieved something no Hopkins team since 1989 had done: they made it to the national championship game. Virginia was the opponent. The key figure, as frequently occurs in lacrosse, was the man in the goal—and in this game, it was Virginia's Tillman Johnson. He had an incredible day, making thirteen saves—several of them spectacular—and ending the Blue Jays' eleven-game winning streak and capturing the championship, 9-7.[55]

The 2004 season's highlight was the one hundredth meeting between Hopkins and the University of Maryland, a game eagerly anticipated by both teams. The build-up to it was remarkable. Pregame press coverage was extensive. *Sports Illustrated* prepared for a major story; the College Sports Television covered the game live; and a standing-room-only crowd of more than 10,000 packed Homewood Field on a perfect spring evening.[56]

Hopkins scored twice in the first two minutes and then unleashed a fusillade of three more goals in under ninety seconds. The Jays were ahead 5–0 before the first television time-out and were leading 8–1 at the end of the first quarter. Maryland managed a comeback later in the game but was never able to take the lead. Hopkins won, 14–10, outshooting the Terps 53–32, winning the ground-ball battle 35–20, and taking 16 of the 26 face-offs. It was a very satisfying victory.[57]

When the playoffs got under way, the Jays were ranked number one for the third year in a row. In the semifinal game, however, Syracuse—which Hopkins had defeated by a combined score of 36–13 in their previous two contests, proved to be the better team. Before 46,923 fans in Baltimore's M&T Bank Stadium, in a game that was tied seven times, the Orangemen ultimately prevailed, 15–9.[58] Despite plenty of postseason All-America and USILA accolades, the '04 players, especially the soon-to-be seniors, were crushed by that semifinal defeat. They vowed that they would not be denied again.[59]

The 2005 season was among the most remarkable in Hopkins lacrosse history. The team was led by seniors who had never lost a game on Home-wood Field: cocaptains Kyle Harrison, Peter LeSueur, Greg Raymond, Matt Rewkowski, and Chris Watson, along with teammates Tom Garvey, Kyle Barrie, Lou Braun, Benson Erwin, James Maimone-Medwick, and Joe "Kip" Malo. With significant contributions by freshmen, sophomores, and juniors, it was a team that refused to lose. They completed a school-re-cord 16–0 season, which included four overtime victories (the most ever in Hopkins history), notched Hopkins' first undefeated campaign since 1984, and won the Blue Jays' first national championship since 1987.[60]

Hopkins' semifinal 9–8 overtime victory against Virginia was the eighty-first game Hopkins had played in thirty-four consecutive NCAA tourna-ments and was a classic. Featuring powerful offense and defense, astonish-ing turnarounds, and sheer, heart-pounding drama, it gave the 45,275 fans in the Philadelphia Eagles' Lincoln Financial Field everything they could have wanted.[61]

Holding a comfortable 6–3 lead heading into the fourth quarter, Hopkins found the weather and Virginia's determination combining for what looked like another disastrous defeat.

As the fourth quarter began, what had been a bright, sunny sky turned ominously dark as thunderstorm clouds began rolling in. High winds buf-feted the stadium, scattering wrappers from Philly cheesesteaks, pretzels, and hot dogs all over the field. With equal suddenness, Virginia rediscovered its offensive power. The Cavaliers launched a four-goal rally and went ahead by one. Moments later, a flash of lightning forced suspension of play, sheets of rain drenched the stadium, and the teams had to go back to their locker rooms to wait out the storm. (Lacrosse often is played in driving rain—but not when there is lightning.)[62]

Following a forty-six-minute delay, Hopkins was about to leave the locker room to resume play when cocaptain Greg Raymond told his team-mates that the Blue Jays would get the first face-off and tie the score—which is exactly what Kyle Harrison did in the first twenty seconds. Virginia wasn't through, however. Their face-off specialist Jack deVilliers won the next battle at the X and the Cavs held the ball tightly for two minutes before calling a time-out with only thirty-seven seconds left to set up a play.[63]

When Virginia's Matt Ward got his fourth goal of the day, giving the Cavaliers an 8–7 lead with 12 seconds left on the clock, many in the stands surely thought Hopkins was toast. Not that '05 team. Greg Peyser beat deVilliers on the next face-off, dashed toward the goal, spotted Jake Byrne about ten yards from the crease, and passed the ball to him. Byrne slipped a left-handed shot through the legs of Kip Turner, the UVA goalie, to tie the game once more with only 1.4 seconds remaining in regulation time.[64]

In overtime, both Turner and Hopkins' goalie Jesse Schwartzman made spectacular saves. After his second save on a shot by Virginia's Kyle Dixon, Schwartzman made a perfect clearing pass to Tom Garvey, who moved the ball forward to Paul Rabil as he sprinted toward the Virginia zone. Rabil found Benson Erwin unguarded some twelve yards from the goal and passed the ball to him. Erwin—a superb defensive middie with just seven career goals—took only a few steps before firing a low shot past Turner to win the game. Erwin later called it "a lucky shot," but along with the other seniors—who together scored seven of Hopkins' nine goals in that game— he had experienced plenty of playoff disappointment in the previous three years. That past heartbreak helped Hopkins rebound to beat Virginia.[65]

Next up for the Blue Jays was a great Duke Blue Devils team. Although Hopkins' seniors had been the motivational backbone of the 2005 team, a pair of sophomores—goalie Jesse Schwartzman and attackman Jake Byrne— were the keys to Hopkins' come-from-behind, 9–8 championship victory over Duke before a crowd of more than 44,000. Schwartzman, who would be named the tournament's MVP, had the solid defense of seniors Watson and Garvey, as well as junior Matt Pinto, in front of him. He made seven of his twelve saves in the second half, stifling the previously potent Duke offense for nearly 28 minutes. Byrne scored the unassisted, game-winning goal with 13:35 remaining in the fourth quarter, putting Hopkins ahead for good.[66]

Hopkins' 2005 team received many postseason honors. Seven Blue Jays were named to All-America teams, and Kyle Harrison hit the trifecta of awards, receiving the Tewaaraton Trophy as the top lacrosse player in the nation, as well as the US Intercollegiate Lacrosse Association's Enners Award as the year's outstanding player, and its McLaughlin Award as the country's best midfielder.[67]

Defending the NCAA title was difficult. The 2006 Hopkins team once again made the NCAA playoffs but lost a 13–12 heartbreaker to Syracuse in the quarterfinals.[68] However, the 2007 team recaptured the NCAA crown— Hopkins' ninth—despite an up-and-down regular season during which the Blue Jays once were just 4-4, and lacrosse's chattering class began to doubt Hopkins would even make the tournament. Instead, Hopkins went on to win its next nine games, including a 12–11 championship victory over Duke before more than 48,000 fans at Baltimore's M&T Bank Stadium.[69]

In 2008, the 125th anniversary season for Hopkins lacrosse, the Blue Jays again recorded a stunning, eight-game winning streak on their way to the championship game but lost 13–10 to Syracuse. In 2010, 2011, and 2012, Hopkins maintained its unequaled record of qualifying for the NCAA playoffs but failed to make the championship game.[70]

A New Era

In the spring of 2012, Dave Pietramala and Hopkins' athletic director, Tom Calder, contemplated the rapidly changing collegiate lacrosse world and began pondering how the Blue Jays could adjust to it. Particularly challenging was a sudden, three-year wave of athletic conference realignments, driven by "TV money, greed, football, crippling intra-institutional insecurity, and the Big Ten," according to Eamonn Brennan, a basketball analyst for ESPN.com.[71] The Big Ten chose to create a TV network solely for its own conference, earning millions for each member school. To increase the reach and profitability of its network, it sought to expand its conference, and "conference expansion" became the goal of other groups as well.[72]

Hopkins was not concerned about television coverage. Since 2005, it had possessed a unique and exclusive, multiyear and multimedia deal with ESPNU to air all regular-season home games, as well as select away games.[73] As an independent athletic program, however, Hopkins did have concerns that the rapidly changing conference realignments might make maintaining a schedule featuring traditional rivals increasingly difficult. Also problematic was the growing number of teams being given automatic qualifying (AQ) berths in the NCAA playoffs based on winning their conference championships—even if their overall season record was a losing one. With half of the sixteen payoff berths now falling into the AQ category, the number of slots available to independents such as Hopkins was dwindling and likely to become even smaller.[74]

Calder and Pietramala took their concerns to Hopkins' president Ronald J. Daniels, a former law school professor, dean, and University of Pennsylvania provost who became Hopkins' fourteenth president in 2009. On March 8, 2013, he appointed a nine-member blue ribbon panel to explore whether Hopkins should end its 130-year history of lacrosse independence and join an athletic conference. The committee was cochaired by his former executive assistant and National Lacrosse Hall of Famer Jerry Schnydman, cocaptain of the 1967 national championship team, and Chris Watson, cocaptain of the 2005 national championship team and a former university trustee.[75]

The committee conducted extensive research into the competiveness of every NCAA Division I men's program from 2005 to 2012, the potential academic impact of conference affiliation, the travel costs associated with it, and how the student-athlete experience and player recruitment would be affected. In addition, profiles were developed of the conferences that fielded lacrosse teams. The implications of remaining independent also were considered.[76]

The views of alumni, faculty, and students and parents were solicited via e-mails and links to the committee's website. More than 330 messages were received, with 65.4 percent of those responding explicitly voicing support for joining a conference, while 34.6 percent preferring Hopkins' independence.[77]

On May 10, 2013, President Daniels announced that the committee had concluded unanimously that Hopkins should seek conference affiliation for the men's lacrosse program. "That conclusion was based on the committee members' conviction that such a move will provide our university and history's most-successful lacrosse program the best opportunity for continued leadership at the highest level of intercollegiate competition," Daniels wrote in an e-mail to the Hopkins community. The pursuit of such an affiliation would be undertaken promptly, he wrote.[78]

It was not a moment too soon to reach that conclusion. A few days earlier, despite being ranked fourteenth in the nation and having a 9-5 record, Hopkins did not qualify for the NCAA playoffs for the first time in forty-two years. Although Hopkins succeeded in returning to the playoffs in 2014, that 2013 break in its unprecedented record of postseason play was due in part to AQ rules. Slots that Hopkins, as an independent, might have obtained instead went to the Metro Atlantic Athletic Conference (MAAC) winner, the University of Detroit, with a 5-9 record, and the Northeast Conference (NEC) champion Bryant University, with an overall 8-10 record.[79]

On June 3, 2013, Daniels, Calder, Pietramala, and Commissioner Jim Delany of the Big Ten Conference held a joint press conference to announce Hopkins' acceptance as an affiliate member of the Big Ten's new lacrosse conference, joining the University of Maryland (also a new Big Ten member), Penn State, Ohio State, Michigan, and Rutgers. Hopkins would remain unique as the Big Ten's first and only affiliate member, joining for just a single sport.

TV money wasn't a motivator for Hopkins' or the Big Ten's decision. Hopkins is pleased with its long-standing agreement with ESPNU and insisted that it remain in place. What the Big Ten wanted was a sixth major lacrosse team in its lineup (the last added had been Penn State in 1992), which would enable its members to vie for an automatic qualifier in the NCAA tournament, explains Ernest Larossa, Hopkins' athletics information director. The newly expanded Big Ten lacrosse conference began play in 2015—and now with six members, it qualifies for one of the NCAA's AQ playoff berths.[80]

The success of lacrosse at Johns Hopkins isn't measured only in championships. The impact that former Hopkins players and coaches continue to have on the sport and the university is not calculated by the numerous athletic honors in the program's trophy cases. Even the coaches in other Hopkins sports are quick to praise the lacrosse team and its success.

For example, football coach Jim Margraff is a 1982 JHU graduate, was a star quarterback as an undergraduate, an avid fan of the lacrosse

In 2015, the Johns Hopkins lacrosse team became a member of the Big 10 conference. Hopkins earned an automatic qualifying bid for the NCAA tournament by beating The Ohio State University, 13–6, for the Big 10 conference title. JHU then walloped the University of Virginia 19–7 in the first round of the playoffs. That win put JHU in the Final Four, where it beat Syracuse University 16–15. JHU's season ended just one goal shy of getting into the championship game when the Blue Jays lost to the University of Maryland, 12–11, in a heartbreaking but inspiring semifinal game. *Courtesy of the Johns Hopkins University Department of Athletics.*

team, and a great admirer of David Pietramala. "Simply, I'm a Hopkins guy. I'm a huge Hopkins lacrosse fan. I'm a bigger David Pietramala fan," says Margraff. When he became football coach in 1990, Margraff says, "everyone recruited against us and said, 'Well, football's not the big sport there,' etc. Now everyone complains that we have all these advantages because we have a Division I lacrosse program and we've got nice facilities and we do things in a first-class manner here."[81] "So to me," Margraff continues, "you can either fight it or look for a symbiotic relationship, and that's what it's turned out to be. I can't put words in David's [Pietramala's] mouth, but I think it helps him to have a good football program, where the school isn't only about lacrosse, but it's good in athletics. It's also powerful to have a flagship sport at a major university, which lacrosse is here."[82]

JHU sports information director Ernest Larossa says, "If you walked down a street in Baltimore and asked 100 people what they think of when you say, 'Johns Hopkins,' 50 percent of them would say 'medicine' and 50 percent would say 'lacrosse.' Lacrosse is part of the fabric of the Johns Hopkins University."[83]

The lacrosse tradition will live on in Baltimore and at Hopkins. The names and faces will change, but the same spirit and enthusiasm will continue for players, coaches, students, alumni, and friends of Johns Hopkins lacrosse.

8

The Bears of Baltimore

Morgan State University Intercollegiate Athletics

JERRY BEMBRY

Morgan State University is one of the nation's best-known Historically Black Colleges and Universities (HBCUs). Founded in 1867 by the Baltimore Conference of the Methodist Episcopal Church, the school, which then was called the Centenary Biblical Institute, had twenty students in its inaugural class. The school was renamed Morgan College after the Reverend Lyttleton Morgan, who donated land in northeast Baltimore to the college. In 1895, the first baccalaureate degree from Morgan College was awarded. Its recipient was George W. F. McMechen, who later went on to earn a law degree from Yale University before returning to Baltimore and becoming the first black member of Baltimore's Board of Commissioners and an active citizen.[1] Morgan College remained a small private school until the state of Maryland, recognizing the need to provide more educational opportunities for black students (in part because it was unwilling to integrate its public universities), acquired the institution in 1939.[2] Morgan received university status in 1975.[3]

Once a tiny school on a small parcel of land in the late 1800s, Morgan State University now occupies 143 acres, has approximately 8,000 students (undergraduate and graduate), and offers a wide array of curricular and extracurricular opportunities. Morgan State has produced a long list of successful alums, including a major magazine publisher (Earl Graves, of *Black Enterprise*), a US Army general who became the first commanding officer of the United States Africa Command (General William "Kip" Ward), talented singers and musicians (Lonnie Liston Smith, Deniece Williams, and Maysa), an Academy Award–nominated actress (Mo'Nique), a national entertainment television host (Kevin Frazier), a *New York Times* columnist (William Rhoden), and US congressmen (Kweisi Mfume and Parren Mitchell).[4]

Morgan alums also include a number of outstanding athletes who realized national and international acclaim. The school has, for instance, four players in the Professional Football Hall of Fame (which ties it with Grambling State University for the most inductees among HBCUs); the first African American pitcher to win a World Series game; numerous Olympians, including several gold medalists; and a great deal of team success, including a national championship in basketball.[5]

Today, Morgan State, the largest HBCU in Maryland, fields twelve intercollegiate athletic teams: five men's teams (basketball, cross country, football, tennis, and track and field) and eight women's teams (basketball, bowling, cross country, softball, tennis, track and field, volleyball, and cheerleading). As a result of significant policy and demographic changes in higher education, the school's athletic program experienced some lean years during the late twentieth century. Nevertheless, there have been signs recently that Morgan's athletic program is on the verge of shifting its fortunes, thus causing some people to wear their Morgan State Blue and Orange attire more proudly.

The Early Years and the Edward Hurt Era

In 1899, Morgan College entered the world of intercollegiate sports by playing its first football game. It competed against Howard University, a prominent HBCU in Washington, DC. The game was in DC on the Howard campus and the score was lopsided: Howard, which had been playing football for six years, destroyed Morgan, 71–0.[6]

It would take some time for Morgan—which fielded teams in men's and women's basketball and men's and women's track in the early 1900s—to be successful athletically. But that did not stop one of Morgan's early coaches, Charles R. Drew, from making an impact on the world.

History knows the Washington, DC, native Dr. Charles Drew as a noted surgeon and researcher who, during World War II, was credited with saving hundreds of lives with the development of the first large-scale blood banks where plasma was stored for transfusions. Drew, who earned his medical degree from McGill University in Montreal, Canada, was the first African American to receive a doctor of medical science from Columbia University.[7]

But before Drew became a world-recognized doctor, he was an athlete and a college football coach. After graduating from Amherst College, where he ran track and played football, Drew wanted to go to medical school, but could not afford it. To save money for his advanced studies, he took a job in 1926 as the first athletic director at Morgan, where he was also the team's football coach for two years. His coaching record was 8-2-2.[8]

The first Morgan coach, however, to earn a lasting reputation for his contributions to athletics came to the school four years later. In 1929, Morgan hired Edward P. Hurt, who would become a legendary jack-of-all trades. A Howard University and Columbia University graduate who taught mathematics at Morgan, Hurt coached the football team for twenty-nine years (1929–1959), the basketball team for eighteen years (1929–1947), and the track team for forty-one years (1929–1970).[9]

A slim, diminutive man who had been a star football player at Howard (1919–1921), Hurt coached numerous dominant teams at Morgan. He led the school to fourteen Colored Intercollegiate Athletic Association (CIAA) titles in football, four CIAA titles in basketball, and eighteen CIAA championships in track.[10] In football, the Hurt-led Bears went fifty-four consecutive games without a loss (from 1931 to 1938) and had three undefeated and untied seasons (1933, 1935, and 1937).[11] The school's first CIAA championship came in 1930, when the Bears went 8-1. The team's most dominant season was in 1933, when Morgan went 9-0 and outscored its opponents by an incredible 319–6 margin.[12]

It might seem incongruous that a man so small was able to direct football teams that were defensive forces.[13] But Hurt's frame belied his toughness and tenacity, which his best squads reflected. His 1934 team, for example, which won the fourth of five straight CIAA titles, was so stingy defensively that it did not give up a single point.

After nearly complete dominance of the CIAA in the 1930s, Morgan won seven more CIAA gridiron titles over the next decade. In 1950, the Bears went undefeated (6-0-2) and it looked like the start of more success. But the 1951 team finished with a disappointing 3-5 record, which was the school's first nonwinning season in twenty-two years. And in 1959, Hurt's final season, the Bears were 1-6-1.[14] All good things come to an end.

At the time, America's racial climate was changing, in the culture at large and in professional football. In 1946, the National Football League (NFL) signed its first black players—Kenny Washington and Woody Strode with the Los Angeles Rams—in almost a generation.[15] This paved the way for the historical moment in 1950 when Len Ford, an offensive and defensive end, became the first Morgan player drafted to play pro football. Ignored by NFL teams, Ford was picked by the Los Angeles Dons of the All-America Football Conference and eventually played eight years with the Cleveland Browns.[16]

The door to the NFL was now open. In the years that followed, Morgan players were drafted and signed into the professional ranks. Many excelled.

In 1951, the Green Bay Packers drafted Charles "Redd" Robinson, an all-conference guard and cocaptain of the 1949 team. He later played for the Baltimore Colts.[17] Two years later, the New York Giants took Roosevelt Brown, a bruising offensive lineman, in the twenty-seventh round of the NFL draft. Despite being such a low pick, Brown enjoyed a long, stellar career, which eventually earned him a spot in the Pro Football Hall of Fame.[18] That Ford, Robinson, and Brown were drafted and played pro football was a testament to the talent that Hurt recruited and cultivated at Morgan.

Yet as good as Hurt was as a football coach, his biggest impact came coaching track—a sport where black runners, unlike football players, often had a chance to compete against their white contemporaries.

While compiling fifteen CIAA track titles against other HBCUs, Hurt also mentored athletes who earned national and international attention. Eight Morgan runners won individual NCAA championships, twelve became national AAU individual champions, and six relay teams won AAU titles.[19] Some of Hurt's athletes also ran in the Olympics. One of his runners, George Rhoden, won Olympic gold (for Jamaica, in the 400 meters and the 4X400 relay at the 1952 games in Helsinki) a year after leaving Morgan.[20]

Hurt's success in track earned him a spot as an assistant track coach on the 1964 and 1968 US Olympic teams; the latter featured the famous (infamous?) sprinters Tommie Smith and John Carlos of raised, black-gloved fame.

In his later years, Hurt reflected on the challenges that he faced: "It was hard to get recognition," he said, "especially in track and field, and we just never had a chance to compete against the better schools. When we first started trying to improve our program, nobody knew we were alive."[21]

By the time he retired in 1970, Hurt was widely appreciated. His Morgan Hall of Fame entry describes Hurt as "the greatest coach to come from a black college."[22] That is high praise, but debatable. After all, basketball coaches John McLendon and Clarence "Big House" Gaines were extremely successful, and Eddie Robinson of Grambling State is among the greatest football coaches in NCAA Division I history. Yet in terms of black coaches who had great success in multiple sports, what Hurt did at Morgan was unprecedented and is unlikely to be duplicated.

Nonetheless, Hurt was not inducted in the US Track and Field and Cross Country Coaches Hall of Fame until 2004, fifteen years after he died. Hurt was also posthumously named the American Football Coaches Association's Trailblazer Award winner in 2011.[23] Herman L. Wade, one of Hurt's athletes, writes in *Run from There: A Biography of Edward P. Hurt* (2004): "The arrival of the black athlete on the national sports scene in the 1940s and 50s goes directly to Edward P. Hurt. There is not a single black sports figure in the world today who is not in some small way in the debt of Coach Hurt."[24]

During Hurt's impressive career there were standout Morgan athletes besides football and track stars. One of the earliest outstanding women athletes at Morgan was Laura Jones, who matriculated in 1934 and was the captain of the basketball team. Like Hurt, she is a member of the Morgan Athletic Hall of Fame—the first woman athlete from that era to join the elite company.[25]

A pioneer and jane-of-all-trades coach on the women's side was Dr. Effietee M. Payne, who spent parts of four decades at Morgan (1946–1973) coaching women's basketball, tennis, and softball. Payne, who is also in the school's Hall of Fame, was a talented, dedicated coach who fought hard for the rights of women students and athletes.[26]

"I was told about one year when mom took the entire [women's] basketball team to sit-in at an athletics awards banquet that they were not invited to," recalled her son, Tom Payne. He also told the story of a group of fans getting out of hand at a game. "And my mom told the referee to stop the game, cleared the gym and started the game again. Most people couldn't believe it," he explained.[27]

On the men's basketball side, Matthew "Mack" Payne, also a member of the Morgan Hall of Fame, was the captain of the Morgan basketball team from 1926 to 1927. That Morgan squad's claim to fame was that it beat the New York Rens, which was the first all-black professional basketball team owned by African Americans.[28]

The Golden Era of Track

Morgan football teams in the 1930s began an era of dominance. But the players on those teams, participating in an acutely segregated sports world, were not able to match their skills against their white counterparts. That was not always the case in the world of track and field.

In 1904, George Poage, a University of Wisconsin student, became the first African American athlete to compete in the Olympics and the first to win a medal, taking the bronze in the 200-meter and 400-meter hurdles in St. Louis.[29] Four years later at the London Olympics, John Baxter Taylor, a University of Pennsylvania graduate, became the first black to win an Olympic gold medal as a member of the 400-meter relay team.[30] The 1936 Olympics in Berlin were a breakout event for black athletes, who won numerous medals in full view of Adolf Hitler, with Jesse Owens of Ohio State University winning an unprecedented four gold medals.[31]

Eventually, Morgan's runners excelled on national and international stages. Two Morgan athletes won Olympic gold medals. As previously noted, George Rhoden won the 400 meters for Jamaica in the 1952 games in Helsinki. Years later, Rochelle Stevens, an eleven-time NCAA All-American while at Morgan, was a member of the 4X400 meter relay team that won the gold for the United States at the 1992 games in Barcelona.[32]

With Morgan track and field athletes having the opportunity to go up against some of the top athletes in the nation, regardless of race, George Spaulding in 1930 was the first from the school to break through on the elite level. Spaulding, competing in the decathlon at the 1930 Penn Relays, finished in second place behind Barney Berlinger, the only three-time college decathlon champion in the meet's history.[33]

Some of the Morgan men at the 1950 Penn Relays achieved excellence when they won the 4X400, establishing a meet record with a time of 3:13.6. That team was comprised of George Rhoden, Sam La Beach, Bob Tyler, and Bill Brown. Their surprising win ended New York University's three-year dominance in the mile relay and broke a Penn Relays record that stood for eleven years.[34] It also marked the first time an HBCU had won the 4X400 title at the prestigious meet.[35]

In 1952, four runners—James Rogers, Otis "Jet" Johnson, Herman Wade, and Joshua Culbreath—entered Morgan and formed a group that would be named "The Flying Four." It was one of the best 4X400 teams of the era.[36] In its four years together, the group won the AAU national championships in 1954 and 1955 at Madison Square Garden and won three CIAA titles between 1953 and 1955. "We kicked everyone's butt," Joshua Culbreath, the team's anchor, said in 2013. "We won every championship from Madison Square Garden to the Boston Garden."[37]

While that foursome proved to be a dominant group in the college ranks, Morgan athletes were also crashing the Olympics in a big way. Four athletes with Morgan connections were named to the US team at the 1952 games in Helsinki. Three of them—George Rhoden and brothers Sam and Byron La Beach—had grown up together in Jamaica.

Even though Sam La Beach had made a name for himself on the Morgan team that won the 4X400 at the 1950 Penn Relays, he was on the Panamanian Olympic team because he was born there. Unfortunately, because he pulled a muscle a few weeks before the Olympics, he never got a chance to run in Helsinki. As a result, the man who was ranked No. 5 in the world at the time of his injury did not even make the trip to Finland.[38] Sam's younger brother, Byron, represented Jamaica's Olympic team and ran in two events: the 400 meters and the 4X400 meter relay. Byron, who was a member of

Some of the stars of the Morgan State track team—Bill Brown, Bob Tyler,
George Rhoden, and Sam La Beach—with legendary coach Edward P. Hurt,
1950. *Courtesy of the Beulah M. Davis Special Collections Department,
Earl S. Richardson Library, Morgan State University.*

Morgan's AAU championship 4X100 team in 1954, did not place in either event at the Olympics.[39]

Another Jamaican from Morgan to reach the Olympics was George Rhoden. He held the world record in the 400 entering the games and was the favorite to win the event in Helsinki. Rhoden, who ran in the 1948 Olympics, lived up to his reputation. Not only did he win the 400 for Jamaica, he also ran the anchor leg for the 4X400 team that won gold by beating the American team by one-tenth of a second.[40]

Of the four Morgan athletes who were on that Olympic team, just one, Art Bragg, represented the United States. Bragg also entered the Olympics as the favorite in his event, the 100 meters, after winning the Olympic trials earlier in the year. But while warming up for the first heat, he pulled a hamstring. He wound up winning that first heat, but he was not 100 percent in the semifinals, in which he finished last.[41]

Bragg was one of the top sprinters in the country. The year before the Olympics, he was a member of the 4X100 team that won gold at the Pan American games. In the years following the Olympics, Bragg won the 100- and 220-yard AAU championships (breaking a twenty-three-year-old AAU record in the 100 and establishing a new record in the 220).[42] Still, he was forever disappointed by what happened in Helsinki. "I cried," Bragg told the Baltimore Sun in 1992 when he recalled the race. "I had successes. That was the major disappointment. Every Olympics when I watch 100 on TV, I break down and cry."[43]

Those early Olympians from Morgan were just the start of a long list that followed. Josh Culbreath was an Olympic bronze medalist for the United States in the 400-meter hurdles during the 1956 games in Melbourne. Paul Winder was a member of the United States 4X400 meter relay team at the 1960 Olympics in Rome (and later a member of the Morgan Athletic Hall of Fame). Neville Hodge competed for the Virgin Islands in the 100 meters at the 1984 Olympics in Los Angeles, the 1988 Olympics in Seoul, and the 1992 games in Barcelona. Hodge, who is now the track coach at Morgan, was also the coach for the Virgin Islands during the 1996 and 2000 games.[44] Jack Pierce won a bronze medal while representing the United States at the 1992 Olympics in Barcelona. Troy McIntosh won a bronze medal for the Bahamas in the 4X400 meters at the 2000 Olympics in Sydney, and competed in the 400 and 4X400 meters at the 1996 Olympics in Atlanta.

The most decorated athlete in Morgan women's track history is Rochelle Stevens, who won a gold medal for the United States in the 4X400 meter relay at the 1996 Olympics in Atlanta, and a silver medal at the 1992 games. While at Morgan, Stevens was the NCAA Division I champion in the 400 meters, won four USA Outdoor Track and Field championships, and earned All-American honors eleven times.[45]

Several other Morgan women participated in the Olympics. Roberta Bell made the 4X400 meter relay team in 1980, but did not run because the United States boycotted the Moscow games that year. Bell was also an alternate on the 4X400 meter relay team at the 1984 games in Los Angeles. Ethlyn Tate was on Jamaica's 4X100 meters relay team that qualified for the Olympic final at the 1988 games in Seoul, but the group had to withdraw after anchor Merlene Ottey suffered an injury. Tate also ran the 100 meters that year. Wendy Vereen-Christopher was an alternate on the United States 4X100 meters relay at the 1984 games. Ameerah Bello ran three events for the Virgin Islands at the 1996 games in Atlanta: the 200 meters, 400 meters, and the 4X100 meters relay. At the 2000 games in Sydney, Bello again ran the 100 meters. Jilma Patrick teamed with Bello to represent the Virgin Islands on the 4X100 meters relay team that ran in Atlanta at the 1996 games.

Morganite Makes Baseball History

Like many of his peers, Joe Black played several sports after entering Morgan in 1939. In track and field he was a hurdler and threw the javelin. On the football field, he was an All-CIAA and All-American end.[46] On the baseball field, he was a topnotch pitcher. Black had good power to go along with a natural slider. Talented and determined, Black seemed destined for the Negro leagues, as Major League Baseball in that era refused to allow black players in its ranks.

Black's Negro league career began in 1944 with the Baltimore Elite Giants. By 1950, Black was the starting pitcher in the Negro league's popular East-West All-Star game. By then, Jackie Robinson, Larry Doby, Satchel Paige, and a few others had integrated Major League Baseball and many teams were scouting Negro league talent. Robinson, in particular, made Black hopeful that he could play in the Majors. "When Rickey signed Jackie, I was 18 all over again," Black said in 1997. "I started dreaming. And that's what happened to most of the guys in the Negro Leagues. You forgot your age. You said, 'If Jackie makes it, I can make it.'"[47]

The Dodgers signed Black in 1952, and he instantly paid dividends by winning fifteen games and being named the National League Rookie of the Year. When the Dodgers reached the World Series that year, Black was named the opening game pitcher, despite having only two starts during the regular season.[48] The Dodgers won the game, 4–2, and Black earned the honor of being the first African American to win a game in the World Series.[49]

Morganites basked in his reflected glory. In the official program for the 1952 annual homecoming football game, Morgan proudly honored the former Bear. "Joe Black has achieved," wrote J. Haywood Harrison. "He has achieved well. His name will indeed be recorded in Morgan's Hall of Fame. Morgan State College salutes Joe Black as a truly worthy and renowned favorite son. To Joe, the College says thanks—thanks for bringing to it thy laurels and placing them at its feet."[50]

The Return of Football Dominance, and Then the Fall

The 1960s was a time of transition for Morgan athletics, as it was for much of the country. In Baltimore, for the first time in thirty years, there was a new Morgan football coach on the sidelines: Earl C. Banks.

Banks was a large man, but he earned the nickname "Papa Bear" around Morgan due to the life lessons that he taught his players and for being a "master motivator."[51] "Coach Banks taught as much about life as he did about football," said Pete Pompey, a former Morgan football player who went on to become coach of a national championship basketball team at Dunbar High School in Baltimore. "That was important to him."[52]

Winning was important as well. During Banks's tenure as coach, from 1960 to 1973, Morgan won a lot. The highlights of Banks's coaching career include ninety-six wins (against thirty-one losses and two ties), four bowl appearances, and a winning streak of thirty-one straight games between 1965 and 1968.[53] Additionally, Banks, who was inducted into the College Football Hall of Fame in 1992, sent forty players to the NFL.[54]

One of the biggest games of Banks's career came on September 28, 1968, a day on which history was made in New York City when Morgan State and Grambling University became the first HBCUs to play a football game in New York City at Yankee Stadium.[55]

There were concerns going into the game. The Reverend Martin Luther King Jr. had been assassinated earlier in the year and the game organizers were worried about maintaining the peace in a stadium filled with more than 60,000 African American fans.[56] "I will never forget when we came out of the dugout and walked out on the field for pre-game warm-up," said Doug Porter, an assistant coach at Grambling, when interviewed for *1st & Goal in the Bronx: Grambling vs. Morgan State, 1968* (2011), a documentary about the game. "A wall of noise hit us. We had never heard that kind of roar come from a crowd. And I looked into the crowd, and the stands were just completely filled with people of color," Porter reminisced.[57] Raymond

Chester, who scored the first touchdown of the game in Morgan's 9–7 win, explains in the documentary, "It was amazing. We were just like in awe."[58]

"That was part of the golden era of black college football," says Ronald Bethea, who was a linebacker on the 1971 Morgan team that won the Mid-Eastern Athletic Conference (MEAC) championship. "Up until 1976, some of the most talented black football players were playing at black institutions."[59] Indeed, some of the most talented played at Morgan. Of the many Morgan players who have played professional football, four have reached the Pro Football Hall of Fame.

Len Ford, who was inducted into the Pro Football Hall of Fame in 1976, played on the Morgan football team in 1944 (standing 6'5", he also played on the basketball team). He left Morgan the next year to join the navy. When his military obligation was over, he transferred to the University of Michigan because of his desire to play football at a higher level. Ford played professionally with the Los Angeles Dons, Cleveland Browns, and Green Bay Packers and earned four Pro Bowl spots and played on three NFL championship teams.[60]

When the New York Giants picked Roosevelt Brown in the twenty-seventh round in 1953, he became the first Morgan player to be selected in the NFL draft. There are not many expectations as a twenty-seventh-round pick, but Brown earned a starting position with the Giants in his first year at offensive tackle and played in nine Pro Bowls during his thirteen-year career. After his retirement in 1965, Brown became an assistant coach with the Giants and later became a scout. In 1999, when the *Sporting News* published a list of the one hundred greatest football players, Brown was listed at number 57. When he was inducted into the Pro Football Hall of Fame in 1975, he was only the second offensive lineman to receive that honor.[61]

Leroy Kelly, who was inducted into the Pro Football Hall of Fame in 1994, was a stud at Morgan. He was a quarterback, kick returner, punter, and a linebacker. But when Earl Banks saw him, he recognized that Kelly could achieve true greatness as a running back.

Although he played both sides of the ball (as many players did in that era), Kelly excelled as a running back. Thanks to a combination of quickness, speed, and intelligence, Kelly was able to explode through any hole and outrun most defenders. He averaged five yards a carry in 1963 at Morgan, and was named the Most Valuable Player of the Orange Blossom Classic game that season—even though Morgan lost the game to Florida A&M, 30–7. Kelly is the running back who replaced Jim Brown, who is widely considered to be the greatest running back in pro football history.[62]

In 1966, when Morgan became the first HBCU to play in the Tangerine Bowl, the game's MVP was a hard-hitting middle linebacker named Willie

Lanier (Pro Football Hall of Fame, 1986).[63] After the Kansas City Chiefs drafted Lanier in 1967, he became the first black player to be a star middle linebacker in the NFL. Lanier still holds the school record for tackles in a game (twenty-six, against Hampton in 1966).[64]

More recently, Morgan football has struggled. Its last great team was in 1979, when the team reached the NCAA Division II playoffs and finished the season with a 9-2 record.[65] Since then, the Morgan football team has had just five seasons in which it has won more than five games, and just one coach—Clarence Thomas—has had a winning record since Banks left the school after the 1973 season.[66]

The school is hoping that the 2014 hiring of head coach Lee Hull will help improve the program. Hull, who is the nineteenth coach in Morgan history, spent the previous six years at the University of Maryland where he helped develop NFL receivers Darrius Heyward-Bey and Torrey Smith. In December 2014, after trouncing Delaware State on the last game of the regular season, 69–7, coupled with North Carolina A&T's season-ending loss, Morgan became MEAC champions for the first time in thirty-five years.[67]

Still, the fact that talented black athletes are now wooed by the top athletic programs in the nation—programs that offer better resources than Morgan—makes it difficult for any HBCU to reach the level of success that schools experienced fifty years ago. Nevertheless, Morgan still intends to field a competitive football team, one that can vie for a MEAC title.

Basketball: The Marvin Webster Era and the Todd Bozeman Renaissance

In terms of individual success, the football team at Morgan State holds campus bragging rights. But in terms of that one shining moment—that one occasion when everyone on campus could walk proudly around campus—there was no bigger moment for the school than March 15, 1974. That was the day Morgan's men's basketball team beat Southwest Missouri State, 67–52, to win the Division II national title.[68]

For generations, beginning in the early twentieth century, Morgan did not have a strong basketball tradition. In the 1960s, Morgan had only one winning season. That was during an era when HBCU teams were still making a tremendous impact on the national basketball scene with competitive squads like Grambling (with future NBA Hall of Famer Willis Reed), Johnson C. Smith University (led by Harlem Globetrotters legend Curly Neal), Norfolk State (featuring future two-time NBA champion Bobby Dandridge), and Winston-Salem State University, which, led by future Hall of Fame guard Earl Monroe, became the first HBCU team to win a Division II national title.[69]

The shift in Morgan's basketball fortunes began the day that a skinny, 6'10" young man named Marvin Webster, the son of a Baltimore preacher, decided to attend Morgan.

Morgan was not Webster's first choice. After a stellar high school career at Baltimore's Edmondson High School, Webster wanted to go to the University of Maryland, the state's top school, which played in the powerful Atlantic Coast Conference. Maryland had just hired head coach Charles "Lefty" Driesell and was about to emerge as a college basketball powerhouse. But Driesell had already signed big men Tom McMillen and Len Elmore (both of whom ended up in the NBA). There was no room for Webster.[70]

So Webster decided to attend Morgan. Initially, he did not do much to impress his future teammates. "I'm going to be honest. The first time I saw Marvin Webster I thought he was a dud," says Joe McIver, a forward on that 1974 team who is now an assistant athletic director at Morgan. "When we first came into the gym, for pick-up games before practices even started, he wasn't exerting himself. I thought he was one of those guys who couldn't run and chew bubble gum at the same time."[71]

When practices finally began, the Webster who would become the 1974 Division II player of the year emerged. Webster averaged 16 rebounds a game as a freshman, and Morgan finished the season with a respectable 16-10 record. As Webster improved, so did the team. With Webster averaging 18.5 points and 23.2 rebounds his sophomore season, the Bears finished with a 20-10 record and reached the 1973 MEAC championship game that ended with a 104–97 loss to the University of Maryland-Eastern Shore.

Webster had a chance to go pro after his sophomore season, but decided to stay in school. As a junior, Webster, now seven feet tall, was unstoppable. He averaged over 21 points a game, along with his 22.4 rebounds per game. These numbers could have been higher had Webster played strictly for statistics. But Webster was a team player, and he bought into the team-first system that was effectively taught by Morgan coach Nat Frazier.

The 1974 Morgan men's squad lost to Maryland-Eastern Shore in the last MEAC game of the season, but was still selected to play in the NCAA tournament. Webster dominated on both ends of the floor, winning the tournament's Most Outstanding Player Award while leading Morgan to the championship.[72] "We were always the smartest team on the floor—that's something that Nat Frazier preached to us," McIver explains. "Having Marvin Webster was a special treat. By that junior year he wouldn't just block shots—he would catch them in mid-air. I had never seen anybody do that before."[73]

There would be no chance to repeat as champions the next season. Webster was infected with hepatitis, and gained weight. His physical condition contributed to his decreased productivity. Still, Morgan finished the season with a respectable 20-8 record, and reached the NCAA tournament for the second straight year. But Morgan's chance to repeat as champion ended with a 64–60 loss to Randolph-Macon in the first round.[74]

The 1970s were the most successful decade for the Morgan men's basketball, as the team recorded a winning record each year. But in 1980 when the teams in the MEAC decided to make the move to Division I, Morgan State stayed in Division II. Departing a league in which Morgan played against familiar competition, the team suffered. The Bears decided to rejoin the MEAC in 1984, but, by that time, the team was in the midst of five straight losing seasons.[75]

Coaches came and went. Frazier, who left Morgan the year after Webster's departure, came back in 1984 to try to revitalize the program. None of his teams had a winning record. At the turn of the century, Morgan hired former NBA player Butch Beard, who had spent a year as a head coach in the NBA in the 1990s and was the MEAC coach of the year in 1992 at Howard, leading the Bison to the MEAC tournament title and the NCAA basketball tournament.[76]

In Beard's first season at Morgan, 2001–2002, the Bears finished 3-25. Under Beard, the team had five straight losing seasons and reached double-digit wins just twice. In his last season, 2005–2006, Morgan State was 4-25.[77] In other words, the men's basketball program, which had not had a winning season since 1989, was in ruins. It would take a coach whose professional life was also in ruins to pull the Bears out of their tailspin.

When Morgan State announced in 2006 that Todd Bozeman was going to be the new men's basketball coach, some eyebrows were raised. In the mid-1990s, Bozeman had been the head coach at the University of California, Berkeley, where he had a point guard named Jason Kidd. In 1993, Cal beat defending national champion Duke in the second round of the NCAA tournament in one of the most shocking upsets the year. With the win, Bozeman, who was just twenty-nine, became the youngest coach to reach the Sweet 16.[78]

Unfortunately, Bozeman's career was sidetracked by a scandal in which he had admitted to paying the parents of one of his players, Jelani Gardner. When Gardner's playing time decreased, his father (who happened to be a Morgan alum) reported the payments to the NCAA.[79] As a result of this malfeasance, the NCAA banned Bozeman for eight years. When the sanctions against Bozeman were lifted in 2005, Morgan was one of the first schools to give him a call. He was hired in 2006.

The results under Bozeman were immediate. The 2006–2007 team won thirteen games, a nine-game improvement from the previous season. The Bears continued to improve in 2007–2008, recording their first winning season since 1989 with a 22-11 record.[80]

As the 2008 MEAC regular-season champions, Morgan earned the top seed in the conference tournament and reached the title game. But the Bears lost at the buzzer in the championship game to cross-town rival Coppin State. The MEAC regular-season championship guaranteed Morgan a spot in the National Invitational Tournament, giving the Bears their first post-season appearance at the Division I level.

Many Morgan players attributed the team's transformation to Bozeman. "He's a great coach and I really liked his style and his patience," said Boubacar Coly, a center on that 2008 team. "He gave you everything he knew and he always put you in a position to succeed."[81]

The success continued. The 2008–2009 team recorded what was, at the time, the biggest win in the school's Division I history, a stunning 66–65 victory over the University of Maryland.[82] The team dominated the regular season and entered the MEAC tournament looking to redeem itself after the previous year's disappointment.

In 2009, the Bears won the conference tournament by an average of seventeen points a game. And on March 14, 2009, the Bears, with their 83–69 win over Norfolk State at the Lawrence Joel Veterans Memorial Coliseum in Winston-Salem, North Carolina, clinched a spot in the NCAA Division I basketball tournament for the first time in school history.[83]

Why did Bozeman succeed where others had failed? He had coached several players who later played in the NBA, so that earned him instant credibility with his players. He convinced several talented players to transfer from established programs, including center Boubacar Coly (Xavier) and Marquise Kately (Cal), and his players matched the level of intensity that he brought to every game and practice.

In four seasons, from 2007–2008 to 2010–2011, the Bears played in consecutive conference tournament championship games, won three straight MEAC regular-season titles, and two tournament titles, which earned the team trips to the 2009 and 2010 NCAA tournaments.[84]

The Ten Bears

During the 1970s, Morgan State had successful programs in football, men's basketball, and, of all sports, lacrosse. Lacrosse? Yes, the sport that was originally a Native American activity, which had come to be perceived as a white, elite sport on the high school and college level emerged as an interesting story in Morgan State's athletic history.

It began in 1970, when athletic director Earl Banks approached Chip Silverman, a Baltimore native and an assistant dean at Morgan State, about starting a lacrosse team. "He said, 'you being white, you must have played lacrosse recently,'" Silverman told *Baltimore Sun* columnist Mike Preston during a 2008 interview conducted weeks before Silverman died of cancer. "I said, 'Earl, that's a racist statement.' He said, 'You are white, aren't you?' And then he asked me if I played lacrosse."[85] When Silverman answered yes, Banks asked him to start a lacrosse team. So Silverman placed flyers around campus and asked students at a historically black institution to play a sport dominated by white kids, many with private school backgrounds.

Of the initial students who tried out for the team, a few had played lacrosse in high school. There were also many who just wanted an opportunity to do something athletic to keep their competitive juices flowing. That is, guys like Stan Cherry, a future NFL player who was a star linebacker on the Morgan football team.

In 1971, thanks to a lot of hard work and dedication, the first Morgan varsity team had a winning record, winning ten out of fourteen games.[86] Having players on the Morgan team with prior lacrosse experience was helpful. The combination of the experienced lacrosse players with the men who had tremendous athletic ability but limited lacrosse skills allowed Morgan to be competitive immediately. "When we took the field, we knew we were the better athletes," says Curt Anderson, who attended Rutgers on a football scholarship before transferring to Morgan. "And [Silverman] stressed to us that this was a contact sport. What helped us compete was the fact that a lot of the guys we played against weren't used to getting hit when they got the ball. And we hit them."[87]

The team played with borrowed sticks and wore old football uniforms. Unfortunately, few fans attended home games. "If I had family in the stands, I would have no problem finding them," Anderson remembers.[88]

On the road, the Morgan team was a novelty. People wanted to see the all-black lacrosse team and, at times, the Bears played in stadiums that had more than 10,000 fans. Remember, the lacrosse team emerged during an era that was racially charged. Blacks marched and demanded equality, and some whites were content to remain in a segregated society. Racial tensions were high at many of the stadiums that Morgan visited.

"They would make comments, you know, like 'Nigger, you don't know how to play this game,'" said Wayne Jackson, who played from 1971 to 1973. "And I would score another goal and say 'well, that's how a nigger scores.'"[89] "We were called racial names, and the first time it happened we didn't respond well," Curt Anderson says. Silverman "explained that it was going to happen and that, in order for us to get games, we were going to have to show that we were above it all. And so we sucked it up. We took the verbal abuse. We just made people pay on the field."[90]

The "Ten Bears," as they were called, accomplished a lot in the ten years that they played. Between 1970 and 1975, the team reached two NCAA tournaments. In 1975, the Bears went on the road and beat a national powerhouse, Washington & Lee University, in Lexington, Virginia. That win was extra special because the historically white Washington & Lee had won twenty-eight straight regular-season games.[91]

Although Silverman left the program after the 1975 season, the Bears continued to play for another five years. But budget issues forced the school to make some difficult decisions in 1980, one of which was to cut the lacrosse team. And thus came the end of an era when the Morgan State lacrosse team had captured the lacrosse world's attention.

"Respect is earned, and we had the good fortune to earn respect," says former Bear Miles Harrison Jr., the first lacrosse player inducted into the Morgan Athletic Hall of Fame. "The satisfaction of watching a team's swagger turn to concern and sometimes fear because of our ability, we considered measures of respect."[92]

Years later, Harrison and Chip Silverman wrote the book *Ten Bears* (2001), which chronicles the team's brief and interesting history. Since the book's release, there have been two documentaries about the team. One of them, *The Morgan Lacrosse Story*, which is narrated by actor Wendell Pierce, aired on PBS on April 4, 2008—less than a month after Silverman died.[93]

Silverman, who was inducted into the Morgan Athletic Hall of Fame in 1991, had a tremendous impact on the lacrosse world. There is even talk of a feature film being made about that incredible decade. Some members of that team are amazed by the story's endurance. "At the time, none of use realized what we were doing was special," Anderson said. "We just wanted to play."[94] At the same time, some former players are disappointed that what they began was discontinued. "They should have kept lacrosse going there," Tony Fulton said in 1990. "We were making history."[95]

"Return to Greatness"

On July 28, 2014, after many years of intercollegiate athletic mediocrity, Morgan State announced its intent "to return to athletic greatness."[96] The announcement came on the heels of a "Return to Greatness" steering committee commissioned by school president David Wilson in 2013.

The group proclaimed its commitment to "help Morgan reclaim its winning legacy." According to President Wilson, "From the 1930s through the early 1970s, the gridiron achievements of Morgan Bears teams coached by Edward P. Hurt and, later, Earl C. Banks were a source of pride for all black Baltimoreans, not only Morganites."[97] Morgan administrators, alums, and boosters hope that athletic success will have positive "repercussions throughout the campus."[98]

At a HBCU in the twenty-first century, even one that can boast a great athletic past like Morgan, is that possible? Is it reasonable to think that pouring resources into intercollegiate athletics is prudent?

When Morgan was producing All-American football players and sending some to the NFL, many of the most-talented African American athletes went to HBCUs because of systematic segregation. In other words, some of the most-talented players in the nation attended Morgan because their options were limited.

That is no longer the case. The best contemporary African American high school athletes can now go to any university. Many of them go to programs that offer the chance to play in big, packed stadiums and on national television.

In this era of college football and men's basketball, money is a huge factor in terms of success. Morgan spent nearly $10 million on athletics during the 2012–2013 season, which ranked 207 out of 230 Division I schools. By comparison, the total expenses at the University of Texas were $146 million—which is more than the entire MEAC conference combined.[99]

In its July 2014 press release, Morgan announced its plans to help its student-athletes:

> The establishment of a training table for scholar-athletes for nutritional guidance during dinner meals; the assignment of customized space for the football team to hold meetings; the renovation of men's and women's basketball locker rooms and the football coaches' offices; and the establishment of programs to connect MSU athletic legends with current Morgan athletes, to help the younger players know the legacy of MSU football.

These proposed changes are positive and will surely be expensive if they are implemented.

But for Morgan State to reach its goal to return to greatness in football, it might have to follow the formula put in place by the men's basketball team. The men's basketball team returned to its winning ways by hiring an established coach, Todd Bozeman, who had a history of making the March Madness tournament and sending players to the NBA. It seems as though the football team has already shifted in this direction by hiring Lee Hull, who has a history of sending players to the pros. In 2014, Hull was named MEAC Coach of the Year.

Perhaps Morgan State can reclaim "its winning legacy," but it will be difficult and expensive to make Morgan athletics the "envy and admiration" of "African-American communities elsewhere."[100]

9

The Team That Made Baltimore Proud

The Baltimore Bullets and the
1947–1948 Championship Season

CHRIS ELZEY

Robert Embry had an idea. As president and co-owner of the Baltimore Bullets, a professional team that played in the American Basketball League (ABL), Embry, a congenial man who went by the nickname "Jake," wanted more exposure for his team—and he knew just how to get it.

It was January 1947, and the Bullets were dominating the ABL and attracting big crowds. For most games, the 3,500-seat Baltimore Coliseum was packed. The only problem was that the ABL was a second-rate league, and Embry, ever the go-getter, had grander aspirations for his club. His ambition was justified. Already that season the Bullets had beaten several teams from the more prominent National Basketball League (NBL), including the Chicago American Gears, which featured star center, George Mikan.

More than any other opponent the Bullets had faced, there was one team Embry would have traded a frontline of first-round draft picks to play. The Washington (DC) Capitols were a talented club that competed in the Basketball Association of America (BAA), a league that, despite having been established just seven months earlier, was recognized as being the premier basketball competition in the country. The Capitols, like the Bullets, were running roughshod over opponents. Soon Baltimoreans were clamoring for a game between their club and the Capitols.

On January 14, Jesse A. Linthicum, sports editor for the *Baltimore Sun*, reported: "Jake Embry, general manager of the Bullets, declares that he not only is willing to play a series with the Washington Capitols, but a move actually has been made toward bringing the teams together." Linthicum was being overly optimistic. The Capitols had no interest in playing the Bullets. What benefit could be gained by beating an inferior team from an inferior league? Besides, BAA regulations banned exhibitions against non-league opponents. As far as the Capitols were concerned, a series against the Bullets was out of the question.[1]

Embry surely knew about the league rule. Yet he refused to let the proposed series die. On January 30, Bob McClean of the *Washington Times-Herald* quoted Embry as saying, the District squad was "avoiding the one team in the country that could give them a real licking." Laying down the proverbial gauntlet, Embry added that the Bullets were prepared to play "anytime and anywhere," and that it was the Capitols, not the Bullets, who were running scared. "They won't play us," Embry bragged, "because we've got the kind of style to lick them. They play a slow, loose game, rely on shot-making rather than team play, and they get awfully tired. We are a fast, close-working club that would run all over them."[2]

Embry may have garnered publicity for his team, but he was not as effective initiating the series. Washington simply could not—and would not—play the Bullets. The rebuff was not easily forgotten. When the Bullets joined the BAA the following season, the animosity generated by the never-realized series—Baltimoreans believed they had been snubbed, Washingtonians did not appreciate Embry's bluster—was on display each time the teams met. The clashes fueled the rivalry between the two cities. And although the Capitols won the majority of games, it would be the Bullets who had the last laugh.

Before the Bullets, professional basketball in Baltimore was a futile venture. The city's first professional club, the Baltimore Orioles of the original ABL, is a good example. Competing in 1926–1927—their only season—the Orioles were a pitiful 6-36. Twelve years later, in 1939–1940, the Baltimore Clippers entered the revamped ABL. Though the Clippers were more successful than the Orioles, by the start of the 1941–1942 season they too had vanished. The Baltimore Mets, an all-black squad barred from playing in the lily-white ABL, were skilled, but not as talented as other independent African American teams, such as the Harlem Globetrotters, the New York Rens, and the Washington (DC) Bears.[3]

In 1944, two Baltimore businessmen, Stanley Behrend and Morton "Babe" Askin, established the Bullets. It was a gutsy move. The failures of previous teams must have weighed heavily on their minds, not to mention that the country was still fighting World War II. With its factories churning out war materiel around the clock, Baltimore itself was an arsenal of democracy. In nearby Middle River, for example, the massive Glenn L. Martin Company was producing hundreds of airplanes, while the shipyard of Bethlehem Steel at Sparrow's Point was constructing, on average, a ship almost every other day. Baltimore's factories also manufactured munitions (hence, the name "Bullets," a moniker that also honored the Shot Tower, a soaring smokestack-like edifice on Fayette Street that at one time had fabricated shot and cannonballs). The need for laborers not only attracted people to the city, it also put more money in Baltimoreans' pockets. Behrend and Askin were hoping residents would spend some of their extra income attending Bullets games.[4]

They guessed right. The Bullets flourished. On most nights, the Baltimore Coliseum, a drafty, dimly lit shell of a building that doubled as a roller skating rink, was filled. The club's drawing power surprised some. "There is no doubt about the fans being interested in pro basketball" in Baltimore, Jesse Linthicum of the *Sun* wrote in December, "attendance and general interest being greater than this column expected." The Bullets finished the regular season a mediocre 14-16—including three wins over the Washington Capitols of the ABL before the Capitols moved to New Jersey—and advanced to the finals. But the Philadelphia SPHAS, coached by the indefatigable Eddie Gottlieb, aka "The Mogul," defeated Baltimore, 2 games to 1. Still, everyone had to admit that the Bullets' first season had been a success.[5]

Behrend, however, wanted out. His sights were set on a different commercial enterprise, and he felt, as club president, he could not oversee it and a sports franchise. Askin, it seems, was unwilling to go it alone. So in July 1945, three months after the Bullets advanced to the finals, the franchise was sold to Jake Embry and Thomas Tinsley Jr., a Baltimore scion and founder of WITH radio, a popular station in the city. Embry and Tinsley paid $7,500. The pair eventually called their partnership All Sports, Inc.[6]

Embry and Tinsley's working relationship had begun in 1943, when Embry, then a successful salesman for WBAL radio in Baltimore, took his silver-tongued talents over to WITH. The 1940s were the heyday of radio, and for an overachiever like Embry, the medium offered him a chance for advancement. A native Mississippian, Embry had been introduced to the business of radio during a sojourn to New York in 1935. Within months, he had scrapped plans of going back to the Deep South and accepted a sales position at WBAL. Good natured and possessed of a warm smile, he quickly built up the station's revenues. In 1943, Tinsley was counting on Embry to do the same at WITH.[7]

He did. Money poured in. Suddenly WITH, which began broadcasting in 1941, was ranked among the most-admired stations in Baltimore. But much of WITH's airtime was devoted to playing music. As an independent station, WITH was not required to follow a network mandate, which kept copyrighted music off affiliates' airwaves—and Embry wanted more variety. Sports seemed like a good choice. And so, not long after arriving at WITH, Embry secured the rights to air Baltimore Orioles games; at the time, the Orioles were the city's popular minor league team. For years, WITH's rival, WCBM, had carried the Orioles. The switch meant that advertising dollars from Orioles broadcasts now went to WITH instead. Bill Dyer, a celebrated sportscaster, was brought over from WCBM as announcer. In addition to his baseball duties, Dyer was a deejay and hosted his own sports show, the "Sports Special," which aired from 4 to 6 p.m. The multitalented Dyer was later named the Bullets' GM.[8]

WITH would go on to carry Bullets games—which might have been why Embry and Tinsley acquired the club in the first place. After all, WITH was looking to diversify its programming, and Embry and Tinsley may have figured that the popular Bullets would help broaden the station's listener- ship (Dyer also announced Bullets games). In 1945–1946, fans had good reason to tune in. Baltimore finished the regular season atop the ABL and claimed the league's title. Attendance was good, even though the Bullets had switched venues and played at the 104th Medical Regiment Armory, aka Baltimore Garden. The pre–Civil War building sat 500 fewer people than did the Coliseum.[9]

Fortunately for Embry and Tinsley, things had fallen into place. The Bullets were champions and the city had supported the team. Still, Embry wanted more. He soon got it. In September 1946, the Bullets acquired Harry Edward Jeannette, a wily 5'11" backcourt star. A graduate of Washington and Jefferson College in Pennsylvania, the twenty-nine-year-old Jeannette— nicknamed "Buddy"—had spent years in the NBL perfecting his game. There, he won multiple championships and was twice named MVP. Accord- ing to Seymour Smith, a former sportswriter for the *Baltimore Sun*, Embry had seen Jeannette play in the prestigious World Professional Basket- ball Tournament in Chicago earlier that spring and was so impressed by Jeannette's skill and poise—Jeannette's club, the Fort Wayne Zollner Pistons, won the title—that he offered him $15,000 to come to Baltimore in 1946–1947 and be player-coach. By comparison, George Mikan—the Wilt Chamberlain of his day—was making $12,000.[10]

That season Jeannette and his teammates took on all comers. Not only did they face the usual ABL competition—which they manhandled—they played several teams from other leagues, as well as clubs with no league affiliation, such as the Harlem Globetrotters and New York Rens. For the

Hall of Fame guard Harry "Buddy" Jeannette during his days as a Baltimore Bullet. *Courtesy of Harvey C. Kasoff.*

Bullets, no matchup was too daunting, no road game too far away. They played in Chicago and upstate New York, in Oregon and Washington State. Home games, meanwhile, were moved back to the Coliseum. The Bullets finished the season a stellar 62-10, including 31-3 in league play. They were odds-on favorites to win the title.[11]

They never got the chance. By April 9, three weeks after Baltimore reached the finals, an opponent had still not been determined. Furious, Embry cut short the Bullets' season and declared that his team was champion, the remaining semifinalists—Philadelphia and Trenton—having forfeited their right to compete. (On April 12, Trenton beat Philadelphia in the third and decisive game of the series; several days later, Trenton was awarded the league title.) The postseason debacle convinced Embry that the Bullets needed to make a change. Luckily, the BAA—the nascent league in which the Capitols played—had an opening.[12]

By all accounts, the BAA had had a rough first season. Gate receipts were less than had been expected, and four of the eleven original franchises ended up disbanding. Still, the league had a lot going for it. Unlike the NBL—which had several teams in smaller cities, such as Anderson, Indiana, and Oshkosh, Wisconsin—the BAA operated exclusively in large metropolises. And whereas the NBL was largely confined to the Midwest, the BAA spanned from St. Louis to Boston, from Chicago to the nation's capital. BAA owners, moreover, had a uniquely vested interest in the league. Not only did they own the franchises, they owned the arenas in which teams played. In the unsettled world of professional basketball, most everyone believed that the BAA represented the future. In June, an elated Embry declared that the Bullets were switching leagues.[13]

The Bullets spent the next few months overhauling their roster. A valuable addition was Paul Hoffman, a brawny 6'2" rookie forward from Purdue. Affectionately dubbed "the Bear," Hoffman, who weighed 205 pounds, had earned all-conference honors in each of his four years in college. His rugged style would spawn several melees with BAA foes. Another important acquisition was Joseph "Chick" Reiser, a 5'11" set-shot specialist who had played with Jeannette in Fort Wayne. The pair comprised a formidable backcourt. Also joining the Bullets were Dick Schulz, a veteran forward with good all-round skills, and Carl Meinhold, a 6'3" rookie from Long Island University. Returning members included Mike Bloom, a high-scoring forward who had been with the Bullets since 1946, and Clarence "Kleggie" Hermsen, a husky 6'8" center who had previously played in the BAA with Cleveland and Toronto. Jeannette would again serve as player-coach.

Baltimoreans eagerly awaited the start of the BAA season. Not since the ABL Orioles embarrassed themselves in 1926–1927 had a Baltimore franchise competed in a major professional basketball league. In other sports it was worse. The last time the city had been represented in baseball's big leagues was 1902, when the Orioles finished dead last in the American League. Baltimore would not acquire a National Football League team until 1950 (the Colts arrived in 1953, after the Dallas Texans were moved). As for a National Hockey League franchise, the city has never had one.

The dearth of big-time sports reinforced Baltimore's negative image and sense of itself—much of which derived from being compared to other East Coast metropolises. Baltimore lacked the gravitas of Washington, DC, and it could not match New York's glitz. Even Philadelphia—a rough-hewn, largely working-class city—was held in higher esteem. In late 1943 and early 1944, a poem ridiculing the city was reprinted in *Newsweek* and *Life*. Titled "Beloved Baltimore, Maryland," it began: "Baltimore, oh Baltimore, you moth-eaten town, / Your brick row houses should all be torn down." (Originally published in the *Baltimore Evening Sun*, the poem elicited a flood of irate letters from Baltimoreans.) Sportswriter Frank Deford, born in 1938, remembered the Baltimore of his youth being "a tentative, defensive place, only a stream or two short of a backwater." In 1947, Baltimoreans craved something they could take pride in.[14]

It did not happen that fall with the original Baltimore Colts, a professional club in the All-America Football Conference (AAFC), a league barely two years old. A founding member of the AAFC, the Colts had originated in Miami, where the franchise was called the Seahawks. But a lousy first season—both in the win-loss column and at the turnstile—compelled a move to Baltimore in late 1946. Apparently, Embry became intrigued with the franchise, and several weeks after the league cleared the transfer, he bought a stake in the team (he would soon become president of the club). The Bullets president probably wished he had held onto his money. The 1947 Colts were terrible. They finished 2-11-1, just ahead of the AAFC's worst team, the 1-13 Chicago Rockets.[15]

The Bullets were placed in the BAA's Western Division, alongside St. Louis, Chicago, and Washington. The Eastern Division consisted of Boston, New York, Philadelphia, and Providence. Divisional opponents played each other eight times. In interdivisional competition, teams faced each other six times. Travel would be difficult. Most players, though, were used to it. Trains and buses would be the main mode of transit, while airplanes would be used for longer trips. Like other top professional leagues, the BAA was entering the modern age.

Still, professional basketball in the 1940s was hardly the slick production it is today. Arenas were dingy. Fans were abusive. Crowds were oftentimes sparse. The playing surface could be treacherous. In several BAA venues, water was known to pool on courts. Temporary wooden floors were placed directly atop ice rinks, and water sloshed up between the boards. Making things worse, fog would sometimes form as the ice underneath melted. So frigid was the arena in Providence that players on the bench donned hats and wore towels as shawls. Minutes after one game in Uline Arena in Washington, DC, the scoreboard hanging over center court became detached and crashed to the ground. No one was hurt, but the mishap took a chunk out of the floor.[16]

People attending games never quite knew what to expect. Before one game in Boston, a backboard broke. It took officials two hours to find another. Players, meanwhile, entertained fans with Harlem Globetrotter-esque dribbling and passing, and engaged in some spirited 3-on-3. The winners received $100, financed by that night's gate. A game at Uline Arena was temporarily halted because a cat and her litter, which had taken up residence inside the arena, wandered onto the floor. When the Capitols played the Bullets at Baltimore's Fifth Regiment Armory in January 1948, a dog interrupted the contest. Paul Hoffman remembered Bullets games in Baltimore Coliseum being rife with bookies hollering and scampering about. No doubt some outcomes of games were affected. A contest between Baltimore and Philadelphia in 1946 saw several brawls erupt in the bleachers and then move onto the court.[17]

Like other BAA teams, the Bullets readied themselves by playing a series of preseason games. Their performance was impressive. On October 21, they beat the Philadelphia Warriors, the defending BAA champions. Nine days later, on Thursday, October 30, the Indianapolis Kautskys, a strong NBL club and victors of that spring's World Professional Basketball Tournament, fell to the BAA's newest entrant. A sign that a new era in sports was dawning: the game against Indianapolis was aired on channel 2, WMAR, Baltimore's first-ever television station. WMAR had begun broadcasting that day, making the Bullets-Kautskys game, which was shown from 9:15 to 10:45 p.m., one of the first telecasts in Baltimore history (the first was two Pimlico races, both of which aired earlier that afternoon). WMAR televised home games throughout the season (Bailey Goss, a much-admired local sports announcer, provided play-by-play). WITH radio likewise carried games.[18]

The Bullets debuted on the road against the Washington Capitols. Most commentators expected a heated battle. The previous year, Washington had shown itself to be the cream of the BAA, compiling a 49-11 record, the league's best. But the Capitols, who were coached by Arnold "Red" Auerbach, future Boston Celtics mentor and Hall of Fame inductee, had lost in the opening round of the playoffs. Auerbach and his men were hoping to redeem themselves in 1947–1948, which was a strong possibility.

Washington had skilled players. Bob Feerick, a 6'3" swingman, for example, possessed a deft shooting touch. In 1946–1947, he averaged 16.3 points per contest—the second most in the league—and made first team all-BAA, as did his teammate, Horace "Bones" McKinney, a beanpole-slim forward known as much for his basketball prowess as for his clownish antics. Another player, Fred Scolari, a chubby 5'10" guard, was voted second team all-BAA. Center John Mahnken provided defense inside. Six-foot three-inch John Norlander, who was released by the Bullets in 1946, contributed offense up front.[19]

The first Baltimore-Washington game was billed as if the Hatfields were to play the McCoys. Much of the bitterness derived from the failed exhibition series earlier that January. Frank Cashen of the *Baltimore News-Post* previewed the matchup using language that could have been printed in *Stars and Stripes*. "Having had things pretty much their own way . . . last year," Cashen wrote, "the Washington Capitols must fight off the invasion of a newcomer . . . tonight at the Uline Arena in Washington." A day earlier, the *Washington Daily News* ran a picture of Baltimore forward Mike Bloom. "Invading Cager," the caption read.[20]

The rancor carried over into the game. From the start, players scrapped. *Washington Post* sportswriter Morris Siegel wrote that "the game was as hard fought as any played here in years." The Bullets controlled the first quarter; the Capitols the second. By halftime, the score was 31–31. In the third period, Baltimore recaptured the lead, but then faltered, and the Caps went on to win, 63–55. Scolari notched a team-high 17 points. Hermsen scored 18. Three thousand five hundred people attended the game. Newspapers did not say how many were Baltimoreans.[21]

Jeannette and his teammates had little time to stew over the loss. The next night they played Boston. Spearheaded by Reiser, who pumped in 19 points, the Bullets prevailed, 85–74. Embry's team followed that up with wins over Chicago and New York, then Boston and Chicago. After Baltimore dismantled Providence, the victory skein totaled six.

It did not stop there. Next the Bullets upended St. Louis, Boston, and Philadelphia, bringing their undefeated streak to nine. Baltimoreans beamed. Frank Cashen of the *News-Post* called the Bullets "the most talked of basketball team in the nation." At 9–1, Embry's team was riding high. Washington, meanwhile, was 4-7, last in the Western Division.[22]

On December 4, the Bullets met St. Louis in Baltimore. It was the Bullets' fifth game in eight days. Jeannette and his men were tired. Their muscles ached. Against St. Louis, it showed. The Bombers dashed out to an early advantage and hung on to win, 65–51. Two nights later, in Chicago, the Bullets lost again.[23]

Next were the Capitols. The game was played in Baltimore, and many Washingtonians made the drive up. Bullets fans flocked to the Coliseum, as a sellout crowd squeezed into the Monroe Street arena. Earlier that day the *Baltimore News-Post* headlined: "Bullets Seek Revenge in Game with Caps." Baltimoreans hoped the headline would be fulfilled.[24]

If Jeannette and his squad wanted to win badly, it was hard to tell. Sluggish, they began poorly. The Capitols, by contrast, came out strong, and by the end of the third quarter, were ahead, 52–40. But Baltimore battled back, eventually sending the game into overtime. In the extra period, though, the Caps were too tough, and the Bullets lost, 71–69. Capturing the testy rivalry between the two clubs—a day earlier the *Washington Evening Star* had termed it an "Intercity Feud"—a picture in the *Baltimore Sun* showed Washington's John Norlander sandwiched between two Baltimore players, arms entwined, wrestling over the ball. "TUG O'WAR," the caption stated.[25]

Two days later, against the Knicks, Baltimore was dealt another loss. Mired in a four-game losing streak, the Bullets desperately needed a win. Unfortunately, the next game was against their arch-nemesis: the dreaded Caps. In front of 2,300 spectators at Uline Arena, Jeannette and his teammates kept the contest close, but Washington prevailed yet again, 66–64. The Bullets, once the toast of professional basketball, were now fighting for their BAA lives.

They would recover. Over the next six weeks, Baltimore played .500 ball. One of the highlights was a victory over New York in front of 16,148 people at Madison Square Garden. Then, on Friday, January 30, they met the Capitols at the capacious Fifth Regiment Armory in Baltimore. In 1912, Democrats had held their national convention inside the imposing stone building. That Friday the great hall reverberated with as much partisanship as it did in 1912. Roughly 6,200 people passed through the turnstiles, and nearly all supported the Bullets. The *Baltimore Evening Sun* later noted that it was the "largest crowd ever to see a basketball game in Baltimore." Originally scheduled for January 29, the contest was moved back a day so it could be included in an athletic program benefiting the March of Dimes Polio Fund.[26]

Spurred on by the rabid crowd, the Bullets began quickly, and by the end of the first quarter, boasted a 25–14 advantage. Washington tried to narrow the margin, but the hosts held firm, and won easily, 95–71. Spectators cheered. The Bullets had finally beaten the Capitols. The game had been physical. Fifty-seven fouls were whistled, and more evidently could have been flagged. According to the *Washington Daily News*, officials had "missed many flagrant violations. Players were flattened on no less than 27 occasions." Still, it was a joyous moment for Bullets supporters.[27]

While Baltimoreans celebrated, Washingtonians complained, suggesting that Embry's team would have never won had it played less physically. Four days after the victory, a reporter for a DC paper wrote: "The Bullets respond to their grandstand clamor with a brand of basketball that includes elements of wrestling, football and water polo. . . . The Bullets evidently have decided the only way to beat the Caps is by outroughing them." The next day, *Washington Daily News* sports editor Ev Gardner observed: "Doubtless [the Bullets] figure their rough style of play, which is reminiscent of the Chicago Bears gridiron bullying, is the prescription necessary to offset the Caps' greater skill."[28]

Such views reflected stark differences between the two cities. Washington was a government city, colonnaded, bureaucratic, bustling with white-collar employees. Baltimore was grittier, rougher. Factories abounded. The city's labor force was predominantly blue collar. According to the 1950 census, 157,592 Baltimoreans worked in manufacturing, compared to 45,277 Washingtonians. In public administration, it was the reverse. Not surprisingly, salaries in the two cities differed greatly. In 1950, the median family income in the nation's capital was $4,262. In Charm City, it was $3,355. If Washington represented power, Baltimore stood for routine. The contrast was visible. Writer Russell Baker, a Baltimore resident in the 1940s, recalled in his memoir, *Growing Up* (1982): "In glamorous Washington, sophisticated men were so much more commonplace than in Baltimore."[29]

Five nights after the Bullets' victory over the Caps, the two clubs were at it again, dueling with gladiatorial gusto. The *Washington Post* noted: "Tempers, at a fever pitch all during the first half, broke anew shortly after intermission and Johnny Norlander, Fred Scolari and Baltimore's Mike Bloom became involved in a fight which threatened to start a full-scale riot on the court." Ev Gardner of the *Daily News* termed the game "a slam-bang, see-saw battle." In the end, the Caps squeaked by, 77–72.[30]

The next time Baltimore and Washington played, on February 21, it was equally brutal. Elbows were thrown. Players collided. In the third quarter, Washington guard Fred Scolari "was slammed to the floor and knocked cold for a few seconds," a reporter wrote. Try as they might, the Bullets could not keep up with the hot-handed Capitols, and succumbed, 85–72. With ten games to go, Baltimore trailed division leader Washington by 2½ games. The situation looked bleak.[31]

It did not stay that way for long. Beneficiaries of a favorable schedule, the Bullets closed out the season with seven victories, including a 97–70 thrashing of the Capitols. Meanwhile, Washington lost six consecutive games. Only a string of five wins at the end—in the penultimate game, the Capitols downed the Bullets in front of a sellout crowd in Baltimore and Paul "the Bear" Hoffman got into several scuffles with different Washington players—saved the Caps from embarrassment. At 29-19, St. Louis claimed the division title. But Baltimore, Washington, and the Chicago Stags all finished with the identical record of 28-20. To determine second and third place in the west, league officials opted to hold a mini playoff, after which three teams from each division would play for the title.[32]

In the divisional draw, the Bullets got lucky. To claim second place, they only had to win one game—and that is what happened. After Chicago defeated Washington in the Windy City, Baltimore beat the Stags in Chicago. (Had the Bullets lost, they would have played Washington for the third play-off spot.) Having thus received what amounted to a first-round bye, Embry's team was awarded second place, and Chicago third. Washingtonians cried foul. Nothing, however, could be done. The Caps' season was over.[33]

The Bullets' first playoff opponent was New York, runners-up in the Eastern Division. The Knicks were a good team, but they had struggled against Baltimore during the season. In six games, they had beaten the Bullets only once. The Knicks' coach, Joe Lapchick, former Original Celtics great, was hoping the postseason would be different. It was not. Led by Connie Simmons, a spindly, 6'8" center whom Embry had obtained from Boston seven weeks earlier, the Bullets beat New York in game 1. After losing the following night, Baltimore closed out the series four days later, knocking off the Knicks, 84–77. In the semifinals, Jeannette and his teammates overwhelmed Chicago, and took the series, two games to none. Incredibly, the Bullets, in only their first BAA season, were going to the finals.[34]

The championship series would be the toughest test yet. Facing Baltimore were the Philadelphia Warriors, defending BAA titleholders. Coached by Eddie "the Mogul" Gottlieb, the Warriors bristled with talent. Howie Dallmar, a 6'4" forward, had recently been voted first-team all-BAA, and George "Doc" Senesky, a crafty point guard from St. Joseph's University, gave opponents fits. Chuck Halbert, a brawny 6'9" post player, was a capable scorer. But the heart of the squad was Joseph "Jumpin' Joe" Fulks, an agile 6'5" forward who had fought in the Pacific during World War II. A basketball trendsetter, the twenty-six-year-old Fulks injected athleticism into the professional game. In an era largely defined by set shots and ball-control offenses, Jumpin' Joe electrified crowds with his acrobatic one-handed shots and scoring barrages. In 1946–1947, and again in 1947–1948, he led the BAA in points per game. He was a defender's nightmare.[35]

Game 1 was played on Saturday, April 10, in the Philadelphia Arena. A crowd of 7,201 watched the Warriors build an early lead and then pull away in the second quarter. Embry's men tried to close the margin in the second half, but with Senesky blanketing Reiser on defense—the normally accurate Reiser finished 0-14 from the field—the effort was in vain. Much to the enjoyment of the hometown audience, Gottlieb's club waltzed past Baltimore, 71–60. Halbert netted 19 points, and Fulks 17. Simmons led the visitors with 15. No other Bullet reached double figures.[36]

It could have been easy for the Bullets to give up. After all, by reaching the finals, they had already surpassed expectations. But if there was one thing Jeannette and his crew had demonstrated all season long, it was that they were not quitters. And they would not quit now. Things did appear hopeless, however, after Philadelphia built a 21-point advantage in the first half of game 2. But a rousing halftime speech by Jeannette—Seymour Smith said that Bullets' player-coach "jumped on" top of a "table and . . . broke" it and Paul Hoffman recalled that "Jeannette tore the dressing room door off the hinges"—helped stave off disaster. Emerging from the locker room reenergized, the Bullets routed the hosts in the second half, and survived, 66–63. Most of the 6,982 spectators left the Philadelphia Arena stunned.[37]

The same was not true in Baltimore. Fans there, watching the game on WMAR-TV, or listening to it on WITH, rejoiced. So, too, did local newspapermen. On April 15, the day game 3 was to be played, C. M. Gibbs, columnist for the *Baltimore Sun*, wrote: "A deep bow is made to our basketball Bullets. In this sterling outfit we have major-league stuff at its very best." Gibbs continued: "Their recovery after a drab start . . . packed enough thrills to start a plague of high-blood pressure among their followers." Then the columnist hazarded a prediction. "If [the Bullets] were to play in the Fifth Regiment Armory tonight, it would be packed. . . . Bullet officials had better make sure the Coliseum roof is nailed down tight."[38]

Gibbs was right. More than 4,000 people filled the Baltimore Coliseum. What they saw was the most exciting game of the series. Both teams started slowly, but the action intensified. In the second half, Baltimore surged ahead, but Philadelphia, behind Fulks's torrid shooting, stormed right back. Eight minutes into the fourth quarter, the Warriors led, 63–55. Fans hooted and screamed. Now it was the Bullets' turn to rally, and they did, drawing even with less than two minutes remaining. A flurry of foul shots followed, upping the score, 70 all. The clock showed 22 seconds. The Bullets had the ball.[39]

Jeannette later called what followed next, "One of the elementary plays in basketball." After Baltimore advanced the ball past midcourt, Reiser passed to Hermsen, who, in turn, threw to a cutting Jeannette. The Bullets' stalwart caught the pass, drove hard to the basket, and laid the ball in. Nine seconds were left. Hastily, Philadelphia put up an attempt, but it missed, and Baltimore prevailed, 72–70. Ecstatic fans poured onto the court. Their squad now led, 2 games to 1.[40]

On April 17, the teams met again. Unlike the previous two games, it was the Bullets who led the majority of the way. Fighting off a Philadelphia rally at the end, Jeannette and his teammates won, 78–75. Fulks and Halbert each scored 20 points. Paul Hoffman, however, was the real star. The Bear tallied 27. Three nights later, the Warriors gave the 6,012 fans inside the Philadelphia Arena plenty to cheer about, downing the Bullets, 91–82. If Jeannette and his men were to win it all, the best chance was game 6, scheduled for Wednesday, April 21, in Baltimore. Game 7 would take place in the City of Brotherly Love.[41]

The next evening, around 9:20, the opening jump ball of game 6 was tossed up. The Baltimore Coliseum bulged with an overflow throng. According to a sportswriter for the *Philadelphia Inquirer,* the crowd totaled 4,500. The noise inside was earsplitting. Earlier, fans had quieted down for a brief ceremony organized by a Citizens Committee honoring Jeannette and his teammates. Players took home several mementos and $200 apiece.[42]

The first half was fiercely fought. The Warriors built an early lead, which the Bullets quickly erased. Then, just before halftime, Jeannette, Hermsen, and Meinhold scored in succession, giving the hosts a 37–31 advantage. The momentum continued into the second half, and by the first few minutes of the fourth quarter, the outcome was clear: Baltimore was going to win. As the crowd celebrated, Embry's men finished off Philadelphia, 88–73, to take the title. Fulks, as usual, was the Warrior's main weapon. Jumpin' Joe scored 28 points. The Bullets, by contrast, benefited from a balanced attack. Five players had reached double figures. The next day, an eight-column-wide headline in the *Baltimore Sun* triumphantly announced: "Bullets Win Championship, Beating Warriors, 88–73." The title of Jesse Linthicum's column read, "Fans Noisy as Game Ends." The subtitle added: "'Cinderella Finish' Reminiscent of 1944 Oriole Success." In 1944, the Orioles had claimed the championship of the International League, then the best minor league in the country. But now it was the Bullets' time to shine, and pride-filled Baltimoreans saluted the club.[43]

On April 23, two days after the Bullets' victory, Rodger H. Pippen, sports editor for the *Baltimore News-Post,* published a letter from two local fans. "As loyal Baltimore Bullets rooters," the missive began, "we feel that the city of Baltimore should support the team and build them an arena seating at least 15,000 people." The letter continued: "After all, we have a championship team and they should have a stadium just like the Orioles and Colts are to get." (Baltimore authorities were considering erecting a new stadium for both clubs; it was never built). Likewise, Pippen's counterpart at the *Baltimore Evening Sun*, Paul Menton, believed that Embry's squad deserved a new venue. "With a modern 9,000 seating capacity arena here, which has been on the drawing board for two years,"—the plans, ultimately, were shelved—"the Bullets probably could have more than doubled the estimated $30,000 gross profit from [their] remarkable season," Menton wrote.[44]

Surprisingly, and somewhat anticlimactically, city leaders organized no public events to celebrate the championship. The only event recognizing the Bullets' achievement took place at the Chanticleer, a well-known lounge located on North Charles Street, on April 26. Underwritten by Gunther Brewing Company—a sponsor of the club—the celebration was a relatively staid function. Seymour Smith, who attended the gala, recalled: "We sat around a big table and watched the floor show."[45]

Baltimoreans expected big things from the Bullets in 1948–1949. Unfortunately, the defending titleholders failed to deliver. Wracked by personnel issues, the Bullets finished 29-31 and lost to the Knicks in the first round of the playoffs. Over the next four seasons, things got progressively worse. In 1953–1954, the Bullets hit rock bottom, managing just sixteen victories—in sixty-two games. By the time the franchise folded in late November 1954, the BAA championship was a distant yet prideful memory for many Baltimoreans.

Jeannette remained Baltimore's player-coach until the end of the 1949–1950 season. By that time, the Bullets were playing in the National Basketball Association (NBA). Several months earlier, in August 1949, the BAA and the NBL had merged, forming the NBA. Jeannette began the 1950–1951 season as the Bullets' coach, but in January he was released. Walt "the Bull" Budko, a member of the Bullets, became player-coach. But he, too, was let go. In the years that followed, Fred Scolari, Chick Reiser, and Clair Bee—the famous coach from Long Island University whose reputation had been tarnished by the recent game-fixing scandal in college basketball—coached the Bullets. Each met with failure. As for Embry, he had wisely bailed out years before. In February 1950, a consortium of executives—"boys from Woodholme," Embry would later call them, a reference to the swanky country club in Pikesville, Maryland—bought the franchise. The men paid $35,000.[46]

In the spring of 1948, however, Baltimoreans had not given up on the Bullets. In many ways, the team—with its never-say-die attitude and pair of victories over its archrival, the Washington Capitols—reflected the city's toughness. The Bullets' accomplishments became Baltimore's. Two days after the Bullets lost the first game of the championship series, *Baltimore News-Post* sportswriter Rodger H. Pippen included a blurb about the team in his column. Under the subhead, "Bullets Put Baltimore in Spotlight," Pippen wrote: "Whether or not the Bullets win the pro basketball championship of the country, Coach Buddy Jeannette and his players deserve all possible credit. . . . They have given Baltimore advertising from coast to coast . . . [and] have added to Baltimore's stature as a sports town, thus keeping up the good work started by the Orioles and the Colts." That stature only grew after the Bullets won the title. It was just what Baltimore needed.[47]

10

Toots Barger

Queen of Duckpins

STACY KARTEN

Little did I know when I was growing up in northwest Baltimore and bowling in an organized youth duckpin bowling league at the Liberty Heights Bowling Academy in the early 1960s that I was being schooled by the greatest female duckpin bowler of all-time—Elizabeth "Toots" Barger. After all, what nine- or ten-year-old, just becoming involved in a sport for the first time, would pay attention to that sort of fact?

It would be around twenty-five years later that I would meet Toots in a professional capacity when I worked for the renowned Baltimore-based bowling center operator, Fair Lanes, Inc., and Toots was active in the proprietor ranks at Riviera Bowl in Pasadena, Maryland. Of course, by that time, Toots was in her seventies and no longer the skilled duckpin bowler that garnered so much acclaim in and beyond Baltimore, but she still bowled in leagues for fun and exercise and loved to promote the game. By this point in my career, I knew about and appreciated all that Toots accomplished on and off the lanes.

Toots Barger was a true Baltimore sports legend who rose to fame during the 1940s, 1950s, and 1960s in a sport that most people believe originated in Baltimore at the turn of the twentieth century and became a part of the city's unique charm, as homespun as marble stoops, snowballs, Berger cookies, coddies, and National Beer.

Duckpin bowling was a big sport during those years, as virtually every neighborhood boasted having duckpin lanes and there were thousands of leagues and tournaments. For the unacquainted, duckpin bowling utilizes a

Elizabeth "Toots" Barger, local duckpin legend, by A. A. Bodine.
Courtesy of the Maryland Historical Society.

short, squat pin, almost 10 inches high, and bowling balls that are 4 7/8" or 5" in diameter, ranging in weights from 3 lb., 6 oz. to 3 lb., 12 oz. The scoring and rules are the same as tenpin bowling except that you get to bowl a third ball in duckpins if you don't get a spare. Achieving high scores in duckpins is very difficult. While the tenpin game sees thousands of perfect (300 score) games every year, the highest duckpin game ever bowled was 279 by Peter Signore Jr. of Newington, Connecticut, on March 5, 1992.[1]

During the 1940s, 1950s, and early 1960s, Baltimore was still considered a heavily industrial, blue-collar city, where hard work was expected, and there were no major professional sports teams. The National Football League Colts moved to Baltimore in 1953 and Major League Baseball's Orioles arrived in 1954, so before fans started gushing over Johnny Unitas's accomplishments as a quarterback and Brooks Robinson's miraculous play as a third baseman, Toots Barger was admired and applauded for dominating her sport. It was not uncommon for Toots's name to be mentioned in the same conversations that included the names Unitas and Robinson. In 1999, when *Sports Illustrated* published its list of the best fifty athletes of all time from every state, Toots made the list for Maryland at number 50.[2]

During her reign as the aptly dubbed "Queen of Duckpins," Toots claimed thirteen National Duckpin Bowling Congress No. 1 rankings as the highest average female duckpinner (1946/47–1950/51, 1952/53–1956/57, 1960/61, 1963/64, and 1964/65). (Note: the bowling season spans two calendar years, typically running from September until May.) She also finished second in the rankings six times and ranked in the top ten twenty-eight times during her career. The highest average Toots ever attained was 126, which she accomplished three times.[3]

Toots won the prestigious Baltimore Evening Sun Duckpin Tournament twelve out of the twenty-two years in which she competed (1942–1963), including six in a row from 1946 to 1951.[4] This invitational tournament got rolling in 1925 and was held annually through 1968. The event generated tremendous coverage and publicity in local print and later on television when the finals were televised in the 1950s and 1960s. The grueling thirty-game elimination format showcased the area's best men and women duckpin bowlers and Toots's dozen championships proved her mettle.

Toots also captured numerous tournament championships, including the Ladies Chesapeake Open five times, the Ladies Baltimore Open twice, and she was a two-time winner of the tournament named for her, the Toots Barger Open. At one point, Toots held every individual woman's duckpin world record, and it is said that she won every duckpin tournament ever held at least one time, except for a Pro Tour title. The Women's National Duckpin Association did not start until 1982, when Toots was sixty-nine years old, well beyond the age she could compete effectively against the younger women bowlers.[5]

Toots was so popular, successful, and respected that she was asked to donate one of her duckpin bowling balls, which she autographed, and a pair of her bowling shoes to the Smithsonian Institution.[6] She was, after all, a local treasure.

Duckpin Bowling History

To appreciate what Toots Barger meant to Baltimore and duckpin bowling, it is important to understand the love affair the city had with the sport, which is believed to have started in Baltimore. The long-accepted version of the game's beginnings has links to Baseball Hall of Famers John McGraw and Wilbert Robinson, who were teammates with the Baltimore Orioles in the National League from 1892 through 1899 and again in 1901 with the Orioles, who switched to the newly formed American League. Both men would go on to enjoy distinguished managerial careers in the National League: McGraw with the New York Giants and Robinson with the Brooklyn Robins (eventually renamed the Dodgers).[7]

McGraw and Robinson were also business partners who owned the Diamond Alleys, a traditional tenpin bowling establishment and saloon, on Howard Street in downtown Baltimore. Around 1900, a Baltimore furniture maker named John Dittmar came up with the idea of whittling the pins into a smaller size and brought a set to the Diamond Alleys. McGraw and Robinson used to give Dittmar the shattered wooden pins so he could use the wood for furniture legs. The pins were set up and a small crowd watched as some people rolled against the smaller pins. Upon being struck, the pins flew off the lanes and McGraw and Robinson, who were avid duck hunters, remarked that "it looked like ducks flying off a pond" and the term duckpins was coined. Dittmar subsequently manufactured smaller bowling balls to go with the pins.[8]

The sport quickly became extremely popular, as duckpin lanes seemed to spring up in every neighborhood. Organized leagues and tournaments developed rapidly and the duckpin game soon spread to other areas when Robinson would introduce the sport to cities to which he traveled per his team's baseball schedule. The sport flourished on the East Coast, from Massachusetts to Georgia. Duckpins became so popular that it pushed tenpin bowling out of Baltimore. The game even attracted the legendary baseball great Babe Ruth, a Baltimorean who occasionally bowled duckpins.[9]

Even during World War II, duckpin bowling did not seem to suffer as much of a decline in participation as other sports in Baltimore. In a February

1943 *Baltimore Sun* article, J. E. Wild reported, "After roughly checking the number of duckpin bowling leagues in the Baltimore area at the present time one is forced to admit this particular sport is not suffering too much from the war."[10] According to Wild, "The check shows that at present there are 506 leagues in existence in town with 5,078 teams on their rolls. Counting regulars and substitutes this makes 35,546 persons who roll regularly in these leagues. This is only a few thousand less than were competing here before Pearl Harbor."[11] Maintaining this level of participation could be attributed to many factors: the fact that there were so many duckpin bowling establishments; the sport could be played year-round; it only took a couple of hours to complete a league match; and women could participate just as easily as men. In addition, duckpin bowling was often a salutary respite for people during a difficult period, especially after a long day on the job.

For over one hundred years, Baltimoreans proudly claimed that duckpin bowling was hatched in their city. However, author Howard Rosenberg has debunked that notion. While researching *Cap Anson 3* (2005), Rosenberg found a reference to the term duckpin bowling in the 1894 *Lowell Sun* (Massachusetts) and subsequently came across an 1892 reference to duckpin in the *Boston Globe*.[12] On the other hand, there have been several articles over the years proclaiming the game's Baltimore pedigree. An article in the *Baltimore Evening Sun* on February 19, 1929, featured the headline, "Uncle Robbie, of Diamond Fame, Inaugurated Duckpin Bowling Fad Back in 1903."[13] Robinson reiterated his claim in the *Pittsburgh Press* in 1929.[14] The birth of duckpin bowling in Baltimore was repeated in a December 24, 1965, *Baltimore Sun* article with the headline, "Duckpin Game Began in 1900."[15]

To complicate matters further, in 1992 John Dittmar's grandson, John Beever, and his nephew, Melvin Bierman, concurred with the Baltimore version of the game's history. They recalled from family discussions that Robinson and McGraw were visiting Dittmar one day and they noticed that one of his products were sofa legs. The ballplayers offered Dittmar their worn and broken tenpins, which could be made into the couch legs and save Dittmar on resource materials. Dittmar was already manufacturing scoreboards, lanes, tenpins, and tenpin balls. When he received the Diamond Alley pins, he experimented and fashioned smaller versions of the pins. Dittmar saw the opportunity for children and ladies to handle smaller bowling balls. He took the new and smaller pins to McGraw and Robinson and the rest is history.[16]

Beever lamented the fact that his grandfather did not stick with the duckpin manufacturing. "We were in the lumber business already and only made the duckpins as a favor to McGraw and Robinson," Beever said.

Dittmar's company correspondence shows that a great effort was made to obtain a US patent on the duckpin, but in 1914 that patent request was denied as the patent office stated the duckpin was just a "cosmetic change to the tenpin."[17]

Ultimately, while historians and duckpin industry officials do not know precisely how and when the sport originated, Baltimore still proudly claims the sport as its own. In fact, the duckpin bowling industry launched a campaign in Annapolis in 1992 to have duckpin bowling named Maryland's Official State Sport—the state sport is jousting—but that legislative effort was defeated. Yet as one would expect, one of the most prominent spokespeople in the campaign in the legislative hearings was "Baltimore legend" Toots Barger.[18]

Toots Gets Rolling

Born in the Hamilton section of Baltimore in 1913, Mary Elizabeth Ryan was given the nickname "Tootsie" by her aunt. She shortened it to "Toots" and when she started bowling she had the name monogrammed on her bowling shirts. A 1931 graduate of Eastern High School, Toots was introduced to duckpin bowling in 1939 when she substituted in a league at Seidel's Lanes on Bel Air Road in Baltimore and averaged 96 her first season. Her second season, she averaged 107 at the Vilma Lanes. The following season Toots's average improved to 115, seventh highest in the nation.[19]

Realizing she had some talent for duckpin bowling, Toots started taking duckpins seriously, practicing daily, and improving her skills. Within a short time, she was competing in the major women's leagues in Baltimore and various tournaments on the East Coast.

Toots married Ernest Barger, a plumber, in the late 1930s and the couple had a son and a daughter. Toots would also venture into the duckpin bowling business with her husband as owners of the Stadium Lanes in the neighborhood near Memorial Stadium and the Liberty Heights Bowling Academy in northwest Baltimore. Toots also worked at Riviera Bowl in Anne Arundel County, where she lived at the time. During her years as a proprietor, Toots taught thousands of children how to bowl, which helped the sport grow.[20]

Toots was in her prime as a bowler during the 1940s, 1950s, and 1960s, when Baltimore was a major population center. According to the US Census, Baltimore was the seventh largest city in 1940 and the sixth largest in 1950 and 1960.[21] Although many people viewed Baltimore as just a stopping-off point between New York or Philadelphia and Washington, DC, the city was full of activity and had much to offer its residents. The city consisted of hard-working blue-collar and middle-class people and major employers such as Bethlehem Steel, Glenn L. Martin, and the shipping port. During World War II, in particular, employment was at peak levels at Bethlehem Steel and Glenn L. Martin.[22] Baltimore was a large city with limited entertainment options, and duckpin bowling was a fun and affordable way for many people to spend their leisure time.

After Toots stopped competing in the Baltimore Evening Sun Bowling Tournament in 1964, she served the tournament on a volunteer basis, her twelve championships hovering over the entrants. Robert Naylor of the *Baltimore Sun* wrote:

> There's a sort of ghost of Christmases past that lurks behind the firing lines of this year's Evening Sun Duckpin Tournament, especially haunting to competitors in the women's division.
> The girls roll tonight at Fair Lanes Dundalk. But keeping an expert eye on the action from the fringes of the gallery and then tabulating scores in the back room will be Mrs. Elizabeth Barger. This ghost of tourneys and titles past they call "Toots," and she's still a lively one.
> "I'm still bowling you know," Toots reminds. Few duckpinners in town need to be reminded. "But I won this tournament 12 times and I've been in it ever since they went to 30 games. That's twenty-some Christmases that I was unable to enjoy with my family like everybody else. When I wasn't bowling, those nights I would be nervous. So I just decided I'd prove what I could do, so that's it," said Toots.[23]

Although Toots continued to bowl in leagues until she was eighty-two—she stopped bowling due to bad knees—the all-time great retired from competitive bowling in the 1970s. Her highest honors included being a charter member of the National Duckpin Bowling Congress Hall of Fame in 1961, the same year she was elected to the Maryland Athletic Hall of Fame; she was only the second woman and the first duckpin bowler to achieve that recognition.[24]

Suffering from dementia, Toots died of cancer at the age of eighty-five in Frederick, Maryland, in 1998. As one would expect, she received a lengthy obituary in the *Baltimore Sun*. Frederick N. Rasmussen wrote, "It was said her very presence in a duckpin alley shook the composure of the women who competed against her."[25] Combing through the *Sun* morgue, Rasmussen added, "When she retired, *The Evening Sun* said, 'Above all, it was an era of sheer brilliance in the clutch, when her competitive spirit more than anything else, provided the decisive ingredient in the capture of her innumerable titles. Far more often than not she came from behind, leaving the feeling that she never was out of contention until the last ball was rolled.'"[26] Longtime Baltimore sports columnist John Steadman, who recalled Toots as being "extremely modest" and "outgoing," was quoted in the obituary: "She dominated her sport and established records in bowling that no other woman approached."[27] Such was Toots's renown that the *Washington Post* and even the august *New York Times* noted her passing, the latter reporting that she was "a perennial world champion in a decidedly regional sport," that she "had long been known as the Queen of Duckpins," and that she "became such an acclaimed figure that she was regarded as the city's premiere athlete until Johnny Unitas came to town."[28] All true. More than twenty-five years removed from competitive bowling and the peak of her celebrity, Toots nonetheless garnered recognition in major metropolitan newspapers and on National Public Radio.[29]

Toots Barger's Impact

What made Toots such an outstanding bowler and a popular sports icon?

With regard to the game, in 1947 Toots cited proper footwork as the key to good bowling. "Most women first taking up the game insist on landing on their right foot, instead of the left, for the slide up to the foul line. That throws them off balance, twists the wrist abnormally as the ball is delivered and the ball does not strike the pins where it is intended to," she said. "That's why I say body balance is the first requisite to good bowling. Acquire that, then bowl naturally, no matter how different from another's style your own style may be. Patience and regular practice will do the rest."[30] Easier said than done for most of us.

Now eighty-three, Joan Corcoran of Baltimore grew up watching Toots bowl and eventually competed against her. "My mother, Audrey Mullaney, bowled in the 1930s and became familiar with Toots Barger back in the day," Corcoran explained. "Later, as I was bowling in leagues and major leagues I bowled with Toots. I bowled against her in later years in the 60s through the 70s. She was quite a champion. Her form was impeccable. Her follow through was so impeccable. She was well known because of her ability, national rankings, her tournament wins. She was the most prominent woman bowler of her day, sort of like Babe Didrikson in the golf world," recalled Corcoran, clearly still impressed with Toots's game.[31] Corcoran continued:

> Many kudos and articles were written about her. She was huge because she remained at the top of her game for such a long time. During the 50s she owned the Stadium Alleys in the Greenmount corridor and due to that fact her whole life could be dedicated to being the best you can be in that sport. Owning the bowling alley as she did, she could practice shooting the 7 pin, the 10 pin, and the 5 pin, any split shot you can

name. She had the time to be able to do this. Her bowling ability was phenomenal. It was her ability to keep that same delivery all the time. The follow through is big.

Corcoran also commented on the game's popularity in Baltimore. "One of the things that made it very popular, Baltimore was like the hub. Duckpins was the thing. Most grade schools had their own youth leagues after school programs. The focus was on local bowling leagues. Women were stay-at-home moms and there were day leagues for them to bowl in. The parking lots were always packed," she said.

A better than average bowler, Corcoran competed against Toots in the Baltimore Evening Sun Tournament and remembered that experience. "When you received an invitation to that tournament, it was an honor, a big deal," she said, adding that trying to defeat Toots was a challenge. "I think she was so intimidating, she scared the pants off a lot of them [opponents]," remarked Corcoran.

Professional bowler and proprietor of Mount Airy Lanes and Greenmount Bowl, Joe Rineer has been involved in duckpin bowling for over five decades. "I grew up in Baltimore. I remember I was delivering the *News American* paper and I would deliver those papers as fast as I could so I could get home in time to watch the Evening Sun Tournament which was televised at that time. The finals were always on TV. It was great. She [i.e., Toots] was a classic as far as form and she was probably like a female Tiger Woods of duckpins," Rineer said.[32]

According to Rineer, there were not many male duckpinners as good as Toots and her following was big. "She was watched as much as any of the men. Definitely. I was told she bowled three games every day. I think just her personality made her popular. People just liked watching her bowl, thinking 'I wish I could do that and act like her.' I don't think you could mention her name to anyone who bowled in Maryland and they wouldn't know who she was," said Rineer.

When Toots competed, duckpin scores were lower due to tougher lane conditions and poorer equipment. The pins and balls were both made of wood as opposed to today's all-plastic pins and urethane covered bowling balls. "She never bowled a 200 game," Rineer recalled. "When I was told that I said you've got to be kidding me. In her days the gutters were deeper, the pins were level, and the pins were all wood. What made her great was that she had the mentality to throw every ball like it was the pin that was going to win her the game. It's a pretty frustrating game. Duckpins and golf are closely related as far as the frustration level," explained Rineer.

"Toots was always the same lady. In her heart she knew she had the ability and the edge because of those three games. She did it every day. I loved picking her brain as a bowler and a proprietor," Rineer said.

Regarding duckpins' popularity in Baltimore, Rineer commented: "At that time she was before Fair Lanes, so until it came along every town had a center or two centers with eight to twelve lanes in them. Then Fair Lanes came along with the Recreation Center. There wasn't an exit that didn't have a duckpin bowling center."

In 1923, the Recreation Center opened on Howard Street in downtown Baltimore, close to where the then-closed Diamond Alleys were located. This duckpin establishment featured one hundred duckpin lanes, five floors with twenty lanes each. The Recreation Center would eventually become the publicly held Fair Lanes, Inc., which at its peak owned and operated 116 bowling centers in thirteen states. Twenty of those bowling centers, totaling over five hundred lane beds, were for duckpins.[33]

Wally Hall, originally from England and now living in Pasadena, Maryland, joined Fair Lanes in the early 1960s. He, too, has fond recollections of Toots. "Toots was the personification of all that was good about Baltimore and Maryland. She was a tough competitor but always fair and gracious in defeat. She had the ability to be friends with everyone and never let her celebrity status as a national champion come between her and her regular bowling pals. She showed that women were capable of holding their own against the best of the male bowlers in this the hardest of all bowling games. Her passion for the sport never left her. She loved duckpin bowling and is truly one of the greats in the sport," said Hall.[34]

Hall said that Toots had a major impact on the sport. "She meant so much to the duckpin game because of her consistent performances. She was a good ambassador for the sport and being local she was good news for the Baltimore press, which helped endear her to Baltimore," he said. Indeed, the approbation many Baltimoreans had for Toots endures.

Hall continued to consider the important link between Baltimore and duckpins. "There is a unique relationship between Baltimore and duckpin bowling because it originated here. I think the fact that for many years it was cheaper than tenpins appealed to many hard-working Baltimore residents, plus I believe between the two World Wars there were more duckpin lanes in the Baltimore area than tenpins. The fact that Baltimore had national duckpin champions and the sport generated local press coverage, as well as press and business sponsorship, also helped," he remarked. Based on my thirty-five years working in the duckpin industry, I think Hall's comments regarding Toots's impact on duckpin bowling are accurate. There is widespread consensus that Toots was a difference maker in the sport's growth and popularity.

Ron Matz, a news and features reporter for Baltimore's WJZ-TV 13, grew up in northwest Baltimore as a big Toots Barger fan and an avid duckpin bowler. Matz also has a good feel for all things Baltimore. "I think what endeared Toots to the city and state was the fact that she was so modest," Matz explains. "She was always easy to talk to and approachable. She was popular because she was one of us, so to speak, just someone who loved to bowl but also excelled at it. She was also a trailblazer. Back in those days we didn't recognize great female athletes, as we should have," recalled Matz.[35]

"I saw her bowl many times and when she got up to bowl she always drew a crowd because everyone wanted to see the best. She was amazing. Toots and her husband, Ernie, ran the Liberty Heights lanes where I bowled in a league. You would see Toots or Ernie in there every day. They were real Baltimore characters," he added.

About the charm of duckpin bowling in Baltimore, Matz said:

There was a certain romanticism about duckpins. It was not unusual to see a "Perfect Game" in tenpins. Duckpins was another story. It was a much bigger challenge. At one time, I bowled in three different leagues. All of my friends were consumed by the sport. It was a religion. Duckpins are just another part of the quirkiness of Baltimore and what makes the city so unique. Here it is 50 years after duckpin bowling was at its zenith here and we still have many lanes devoted to duckpins. The Patterson on Eastern Avenue, Stoneleigh Lanes on York Road, Pinland in Dundalk and probably others I can't remember. Duckpins, like Natty Boh, John Waters and our white marble steps are Baltimore personified.

If Toots Barger is the greatest woman duckpin bowler of all time, Pat Rinaldi of Chevy Chase, Maryland, is in the next tier of outstanding bowlers. Rinaldi was the National Duckpin Bowling Congress No. 1 ranked woman bowler six times and won numerous tournament titles.[36] Rinaldi also has pleasant memories of Toots. "I bowled in Washington and she was up in Baltimore, so I did not bowl a lot directly with her, plus I was much younger. Of course, I did bowl against her in some tournaments in Baltimore. I knew she was a legend and a force to be reckoned with. She was a fierce competitor and someone you would want to be like when I grew up," Rinaldi remembered. "One thing she always said, that one hint she always gave me about bowling, was stay down and get the ball out. Down and out and loose as a goose. That is what she would always say. I still remember that and keep trying to do it. She was very focused on being the greatest bowler and she was the greatest bowler. She was always someone everybody tried to be as good as."[37] For many bowlers, Toots set the standard of excellence.

Twenty-six years after her death, and almost five decades since her stellar bowling kept her in the public eye, Toots Barger may be waning as a local sports legend. Memories fade, after all. Those who compete in duckpin bowling and most native Baltimoreans over the age of fifty fondly recall her. But those who are not in that demographic don't know much if anything about the woman the *Baltimore Sun* once called "duckpin bowling's equivalent of Babe Ruth."[38] Add to that the decline in the number of duckpin bowling centers—there is only one establishment within the city limits and just nineteen facilities in the state—and the industry does not have the wherewithal, and perhaps the need, to perpetuate Toots's celebrity and memory. The Orioles and the Ravens, on the other hand, who have the resources to celebrate and market their all-time greats, keep their memories alive for younger fans.

One could argue that Toots Barger impacted her sport as much as any athlete in any sport. For over thirty years, she dominated on the lanes and in the media, sparked legions of fans and participants, and was considered an all-time great Maryland athlete. Toots accomplished this with tremendous humility and style, which was a byproduct of her simply doing what she enjoyed most, rolling a small ball down a sixty-foot lane and knocking down some small pins. No one did it better than Toots. She was a hometown original, "Babe Ruth without the swagger," one of us.[39]

11

"The Best Ambassador Baltimore Ever Had"

Art Donovan and the Colts

MICHAEL OLESKER

In Baltimore, even the sorriest of days—floods in Fells Point, six-car pileups on the Jones Falls Expressway, your favorite aunt Minnie passed away—still get measured against a civic catastrophe now three decades old.

"This," goes the overheard conversation, "is one of the two worst days of my life."

"What's the other one?"

"The day the Colts left town."

That day of constant sorrow was March 29, 1984. It's the dark hour when a drunken air-conditioning magnate named Robert Irsay sneaked the football team he owned all the way from Baltimore to Indianapolis while everybody had their backs turned.

This day, August 9, 2013, feels like some sorrowful postscript of departure.

This day, what feels like half the town has crowded into the massive Cathedral of Mary Our Queen, up on north Baltimore's Charles Street, to say goodbye to Arthur Donovan Jr., aka Artie, aka Fatso, aka the man who kept the laughs alive.

This crowd is saying farewell to a generation, as well. It's a generation that helped give a city its identity, that helped bring together a bunch of communities that were oblivious to each other but found common ground in that era's Colts.

Baltimore Colts defensive tackle Art Donovan runs onto field on September 16, 1962, to the salute of Colts drum majorettes and cheerleaders. He was honored prior to the Baltimore–Los Angeles Rams game.
Courtesy of the Associated Press.

Donovan played football in that long-ago time. He played for the vanished Baltimore Colts in a ballpark on Thirty-Third Street called Memorial Stadium, also vanished. The ballpark was replaced by an old-age home. Donovan cannot be replaced. He played here from 1953 to 1962, and he played on a couple of legendary championship teams, and he's up there in professional football's Hall of Fame.

But that's the least of the Donovan story.

He was Baltimore's great raconteur. As we now live in a time when professional athletes speak in dialect comprised strictly of the hoariest of clichés —"It was a team effort," "We just play 'em one at a time," thus driving all listeners comatose—Donovan's open mouth, and his open heart, are ever more to be missed as such characters fade from the landscape.

He was the comic storyteller around whose beefy frame everyone gathered for shared laughs. He was Santa Claus in a football jersey. The gift he gave was ecumenical: he made an entire metropolitan area realize it had a shared history, and made everybody fall in love with each telling of the gladdest pieces of that history.

And now, on this muggy August morning, he goes to his grave and takes with him the tales that helped define a generation.

In Baltimore, we were earlier than most towns in our love of professional football. In the 1950s other cities struggled to build a fan base, to fill their ballparks each week. The college boys grabbed the big headlines back then: Army-Navy, and Notre Dame, and Harvard-Yale. The professional game was considered a step down, a payday for postgraduate Cro-Magnons to strain a few ligaments before getting on with real adult lives.

"The pros are potbellies," a sportswriter once disparaged. "A bunch of beer swizzlers playing lazy football. And the only thing worse is the bunch of beer swizzlers watching."[1]

If any Baltimoreans had read those words, they might have asked, "Yeah? So?" We were hungry for big-league athletics of any kind, and so we bought into the whole business. We filled our Memorial Stadium Sunday after Sunday. The Colts were among the first pro teams with their own cheerleaders, and a devoted marching band—and a horse named Dixie that galloped around the field whenever the team scored.

Fact is, all of this helped define the town.

And Donovan was right there at the heart of it. His team was the Colts of John Unitas, who threw footballs across the horizon; of Lenny Moore who ran away from tacklers and Alan (the Horse) Ameche, who ran over them; of Gino Marchetti and Big Daddy Lipscomb and Donovan himself smothering all opposing offenses; of Raymond Berry, who caught more passes than anyone else of his era and did it most famously with the whole country watching in the frigid twilight of long-ago Yankee Stadium; and of all those Colts who won football's first Sudden Death game, the 1958 championship contest: the one that made professional football America's obsession instead of its afterthought, the one that many still call the Greatest Game Ever Played.

These people gathering here today—they remember all of it. They're the ones who came of age with the Colts. They filled every seat at Memorial Stadium for years before Irsay killed the love affair. They cheered the Colts band ("The Band That Wouldn't Die," the one that kept playing even after Irsay stole the team away, and played insistently enough for the big shots up at league headquarters to understand how fiercely Baltimore wanted back in the game). They formed their Colts Corrals all over town—clubs whose gatherings became a way of life. (Even the inmates at the state penitentiary had their corral.)

These were the folks who turned their old ballpark into the place known as "the world's largest outdoor insane asylum." They're the ones who spilled out onto the tarmac of the old Friendship Airport, 30,000 of them that night in the late December cold, to welcome the Colts home after the championship game in '58. Many were part of a generation of school kids, some of whose daily classroom opening exercises included the Pledge of Allegiance, the reading of the Lord's Prayer—and the singing of the Colts Marching Song.

And they kept coming, Sunday after Sunday. They were there when the Colts won a second title in '59, and they were there when coach Weeb Ewbank was replaced by Don Shula and the team kept winning and winning. Over one stretch, Shula's Colts lost a total of twelve games—in five years. Decades later, they can still tell you about Tom Matte's wrist band and a corner of the end zone called Orrsville and the way John Mackey would catch a pass and then obliterate would-be tacklers. They were around when Marchetti and Donovan's generation was replaced by the behemoth Bubba Smith and the killer linebackers Mike Curtis and Ted Hendricks who led them to a couple of Super Bowls, and they were still there when Ted Marchibroda's Sack Pack kids and Bert Jones won three straight division titles.

Hell, some of them still bleed when you mention Super Bowl III, and that damned upset to Joe Namath and his Jets.

And they still remember when the love affair ended, when the despised Irsay took the team away and all of the NFL big shots let him get away with it.

In that moment, Irsay did two things: He drove a stake into the heart of Baltimore football fans, much the same as Walter O'Malley killed something in Brooklyn years earlier when he moved the beloved Dodgers to Los Angeles.

And he legitimized the art of blackmail in sports.

He legitimized it for every other owner of a professional sports team: Give me what I want—a new ballpark, higher ticket prices, luxury boxes, tax breaks, personal seat licenses, higher and higher revenues, whatever I feel like demanding—or I take my team somewhere else.

So they've come to the cathedral today, all these old Colts fans, to remember happier days—and Donovan at the heart of so much of it.

Never mind football itself. It's an animal occupation where forearms are thrown into Adam's apples. But Donovan reminded us why the game truly matters to the cities where it's played: It takes thousands who grind out their lives on assembly lines and loading docks and insurance offices and lifts them out of the numbing rut for a few hours each week. It takes those who live in close geographic proximity but otherwise go their separate ways and gives them common emotional ground. It offers, at its heart, a sense of belonging.

Take the Sudden Death game. Everybody knows the impact it had on America's sports culture. In a heartbeat, baseball was no longer the national pastime. There in the twilight of Yankee Stadium, with a national television audience tuned in, Unitas led the Colts to a tying field goal in the closing seconds of regulation time; and, in dramatic overtime, sent the fullback Ameche barreling into the New York Giants' end zone for heart-stopping victory.

Suddenly the Colts of scruffy Bawlamer were champions of the world; suddenly each ballplayer was held aloft as a paragon of home-town godliness.

Who could go on living at such an altitude? The air was too thin up there for actual breathing.

So here was Donovan, putting it all into comic perspective.

He'd grown up in the Bronx, barely beyond the shadows of Yankee Stadium itself. Now he told the story of the day after the great game, about returning triumphantly to his old neighborhood's corner store—Goldberg's candy store where he'd regularly hung out in his younger days—to take a few championship bows for old pals.

Whereupon old man Goldberg, who hadn't seen Donovan since he moved off the block, spots him and says, "Donovan, you big bum, you out of work again?"

Nobody laughed louder than Donovan.

The story took everybody beyond descriptions of trap plays and hook patterns and blitzing linebackers. It humanized one of our gods. We imagined ourselves in Donovan's shoes, in the afterglow of victory.

And it wasn't merely self-deprecating humor, a Donovan specialty. He recited the story countless times across the years, and you laughed each time—because hearing it repeated was part of the kick.

It meant you were already an insider.

Each familiar retelling made all listeners part of a community of shared histories, and that inner circle kept widening with each telling. And it happened each time Donovan shared a tale of those Colts.

"Hey, Artie, tell us about the time . . ."

Like the time in Los Angeles, when the Colts played the Rams a few days after the circus left town. Left behind, all over the field, were random elephant droppings.

"So every time the Rams line up," Donovan laughed, "and they're in the set position, we're picking up elephant dung and flinging it at 'em. They flinch, and it's illegal procedure every time."

Or, "Hey, Artie, how about the time . . . ?"

Like that time against the Detroit Lions, who were quarterbacked by Bobby Layne, known as a great passer and, never to be minimized, a great drinker.

"I tackled him one time late in the third quarter," Donovan remembered, "and I get up and tell him, 'Geez, Layne, your breath reeks. What did you do, tie one on last night?' And Layne says, 'Hell, no. Halftime.'"

Or, "Hey, Artie, how about the time . . . ?" Like the time Donovan broke his leg but coaches insisted he play anyway.

"They told me, 'When they snap the ball, fall down. Maybe somebody'll trip over you.'"

Such tales took us beyond X's and O's. Now you knew the rest of the story. He told his stuff on radio shows, in TV interviews, at CYO dinners and Chamber of Commerce luncheons and synagogue brotherhood breakfasts and corner bars all over the Baltimore area. (Later, Donovan unburdened himself to Johnny Carson and to David Letterman, who invited him back a dozen times.)

For years, Donovan shared a radio program with the defensive end Ordell Braase. "Easiest job I ever had in my life," Braase remembered. "All I had to say was, 'Remember?' And Artie took off."

The stories drew everyone into the great fellowship at the emotional heart of all sports. They became a giddy common denominator and made all the Colts, by extension, feel like everybody's pals.

The Colts of Donovan's era gave rowhouse Baltimore, stuck along a highway between New York and Washington, a reason to feel terrific about itself when we mostly suspected the rest of the country was sort of sneering at us (if they noticed us at all).

OK, maybe we didn't have Manhattan's glamour or Washington's self-importance, but how 'bout them Colts, hon?

That feeling existed right up to the Era of Irsay.

And so, on this muggy August morning half a century since the big lug hung up his cleats, Donovan's old teammates now arrive among all those filing into the cathedral to pay their last respects.

"Look at this," says Ordell Braase, who played defensive end for the Colts for ten seasons. Braase can't get over the size of this crowd. "Here's Donovan, he's a defensive tackle, he's not a quarterback, not a running back, but a tackle. He wasn't one of those glamour guys. And yet, 50 years later, look at all these people. You know why? He brought everybody together. He showed us what we had in common."

Even the dim bulbs who run television news outlets understand the significance of the moment. Can you believe this? They've all assigned crews here, and they're giving the church service wall-to-wall live coverage, like it's the pope himself who's passed.

Now comes Lenny Moore, the Hall of Fame halfback. Lenny, too, seems stunned by the size of the crowd. He's seventy-nine now and gone gray, but still looks like he could slip a couple of tacklers. He pauses as people gather around him.

"What do you remember about Artie?" somebody asks.

"Oh, my," says Moore, shaking his head. "The jokes, the laughter. I mean, football's a game where your mind's tied with so many things. Somebody's trying to tear somebody else's head off. Donovan kept everybody loose. He kept the whole town loose."

A few moments later Gino Marchetti, the Hall of Fame defensive end who played here for a dozen years, nods his head in agreement. Gino's shuffling a little slowly toward the cathedral. He's eighty-six, but he's still built along the lines of a municipal statue.

"Oh, Fatso," Marchetti says, a smile spreading across his face. "I loved the guy. Hell, the first time I saw him, back at our first training camp, I hear a guy yell, 'Hey, kid, come over here.' I'm thinking, 'Who's calling me a kid?'"

Fact was, they were a couple of World War II veterans. Gino fought at the Battle of the Bulge, while Artie was out there in the South Pacific with the marines. But now they were back on a football field again, where everybody could be a kid for a while.

You think the town loved these guys? The ones like Gino and Artie were happy just to be alive.

"Oh, I loved Fatso," Gino says again. "You know what? He was the best ambassador Baltimore ever had."

He was, in fact, the Colts' ambassador-at-large to Baltimore.

Go back to the beginning of the whole thing. It's 1953, a time when Baltimore's the sixth-biggest city in the whole country but doesn't seem to realize it. As always, the town's suffering from a severe case of municipal inferiority complex.

The World War II years brought a quarter-million newcomers here to work the steel mills and the shipyards and the factories that were churning out battleships and bombers. These are people who barely survived the Depression and can't believe they finally found steady work. They made it through the war crammed into these little rowhouses all over Baltimore.

Many of them shared bedrooms and slept in shifts, and they lined up in hallways just to go to the bathroom. And by mid-century they swelled the city's population to just under a million.

But, in the postwar years, there's nothing that binds the town. The Italians are down in southeast Baltimore's Little Italy, a few blocks north of the scruffy harbor. The Poles and the Germans and the Greeks and the Slovaks are further east, each group cloistered in its own protective little ethnic enclave. The blacks are jammed together over in their west-side ghettos, not exactly by choice. The Jews are huddled out in northwest Baltimore because they can't fit in anywhere else. That's the mood of the era. We're a hundred neighborhoods in search of a sense of community.

Until '53 there was no professional football here, and baseball's pitiful St. Louis Browns were still a year away from becoming the pitiful Baltimore Orioles. Sports die-hards grumbled through winters watching professional wrestlers like Haystacks Calhoun and Rocco the Flying Italian perform at a dump preposterously called the Coliseum, down on Monroe Street. The town's biggest indoor sport was bowling; the biggest outdoor sport was the illegal crap game, preferably one step ahead of the cops. The town's best-known athlete was Elizabeth "Toots" Barger, a duckpin bowler.

But then the Colts arrived, including the boisterous Donovan.

They were awful for a while. They lost by preposterous scores, like 70 to 27. In their first year, they won three games. In their second year, they won another three. But the action, and the game's shot-in-the-mouth aggressiveness, and the club's characters, found a following almost immediately.

Never mind the losing. Suddenly you had people from every part of town with something to cheer about—or despair over—in unison. You slipped into any part of Baltimore, any corner bar, any schoolyard, any bowling alley, and that's all people were talking about: the Colts, the Colts.

They gave us a common language.

When the club's coaches geared up for the 1955 college draft, they did it in the usual inept way: they examined the newest copy of *Street & Smith*'s football magazine.

But they were smart enough to start that winter by drafting Alan Ameche, the great fullback out of Wisconsin. The whole town couldn't get over it—a Heisman Trophy winner, and he's coming here? When Ameche ran seventy-nine yards from scrimmage the first time he touched the ball, he lit a fire in everyone's imagination.

A year later, the Colts drafted Lenny Moore, whom Donovan called the greatest football player he ever saw. Moore ran controlled, and he ran blazingly fast. When tacklers came, he gave a hip and then took it away. It looked like magic. On occasion, he ran backward. He caught passes all over the place. His skills were so otherworldly that his teammates called him Sputnik, after the Russian satellite.

And then the Colts got lucky with the most famous long-distance telephone call in Baltimore sports history.

When their promising young quarterback, George Shaw, was injured, they got a tip on some kid named Unitas, who couldn't even make the lowly Pittsburgh club. The Steelers cut him from training camp. They never bothered to give him a legitimate tryout. So he's playing with the Bloomfield Rams of the Greater Pittsburgh League for six bucks a game, until the Colts place an eighty-five-cent phone call and ask John if he'd like to drive down and try out for the Colts. His first contract is $7,000. Even for 1956, it's pretty pathetic.

Do we need a recitation of the rest of Unitas's story here? Over the next decade and a half, all he does is revolutionize the game. He wins championships and sets passing records. He practically invents the two-minute drill in that nerve-wracking '58 title game with the whole country watching. He throws touchdown passes in an unbelievable forty-seven consecutive games. He throws them with tacklers draped all over him, and he does it with almost no time left on the clock, and he seems impervious to all pressure and pain.

Once, late in his career, he throws a last-second touchdown pass to Roy Jefferson to beat Oakland. Head down, he trots off the field—without apparently watching to see if Jefferson catches the ball. The Colts' general manager, Ernie Accorsi, pulls Unitas aside after the game.

"John, did I imagine it, or were you running off the field before Jefferson even caught the ball?"

"Yup," the laconic Unitas says.

"How could you do that?"

"I did my part," says Unitas. "Wasn't anything else I could do."

Just another day on the job, and his workday was over. For a generation of Baltimoreans, who stand on assembly lines, who punch time clocks down at the plant (and feel underpaid, like Unitas), such words resonate: "Hey, man, John's a working guy, just like us."

And he's tough like a working guy, too.

Once, he astonishes everyone in Chicago after the Bears' Doug Atkins breaks Unitas's nose and busts his teeth. The Colts call time-out but can't stop the bleeding until somebody shoves a clump of mud up John's nose. Seconds remain in the game. Unitas's face is so grotesque, his teammates can't bear to look at him in the huddle. The Colts' coach, Weeb Ewbank, tries to take John out of the game.

"You do," says John, "and I'll kill you."

On the next play, with time running out, Unitas throws the touchdown bomb to Moore to win the game.

"That game was tougher than World War II," says Donovan, who spent the war years fighting with the marines in the South Pacific.

Once, Donovan was asked, who was the toughest Colt of them all? Surely it was Marchetti, or perhaps the massive Big Daddy Lipscomb or Don Joyce, who wrestled as tag-team professionals in the off-season; or Donovan himself, maybe?

Nope.

"Unitas," says Donovan. "Because he took the most punishment. And never said a word."

That's the symbiotic connection between those Colts and that era's Baltimore, the thing beyond the championships and the national spotlight they'll bring.

They're working-class guys. In postwar America, this is a city of sweaty people who go to work with their sleeves rolled up, minus coats and ties. We're not Los Angeles, where they make flashy movies and television shows, and we're not New York where they make Wall Street money and slick Madison Avenue commercials and consider this actual work.

We're postwar Baltimore, where 40,000 people have jobs connected to the city's port. We're mid-century Baltimore, whose 1,600 manufacturing establishments employ 130,000 people and produce steel for power tools and metal cans and car and truck bodies and hydraulic pumps. We're Baltimore where 30,000 people go to work every morning at Sparrows Point's Bethlehem Steel, where the jobs are handed down through the generations like family heirlooms and the mills' blast furnaces send columns of smoke and soot into the air, and it drizzles over everything in the vicinity. Nobody calls this pollution; they call it a blessing. It means people are working.

That's what we do in Baltimore. Nobody imagines a future Harborplace, with millions of tourists. You gotta be kidding! Tourists? In Bawlamer, hon? In Bawlamer, we get our hands dirty for a living.

Like these Colts of ours.

Unitas wears a crewcut and spends an off-season working down at the Sparrows Point steel mill to make extra money. Donovan hustles whiskey. The great lineman Jim Parker sells cemetery plots, and Marchetti sets pins at a cousin's bowling alley. They're scuffling for the buck, like everybody else in town.

And these Colts are a common denominator in another way, which few people mention out loud but everybody can't help but notice.

From the start, they're a racially integrated team. In America, this is a time when the so-called public schools have just begun to integrate. In much of the country, black people are still fighting for equal employment, for the right to decent housing, for the right to enter any restaurant or theater the same as any white person.

In Baltimore, entire neighborhoods have begun changing color with the integration of schools. Nobody knows how this is going to work out. Maybe the Supreme Court ordered the public schools to integrate, but the private schools are still dragging their heels, and so are the colleges. The city's liquor board has a regulation against serving drinks to "mixed clientele." It's a way to keep bars segregated. The city's hotels still turn away blacks, even after the Orioles arrive in 1954.

The Orioles are a story of complete racial insensitivity and stupidity. Across the 1950s, they have a first baseman named Bob Boyd and a pitcher named Connie Johnson who are African American, and almost nobody else. A couple of utility players come and go without notice. One year, they run fifty-four players through the roster. Every one of them is white.

But the Colts are different. They not only have black players, but they're high-profile guys. First there's Buddy Young, the speedy running back. Then there's Lenny Moore running circles around everybody, and Jim Parker opening the holes for him to dart through. There's Big Daddy Lipscomb, who crushes opposing running backs. There's Leonard Lyles, who runs two kickoffs back for touchdowns in his rookie year, and Johnny Sample, who intercepts two passes in the 1959 championship game, and the elegant defensive back Milt Davis.

For black fans, who quickly became indifferent to the Orioles, these Colts signaled the beginning of a new day. Big Daddy's knocking down white guys, and white Baltimoreans are cheering! Moore's outrunning white tacklers, and white Baltimoreans are roaring happily! Such a thing has never happened before. And in the morning newspapers there are — locker-room photos of black and white ballplayers embracing each other while half-dressed.

The message is unspoken but clear to everyone: if these tough guys, who make their living in violent action, and embrace each other like brothers—if these guys can make it work, maybe there's a lesson here for all of us.

And everybody knows their stories because these guys are out there in the community all the time. The Colts' front office types are pretty smart this way. They send the ballplayers out on goodwill missions all over town:

to schools and churches and synagogues, to parades, to country clubs. They're mixing it up, they're telling stories, and they look like everybody's neighbors.

What's more, that's exactly who they are. It's a time when the athletes live among their fans.

"We were connected at the hip with these people," the great linebacker Mike Curtis says one night, years after he retired. Typically, he says it at a neighborhood bar.

"It felt," he says, "like we were attached to this town at our very core. You understand what I'm saying? It felt like we were attached at our souls. You know what I used to do after games? I used to drive down to east Baltimore and find a bar and sit there with all those guys from Highlandtown and Middle River. They were our people, see? They were hardworking guys like us, and they loved us. I don't know if you can have that any more. These guys move around so much now, and they're making all that money. It's two different worlds, isn't it? It's like royalty. What we had was different."

Take a place like the Seton Apartments, out in northwest Baltimore. Every afternoon back in the Colts' era, all these teenage boys are out there in their black high-top Keds and their beat-up sweatshirts playing their games of tackle. One afternoon in the mid-fifties, there's a loud argument.

"Did you hear who moved into the apartments?" one kid asks.

"Who?"

"Joe Campanella and Jack Call."

"No!"

"Yeah!"

"Bullshit artist," comes a chorus of voices.

Nobody can believe this is possible. Campanella's a backup linebacker and Call's a reserve halfback, neither exactly a household name. But they're Baltimore Colts. Colts don't live at the $60-a-month Seton Apartments, they live on Olympus, don't they?

Well, no, they don't. They aren't cloistered in some gated community like today's millionaires, they're living down there in working-class apartments, or they've rented a room or two in somebody's house, where a family's happy to take in a few extra bucks during football season.

And they're hanging out in some neighborhood bar—because football's not just a place for cashing in back then. These guys really are part of the town.

Like Gino and Artie, hanging out at this joint over on the east side of town, over on Eastern Avenue, at a night spot called Gussie's Downbeat, which is fashionably located directly beneath a Chinese laundry.

They say that Marchetti would drop in the night before a game, and get a load on, and play his best ball the next day. Or Donovan. He came home from Gussie's four o'clock one morning.

"Where were you?" said his wife, Dorothy, the decibels rising with each syllable.

"I went out for an early haircut," Donovan explained. "There was a line."

That's the Donovan they're remembering at the chapel this morning. That's the generation that's slipping away. It's the one that gave Baltimore its identity a long time ago, before Irsay stole it away.

Now the town has its football Ravens, and loves them passionately. We're a football town, no doubt about it. We've got a history here. Artie Donovan kept telling us all about it, kept reminding us we were all part of the same community.

That's why so many turned out to say goodbye—to Artie, and to a generation's sweet stories.

12

Sam Lacy and John Steadman

Empathy and a Conscience on the Sports Pages

DENNIS GILDEA

When Baltimore sportswriter John Steadman and 1,600 others gathered at a dinner in 1979 honoring another Baltimore sportswriter, Sam Lacy, Steadman noted that he and those in attendance were there to celebrate "what [Lacy] has accomplished as a writer, cheerleader and a citizen."[1] In a newspaper career that spanned from 1918 to the dawn of the twenty-first century, Lacy had accomplished a great deal, as, for that matter, had the man offering the tribute, Steadman. In fact, the three categories Steadman chose to emphasize concerning his friend's career provide a worthwhile guide to examine both of their lives and contributions to Baltimore journalism.

The "writer" and "citizen" categories fit perfectly with a description of an ideal newspaper reporter, who must be both a wordsmith and a crusader for social justice. But a "cheerleader?" Would any reporter worth the ink that stained his very being want to be known as a cheerleader or a homer? Aren't reporters, even sports reporters, supposed to be objective? Or could it be that journalistic objectivity is an impossible, even ridiculous concept? In a tribute to Steadman following his death on January 1, 2001, Bill Hughes observed that Steadman was "too much of a homer to be a great writer." Steadman's failing, according to Hughes, was that he "had crossed the line as a journalist" and came to identify too readily with Baltimore teams, most notably the Colts.[2]

For his part, Sam Lacy made no bones about arguing in print for the racial integration of sports, especially advocating and even cheering for the pioneering role Jackie Robinson was playing in breaking the color barrier in Major League Baseball. Had Lacy crossed the journalistic line separating the press box from the player and the team? Were two of the most prominent and prolific sportswriters in the history of Baltimore journalism failures because they were blinded by the causes, the athletes, and the teams they covered? This chapter examines the work of Lacy and Steadman by using the three categories—writer, cheerleader, and citizen—to answer that question.

Biographical Backgrounds

Sam Lacy was born in 1903 or possibly 1905 in Mystic, Connecticut. His mother was a Shinnecock Indian, and his father, Samuel Erskine Lacy, moved the family to Washington, DC, when Lacy was still young. Samuel Lacy distinguished himself by becoming the first African American detective on the District of Columbia police force. More importantly for his son, he

From left to right, sportscaster Vince Bagli, Sam Lacy, publisher John Oliver Sr., John Steadman, and Michael Olesker at the ***Baltimore Afro-American*** office to celebrate Sam Lacy's ninety-seventh birthday, October 23, 2000.
Ray Gilbert, *courtesy of the Baltimore Afro-American.*

was a baseball fan who regularly sat in the Jim Crow Negro section of the right field stands to watch the Washington Nationals (who became known as the Senators in 1919). On more than a few occasions, his young son joined him.[3]

The senior Lacy became friendly with Nationals owner Clark Griffith, and that friendship enabled young Sam to land a job catching batting practice balls hit to the outfield, as well as serving as a gofer for team members and the manager. Once the game began, Sam worked as a vendor, who kept at least one eye on the play on the field even as he was hawking his wares.[4]

Lacy became an accomplished player himself, starring at Armstrong High School, where he was also a good student. In fact, he was good enough in the classroom and experienced enough in sports to gain a sports reporting job, while he was still in high school, with the city's African American newspaper, the weekly *Washington Tribune*.[5]

In 1920, Lacy infuriated and bewildered his parents by refusing admission to Howard University in favor of a chance to play baseball in the Negro leagues. He spent two seasons with the Atlantic City Bachrachs and the Baltimore Black Sox before finally acquiescing to his parents' wishes and enrolling at Howard. While he loved baseball, Lacy was disturbed by other aspects of the professional athlete's life. "When the games ended, all of the players would go back to the boarding houses and smoke and drink," he recalled, and, putting it as delicately as possible, "have women in their company."[6] It was not, he decided, the life for him.[7]

Lacy eventually graduated from Howard University, and in 1923 he began covering sports for the *Washington Tribune*. In 1934 he became sports and managing editor, and in 1939 he joined the *Baltimore Afro-American* when that publication absorbed the *Tribune*. However, in 1940, he left the *Afro-American* to become the national editor of the widely respected *Chicago Defender*, a position he held until 1943, when he returned to the *Afro-American* as sports editor and columnist. He stayed active as a journalist until his death on May 8, 2003, having spent a remarkable eighty-five years in the newspaper business.

Toward the end of his life, Lacy was recognized as one of the truly greats in the profession. In 1997, he won the J. G. Taylor Spink Award for meritorious contributions to baseball writing, and a year later he was inducted into the writers' wing of the Baseball Hall of Fame. In 2002, Martin O'Malley, the mayor of Baltimore, praised Lacy "for challenging the American conscience and demanding that we live up to our promise as a people."[8]

Like Lacy, John Steadman knew the people and culture of Baltimore, and like Lacy, he often challenged the values of Baltimore's culture. Actually, it is hard to imagine anyone more quintessentially representative of Baltimore than John Steadman. He was born in the city on Valentine's Day in 1927, the son of Baltimore's deputy fire chief. In fact, the John F. Steadman firehouse was named for his father in 1973. For young John, the city's streets and vacant lots became his playground. He wrote of sledding around Baltimore by "hopping on the rear extension of an automobile bumper and getting pulled up the 41st Street hill. Sometimes you'd go for miles—until your arms got tired or you ran out of snow on the highway and then the runners of the sled made sparks and the grinding noise made the driver alert that he had trailers he didn't know about."[9]

Those sledding trips around the city were one of the few free rides Steadman ever got. He began to earn his keep at an early age. After graduating from City College High School, he was signed as a catcher by the Pittsburgh Pirates. He spent just one season in the minors, where his .125 batting average persuaded him that he might find more success as a sportswriter. When Steadman received the Associated Press' Red Smith Award posthumously in 2001, his brother Tom accepted it for him, noting, "When you hit .125 in the minors, you'd better find another field of dreams."[10] Steadman did. He landed a job with the *Baltimore News-Post* in 1945, earning $14 a week. He became publicity director and assistant general manager for the Baltimore Colts in 1954, but three years later, he returned to the news business. "Once you've worked on a newspaper, it's like a man who goes to sea and eternally loves the roll of a ship and where it's going," he explained.[11]

Steadman became the youngest sports editor of a metropolitan United States newspaper in 1958, a position he held at what was then the *News-American* until that paper folded in 1986. He then joined the sports staff of the *Evening Sun*, noting wryly in his first column for that paper, "Our profound wish is *The Baltimore Sun* and you, the readership, have the tolerance to put up with the 'new kid' who has appeared in your midst."[12] Of course, by this time he had been covering Baltimore sports for more than forty years.

The *Evening Sun* met the fate of many metropolitan evening newspapers when it went under in 1995, at which time Steadman joined the staff of the *Sun*. He wrote his last column—in his prime he wrote six columns per week—on December 3, 2000, a tribute to the late Naval Academy football coach and war veteran Emery "Swede" Larson. Steadman's final paragraph read: "Larson is buried only 100 yards from John F. Kennedy at Arlington National Cemetery. Let his epitaph be written: He never lost to Army."[13]

Steadman was diagnosed with cancer in 1998, and following his death in 2001 the American Cancer Society renamed its annual Hope Lodge golf tournament the John Steadman Tournament of Hope.[14]

Writers

John Steadman devoted a 1993 column to Sam Lacy and his distinguished contributions to Baltimore journalism, noting that in addition to his life-long fight for social justice, Lacy "has continually produced quality work—columns that were hard-hitting when need be," work that was marked by "distinctive phrasing, insightful opinions and—bottom line—an inherent desire to make things better for his fellow man."[15]

Another commentator on Lacy as a writer concluded, "His literary style might best be described as sardonic honesty," a character of mind that may well be attributed to his struggle for acceptance and even admission as a reporter to a multitude of Jim Crow press boxes. "Lacy's outsider status and critical attitude certainly led to a rather muted reception of his work by those other than his colleagues at the major black presses," writes J. Douglas English in the *Dictionary of Literary Biography*. "While he had won four National Newspaper Awards at *The Afro-American*, the distinguished quality of his career was not widely acknowledged until late in his life."[16]

At his journalistic best—and his best often occurred when his blood boiled over a racial injustice in the world of sports—Lacy could turn a phrase calculated to rivet a reader's attention to his cause. For example, he led one of his "A to Z" columns on Lee Elder's second entry into the field at the previously segregated Masters golf tournament in Augusta with these lines:

> There is this haunting melody of sometime back that comes to mind as Lee Elder returns to the Master's golf tournament. Written in the Fifties, its lyrics describe the pleasure and advantages of another chance. It goes in part: Love is lovelier, the second time around; love is beautiful with both feet on the ground; love's more comfortable the second time you fall, like a friendly home the second time you call.[17]

The 1977 Masters was African American pioneering golfer Lee Elder's second appearance on the Augusta links. The first, two years previous, was not as successful as it could have been, Lacy argued, because of the intense pressure Elder felt as he broke the golfing color barrier:

> He endured a fishbowl existence, plagued by the curious, the critical and the hopeful. His anxiety to answer the curious, slap down the critics and vindicate the hopeful destroyed his concentration and magnified the insecurity which accompanies all players facing Augusta for the first time.[18]

Elder missed the cut in his first Masters. Lacy's column, certainly representative of the wishes of the "hopeful," reveals another quality that marked his writing, one not seen in the majority of sports reports: empathy.

John Steadman was the master of a straightforward style. His readers never doubted about where he stood on a topic. "He was certainly not a poet," sportswriter and Baltimore native Frank Deford once said. However, "He was a good reporter. John could write a feisty and entertaining column. He could not have survived as a stylist, but he was very good at what he did."[19] What Steadman did better than most sportswriters was function as a solid reporter who diligently did his legwork, checking and cross-checking his facts with a legion of sources who trusted him and were willing to tell him their stories. More than anything, Steadman was the consummate storyteller.[20]

The stories Steadman favored involved underdogs, the people whom society had shunted to the sidelines of life. "He wrote about [underdogs] with passion; but he cultivated characters, and he saw the world with a twinkle in his eye," Michael Olesker writes.[21] Throughout his career, Steadman remained, Olesker contends, "The conscience of the press box, the carrier of legends, the man who looked for the heart beating behind the box scores."[22] As evidence, Olesker, who got his start in journalism under Steadman, points out a late-season game when the Orioles were in the thick of the American League pennant race with the Yankees. With the outcome of a key game in Yankee Stadium in doubt, Mickey Mantle hit a high foul ball that catcher Clint Courtney of the Orioles muffed. One pitch later, Mantle hit a game-winning home run, giving sportswriters all the reason in the world to unload their venom on Courtney. Not Steadman. "While the rest vilified poor Courtney," writes Olesker, "John had his own perspective. Imagine, he wrote the next day, poor Courtney's utter humiliation."[23] Like Lacy, Steadman could empathize and sympathize.

An editorial dedicated to Steadman in the *Baltimore Sun* made a telling observation on his writing style and his worldview: "His columns struck some as sugary in their adoration of athletes, overwrought in their prose. But that's the way John Steadman ran his life. He wore his heart on his sleeve. Indeed, he was so polite that he apologized to his dentist during surgical procedures."[24] His column about Cal Ripken Jr.'s breaking Lou Gehrig's consecutive games played streak serves as an example of both his tendency to "sugary" prose and his heartfelt emotion. Steadman wrote: "Fittingly enough, a marshmallow Maryland moon lit up the sky, accompanied by a canopy of twinkling of stars, but the one that shone the brightest was the man wearing a baseball uniform with Orioles scripted across the front and a block 8 on his back."[25] Steadman makes clear his admiration for Ripken, although for many readers it may be difficult to see past that "marshmallow Maryland moon."

Like Ripken, Steadman compiled his own ironman record. He covered every football game played by the Colts and then the Ravens: 719 games in all. In addition, he was one of only eight reporters in the nation to have attended all thirty-four Super Bowls contested up to the time of his death.[26]

Citizens

John Steadman knew Baltimore's history, and one of the major events that occurred in the city was the 1944 fire that "destroyed the wooden bandbox known as Oriole Park."[27] It was a blaze, Steadman wrote fifty years later, that "became the catalyst that burned Baltimore out of its minor-league confinement and ignited a desire for major league franchises in both baseball and football."[28] While the minor league Orioles lost their ballpark, their uniforms, and all of their baseball equipment, the loss proved to be a blessing, because, as Steadman maintained, it meant an emergency move to what was then known as Municipal Stadium, "which accommodated huge crowds and helped create an enthusiasm that notified the nation that spectacular change was underway."[29]

Oriole Park was built in 1914, and as its rubble still smoldered, Steadman noted that *Baltimore News-Post* and *Sunday American* editor Rodger H. Pippen wrote prophetically, "Baltimore rose from the ashes of its great fire in 1904 to be a bigger and better city. Our Orioles will come through just as soon as war conditions permit, with a bigger and better place for their games."[30] The spectacular fire, Steadman concluded, "sent Baltimore into a renaissance of monumental proportion."[31] The Colts, whose team colors were green and silver and who were members of the All-America Football Conference, began playing in Baltimore in 1947, and the St. Louis Browns became the Major League Baltimore Orioles in 1953. The Colts of the National Football League arrived in Baltimore by way of Dallas, Texas, also in 1953. The professional teams, of course, played in Municipal Stadium.

It was 1954 when Steadman became for a period of three years the publicity director and assistant general manager of the Colts. He was back in the sportswriting business in 1958 when the Colts won the NFL championship in the legendary overtime game against the New York Giants, 23–17, on the strength of Alan Ameche's plunge into the end zone. Steadman chronicled the game in his 1959 book *The Greatest Football Game Ever Played: When the Baltimore Colts and New York Giants Faced Sudden Death*. The nationally televised game proved to be central in building interest in the NFL. "It was the day the sport turned the corner," Steadman quoted Alex Webster of the Colts as saying. Moreover, it was a victory that did wonders for Baltimore's civic morale. "It's a game Baltimore won't let die," Steadman wrote thirty years later, "because it was the city's first major championship in 62 years and came in New York against the Giants, one of the league's most consistent winners."[32] The character of that Colts team made it special, and it was that character and that victory that led to a city's falling "in love" with them.[33]

One of the ironies of Steadman's relationship with the Colts is that, as one reporter argues, his criticism of Colts owner Bob Irsay contributed to the owner's decision to move the team to Indianapolis in 1984. "Steadman, more than anyone else in Baltimore, was responsible for driving [Irsay] out of town and for demonizing the persona of that poor devil," Bill Hughes writes.[34] The point is debatable.

Sam Lacy was a reporter who devoted his writing and his life to improving opportunities for African Americans, and even that is an understatement. He lived through the Jim Crow days early in the twentieth century, through Jackie Robinson's struggles to be accepted during his Major League baseball career, and through the civil rights movement of the 1960s. He both chronicled and was part of the long struggle. In 1979, he could survey the progress made by African Americans in sports and in American life, and thus wrote the following about young black athletes: "I don't look at them as sports heroes but as leaders of the future who will become corporate executives and mayors of cities. They shouldn't just look to the tree tops, but should reach for the stars."[35]

When he made that statement, Lacy was almost eighty, but he was more interested in what lay ahead for African Americans than he was in what came earlier. "I'm not interested any more in what Jackie [Robinson] did. That issue is dead. I now want to see young people make themselves worthy of so many opportunities."[36] Those opportunities did not exist decades earlier. In 1937, Lacy began his campaign to integrate baseball when he urged, unsuccessfully, Washington Senators owner Clark Griffith to sign black ballplayers. When he was writing for the *Chicago Defender* in 1943, he convinced baseball commissioner Judge Kenesaw Mountain Landis to meet with prominent members of the Negro Newspaper Publishers Association to discuss the possibility of desegregating baseball. Oddly, Lacy was not included in the group. Rather, the publishers chose Paul Robeson to accompany them because "it was believed that handing a speaking role to Robeson would have a greater impact on the moguls of baseball."[37] Choosing Robeson as a spokesman, however, was "the kiss of death," Lacy thought, because, "Paul was considered by many to be a communist."[38] Lacy was right; the effort failed.

Lacy, though, was not easily discouraged. In 1945, he was the force behind establishing a four-member committee to explore the possibility of integrating the Major Leagues. Branch Rickey of the Dodgers, Larry MacPhail of the Yankees, and Joseph H. Rainey of Philadelphia joined Lacy on the committee. MacPhail, however, seemed to be disinterested; he never appeared for any meetings. Lacy and Rickey held discussions without him, and in early 1945 the Dodgers co-owner and general manager told Lacy that he was ready to sign a black player, although he had not selected the individual. The point is that even before Robinson became a Dodger, Lacy was instrumental in making the historical event happen.[39]

After a while, Lacy's involvement in breaking baseball's color barrier became more than strictly intellectual. In 1946, when Robinson—in addition to Johnny Wright, a pitcher the Dodgers bought from the Homestead Grays of the Negro National League—reported to spring training with the Dodgers and the club's triple A minor league team, the Montreal Royals, in Florida, Lacy dealt with almost as much discrimination and acrimony as Robinson did. Lacy rode with Robinson to the stadium in Sanford, Florida, for the start of spring training. Sean Yoes of the *Afro-American* wrote: "a large crowd of Sanford's White citizens had gathered—some of them members of the Ku Klux Klan, which was very active in that region of the state—and they were determined to keep Robinson out of 'their' ballpark."[40]

Robinson had come too far to turn back; he walked the gauntlet and entered the stadium. Lacy tried to do the same, but Florida state police turned him away, his press credential notwithstanding. Robinson became aware of Lacy's plight, and he went with him around the perimeter of the stadium until they found a loose board in the fence. Like kids sneaking into a game, the two sports pioneers crawled through the crack in the fence. "It was Jackie's shoulder that went against the plank, not mine, as we found a way to get inside," Lacy remembered.[41]

On April 15, 1947, when Robinson played his first game for the Dodgers in Ebbets Field against the Boston Braves, Lacy was there to cover the event, which he did from the press box, not from a segregated seating area. In 1948, when the Dodgers, which by this time had Roy Campanella on the roster joining Robinson, played the New York Giants, both teams featured "black men who were selected on their merits as ballplayers," Lacy wrote. Moreover, "In the stands, persons of all races sat together. In the field boxes, Mrs. Rachel Robinson and Mrs. Ruthe Campanella occupied seats with other players' wives, near Mrs. Laraine Day [manager Leo Durocher's wife] and Mrs. Branch Rickey. Yes, it was different. I can't recall ever having felt the same about the playing of the national anthem."[42]

It is impossible in a single chapter to account for even a smattering of the journalistic campaigns Lacy undertook in his ongoing quest to achieve equal treatment for African American athletes. His autobiography, written with Moses J. Newson, *Fighting for Fairness* (1998), is the best source for fuller accounts of his efforts. But a cause and a case he fought for in 1937 deserves to be mentioned. In October of that year, Syracuse University's undefeated football team came to Baltimore to play the University of Maryland. A star on the Syracuse squad was Wilmeth Sidat-Singh. He was an African American who, as the Maryland game approached, was publicly identified as an Indian, an identity that stemmed from his surname and one that was encouraged by both Syracuse and Maryland sports administrators.

Sam Lacy blew the lid off that bogus story. Writing at the time for the *Washington Tribune*, Lacy produced a page-one story that ran under the headline, "Negro to Play U. of Maryland; Boy Called Hindu by Papers." Lacy knew Wilmeth's birth father, Elias Webb, a Washington pharmacist, and he knew that following Webb's death, his wife married a medical doctor from the West Indies, Samuel Sidat-Singh. Wilmeth had never tried to suggest that he was an Indian, and no white college in the South had ever permitted an African American to play on its home venue.

Lacy's revelation created a racial tempest, and Sidat-Singh dressed for the game but did not play, despite the fact that he was a star. Maryland won, 13-0. Lacy led his game story with the following: "An unsullied football record went by the boards here today as racial bigotry substituted for sportsmanship and resulted in the removal of the spark-plug from the machine which was Syracuse University's football team."[43] Some in the African American community criticized Lacy for exposing Sidat-Singh's racial background, maintaining that it would have been preferable to let him play in the game. Lacy rebutted that position in print: "To me, such a contention seems only to be a weak-livered admission that we are willing to see our boys progress under any kind of masquerade, that we agree with the Nordic observation that ANYTHING BUT A NEGRO is okay."[44] Sam Lacy was anything but weak livered.

Cheerleaders

As sportswriter Jerome Holtzman famously declared, there should be "No Cheering in the Press Box."[45] The age-old dictum meant to curtail "homers" and regulate press box behavior was something Lacy and Steadman adhered to as professionals. Nevertheless, both could be classified as "cheerleaders" in the finest sense of the word, because they approached sports and the sportswriting as important to their community of readers and something that should celebrate the positive aspects of their regions and, in Lacy's case, his race.

Vi Ripken, Cal Ripken Jr.'s mother, made a perceptive observation regarding John Steadman's influence on the morale of Baltimoreans. "There are positives in this world," she said, "but without John in Baltimore, we'd never have heard about them."[46] As evidence, consider the column he devoted to August Waibel, who for almost forty years coached high school football at Baltimore Polytechnic Institute and before that Edmondson High School. Waibel, Steadman wrote, was both a "disciplinarian and a cheerleader," and despite the fact that his all-time record of 280 wins and 75 defeats made him the most successful coach in the history of Baltimore scholastic football, he never sought to "embarrass a rival coach and players on the other side of the field—only to beat them, without aspiring to huge numbers on the scoreboard to satisfy an out-of-control ego." Waibel coached by a single slogan, Steadman noted, "Poly first, me second." He was a man who exemplified "what football was about in its purest perspective."[47]

Steadman's story on Waibel, a high school coach working in a city in which coaches such as Weeb Ewbank and Don Shula of the Colts deservedly received barrels of ink, stands as an example of his discovering and telling the stories of the little guys, society's underdogs, as Michael Olesker observed.[48] Over the course of his career, Steadman wrote about a blind baseball announcer, an ice-skating coach who had lost both legs, and the story of Mary Dobkin, who, despite her own health struggles (117 operations on her deformed legs), did everything in her power to help children who needed a break in life. "The Mary Dobkin A.C. sponsored football, basketball, baseball and softball teams in Baltimore, and remarkable success came about because," Steadman wrote, "Mary refused to accept explanations over why something couldn't be done if kids were concerned."[49]

Steadman's obituary in the *Sun* made an observation about him and his journalism that could just as easily apply to Sam Lacy: "He'd get personally involved in stories, trying to make a difference for a needy individual or a cause."[50] Was Lacy personally involved in Jackie Robinson's story? Most definitely. Both he and Robinson had to tolerate separate housing from their white colleagues. "Sam was [Robinson's] roommate when the Dodgers were on the road," his son Tim Lacy recalled, "and he tells horror stories of some of the adventures they were a part of. One morning, emerging from the rooming house where they stayed, they found a cross burning in the yard, an indicator that the Ku Klux Klan had visited overnight."[51]

Did Lacy cheer in print for golfer Lee Elder or tennis player Arthur Ashe? Of course. Did that result in stories that lacked balance? Not at all. Would he work political and racial controversies into his coverage? Most definitely. When thirty-two newly independent nations in Africa were threatening to boycott the 1964 Summer Olympics in Tokyo if South Africa and Portugal were permitted to participate, Lacy sided with the potential boycotters. To those who criticized him for mixing sports and politics, Lacy responded: "What my colleagues don't seem to understand is that colored people have never regarded morality and human dignity as being related to politics. They belong in the political arena, of course, but in the sense that they should be in the conscience of those practicing politics."[52]

Lacy refers to the collective conscience of mankind, and it can be said that both he and Steadman did everything in their power in their stories over the years to nudge the conscience of their readers to an awareness of the problems facing society and to the brave attempts of those who fought within sport to solve those problems. As a result, Baltimore and several generations of Baltimoreans were enriched by their efforts and heartfelt prose.

13

Baltimore's Bard of Baseball

Jim Bready Remembers the O's of Old

RAFAEL ALVAREZ

Most things sprout unseen—but not serious baseball in Baltimore.
Its start can be dated, placed and named. The very man who started
it can be identified and his picture printed, whiskers and all.
He was Henry B. Polhemus . . .
                                   —James H. Bready, *The Home Team* (1958)

The jacket of Jim Bready's encyclopedic narrative of baseball in Crabtown—
The Home Team, published in 1958 at the author's expense—shows a ball-
field through a knothole in a wooden fence. It's a classic folk image of the
national pastime, one known to old-timers in big cities, farm towns, and
railroad hamlets across the United States.

On one side of the fence is the street.

On the other: *the game!*

"The game of throwing, hitting, catching, running—counting," wrote
Bready. "The game of thinking ahead on the diamond, of reliving afterward
in the mind."[1]

The photo and the layout—selected and designed by Bready, as was
everything in the book, for which he took a second mortgage to publish—
shows Union Park near the corner of Twenty-Fourth Street and Barclay in
Baltimore's Waverly neighborhood.

Union Park was the short-lived home (1892–1899) of the fabled
National League Orioles, a team of skilled roughnecks featuring manager

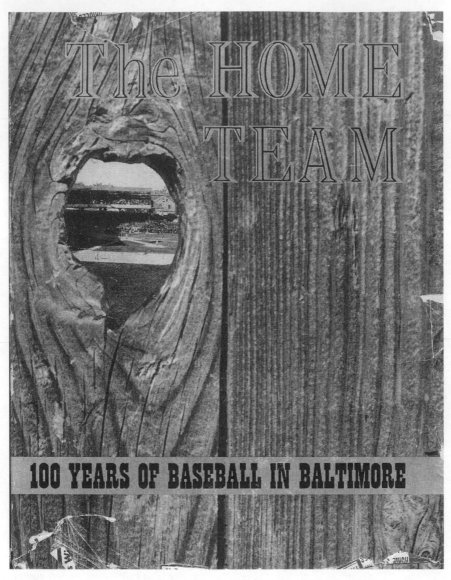

The HOME TEAM

TEAM

100 YEARS OF BASEBALL IN BALTIMORE

The cover of James Bready's *The Home Team* (1958). *Courtesy of Chris Bready.*

Ned Hanlon and star players John McGraw (a brawler who could make Ty Cobb look like a diplomat), the beloved Wee Willie Keeler (indeed wee and a good saloon singer), Wilbert Robinson, and Hughie Jennings.

The greater Waverly area east of Johns Hopkins University was home to many ballparks and Oriole teams from the late nineteenth century through the 2002 demolition of Memorial Stadium.[2]

One of the early neighborhood ball fields—the completely wooden Terrapin Park—was the fifth incarnation of Oriole Park, the brief home of the Baltimore Terrapins of the Federal League. From 1916 to the Fourth of July holiday in 1944 it housed the International League Orioles.[3] The address is now the site of a brewery called Peabody Heights in honor of the neighborhood's nineteenth-century name.

"The old left field fence is our north side property line," said J. Hollis B Albert III, general manager and, in the 1970s, a prep school ballplayer. "We have a photo of players on the field with St. John's church behind it that lets us know exactly where everything used to be."[4]

A baseball themed brew is in the works. Albert bought a couple of straw-filled bases from the 1920s to lend authenticity to the nostalgia (bags from the Midwest, found on the Internet), and a surveyor will be brought in to tell the beer barons precisely where home plate once lay.

Long before the site was a brewery it was a soda-pop bottling company and before that, a ballpark worthy of Rockwell with knotholes in the fence.

Fred Koenig knew the thrill of being on both sides of the lumber in the early twentieth century, back when his mother ran a 1930s boardinghouse for ballplayers. It was the days, he said in a 2013 interview in Baltimore, "When men wore straw hats and threw them out on the field after the game." Win or lose, Koenig didn't say, just that the lids would sail toward the diamond after the final out.[5]

"I remember peeping through the knotholes [at Oriole Park] to watch a game," said Koenig, born in 1920 and raised just a block from the hardball action at 418 East Twenty-Eighth Street. His father ran a North Avenue lunchroom and his mother knew enough not to make suppertime small talk with a pitcher who'd just lost a game. "They used to hose down the wooden stands after each game to make sure no one dropped a cigar or cigarette," said Koenig. "We'd go under the stands after games and look for coins and soda bottles to return for the deposit."

Like longtime Orioles trainer Edward P. "Doc" Weidner Jr., who died at age ninety-two in 1994 after a half century with the team (going back to the International League), Koenig was born within a fungo fly of old Oriole Park.

His father, Frederick Leopold Koenig, was born in Vienna and ran a lunchroom—"they served chicken dinners," he said—on North Avenue near Eutaw Place in west Baltimore. His mother, the former Josephine Erjautz, provided room and board to ballplayers looking to make the bigs. Some were on the way up; some going nowhere; others headed for factory work.

"The players would tie our shoelaces in knots before we got up for school," said Koenig, a batboy who worked for tips as a gopher in the visitor's clubhouse at old Oriole Park, often running to the corner to get chewing tobacco for the players. Other chores included taking the sweaty uniforms of the opposing team and hanging them over the ballpark seats to dry in the sun. Before the games, fans would rent pillows to cushion their derrieres across nine innings and the then-frequent doubleheader. "Some [of the ballplayers] came back to our house after they were out of baseball because they loved my Mom and her cooking," said Koenig.

On that long ago Independence Day in '44, a smoldering cigarette near Oriole Park's third-base grandstand escaped the postgame hosing and the tinderbox burned to cinders a few hours before dawn on the Fourth of July. The blaze was described by a witness as "a sheet of fire."[6]

Fred Koenig was in New York City at the time, reporting for army service. Jim Bready had already served several years, mailing war memorabilia like German helmets to his sweetheart and future wife, Mary Hatop, at her parents' home in Govans, with the same zeal he would later apply to baseball treasures.

A dozen years before the Oriole Park fire, Koenig was there for a Fourth of July doubleheader pitting the hometown nine against the Reading Keystones. In that 1932 game, a minor-league legend named Russell "Buzz" Arlett hit four home runs for the Orioles and followed it the next day with a round-tripper in an exhibition against the New York Yankees. Arlett (1899–1964) left baseball in 1937 with 432 minor league home runs, a record that held for decades.[7]

Buzz is in Jim Bready's great book. Alas, Fred Koenig is not. The omission is one of the few things related to baseball in Baltimore before the Camden Yards era that Bready did not chase, capture, document, and wax about in idiosyncratic prose approaching Joycean verse: "for the many-games fan, the watcher-reader-rememberer, a baseball splendor needn't be obvious, or frequent."[8]

"Dad tried to get as much into a sentence as you can," said Chris Bready, the book monger son of a newspaperman and a librarian. "He also made up words and wrote sentences 50 words long. You'll read it, know what it means, but won't be able to find it in the dictionary."[9]

In this way, said Chris, "He amused himself."

Jim Bready saw his first professional baseball game with his father, who was a newspaperman, the city editor on lobster shift at the *Philadelphia Public Ledger*. They went to see Connie Mack's Athletics play at old Forbes, Twenty-First and Lehigh. The family lived in Woodbury, New Jersey, just south of Philadelphia.

Bready's father—James Ely Bready—died when his first-born was about thirteen. His mother, the former Mabel McIlvaine, a newsroom staffer who met her husband at the *Public Ledger*, took over the job of raising Jim and his younger brother Gerald.

"He didn't see a lot of his old man," said Chris. "But there'd be times when they'd go see the A's together."

Bready, who ran cross-country while studying history at Haverford College, started making plans for *The Home Team* near the end of a half-century lull of Major League Baseball in Baltimore. From the bankruptcy of the 1902 American League Orioles to the dawn of Elvis Presley, there was no big league baseball in Crabtown save for the odd exhibition.

Bready's plan was to have the book ready for an Opening Day release in 1954, when the former St. Louis Browns took the field against the Chicago White Sox on Thirty-Third Street as the modern-day Baltimore Orioles. "Unfortunately, Dad didn't write fast," recalled his son Chris, and the book did not appear until 1958, which made a nifty one-hundred-year bookend from 1858, the year the game migrated from New York to the shores of the Patapsco.

Bready was keen to have the commissioner of the game—Ford Frick, under whom the regular season expanded from 154 games to 162—boost Baltimore with a letter congratulating the city on its new team. The thought apparently had not occurred to Frick and, as he did with so many people he either admired or wanted something from (often both), Bready wrote a letter.

"And Frick doesn't give a shit," laughed Chris Bready. "So my father takes the commissioner's letterhead and a sample of Frick's signature, sets it in type and that becomes the letter from Ford Frick to Baltimore for the book. After a relatively isolated childhood, my Dad was having the time of his life."

Raymond Daniel Burke, a Baltimore attorney, writes essays about baseball in Baltimore with a heart that knows the game cannot be separated from home and family.

"My grandfather was born in 1876 and lived with us when I was a child," said Burke. "He saw the legendary 1890s Orioles teams that won three straight National League pennants and Bready writes so lovingly about."[10]

On Opening Day in 2010, Burke filed a piece for the *Baltimore Sun* about listening to the game on the radio—when he was a kid—as the imposing old man sat smoking in his armchair.

"The game was in the late innings by then, and each pitch became a matter of critical analysis," wrote Burke. "My favored position was sprawled across the foot of his bed, in the spot where the humid scents of the summer night air flowed in from the open window. It was during such nights that I discovered that baseball, in its many moments of pause, was a game of conversation and reflection."[11]

In one of his own Opening Day essays—published in 1996, some dozen years after the final edition of *The Home Team* was released to honor the Orioles' 1983 World Series win over the Phillies—Jim Bready reflected on his favorite play in the game.

The steal of home—"the maximum thrill," Bready called it—for which Ty Cobb holds the Major League record with fifty-four.[12] "Think of him, sliding into home, feet aimed at the catcher's knee, then when cleats were still metallic, and sharpened," Bready wrote of Cobb. "It's exciting when a home run wins a 1–0 game, but after the majors' 530 such outcomes so far, it's not extraordinary. Fifteen times, a steal of home has won a 1–0 game."

And then, he made a call to the bullpen, his own deep archives of lore:

The SOH [steal of home] goes back a long way. John McGraw, third-baseman for the Other-'90s Orioles, included the SOH in his bag of tricks, perhaps also reaching for the umpire's shoelaces as he slid by. Since April 15, 1954, the Orioles have pulled off a successful SOH about 20 times. On May 31, 1982, Cal Ripken stole home; Brooks Robinson stole home twice. So did Don Buford. On August 15, 1979, against the White Sox, Eddie Murray stole home in the 12th inning, winning the game.[13]

And the beat goes on. In June of 2014, Orioles designated hitter Nelson Cruz attempted an extra-inning steal of home at Camden Yards against the Oakland Athletics. Cruz failed, as did the Orioles that night, 4–3 in eleven innings.

To appropriate a Bready quote about diamond heroics you don't see every day: "Ostentation goes with many of the rarities . . ."[14]

On a Wednesday afternoon—June 12, 2013—Chris Bready sat in the upper deck of Camden Yards, on the third base side, as the Orioles played the Angels of Anaheim. Next to Bready sat Michael Olesker, longtime Baltimore newspaperman and author who attended Baltimore City College high school with Chris Bready's older brother, Richard.

As the pair bantered about early 1960s Orioles teams—the Paul Richards's rosters of Gentleman Jim Gentile and the Greek American battery of Milt Pappas and Gus Triandos—Olesker mentioned that Jim Bready's baseball book got him through a tough time when he was a kid.

It was 1960, a year of legitimate baseball optimism in Crabtown, an 89-win season at the dawning of a New Frontier and the "Baby Birds" on Thirty-Third Street. Chuck Estrada won 18 games as a twenty-two-year-old rookie, Brooks Robinson, just twenty-three, was laying a hot corner foundation for a cathedral made of gold and, at the far end of the game, Bobby Thomson—he of "The Giants win the pennant! The Giants win the pennant! Shot-Heard-Round-the-World" fame—played his last game that year with the Orioles.

Olesker, just fifteen, was laid up in bed, recovering from an operation to remove a tumor in his back.

"I spent about a week recuperating at Bon Secours hospital and one of our neighbors brought me a copy of Bready's book after I came out of surgery," said Olesker. "I was miserable in that hospital room, bored, my entire torso wrapped in heavy bandages for a month. And here was a book that handed me the entire history of the beloved O's. It was the spring of 1960, when the Orioles were just beginning to blossom and the town was turned on by Brooksie, Ron Hansen, Gentile and Triandos, Marv Breeding, and the Kiddie Corps of pitchers."

Olesker had been given a first edition, $1.50 to print and sold for five bucks out of the back of the family station wagon. It featured an orange cloth hardcover with 1950s sports section headlines about the Orioles—and the woeful Browns moving to Baltimore—as endpapers.

"The book helped link me not only to the modern Orioles, but to a sporting history of my home town," said Olesker, who as a youngster lived in Grove Park in northwest Baltimore. "A few years earlier, in a neighborhood ballgame, I dove to my left for a grounder and a grownup from my block said, 'You're playing like one of the old Orioles'—meaning, I think, that I wasn't afraid to get myself a little dirty."

"At that point," said Olesker, "I'd never heard of Wee Willie Keller and Hugh Jennings and Uncle Wilbert Robinson and those turn-of-the-century Orioles."

Those Orioles—bad asses afraid not of dirt or blood, progenitors of the "Baltimore Chop," and dead-ball adherents to the rule that all is fair—are duly heralded in the Bready book.

"It was like a light going on, connecting me to the dark past previously hidden," said Olesker. "The book was written with such loving care, and illustrated so beautifully."

Long before the Internet turned baseball into a wing of Borges' Library of Babel—a stack of diamonds in which the most obscure and arcane facts can be found quicker than a Steve Dalkowski fastball sailed over the umpire's head—*The Home Team* was the go-to reference.

Born in south New Jersey in 1919, James Hall Bready died in Baltimore at the age of ninety-two in October of 2011.[15] His ashes lie in the columbarium of the Episcopal Church of the Redeemer, a North Charles Street congregation for which he wrote the history *This Parish Under God* (1955).

"My father taught me that you could become somebody without having to be famous," said Chris Bready. "That you should help someone out if you can and then forget about it."

Lauded by colleague Ernie Imhoff as "the *Evening Sun*'s grand old editorial writer, book columnist, reporter and Guildsman," Bready's passing was mourned in many spheres. Not the least of them baseball where a farewell "salute" came from the Society for American Baseball Research for his "great contributions to baseball historical research."[16] The first Marylander accepted into the organization—grown geeks taking childhood enthusiasm for the stats on the back of baseball cards as far as their computers will take them—Bready was one of the group's early members.

If there is a hole in the verity that you can't take it with you—neither golden calf nor golden glove—it is this. When someone dies, whether Earl Warren or Earl Weaver, they take their stories with them.

Jim Bready left some of his behind in *The Home Team*, sixty-eight oversized pages—10.2 inches by 9.1 inches—crowded with duplicates of original headlines and gray agate type; tales of beautiful blasts and bonehead plays culled from the author's eighty years in the stands.

In his wake, the guts of his book—some fifty-two cardboard file boxes holding nearly 2,000 items ("box after box after box," said Chris Bready, "my father kept stuff")—were given to the Babe Ruth Birthplace and Sports Legends Museum at Camden Yards.

Greg Schwalenberg, a longtime curator and Orioles' beer vendor, had the privilege of culling, collating, and cataloguing the Bready treasures at the museum, which is housed in a building built by the B&O Railroad in 1856 as a train station. Since 1992, it has been the entrance to Oriole Park at Camden Yards. "I never knew [Bready] had this much stuff," Schwalenberg said, hands in white cotton curator's gloves, bringing file upon folder upon fabulous factoid from a back room near his desk. "Jim had Babe Ruth's first box score when he pitched for the [International League] Orioles in 1914. The first time the Babe came to bat he got a hit to right field."

Visitors to Schwalenberg's underground treasure chest are sometimes invited to take a few cuts with one of the Babe's dark brown bats. Of particular fascination to Schwalenberg is the stuff Bready collected that is more than a century old, back when the home nine looked like the guy on the orange-cloth cover of *The Home Team*—baggy pants and bushy mustache, about to catch a ball bare-handed.[17] "I was totally fascinated by the 1890s stuff: pictures, pins, invitations to banquets . . . a lot of handwritten stuff and stock certificates from people who invested in teams in the [1914–1915] Federal League . . . not only did Bready save the letters, he saved the envelopes," said Schwalenberg.

One of the great stories from the book, a snapshot of the resentments that accompany the serious business of baseball, concerns Tommy Murphy, a groundskeeper for the mighty National League Orioles. McGraw—the "Little Napoleon" who both played the hot corner and managed the team—was so beloved in Crabtown that Murphy had a bed of white posies near the home team's dugout that spelled McGRAW. When McGraw dumped the Birds for the New York Giants in the middle of the 1902 season, Murphy got down on his hands and knees to rip out the flowering letters. "Making it official," wrote Bready, "that McGraw had been uprooted."[18]

Chris Bready likened his father's files to the archives of a newspaper morgue: "very detailed, kept by slipping ephemera on subjects that mattered most to him into 8.5 x 11 manila folders." In addition to baseball, subjects amassed at the Bready home on Gladstone Avenue included H. L. Mencken, with whom Bready struck up a friendship based on newsroom gossip late in the fabled writer's life, Baltimore buildings that no longer existed, and Maryland Rye Whiskey.[19] Bready's fifty-page paper on pre-Prohibition Maryland Rye, written in 1990, is considered the standard history on the subject and is on file at the Maryland Historical Society.

Nonetheless, Bready's baseball files were voluminous. "He kept receipts on everything to do with the [baseball] book," said Schwalenberg. "We have notes he took on the back of envelopes from his gas and electric bills."

"All of his notes, production items, and whatever was still around regarding printing and publishing of *The Home Team* and later *Baseball in Baltimore*," said Chris, the latter published in 1998 by Johns Hopkins University Press and solely concerning the local game through the nineteenth century.

In 2000, the mother lode was gathered from the north Baltimore condominium where Jim and Mary Bready moved after leaving the Roland Park home where they raised their family. "Every time we thought we'd gotten it all, Chris would call and say, 'Come back, I found something else,'" Schwalenberg recalled.

Something else included an original copy of the Constitution of the American League of Professional Baseball Clubs; handwritten notes from Baltimore fans willing to pay $250 apiece to hire an attorney in an effort to force the major leagues to absorb the Federal League Orioles; pen pal letters from long-retired ballplayers, correspondence Bready initiated.

"Jim would track old players down and write letters to them, guys like Bill Clarke," said Schwalenberg, noting that on page 118 of *The Home Team* is a picture of Clarke's lifetime pass from Major League Baseball. "Clarke was a catcher/first baseman who played for the National League Orioles for five years," Schwalenberg explained. "He was on the three consecutive championship teams of 1894, '95, and '96.'"

Bready and Clarke stayed in touch for years. In one of the letters, the ballplayer asks the newspaperman if he has an address for Bill Hoffer, an old teammate. The letter is dated January 26, 1959. Six months later, both Clarke and Hoffer would be dead.

"When the museum wanted to trace the location of all of the ballparks in Baltimore, Mr. Bready knew where all of the photographs were," said Schwalenberg. "Every time we went looking for specific information to fill a hole, it was either scattered all over town or Jim Bready had it."

Jim Bready was already about sixty—an affable, nerdy man darting through the newsroom with an urgency not always related to deadlines—when I landed on the *Baltimore Sun* sports desk in 1978. I had just turned twenty, and Bready's book was about to claim its twentieth year on shelves like the one in Pete Kerzel's home where, he said, "it holds a permanent and reachable place of honor."[20]

"Back in 1973 that book cost me the equivalent of two summer lawn cutting jobs," said Kerzel, the managing editor of MASNsports.com. "None of my friends understood why I'd spend that hard-earned money on a baseball book instead of Linda Ronstadt or Elton John. I read it until the pages came loose from the spine and kept it together with a large binder clip."

I was buying Muddy Waters's records from the cut-out bin when I first met the man most people referred to as "Mr. Bready." Loaded down with books and papers and canvas bags filled with more books and papers, he'd dash past my desk in the sports department, where I spent a year compiling horse racing results before moving over to the City Desk.

I remember amiable chats, as he seemed more interested in young reporters than some of my generation (high school sports and future London correspondent Bill Glauber; crime news and future college dean Catherine D. Gunther) was curious about him.

But I don't recall connecting him to "the book," which I first encountered in the Mount St. Joseph High School library a few years earlier, too impatient for its charms because the 1969 Birds were more important to me than those of 1889.

At a historic paper with correspondents around the globe, the newsroom could be stern and aloof, at least to the sensibilities of a twenty-year-old horse race clerk writing about rock music as often as he could get away with it. Yet there was an openness to Mr. Bready, a certain goofy charm underscored by honesty and intellectual rigor. He seemed more like an absent-minded professor than a newspaperman back in the days when the difference was negligible in putting a good daily read on the street three times a day.

Bready had a helping hand in that daily miracle for more than six decades in Baltimore. First, he was a copy editor in the marble-tiled and limestone-columned *Sun* building at Charles and Baltimore Streets not long after Victory over Japan, and then writing general assignment and features when the A. S. Abell Company built an ugly brick newsprint factory at 501 North Calvert Street.

He'd often stay well past his shift and when the family would arrive to collect him—his wife, Mary, driving the station wagon out of which first editions of *The Home Team* were sold—the three Bready boys—Richard (born 1947), Chris (born 1948), and Stephen (born 1951)—would take turns trying to get Dad to walk away from the action. "Family was paramount," said Chris, "as long as he got the chance to do some of the things he liked."

In 1949, Bready was sent to interview the famous British author Evelyn Waugh (1903–1966), who was passing through Baltimore. In the midst of their conversation, Russell Baker, then a twenty-four-year-old staffer on the *Sun*—the Abell's morning paper—arrived to do the same.

Baker, who would go on to win two Pulitzer Prizes—one for commentary in the *New York Times* and one for his autobiography *Growing Up* (1982)—was flummoxed to see Bready at work. "He was James Bready, one of the *Evening Sun*'s brilliant cadre of feature writers, all of whom I admired with a respect close to awe. Bready was major league," wrote Baker in his newspaper memoir, *The Good Times* (1989).[21] Baker continued:

> The imagination, wit, and graceful lilt of his writing made him one of the glories of the *Evening Sun*. He was the kind of newspaper writer I wanted to be, but until this moment I had never met him. Thin, pale, and as ascetic-looking as a metaphysical poet, he gave me a wide, impish smile. He probably meant it to be genial, but in my frantic state

of mind it seemed satanic and malevolent, as though he relished this chance to watch me humiliate myself.[22]

It *was* genial, in keeping with similar adjectives used to describe Bready by coworkers who saw him more than his family did: upbeat, optimistic, curious, humorous, nostalgic, friendly, and grateful to be making a living at a job that, as the newsroom saying goes, "sure beats working."

From 1952 until his retirement in 1986, Bready wrote editorials—arts and literary issues, the demise of the Diamondback Terrapin—and on the days when Mary and the kids didn't pick him up curbside, hauled his passions home to Roland Park on a transit bus after the evening paper was put to bed in the early afternoon.

"After dinner, I would peer into [Dad's] room and find him perched over the typewriter," said Chris Bready in 2010 to reporter Jason Policastro. "Sometimes [he was] nodding off, other times searching for the right word, or a way to put them together."[23]

Bready's influential "Books and Authors" column debuted in the *Sunday Sun* in October of 1954 and ran regularly through 2005, some twenty years after he'd officially retired.[24] Long after I had matriculated from the horse-race desk to the City Desk, Bready wrote kindly of my collections of short stories set in the city he'd adopted as his own before I was born.

With the early 1980s retirement and deaths of people like John T. Ward (who wore a pocket watch and worked the business desk until he was ninety) and rewrite man emeritus Jay Spry (who taught the trade to David Michael Ettlin and Joe Challmes, local ruffians who did not wear pocket watches), Bready became the dean of Baltimore journalism.

Conferring respect and affection, the title was once common in big city newsrooms. Baseball writer Lou Hatter, who as a rookie covered a hanging at the Maryland Penitentiary, was the sports department "Dean" when I landed on morning *Sun* race desk.

Bready's honor was codified in a history of the paper, *The Baltimore Sun: 1837–1987* (1987), by the late *Sunday Sun* editor Harold A. Williams.[25]

The last time I saw Mr. Bready was sometime in 2010 at the weekly gathering of the Aging Newspapermen of Baltimore, an informal luncheon then held at Enrico's on the corner of East Pratt and Haven Streets. He stood and told a few stories, finger in the air, and everyone set down their soupspoons to listen.

It didn't matter what he was saying—something relatively inane about "news hens" (of which his mother was one), antiquated 1940s slang for female reporters—except that Jim Bready was saying it.

It was time to get someone over to the Bready home to take down whatever the "Calvert Street whirlwind" cared to talk about and I dispatched Policastro, a novice who now and again dined with the Aging Ones.

Now a financial writer, Policastro visited Bready at home three times in 2010, twice alone and once with former *Sun* Moscow correspondent and Bready admirer Antero Pietila.

Perhaps he saw the specter of his younger self at the knee of Mencken as Policastro took down his every word, telling the young reporter that he had "traded a life of analysis, for dialysis," insisting that every day his name didn't appear in the death notices was "a nice day."

"We traced the outline of his career," said Policastro. "The interplay between him and his wife was fantastic too, finishing each other's sentences and then applauding when one of them remembered an elusive answer to one of my questions. The thing I remember most clearly was Mr. Bready's emphasis on being curious about everything. I think that's what made him the writer he was."

One of the great anecdotes in the Policastro profile came from Robert A. Erlandson, who started at the *Sun* in 1955, was stationed in Saigon—1966 through 1968—during the Vietnam War and met Bready while filing book reviews. Once, Erlandson recalled, he saw Bready running through the streets of downtown. "He never walked when he could run," said Erlandson.

"Walking fast, bicycling quickly," remembered Imhoff, the last managing editor of the *Evening Sun*, in the same profile, "always talking in a hurry, sometimes quicker than his thoughts were lined up to come out."

On this occasion, said Erlandson, Bready was running with a brick in each hand, having pinched them from the rubble of two old buildings that had come down to make way for alleged progress. "That was Jim," Erlandson told Policastro, "trying his best to preserve some part of old Baltimore."

You Can't Kill an Oriole

Wee Willie Keeler
Runs through the town,
All along Charles Street
In his nightgown
Belling like a hound dog,
Gathering the pack
Hey, Wilbert Robinson,
The Orioles are back!
Hey, Hughie Jennings!

Hey, John McGraw!
I got fire in my eye
And tobacco in my jaw!
Hughie, hold my halo.
I'm sick of being a saint:
Got to teach youngsters
To hit'em where they ain't
                    —Ogden Nash, published in *The Home Team*

14

Black Sport and Baltimore

Spats, the Judge, and the Pearl

JAMES COATES, HANNAH DOBAN,

AND NEVON KIPPERMAN

Sometimes stars align. Such was the case in Baltimore in 1967, when three talented, accomplished African American athletes at different stages in their careers played for local professional teams. Lenny Moore of the Colts, Frank Robinson of the Orioles, and Earl Monroe of the Bullets all excelled in Baltimore and eventually became Hall of Famers. Unsurprisingly, they got to know one another while playing and living in Charm City.

"Baltimore was like a small town when I got there—the Colts, the Orioles, guys like Frank Robinson, we all knew and respected each other," Earl Monroe, a Philadelphia native, once said. "Everyone would cross paths at one point at Lenny Moore's Sportsman's Lounge, trading stories and having some fun. The baseball players—Paul Blair, Don Buford—we all had some great times together, and of course the Orioles were at the top of their game then."[1]

Lenny Moore's Sportsman's Lounge was located on Gwynn Oak Avenue, near Liberty Heights Avenue, and was a popular gathering spot for sports and music fans. Like many things in Baltimore of that vintage, the lounge is long gone. Today, Moore, Robinson, and Monroe are old men, their glory days long gone, too. But as it used to say on the façade of Memorial Stadium, "Time will not dim the glory of their deeds." For many Baltimoreans, black and white, this is certainly true regarding Moore, Robinson, and Monroe, who signified different things to the city's disparate

181

communities and yet, due to their racial identity and to racial prejudice and discrimination, shared certain experiences.

First, though, some context is useful.

Black Sports in Baltimore

African Americans have a long, rich sporting history in Baltimore. It dates back to at least the eighteenth century, when enslaved blacks managed to find ways to participate in different forms of recreation.[2] In 1867, after the Civil War and long before Negro baseball leagues flourished in the 1920s and 1930s, "Baltimore had two early African American teams called the Lord Hannibals, or Baltimores, and the Orientals."[3] By the end of the nineteenth century, in 1889, George "Spider" Anderson rode a horse named Buddhist to become the first black jockey to win the Preakness Stakes at Pimlico.[4]

At the dawn of the twentieth century, African Americans in Baltimore gained opportunities and rights that they had never experienced. In the field of education, for example, the city began to provide a more comprehensive system of public schools for black children, and black teachers were poised to assume more positions in those schools.[5] Politics, city and statewide, were also about to become more accessible to African Americans. The same was true of recreation. In fact, public and private facilities and programs for sport and other forms of leisure appeared at an unprecedented rate.[6]

One of the most notable of these programs was the Interscholastic Athletic Association, which was "organized with the purpose of fostering sports in the Baltimore/Washington, D.C., area."[7] In Baltimore, the Dunbar Athletic Association and the Colored High and Training School teams earned some early fame, especially in boy's basketball. The game's popularity in Baltimore was also due in part to the Public Athletic League. The league's 1910 tournament featuring various schools gave youth citywide the opportunity to compete. A white man, W. S. Pittman, organized these tournaments for Baltimore's African American youth. In 1910, Pittman resigned his post with the Playground Athletic League (PAL) because of its practice of not allowing organized competitive team athletics. PAL teams played their games at Commonwealth Hall and School No. 110, the latter of which won several consecutive PAL championships. Some of 110's members later joined the Dunbar Athletic Association team.[8]

The Colored High and Training School developed an outstanding team. In 1917, it defeated the Dunbar Athletic Association for the city championship. Two years later, several of the Colored High and Training School players formed the nucleus of the Druid Hill YMCA team, bringing local fame to themselves and the Y with their winning ways. Some of these players would go on to form the famous Athenian Athletic Association. The Athenians traveled the East Coast and the Midwest, playing college and club teams.[9] By the mid-1920s, the Athenians started advertising themselves as "Baltimore's favorites," and played on a circuit that included clubs in the Midwest.[10]

The Athenians were extremely popular with black Baltimoreans, not just because of their winning tradition, but also because of the teams they played against and the postgame entertainment. The Athenians competed against teams such as the Harlem Big Five, known at the time as "Basketball's Greatest Attraction." Interestingly, the Athenians also played the Alert Club, a white team advertised as South Atlantic Champions during the 1920s. By the mid-twenties, rivalries between the Athenians and Washington, DC, teams were well entrenched. Coupled with the lively, popular dances held after games, the Athenians were an attractive draw.[11]

Although *Brown* v. *The Board of Education of Topeka, Kansas* (1954) did not immediately cause most American institutions to integrate, many people in the sporting world had already begun to recognize the rewards that could be gained from racial integration. Branch Rickey of the Brooklyn Dodgers is an obvious example. Rickey and others smartly envisioned the benefits of having an infusion of new talent. New revenue streams would be created as black fans continued to follow their favorite black players. Colleges and universities also recognized this potential financial windfall and began to change not only entrance requirements, but also rules, regulations, and requirements for participation in sporting competitions.

Despite the increasing involvement of African Americans in Baltimore's sports world, the city remained a racially divided place for most members of the black community in the 1940s and 1950s. No amount of athletic success could wash away the city's long and complicated racial history.

Although African Americans were participating more in Baltimore's civic life—in terms of politics, education, and recreation—legalized segregation remained the law, just as it had been at the turn of the twentieth century. On a national level, during World War II the "Double V" campaign "sensitized" African Americans and some whites to racial injustice.[12] As tensions increased around the country, many of Baltimore's African American residents and the city's black leaders "understood the importance of organization."[13] While civil disturbances went on elsewhere, the Baltimore NAACP registered voters.[14] Other organizations that garnered black support in Baltimore included Activists for Fair Housing and CORE (Congress of Racial Equality), which continued through the 1950s. The emphasis on organization in the 1940s and 1950s illustrates the ways in which members of the city's African American communities understood their civic identity in Baltimore. In 1942, 17 percent of the city's voters were African American, and yet African Americans were granted few of the same rights as their white contemporaries.[15] The myriad experiences shared by Baltimore's residents in the 1940s and 1950s exemplify what author Eden Unger Bowditch has called Baltimore's "parallel worlds."[16]

Even when the city's white professional athletic teams finally allowed African Americans on their rosters, the participating black athletes still found it exceedingly difficult, if not impossible, to associate with their white teammates off the field or court. Regardless of any legal strides that had been made toward equality, the city remained culturally segregated. While Baltimore offered recreation and opportunities for African Americans, they were segregated along racial lines. Colleges and universities did not look past race until the mid-1960s, and the University of Maryland did not admit its first black player until 1965. The city's professional sports teams, however, saw the financial benefits of signing black players as early as the 1950s. They did not provide complete equality for players and fans, and instead offered segregated seating for any black fans that attended games.

Realizing the potential on-field success and financial gain of playing black athletes, a National Football League (NFL) team signed the first African American player in 1946, when the Los Angeles Rams added Kenny Washington of UCLA to its roster. A few years later, the Baltimore Colts signed Mel Embree, George Taliaferro, and Claude "Buddy" Young, the first African Americans to play for the franchise. In the 1950s, NFL teams increasingly drafted African American players; in 1956, the Colts signed Lenny Moore, an African American player who, like those before him, helped integrate the NFL and simultaneously faced difficulties due to the era's racism and racial tensions.

Lenny "Spats" Moore

From the mid-1950s until 1984, many Baltimoreans derived a great deal of pride from the city's professional football team.[17] The Baltimore Colts were "part of the city's fabric," emblematic of its blue-collar work ethic and sensibility.[18] The players were not just players; they were Baltimoreans. A local fan from the era recalled, "The players lived in the area. You would see them in the offseason."[19] When they were not on the field, the Colts were working jobs in the city just like their fellow citizens. The Baltimore Colts' players reflected the average people of the city and simultaneously bestowed "big-league status" to Baltimore.[20] To many fans, Memorial Stadium—where the Colts played—represented the city's soul. According to the narrator of the documentary *Colts: The Complete History* (2006), "nowhere did the heart of the city ever beat stronger."[21] While many Baltimoreans constructed their community's sense of civic identity via the Colts, this civic identity was neither inclusive nor colorblind.

Although most Colts were considered Baltimoreans, not all were treated equally. The team seemed to be a unified "family" on the field; however, off it things were different. Lenny Moore's career with the Baltimore Colts reflected the disparities and discrimination that professional black athletes experienced at the time when racial tensions permeated the NFL and American society. His years with the team were hardly comparable to those of his white teammates. Recounting his early days with the team, Moore explained, "When I came to Baltimore, we couldn't go downtown to the movies. We couldn't go to any of the eating houses. In fact, all of downtown Baltimore was taboo to blacks."[22] Moore felt that the black community in Baltimore had become "strong and self-sufficient," but there was no doubt in his mind that "white privilege ruled the day in the 1950s" when he made Baltimore his home.[23] Despite the important role that Moore played on the Colts, he could not enjoy life in Baltimore. Still, he was an athletic hero to many fans who, like other black athletes at the time, had to overcome racial boundaries and discrimination. His prominence came to symbolize a hopeful future for black athletes and perhaps fans. Moore's history with Baltimore and with the Colts illustrates the ways in which the NFL challenged and simultaneously perpetuated racial anxieties in the 1950s and 1960s.

Lenny Moore grew up in Reading, Pennsylvania, a blue-collar, steel-manufacturing town. His father was a steelworker, and his mother a domestic. Moore was one of eleven children and the only one to pursue his education past high school. After graduating from high school, Moore attended Penn State University on a football scholarship. He stood out as a college player, but even at Penn State Moore experienced racism and discrimination. Sportswriter Dave Klein notes, "Moore was totally unprepared for the more virulent form of prejudice he found once he joined the NFL," despite having experienced bigotry in college.[24] In 1956, the Colts selected Moore in the first round of the NFL draft.

With the Colts, Moore was a combination flanker and running back. He was named NFL Rookie of the Year in 1956. His speed, paired with teammate Johnny Unitas's passing skills, and a first-rate defense, made the Colts the dominant team in the NFL during the late 1950s.[25]

The Baltimore Colts' most famous game has a special place in NFL history and Lenny Moore played a large part in it. The Colts faced the New York Giants at Yankee Stadium on December 28, 1958, in what became known as "the greatest game ever played." On that memorable late after-noon, the Colts were "a young team of castoffs from a small city that had never participated in a national championship in any sport."[26] To many Baltimoreans, this game was everything; it solidified the city's place in the national spotlight. It was also the first NFL title game to be settled in sudden-death overtime.[27] Moore's main contribution to the game was to act as a decoy and allow Colts' wide receiver Raymond Berry to get open, which he did. Moore's chest and ribs were injured in the second quarter, but he played the entire second half and kept his injuries a secret so as to prevent the Giants from making defensive adjustments.

On Alan Ameche's game-winning touchdown, Moore's key block helped pave the way to victory. Moore was instrumental in other ways too. Former

Colts running back Lenny Moore at the team's training camp in Baltimore, August 1964. *Courtesy of the Associated Press.*

Colts player Gino Marchetti recalls the 1958 game: "I can remember Lenny Moore making one of the greatest catches I've ever seen."[28] Baltimorean and filmmaker Barry Levinson admits, "It was more than a game . . . We had no real identity. And all of a sudden we get to be in a championship game with the New York team, the Giants. It was like the top of the world."[29] For many Baltimoreans, winning the championship legitimized their city. Moore remembers the Colts' win against the Giants and explains that after that game "none of us would ever appear at any event, or even walk down the street in Baltimore, without being recognized."[30] For Moore, however, fame couldn't "crack racial prejudice."[31] In his autobiography *All Things Being Equal* (2005), Moore recounts that by "being a member of the celebrated Colts," he thought that things would be different. But some things never change.[32]

As Moore once explained, "People say we were one family. Well, we weren't."[33] According to Moore, "We knew each other as ball players. But we didn't know each other as men."[34] Once the whistle blew and the game was over, Moore and his white teammates went their separate ways. Journalist Michael Olesker writes that a "pattern had developed." The Colts were "warriors in battle," but their camaraderie and social interaction were limited.[35]

Race relations had much to do with it. During the 1959 preseason, the Colts met the Giants for an exhibition game in Dallas. When the team arrived at the airport, a special bus was sent to retrieve the black players from the plane, as the airport did not allow black people. The black players were also forced to stay at an all-black motel in the black section of town while their white teammates stayed at the Sheraton Hotel in Dallas.[36] The black players on the Giants were also staying at an all-black motel just up the street from Moore's motel. The black Colts players met with the black Giants players and considered boycotting the game in response to the discriminatory treatment. Moore recalls that the next day it "was just the funniest feeling when we showed up at the Cotton Bowl for the game."[37] The Colts won, 28–3, but Moore recalled: "We blacks, on both teams," he said, "had been treated like animals. Like dirt. And we were the champions."[38]

Moore's first coach with the Colts, Weeb Ewbank, tried his best to ignore that he had black and white players on his team. His attitude did not encourage a shift in the racially divided atmosphere of the NFL or Baltimore. Moore states that Ewbank did not want to deal with it. The team was organized in such a way that most of the black players were wide receivers, running backs, or defensive backs, while white players were "awarded the positions closest to the ball."[39] Moore felt that this deliberate practice (known as "stacking") made it easy to cut black players without greatly disturbing the team's "cohesiveness."[40]

Although his relationship with the Colts and Baltimore was challenged by the racial tensions that characterized the era in which he played, Lenny Moore still represented hope for some people in Baltimore's black community, and reflected a future for increased racial integration in athletics. Moore played hard and well for the Colts, and he inspired many Baltimoreans, black and white, and gave them a reason to be proud of their city. At a time when players' names were not featured on the back of their jerseys, and when commentators were not selling individual players as marketing tools to the extent they do today, Lenny Moore stood out among other players in the league—perhaps with the exception of Johnny Unitas. Unitas donned his signature black high tops, but it was Moore's trademark white spats— hence his nickname—that came to "symbolize the syncopated rhythm of the Baltimore offense."[41]

Lenny Moore's time with the Colts came to an end in 1967. He was a seven-time All-Pro and a five-time All-NFL selection. During his twelve-year career with the Colts, Moore gained nearly 12,500 combined yards and scored 113 career touchdowns.[42] Moore's success in the late 1950s was hindered due to injuries, but beginning in 1963 he launched a comeback. During one especially impressive stretch, Moore scored a touchdown in eighteen straight games, an NFL record. In 1964, he was named the NFL Player of the Year, as well as the Associated Press Comeback Player of the Year. The 1964 season came just after two injury-plagued seasons, and sportswriters were skeptical of Moore's return. In response to the dubious sportswriters, Moore had one thing to say. He remembers, "I said, 'I'm going to prove to those that don't think I have it anymore.'"[43] Moore did just that. He was truly deserving of the comeback award in 1964. Eleven years later, he was inducted into the Pro Football Hall of Fame.

Although Moore's Hall of Fame induction is proof of his professional success, Baltimore has recognized Moore as more than an athlete. In a 2008 article, "Old Colt Is Still a Good Team Player," *Baltimore Sun* reporter Julie Bykowicz noted Moore's involvement with the Baltimore community. "Better known for star turn as a halfback in the 1950s and 1960s," Bykowicz wrote, "Lenny Moore has spent the past two dozen years helping troubled teenagers."[44] Since taking a position with Juvenile Services in 1984, Moore has used his NFL connections to arrange trips to training camps and exhibition games with local youth. His years as a football player are over, but Moore has remained an important figure in Baltimore. In 2013, a street in nearby Randallstown, Maryland, was named after him. The street is a testament not only to his athletic success, but also to his commitment to Baltimore. The Pennsylvania native is recognized as an icon within the city that became his adoptive hometown. Additionally, there has been talk about a statue to honor Moore. "After Lenny Moore left the Baltimore Colts, he has spent almost two lifetimes basically helping here in Baltimore City," said Marvin "Doc" Cheatham, president of the Baltimore chapter of the National Action Network and coordinator of a committee to erect a commemorative statue honoring Moore, similar to the one of Frank Robinson at Oriole Park at Camden Yards.[45]

Frank Robinson: Here Comes the Judge

Outfielder Frank Robinson of the Cincinnati Reds was traded to the Baltimore Orioles in December 1965—two seasons before Lenny Moore retired and a year before Earl Monroe joined the Bullets. It was a historically lopsided trade that transformed the Orioles from a good team to a consistent pennant winner.[46] It also surprised and upset Robinson, who was a ten-year veteran with the Reds, muscular and "spindly-legged, high-shouldered, somehow ungainly looking," a former National League Rookie of the Year (1956) and Most Valuable Player (1961).[47] Besides his power hitting, Robinson brought a combativeness and fire to the Orioles, qualities that the team lacked.

"Frank was the most intense ballplayer I've ever seen," said Orioles manager Earl Weaver. "He played the game as hard as anybody. He never, ever gave up on an at-bat no matter what the score was. He'd get a big hit. He went into the stands in New York to make a catch. But what's important is, he did these things every day."[48] Outspoken (if sometimes abrasive) and a leader, Robinson played baseball with passion. "Hard-nosed, no-nonsense baseball. That's the way I've always played the game. That's the way I'll continue to play the game," Robinson explained in his autobiography *My Life is Baseball* (1968).[49]

Certainly Robinson's first season with the Orioles was impressive and historic. He led the American League with a .316 batting average, 49 home runs, and 122 runs batted in, thus becoming one of only thirteen Triple Crown winners and the first since Mickey Mantle in 1956. When he was named the league's Most Valuable Player, Robinson became the only ballplayer to win the award in both circuits.

That same year the underdog Orioles won the World Series, sweeping the Los Angeles Dodgers. Baltimore won the final game 1–0, thanks to Robinson's home run off future Hall of Fame pitcher Don Drysdale. Robinson's heroics earned him the World Series MVP award.[50] In its World Series roundup, *Sports Illustrated* concluded, "in the final evaluation, Frank Robinson was the difference. He won the pennant for Baltimore. He won the Series."[51] Baltimore's superb pitching and defense also helped.

Looking back in 2005, William Gildea, a Baltimorean writing for the *Washington Post,* argued: "That year, 1966, of all his years in baseball, which includes 21 as a major league player and four managerial stints, best defines Robinson's very reason for being, which exists to this notable day in his life: to go all out in every game until opponents feel nothing but sorrow in their hearts, and to do it every day until he has done what he set out to do, winning all there is to win."[52] During his six years with the Orioles (1966–1971), the team won four American League pennants and two World Series and Robinson was a five-time All-Star.

In addition to his stellar, aggressive play, Robinson was a respected team leader. Years later, he reminisced, "I remember [Orioles shortstop] Luis Aparicio once saying to the press, 'Here's a superstar who's always throwing his body around. We felt like if Frank could play that way, we could play that way.' My idea was that just by being myself, I could maybe get people to come together."[53] It worked. Many Orioles gravitated to Robinson. They sought his counsel and approval. "Everybody," said Don Baylor, who was an up-and-coming outfielder with the Orioles in the early 1970s, "flocked to Frank with his problems. How to run the bases, how to play certain stadium walls, how to hit, or whatever. And the way he played the game was the way it should be taught. He was an intimidating, awesome player and if you couldn't learn from watching him, you couldn't learn anything."[54] Baylor evidently learned a great deal. He won the American League MVP with the California Angels in 1979, had a nineteen-year playing career, and, like Robinson, became a Major League manager.

Like many effective teachers, Robinson was not always popular. In 1970, *Look* magazine reported, "He is not, his teammates say, the easiest man in America to deal with."[55] Despite his reputation for being moody and sometimes surly, Robinson could be fun. "At the urging of the coaches," journalist John Eisenberg writes, "he named himself the judge of a kangaroo court, a lighthearted team meeting that convened in the clubhouse after wins and levied fines on players for making stupid comments or bonehead plays."[56] Wearing a mop as a judicial wig and brandishing a gavel, Robinson levied fines for all manner of miscues: missing a signal, failing to get a bunt down, missing the cutoff man, and even showboating.[57] Many Orioles looked forward to this Robinson-led, camaraderie-building, postgame activity. It showed the team how to relax and have a sense of humor in the clubhouse and how to be all business on the field.

While Orioles fans cheered Robinson on the field, he was not always popular with Baltimoreans. *In Black and Blue: The Golden Arm, the Robinson Boys and the 1966 World Series That Stunned America* (2006), Tom Adelman asserts, "A loner who rarely smiled, Robinson was always admired but seldom liked."[58] A proud black man, who had suffered racist taunting and discrimination while in the minor leagues, in Cincinnati when he played for the Reds, and in Baltimore, particularly when he and his wife first moved to town, Robinson was a self-described "loner."[59] He lived an insular life and was not interested in becoming popular with sportswriters or fans. Robinson was candid: "Baseball, really, is all that matters with me. It's what my life is all about."[60] That seems to have been the case. As a result of this singular focus there were and are Baltimoreans, like Harvey Polston, an African American octogenarian, who think Robinson was "on the snooty side," aloof, too removed from the black community.[61] Likewise, Willard Wright, a Dunbar High 1956 graduate, says that Lenny Moore and Frank Robinson did not hang out with or make strong connections with many local black folks.[62]

This is unfortunate, as Robinson was and remains a strong, straightforward man who champions racial justice when it comes to Major League Baseball. He is defined, contends sportswriter Thomas Boswell, by "his glowingly upright character, his authentic, often uncompromising integrity."[63] These qualities were often on display throughout his Orioles playing career and again years later when he managed the team, from 1988 to 1991. Over time, Robinson "made an effort to be more outgoing, to be more relaxed, and to smile more." He mellowed and developed some perspective.[64] Yet through it all he never lost his desire to win—and to be respected as a man.

"The trade to the Orioles worked out very well for me," Robinson mused in 2006. "I played hard, but sometimes you need a jolt in life—and that gave me one. Sometimes a bump in the road is painful, but this turned out to be the best thing that ever happened to me."[65] And one of the best things that ever happened to the Baltimore Orioles and its fans.

Not long after the April 2015 riots that seared Baltimore, Robinson returned to the city. Along with current Orioles outfielders Adam Jones and Delmon Young, executive director of the Major League Baseball Players Association Tony Clark, Mayor Stephanie Rawlings-Blake, and others, the seventy-nine-year-old Robinson was on hand to donate equipment, do some coaching, sign autographs, and to mentor James Mosher Little Leaguers in west Baltimore. Standing in front of the crowd, his hand resting on a young ballplayer's shoulder, Robinson said: "This is the perfect time after the situation here [i.e., the recent riots] for the sports families to get in here and let these people know that we are staying with them, and we are here to try to help them. We want these kids to understand that they have someone to look up to and someone that cares about them and wants to be involved with them."[66] Robinson is not from Baltimore and no longer lives there. But there he was, on a hot summer day, giving back to the city that gave him so much.

Earl "the Pearl" Monroe

Whenever the 6-foot-3 guard Earl "the Pearl" Monroe entered the Baltimore Civic Center in 1967 and beyond, chants of "Earl, Earl, Best in the World!" would echo throughout the arena. Monroe was a legendary basketball player with the Baltimore Bullets from 1967 to 1971. His time in Baltimore was relatively short yet impactful on the community. Years later, the *Baltimore Sun* reported that despite Monroe's "knobby knees, a skinny frame and elbows that looked like sharpened pencils," his "reverse spins, no-look passes and between-the-legs dribbles juiced the Baltimore Bullets, and their fans, for four seasons and carried the team to the NBA Finals in 1971."[67] He was known for his flashy, improvisational play, such as his famed "flukey-dukey" shots.[68] Fellow Bullets teammate Ray Scott once said, "God couldn't go one-on-one with Earl Monroe."[69] At the time, it barely seemed like hyperbole.

Monroe's perseverance and talent inspired audiences of every race, but the African American community especially took pride in having a black superstar athlete who could awe basketball fans all over. In almost every description of or statement about Monroe, his race is mentioned only once or twice, if at all. What made him different was not his racial identity. It was, as filmmaker and basketball fan Woody Allen wrote, "the indescribable heat of genius that burns deep inside him. Some kind of diabolical intensity comes across his face when he has the ball."[70] Ultimately, Monroe, nicknamed "Black Magic" (and "The Black Jesus"), transcended race and became a popular icon in Baltimore.

Monroe was born and raised in Philadelphia, Pennsylvania, and was known by his high school teammates as "Thomas Edison," due to the many moves he invented on the court.[71] By his senior year of high school, Monroe's statewide reputation had established NBA players stopping by to see him play.[72] After graduating from high school, Monroe played under the legendary Clarence "Big House" Gaines at Winston-Salem State College in North Carolina, originally as center and later as a point guard.[73] Monroe averaged 7.1 points as a freshman, 23.2 his sophomore year, 29.8 during his junior year, and an unheard of 41.5 as a senior.[74] In 1967, he earned the NCAA College Division Player of the Year award.[75] NBA scouts scurried to every game to see him play. "Earl's Pearls," as newspapers dubbed his record-breaking statistics, not only gave him his nickname, but a start in the NBA.[76]

The Baltimore Bullets had a mixed past. In the beginning, they were not a winning team, and were disbanded after two straight dismal seasons (1952–1954).[77] Many Baltimoreans figured that the team reflected poorly on the city. Then, in 1963, the Chicago Zephyrs (originally the Packers) moved to Baltimore after two years of being last in the league. The Zephyrs arrived in a new town with new coaches and a new building (the Baltimore Civic Center) for the 1963–1964 season, and the team was renamed the Baltimore Bullets. Slowly improving season after season, they went from fourth in the NBA's Western Division during the 1964–1965 season to a surprising second place in 1965–1966.[78] Then, in 1967, Earl Monroe arrived.

Monroe was the second pick in the NBA draft and signed a two-year contract with the Bullets.[79] In the Bullets' opening game against the New York Knicks, Monroe established himself as a crowd favorite. He wowed the audience with his tricky plays, dribbling between his legs, and passing behind his back. His "unique shooting and dashing ball control" amazed everyone who saw him.[80] Due to Monroe's fame, ticket sales for the Bullets grew substantially, setting new attendance records. His flashy style made fans optimistic about Baltimore's chances for the rest of the season. The optimism briefly died down when the Bullets hit a losing streak, and it became clear that each man was playing for himself rather than for the team. Monroe was the biggest factor in getting the Bullets to function as a team.[81] He became the team's "quarterback," as his teammates looked to him for leadership. Monroe delivered and the Bullets improved.[82]

Monroe had an outstanding rookie season, though the Bullets finished last in the Eastern Division. He averaged 24.3 points per game and led Baltimore in games played, minutes played, field goals attempted, field goals made, free throws attempted, free throws made, and assists.[83] He was also the Bullets' top scorer. All of this contributed to him winning the NBA's Rookie of the Year award. Monroe was famous for saying, "The thing is, I don't know what I'm going to do with the ball, and if I don't know, I'm quite sure the guy guarding me doesn't know either."[84]

Today, Earl Monroe may not be a household name like Earvin "Magic" Johnson or Larry Bird, but sportswriter Mike Wise explains, "Monroe spun his body 360 degrees in midair before [Michael] Jordan or LeBron James's *mother* were born. So unpredictable, so original. Monroe painted more than he played, and the court was his canvas."[85] Many Baltimoreans were enamored with Monroe's playing style. Perhaps it was because the city gained recognition due to Monroe's and the team's success.

Perhaps it was also because the African American community considered Monroe to be an icon during the turbulent 1960s and early 1970s, just as Lenny Moore and Frank Robinson were in the 1950s and 1960s. Monroe grew up in a rough Philadelphia neighborhood where the slums were some of the worst in the country. According to writer Robert B. Jackson, "the poverty, crime, and dreary hopelessness—not to mention the segregation— of the ghetto made a strong impression on [Monroe] as a young boy."[86] Monroe thus identified with the racial tensions in Baltimore because they echoed some of his experiences in Philadelphia.

Regarding racism in basketball, Monroe writes in his autobiography *Earl the Pearl: My Story* (2013), "You can't really appreciate good things that happen to you unless you've had a lot of problems in your life that you've been able to work through. I understood that some of my motivation to succeed was a desire to become good at something a lot of people thought I couldn't do, and that some of my drive came from being very dark skinned."[87] Monroe faced many obstacles growing up because of his racial identity and the culture's discriminatory practices.

When he started getting national recognition, some of those obstacles intensified. Monroe showed fans in Baltimore that it was possible to overcome those challenges. Perhaps "from exclusions comes invention," says the narrator in the ESPN documentary *Black Magic* (2008), which examines the struggle for civil rights on the court as experienced by African American basketball players, particularly those from historically black colleges.[88] Monroe gave hope and optimism to disenfranchised people and a community that deeply needed it. As "the Black Jesus," Monroe instilled faith in Baltimore basketball fans by invigorating the community, as well as communities near Baltimore—down-on-their-luck communities that needed healthy doses of Monroe's "Black Magic" too.

Journalist Wil Haygood, for example, recounts the first time he saw Monroe play as "new, vivid, and soulful . . . he was Houdini on the court, hiding the ball behind his back, revealing it at the last moment. But he also had the coolness of a white-gloved butler circling the dinner table."[89] Haygood recounts the morning he and his friends found out the Bullets were coming to play in his hometown of Columbus, Ohio. As a thirteen-year-old African American boy, Haygood was thrilled. After all, his hero was coming to town. Haygood was not the only one excited by the news. Whole neighborhoods in Columbus changed once people found out Monroe would be arriving. People were running around, scrounging together their last paychecks in order to obtain a ticket to see Monroe play. Haygood explains that in Monroe, as well as other athletes of the era, some people "found freedom in [his] expressions."[90] They found his play not just joyful, but liberating.

During the 1970–1971 season, after a contract squabble, Monroe was traded to the New York Knicks. Monroe would later blame the trade on "the naiveté of his younger self."[91] In return, he got more money and a longer contract. This news was widely publicized, as the Bullets and the Knicks were rivals. It was sometimes reported as a story of betrayal; how could Monroe abandon Baltimore? His defection from the Bullets to the Knicks was unimaginable to some Baltimore fans. Monroe later regretted the trade. While he arguably achieved more fame and success with the Knicks, New York was not Baltimore.[92] For better or worse, depending on whom one asks, Monroe's playing style changed as well.

According to some NBA insiders, Monroe was conflicted because he really wanted to stay in Baltimore. He wanted to remain with the team that he helped build in the city that accepted him. Of course, he wanted to get paid too. When discussing the dramatic career shift with friends, he was constantly asked, "Can you go to New York and fit into that style? Can you fit in?"[93] The implication that Monroe could not fit in somewhere annoyed him. The Knicks style of play was the antithesis to the type of schoolyard basketball Monroe grew up playing.[94] The Knicks were more structured, organized, and corporate, and thus many doubted whether Monroe would be able to adapt. Once he debuted with the Knicks, the skepticism subsided. Earl Monroe knew how to play basketball, and on his debut with the Knicks he received a standing ovation and lived up to the hype.[95]

Monroe spent twice as many seasons with the Knicks than with the Bullets and won a championship with New York in 1973. But New York only saw flashes of the Black Jesus.[96] The sacrifice he made to fit in with the Knicks—giving up his showmanship and superstardom for traditional play—became painful for some of his fans to watch. Those who grew up playing with him or watching him during his college or Bullets days hardly recognized "the role player he'd become in New York."[97] It seemed that Monroe cheated himself by giving up his individuality to become part of the Red Holzman–coached Knicks. Monroe spoke of the difficulties of being just another cog in the Knicks machine, saying, "As far as my game, it went from spectacular to being like a student. It was very hard . . . I'd always played at a certain pace and rhythm, managed the game as opposed to just playing it."[98] Monroe's time with the Knicks seemed to squash the joy Monroe had for the sport. The Bullets embraced Monroe's creativity and encouraged his flash and flare. Baltimore *needed* him; the team needed someone to enliven the entire Baltimore community.

Earl Monroe did just that. Unlike the Bullets, the Knicks did not need or want Monroe's hardwood magic. Even Monroe never thought of himself as a real Knick. His heart always remained with Baltimore. Monroe once said, "I always felt as though the Bullets and Baltimore was the way I made my name."[99] When the Basketball Hall of Fame came calling in 1990, Monroe went in as a Bullet. "I felt that was the way to go," Monroe said on his induction, "Baltimore took a chance on me and gave me the opportunity to be 'Earl The Pearl.'"[100]

Even though Earl Monroe only spent four years in Baltimore, he made an impact on the community. He certainly helped shape the culture of modern basketball. At the same time, he was "less a symbol of basketball's evolution than society's," suggests Mike Wise.[101] Monroe represented more than stunning plays on the court: he represented black empowerment and an improvisational, freewheeling aesthetic. Wise argues that Monroe "married sport and pop culture long before" Michael Jordan.[102] He was an "anti-establishment cult figure in a sport fast becoming a bastion of black expression."[103] To many Baltimoreans, Monroe will always be a Bullet.

Conclusion

Lenny Moore, Frank Robinson, and Earl Monroe accomplished exactly what their teams had hoped for and more. They made the Colts, Orioles, and Bullets extremely competitive, and, in the cases of Moore and Robinson, helped their teams win championships. They also helped generate local and national attention and revenue for their teams. Of course, much of this occurred during some of the most turbulent times of the civil rights movement and the fight for racial equality and integration. According to some but not all black Baltimoreans, these three sports icons were excellent role models who provided inspiration and pride in local black communities. Other people saw them as outsiders, non-Baltimoreans, men who merely worked in the city, lived there part time, and did not become enmeshed in the community or its social life. Both perspectives coexist.

Nonetheless, Moore, Robinson, and Monroe's collective accomplishments served Baltimore in at least two ways. First, the city undoubtedly achieved national prominence due to their individual and team successes. The Colts were regularly on TV during Moore's career, for example, as were the Orioles when they reached the postseason. Second, the achievements of these men and their teams fostered pride in some African American community members that brought about a sense of belonging that transcended racial barriers. Blacks and whites, from all over Baltimore, cheered and rooted for Moore, Robinson, and Monroe. That is, the pride that some people felt in Moore, Robinson, and Monroe was not a one-way street. Thanks to the contributions of these men, some white people and communities began to be more accepting of black people. In other words, the accomplishments of these athletes, in some small way, promoted racial tolerance and acceptance in and beyond Baltimore.

To their credit, Lenny Moore, Frank Robinson, and Earl Monroe navigated the racial tensions that persisted during the years in which they played in Baltimore—sometimes deftly, sometimes with difficulty—and their play was consistently great and frequently superlative. As this book makes clear, Baltimore has a rich athletic and cultural history. Moore, Robinson, and Monroe are enmeshed within both of them. Their careers as athletes are emblematic not only of the city's impressive athletic success, but of the cultural changes that occurred as all three players participated in their respective sports during a time characterized by political and social tension and inequality. In the process they became Baltimore and African American athletic icons and incandescent stars, which all these years later still burn in many memories.

15

Orange and Black Forever

How a New Yorker Fell in Love with
Earl Weaver's Baltimore Orioles

LEE LOWENFISH

*In her old age, she had become a great Orioles fan. She would listen on
the radio if she couldn't attend in person, even staying up past her bed-
time if the game went into extra innings. Baseball was the only sport that
made sense, she said: clear as Parcheesi, clever as chess. . . . She liked to
think of the Orioles as poverty-stricken and virtuous, unable to simply buy
their talent as richer teams did. Players' looks mattered to her as deeply
as if they were movie stars: Ken Singleton's high, shining cheekbones, as
described by one of her granddaughters, sent her into a little trance of
admiration. . . . She thought Earl Weaver was not fatherly enough
to be a proper manager and often, when he replaced some poor sad
pitcher, who'd barely had a chance, she would speak severely
into the radio, calling him "Merle Beaver" for spite and spitting
out her words. "Just because he grows his own tomatoes," she said,
"doesn't necessarily mean a person has a heart."*
—Anne Tyler, *Dinner at the Homesick Restaurant*

People have often asked me, "How can a New Yorker root so passionately
for the Baltimore Orioles?" The explanation goes "way back in the way
back," a folksy expression for the good old days that I first heard from Paul
Richards, the Texas-reared baseball brain who established the foundation

199

of the modern Orioles organization in the 1950s. You see, I grew up in New York City, the son of a New York Giants fan who never could accept the rise of the Yankees and their fans' outrageous sense of entitlement. I inherited early on this proud passion as a life principle.

I enjoyed some moments of glory when Bobby Thomson hit his dramatic playoff home run against the Brooklyn Dodgers. Over sixty years later I can still picture where I was standing in my parents' living room listening on their Crosley floor model radio as broadcaster Russ Hodges screamed four times, "The Giants win the pennant!" However, the joy wore off when the Yankees foiled the Giants in the World Series. Three years later the 1954 Giants, skippered by Leo Durocher and led by the irrepressible Willie Mays, thrilled this young teenager by winning another pennant. Their World Series sweep came against the Cleveland Indians, not the Yankees, so it didn't taste as good.

After the 1957 season, the Giants and the Dodgers fled to the West Coast. I was cast adrift without a team to call my own. Of course, I continued rooting against the Yankees, but my formative years were frustrating because the Yankees appeared in every World Series between 1949 and 1964 except for 1954 and 1959, when the Cleveland Indians and the Chicago White Sox won American League pennants.

Happily, there were signs that the current Yankees dynasty was coming to an end. I was elated when Bill Mazeroski hit his glorious walk-off home run in the seventh game of the 1960 World Series to win it all for the Pirates. I relished the Dodgers' humiliation of the haughty Yankees in four straight games in the 1963 World Series and, though the Yankees did stretch the 1964 Series to seven games, in the end the St. Louis Cardinals prevailed. Starting in 1965, the Yankees' eleven-year pennant drought commenced. "At long last you spoiled princes of entitlement have to join the human race of scuffling mortals," I thought happily.

Yet for all my genuine *schadenfreude* at the Yankees' new predicament, I knew that baseball is best enjoyed by having a team to root *for*, not just against. From hundreds of miles away in Madison, Wisconsin, where I was studying American history in graduate school at the University of Wisconsin, I began to take notice of the emerging Baltimore Orioles. They wore similar colors, orange and black, that my departed Giants sported, and, more important, they showed signs of becoming a regular contender for the American League pennant. In 1966 they shocked the baseball world by sweeping the Dodgers in the World Series. Back-to-back home runs by Frank and Brooks Robinson in the first inning of the first game of the Series set the tone and shutout pitching by Jim Palmer, Wally Bunker, and Dave

McNally closed the deal. So much for the invincibility of future Hall of Fame L.A. mound aces Don Drysdale and Sandy Koufax.[1]

The Orioles seemed like a promising team: a mixture of youngsters developed in the farm system, such as Brooks Robinson, Palmer, and McNally, and players obtained in savvy trades, like Frank Robinson, who in 1966 became the first player to win the Most Valuable Player award in both Major Leagues after foolishly being described as "an old thirty" and traded by the Cincinnati Reds after the 1965 season.[2] I became even more enamored by the Orioles' success when I learned in Baltimore sportswriter Gordon Beard's wonderful book about the 1966 Orioles, *Birds on the Wing* (1967), that from mid-July 1964 through the entire 1966 season they conquered the Yankees twenty-one out of twenty-five games at Yankee Stadium.[3]

Could my quest for a team to call my own have been answered? The Orioles seemed like Cinderella, a team emerging from the woebegone shell of a St. Louis Browns franchise so poor that it wore unwashed uniforms and used dirty baseballs in its last home game and now a mere twelve years later were World Series champions.[4]

However, I knew that the real test of a successful franchise is competing for a pennant every September, and the Orioles had not yet reached that rarefied atmosphere. The Orioles fell under .500 in 1967, partly due to injuries suffered by Jim Palmer and Frank Robinson. At the All-Star Game break in 1968, with the team only six games over .500 and already 10½ games behind the high-flying Detroit Tigers, manager Hank Bauer, who led the 1966 team to its title, was fired. He was replaced by one of his coaches, Earl Weaver, a onetime minor league second baseman that had served a long apprenticeship as a manager in the Orioles minor league system. That seemed a wise choice to me given that Weaver was homegrown and, for heaven's sake, Bauer's roots were with the enemy; he was a former Yankee right fielder who had won seven World Series championship rings in New York.[5]

Just a few weeks after Earl Weaver took the helm in Baltimore, I arrived in town, a newly minted PhD from Wisconsin starting a teaching job at Goucher College in Towson, Maryland, just north of Baltimore. It was purely coincidence, of course, but I like to think that kismet played a role in bringing me to Baltimore. Starting with Weaver's first full season in 1969 and through 1982, the Orioles enjoyed an enviable run of three straight 100-plus-win seasons, three straight appearances in the World Series, including a 1970 World Series title, six American League East division titles, and an amazing average of more than 95 wins a season.[6]

Earl Weaver's Orioles didn't win enough in October to be ranked in baseball history as a dynasty—he actually won only the 1970 World Series—but they sure played fundamentally sound baseball. His formula was the simple one of Pitching, Defense, and Three-Run Homers. Looking back on his career shortly before his induction into the Baseball Hall of Fame in 1996, Weaver reflected, "I came here in 1968 when urban areas were being demolished by riots and fires, . . . but, after the turmoil subsided, it didn't take me long to find out I was in a baseball town."[7]

He certainly was right about Baltimore as a baseball town. It welcomed excellence at the highest level without taking on self-important big city airs. Memorial Stadium may have lacked grandeur and quirkiness but it was a substantial edifice that took the name "Memorial" seriously. In *Ballpark: Camden Yards and the Building of an American Dream* (1994), Peter Richmond notes that in a glass case in the old stadium lobby there resided a brass urn "containing a teaspoon of dirt from every foreign cemetery on earth where an American serviceman or woman is buried."[8] Fans who crossed Thirty-Third Street to enter the ballpark could look up and see atop the façade a stirring paean that began, "To All Who So Valiantly Fought And Served In The World Wars," and ended, "Time Will Not Dim The Glory of Their Deeds."

Memorial Stadium was located in a residential neighborhood not far from one of the classiest and most verdant thoroughfares in Baltimore, Charles Street. Right fielder Ken Singleton, who came to Baltimore from the Montreal Expos in a trade before the 1975 season and became a stalwart player for a decade, told Peter Richmond: "Charles Street was a street that dictated baseball. It'd start with the early leaves, then full bloom, and then in the fall, as the season was ending, the leaves were falling. And every year you wished it would go on forever."[9]

Though I returned to live in my hometown of New York during the 1976 season, I made regular trips to Baltimore to see my team continue its winning ways. I cherish memories of sitting in inexpensive upper-deck seats at Memorial Stadium and looking out at the cluster of stately trees beyond the scoreboard and the center field fence that provided a good backdrop for the hitters. There was also enough soil in left field foul territory for Weaver to engage in tomato-growing contests with head groundskeeper Pat Santarone, who had worked with Weaver at the Orioles' farm club in Elmira, New York. Unlike Anne Tyler's fictional Pearl Tull, I found Weaver's gardening hobby humanizing.

One night walking down Thirty-Third Street on my way to the ballpark, I nodded approval at a billboard that advertised: "Orioles Baseball—A

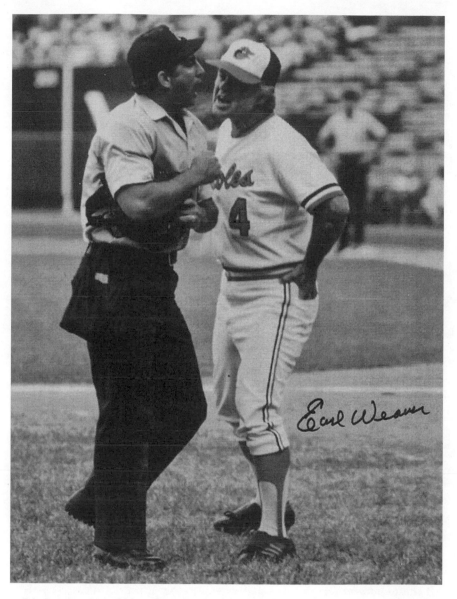

Diminutive, irascible, and a winner, Baltimore Orioles manager Earl Weaver.
Image by and courtesy of Scott Hubert.

Drama in 18 Acts . . . At Least." On another night, I was sitting in the upper deck and caught a foul ball hit by Brooks Robinson. To be completely honest, I didn't exactly catch it but grabbed it when it lodged in the slats of a chair a few empty seats away. Attendance was sparse that night and the lack of fans would always be an issue in a town without a long heritage of Major League Baseball. In his memoir *Over Time: My Life as a Sportswriter* (2012), Baltimore-bred Frank Deford admits to "the defensive spirit of my city, the sense that we were an ugly duckling."[10] Yet the Orioles played proud and intelligent baseball at Memorial Stadium, where pitching and defense could shine because, although it was only 309 feet down the foul lines, the power alleys were 376 feet away, and it was 405 to dead center. (When Memorial Stadium first opened for the Orioles in 1954, the dimensions were truly staggering: 445 feet to dead center field with both power alleys over 400 feet.)[11]

One never knew when umpire-baiter extraordinaire Earl Weaver would explode. I recall one game against the Oakland Athletics, the Orioles' nemesis in 1973 and 1974 who beat them in the playoffs and kept them from the World Series both years. The A's shortstop Bert Campaneris hit a high fly ball down the left field line that the umpires ruled a home run. Angry fans started throwing paper cups along the third base line in foul territory as Weaver raced out with his hat turned backward protesting the call. (He turned his hat around to make sure the bill of his cap wouldn't make contact with the umpire, an offense that would mean immediate ejection.) He took the discarded cups and created his own foul line to indicate how far off the umps' call had been. Several times he pointed his hands melodramatically into foul territory. Then, on his way back to the dugout en route to his banishment to the clubhouse, he kicked aside many of those cups.

Then there was the night in late June 1977 when I was listening to the second game of an Orioles doubleheader in Cleveland on the radio back in New York. I was tuned into Washington's WTOP 1500 AM station. When broadcaster Bill O'Donnell—or perhaps it was Chuck Thompson of "Go to war, Miss Agnes" fame—informed me that the Orioles lost the second game on a throwing error by rookie second baseman Rich Dauer, I angrily turned off the radio and went to bed. I awoke the next morning to discover that, thanks to Weaver's knowledge of the rules, the umpires had been mistaken when they awarded two bases and the winning run to Cleveland on Dauer's error. An infielder's errant throw costs only one base; an outfielder's throw into the stands costs two bases. The Orioles wound up winning the game in extra innings to salvage a split of the doubleheader.

In 1977, the Orioles won ninety-seven games despite the loss of All-Star second baseman Bobby Grich and slugger Reggie Jackson to the first year of free agency. The Birds still battled the Red Sox and Yankees down to the last weekend of the season before they fell just short of the revived Bronx Bombers under manager Billy Martin. It was the rookie season of switch-hitting Eddie Murray, and Weaver wisely broke him in at designated hitter while Lee May, who became a great mentor to the future Hall of Famer, continued to play first base. During this surprisingly competitive season, obscure players called up from the minor leagues made major contributions. In a late July game at Memorial Stadium, for instance, third-string catcher Dave Criscione hit the only home run of his career to win an extra-inning game.[12] Later in September, in a game against the Chicago White Sox, in his first Major League chance in the field, outfielder Mike Dimmel threw out the potential game-tying run at home plate and one out later the Orioles won the game.[13]

After winning the pennant convincingly in 1979 but losing a tough seven-game World Series to the Pittsburgh Pirates, the Orioles contended again in 1980, engaging in a fierce battle with the Yankees for the AL East title. Because of rainouts, the teams had to play eight games in eleven days in the middle of August. I attended seven of the games, six of which were won by the Orioles, including a three-game sweep at Yankee Stadium. I missed the last game of this remarkable eight-game stretch because I was in a Washington, DC, radio studio doing an interview promoting my first book, *The Imperfect Diamond: The Story of Baseball's Reserve System and the Men Who Fought to Change It* (1980).

The jacket copy contained a drawing of a baseball infield torn asunder, ripped apart because of labor-management disputes. Earl Weaver had been a rare management figure that sided with the players on the issue of free agency, agreeing with them that at some point in one's career a player should be able to choose his next employer. He felt that a good organization should be able to make up for lost players with a good farm system and additions by trades—if other organizations lacked the intelligence and talent, they should learn from the successful ones or go out of business.

During the Orioles' next Florida spring training in Fort Lauderdale, I gave a copy of my book to Orioles press secretary Phil Itzoe to give to Weaver. I came back the next day, introduced myself to Weaver, and asked if he had received my book. "Do you mean 'Broken Diamond?'" he said. To my astonishment he started reciting to longtime Orioles coach Cal Ripken Sr. chapter and verse from my book about the early history of pro baseball when the American League was a rebel circuit against the established National League. Referring to two of the most conservative later owners, Weaver chortled, "Can you believe that Connie Mack and Clark Griffith were once on the side of a players' union?"

I shouldn't have been surprised that Earl Weaver had begun to read *The Imperfect Diamond*. After all, once he became nationally famous for his three 100-win seasons from 1969 through 1971, he became a darling of many publishers. His titles included *Winning!* (1972), *Weaver on Strategy* (1984), and the one with the title lifted from one of President Harry Truman's favorite sayings, *It's What You Learn After You Know It All That Counts* (1982). Long before statistical analysts began to infiltrate baseball organizations, Weaver was keeping batter-pitcher matchup information on index cards to make better judgments on who should bat against what pitcher.[14]

Not surprisingly, the rest of the Orioles management was not as sanguine as Weaver about the future of the game under free agency. During some of my trips to Baltimore toward the end of Weaver's glory years, I occasionally dropped by the Orioles offices to chat with Jack Dunn III, a team business manager who had started in baseball working for the International League Orioles. Dunn's grandfather, Jack Dunn, was the man who sold Babe Ruth to the Red Sox in 1914 to keep the minor league Orioles afloat during the competition from the short-lived Federal League challenge.[15]

Jack Dunn III doubted baseball could survive unlimited free agency. He questioned whether the desire to excel would continue to motivate players if they received huge salaries and long-term contracts. He quoted jockey Eddie Arcaro's cautionary statement: "It's hard to get up early in the morning when you are wearing silk pajamas." I didn't accept this argument at the time but as the years have passed and the salaries in baseball have become mind-boggling, I have become more sympathetic to Dunn's point of view. Despite our differences on free agency, I loved talking baseball with Dunn. We both admired how Weaver could get the best out of a twenty-five-man roster, but Dunn told me that the greatest baseball mind he ever encountered was Paul Richards.

So I decided to look up the story of the man from a farming community outside of Dallas, Texas, who became known as the Wizard of Waxahachie.[16] It is true that Paul Richards never won a pennant as a Major League manager and his views on free agency were even more apoplectic than Jack Dunn's; he famously called the demise of the perpetual reserve system "the end of baseball as we know it."[17] Yet there is no doubt that Richards was one of the finest minds in the game's history. He wrote many articles about baseball and the book *Modern Baseball Strategy* (1955), in which he preached the importance of pitching and defense and the need for constant repetition of fundamentals.

After the Orioles' 100-loss season in 1954, Richards was lured to Maryland when Baltimore's first community ownership group, headed by local securities lawyer Clarence Miles, offered him the positions of both field and general manager. It placed Richards in the select company of Hall of Famers John McGraw and Connie Mack, who also simultaneously held both plum jobs.[18]

The Orioles' ownership provided Richards with an unlimited budget that he immediately spent on young players. Most of his "bonus babies" did not wind up contributing in Baltimore, but Richards did sign the nucleus of the so-called Kiddie Korps pitching staff that first brought the Orioles to pennant contention in 1960: Steve Barber, Chuck Estrada, Jack Fisher, Jerry Walker, and eighteen-year-old Milt Pappas, who came directly to Baltimore after his high school graduation in Detroit.[19]

Richards's greatest early find for the Orioles cost only a $4,000 bonus, Brooks Calbert Robinson Jr., who was signed in June 1955 upon graduation from high school in Little Rock, Arkansas.[20] Richards rushed Robinson to Baltimore when he was only eighteen, and he needed a few more years of minor league seasoning before he arrived to stay in the middle of the 1959 season. He became the first of the franchise's core players that would lead the Orioles into their glory years—a shining example of the Oriole Way of playing good baseball on the field and serving as a role model in the community off it.

The 1960 season in Baltimore provided the first glimpse of the Birds' bright future. The Orioles won eighty-nine games, finishing over .500 for the first time. Farm-raised players were a big reason for their success, especially Brooks Robinson, the Kiddie Korps pitchers, and American League Rookie of the Year, shortstop Ron Hansen. Attendance soared over the million mark in a city that had fallen in love with the Baltimore Colts, who in December 1958 had won the National Football League championship over the New York Giants in a nationally televised "sudden death" overtime game. Until the Orioles proved they were winners, too, they were destined to play second fiddle to the Colts.[21]

Hopes were high in Baltimore for the 1961 season. "It Can Be Done in '61" was adopted as a slogan by team marketers and the Orioles amassed an impressive 95-67 record, but it was only good for third place behind the Yankees and the Detroit Tigers. Attendance dropped from nearly 1,200,000 in 1960 to slightly more than 950,000 in 1961.[22] Before the season was over, Paul Richards resigned to return home to Texas to take over the expansion Houston Colt 45s franchise in the National League.

The handwriting had been on the wall about Richards's departure for some time. Before the start of the 1959 season, Orioles ownership, concerned about his excessive spending on bonuses to young players, removed Richards as general manager and replaced him with Lee MacPhail, who had been director of the highly successful Yankees' farm system.[23] One of MacPhail's assignments was to try to bridge the gap between Richards and the Orioles farm director Jim McLaughlin, a rare holdover who had worked for the St. Louis Browns before the franchise moved to Baltimore. McLaughlin had never been a baseball player, but he was a good administrator who believed deeply in the importance of the mental aspects of baseball. He stressed to all his scouts that they must consider makeup, competitiveness, and family background in evaluating talent.[24]

MacPhail was not successful in getting McLaughlin and Richards to work together and eliminate the factions that had developed within the organization. So after the 1960 season MacPhail dismissed McLaughlin, the last straw probably being that he admittedly "overstepped" his authority by committing $80,000 to the signing of the sensational Billings, Montana, high school southpaw Dave McNally.[25] Thus by the start of the 1962 season both key architects of the Orioles system, Jim McLaughlin and Paul Richards, were no longer with the team. Yet Baltimore's farm system did not miss a beat under McLaughlin's former assistant Harry Dalton.

Dalton, a graduate of Amherst College and a Korean War veteran who started working in Baltimore as an intern, deeply respected the work of baseball scouts and those who worked in player development. He convinced Orioles ownership to reward them with salaries and bonuses higher than those offered by most teams. Gifted Orioles talent hunters were sprinkled all across the United States—Dee Phillips in Texas, Ray Scarborough in the Carolinas, Al Kubski and Donald Pries in California, Walter Youse in Maryland and Pennsylvania, and Frank "Beauty" McGowan in New England, who was so nicknamed because he always dressed impeccably, feeling it was a great advantage when he met the parents of prospective players.

Another reason for Dalton's success was his ability to absorb points of view from a variety of baseball backgrounds. His first scouting director, Walter Shannon, came to the Orioles after nearly thirty years of working for the St. Louis Cardinals, where he learned the ropes under Branch Rickey. Before he left St. Louis, Shannon signed Bob Gibson, Dal Maxvill, and Tim McCarver: three stars of the Cardinals' world champions of 1964 and 1967. Shannon made it a point to speak every day with his farm director Donald Pries, who appreciated the care and the camaraderie that came from the top. "You [felt like you] were an Oriole for life—your bloodstream was in the organization," Pries remembered in 2013, not long before his August 2013 induction into the Orioles Hall of Fame. Pries was the primary author of "The Oriole Way," a thick binder that provided essential information for every player, manager, coach, scout, and player developer in the organization.[26]

Like all good executives working in player development, Walter Shannon believed in the importance of scouting the scouts as well as the players. "I won't know for three to five years and you won't know for three to five years how good a scout you will be," he told former minor league southpaw John Stokoe at the start of Stokoe's nearly thirty-year career as an Orioles scout and scouting supervisor. But if one followed the tenets of the Oriole Way with its focus on fundamentals, athleticism, and intelligence, there was a good chance you would become a valued member of the organization.[27]

Under Dalton, the Orioles soon became the desired destination for many aspiring young executives, several of whom became general managers. Among those who started out as members of the so-called Dalton Gang were Hall of Famer Pat Gillick, a onetime Orioles minor league pitcher, who won World Series rings with the Toronto Blue Jays and Philadelphia Phillies; Lou Gorman, who served as general manager of the Seattle Mariners and the Boston Red Sox; and Baltimore native John Schuerholz, who built champions with the Kansas City Royals and the Atlanta Braves. In Gorman's memoir *High and Inside: My Life in the Front Offices of Baseball* (2007), he said of Dalton, "He welcomed everyone's opinion and judgments but carefully and brilliantly distilled their judgments to make his final decisions."[28]

Harry Dalton also displayed a keen talent for finding the most promising minor league instructors. He convinced two mediocre players, catcher Cal Ripken Sr. and second baseman Earl Weaver, that their future was best served in teaching. They became fixtures at the Orioles' Thomasville, Georgia, minor league training facility where they started their climb toward the Major Leagues. As Paul Hensler has written in his valuable book *The American League in Transition, 1965–1975* (2012), "Thomasville was to the Orioles franchise what Parris Island was to the Marine Corps."[29] No one played the role of drill instructor more diligently and frankly than Earl Weaver.

Harry Dalton first met Earl Weaver in minor league camp, where he spotted him as managerial material. Scouting director Walter Shannon's connection with Weaver went back even further. He had first observed him riding the Weaver family's laundry truck as the baseball-loving lad delivered uniforms to the Cardinals.[30] After Weaver graduated from Beaumont High School in St. Louis, Shannon signed him to his first professional contract, but when it became clear after a few seasons that the scrappy second baseman lacked the goods for the Majors, he encouraged him to try managing. Shannon and Dalton followed Weaver's minor league managing career closely, noting that he won pennants or finished second wherever he worked. They understood that he was blunt, opinionated, and especially pugnacious when influenced by strong waters. But he possessed the saving grace of never carrying a grudge over to the next game, a vital trait in a sport where there was another game the next day and the day after.

When the 1968 season started, Weaver was already on manager Hank Bauer's coaching staff in Baltimore. He had managed in the minors fifteen of the twenty-five Orioles on the 1968 Major League roster and it was only a matter of time before his elevation. With the team only six games over .500 at the All-Star Game break, Harry Dalton won the approval of general manager Frank Cashen and owner Jerry Hoffberger, the local brewery magnate who had become majority owner three years earlier, to make a managerial change. At the age of thirty-seven, Earl Weaver became the youngest manager in the game and was headed for the three best regular seasons of any manager in baseball history.[31]

Though the Orioles did not return to the World Series from 1972 through 1978, the team stayed in contention despite more key changes in the front office. After the 1971 World Series, evidently feeling that he needed new worlds to conquer, Harry Dalton accepted an offer to head the front office of the California Angels. He took many loyal members of the so-called Dalton Gang with him, including key scouts Walter Shannon, Ray Poitevint, and Walter Youse.[32]

After the 1975 season another major change occurred in the front office when Frank Cashen was called back to the brewery by Jerry Hoffberger, who was contemplating selling the team. Henry "Hank" Peters came in as the new general manager, coming over after a stint as chief executive officer of the minor league ruling body, the National Association. Peters was faced almost immediately with the consequences of the Andy Messersmith-Dave McNally decision that, beginning with the end of the 1976 season, created a historic new arrangement under which Major League players with six years of experience could be free agents.[33] (Orioles executives ruefully conceded that McNally brought the same competitive intensity to his historic arbitration case that made him a great pitcher.)

Hank Peters was a calm man at the helm, having previously worked for the volatile Charlie O. Finley of the A's, once in Kansas City and once in Oakland. Peters knew that a big salary tidal wave was coming, but at the end of spring training in 1976 it did not stop him from trading Don Baylor for Reggie Jackson. When Earl Weaver broke the news of the trade to Baylor, the outfielder broke into tears. "It was like being kicked out of the family," explained the team's number two pick in the 1968 amateur draft and whose potential had been a big factor in the team's decision to trade Frank Robinson after the 1971 season.[34]

When Reggie Jackson left Baltimore in the first professional "re-entry" draft to join the Yankees after the 1976 season, the Orioles did not panic, because before the June 15, 1976, trade deadline Hank Peters had pulled the switch on a ten-player deal that landed a solid core of the forthcoming Baltimore World Series teams of 1979 and 1983: catcher Rick Dempsey and southpaw pitchers Scott McGregor and Tippy Martinez. Peters also knew that Eddie Murray was emerging from the Orioles' farm system after serving his minor league apprenticeship.

Before the end of the 1979 season, after years of hesitation, Jerry Hoffberger sold the team to noted Washington attorney Edward Bennett Williams. (Baltimoreans began to live in fear that Williams planned to move the Orioles to DC, which had lost its Washington Senators to Texas after the 1971 season.) It turned out that 1979 was a bad year for Hoffberger to sell because the latest edition of the Orioles was beginning to flower. Farm system products Eddie Murray and Doug DeCinces, who replaced Brooks Robinson at third base, developed nicely, and the homegrown pitching of Mike Flanagan and Dennis Martinez, aided by McGregor and Tippy Martinez, who were pilfered from the Yankees in the 1976 trade, was becoming dominant.

On the business side, the team profited from two decisions made by the usually conservative Hank Peters and his business manager Al Harazin. They moved the team from its longtime radio station WBAL to the more youth-oriented WFBR. They also approved the introduction of an Orioles mascot that cavorted around the stadium to the delight of the younger fans. The pennant-winning 1979 Orioles drew a record number of fans, nearly 1,700,000, over a half-million more than the previous record.[35]

In 1980 the Orioles did not repeat as pennant winners but won 100 games, missing out on the playoffs because the Yankees won 103. In 1981, the Orioles played well but not well enough during the strike-interrupted season to make the playoffs. It spoke volumes about the executive talent developed in the organization that two former Orioles front office leaders, Frank Cashen and Harry Dalton, served on a committee with players Sal Bando and Bob Boone to try to avert the strike. Conciliatory heads on both sides of the labor-management table were too rare and the strike cut two months out of the middle of the 1981 season.

In 1982, the Orioles roared from behind to make a late run at the Milwaukee Brewers in another hotly contested AL East race. They needed to sweep the last four games of the season at home to edge out the power-hitting Brew Crew. After winning the first three games convincingly, they fell short in the final game of the season when, in a matchup of future Hall of Famers, Don Sutton outpitched Jim Palmer on the last day of the season. Early in 1982, Earl Weaver had announced he would retire at the end of the season, but the fans wouldn't leave Memorial Stadium until he came back for a final bow.[36]

Under new manager Joe Altobelli, who had managed many of the Baltimore players in the minors, the 1983 Orioles won the pennant and the World Series with essentially the same personnel that Weaver had come up short with in 1982. It was almost as if the players were saying that they could win without Weaver.[37]

The dark years commenced in 1984, as owner Edward Bennett Williams, terminally ill with cancer, grew more and more impatient. Williams lured Weaver back to manage the team in the middle of the 1985 season. It was an ill-advised decision on both parts. Weaver resigned at the end of the 1986 season in which the Orioles lost a staggering forty-two out of their last fifty-six games. The 1988 season opened with twenty-one straight losses, an embarrassing Major League record, but such was Baltimore's love for the Orioles that 50,000 fans came to a Second Opening Day after the team won their first game on the road.[38] Except for exciting appearances in the 1996 and 1997 playoffs, the Orioles had become a chronic noncontender. Even worse, the Orioles only won one series against the Yankees from 1984 through 2011.

Then in 2012, baseball rebirth came to Charm City.

Under the steady managerial hand of onetime Yankees skipper Nathaniel "Buck" Showalter, the Orioles reversed their 2011 losing record of 69-93 and made the playoffs for the first time since 1997. Then, on the road at Texas, they won the first ever wild-card "play-in" game before losing a tough five-game divisional series to the Yankees.

As a historian and an Orioles fan, I like to think it was more than coincidence that 2012 was also the year that the team unveiled statues at Oriole Park at Camden Yards of six Baltimore Hall of Famers: Brooks and Frank Robinson, Jim Palmer, Eddie Murray, Cal Ripken Jr., and Earl Weaver—who managed them all to triumph in his heyday from 1968 through 1982. The word magic is overused in sports, but the confluence of saluting the past as the present and future suddenly looked brighter struck me as relevant in 2012.

It was the twentieth anniversary of Oriole Park at Camden Yards, the first of the new "retro" ballparks. (Before Edward Bennett Williams died in 1988, he succeeded in tough negotiations with the state of Maryland in arranging for the building of a baseball-only ballpark that assured the Orioles would remain in Baltimore indefinitely.)[39] In addition to refurbishing the ballpark's brick-and-mortar structure and modernizing the concessions stands, owner Peter Angelos, a local lawyer who had bought the team at a bankruptcy auction in 1994, made a strong commitment to honoring Orioles greats by commissioning Maryland-based sculptor Toby Mendez. Mendez had drawn accolades for his previous work: realistic statues of

Nolan Ryan at the Texas Rangers' ballpark in Arlington, football coach Don Shula at the Miami Dolphins stadium, and Johnny Pesky and Dom DiMaggio at Fenway Park.[40]

"Always buy local when you can choose local," said architect Janet Marie Smith, explaining the choice of Mendez.[41] Smith had been intimately involved with the original construction of Oriole Park at Camden Yards and, after working on the 1996 Atlanta Olympic stadium and its conversion into baseball's Turner Field and improvements to Fenway Park, returned to Baltimore in 2009 to oversee renovations.

"It was my most thoroughly reviewed project," sculptor Toby Mendez said. Many players, including Terry Crowley, a valuable Oriole reserve in the glory years and later the team's hitting coach, came to examine the drawings to make sure the most minute detail of muscle and movement was just right, Mendez recalled.[42]

In six separate ceremonies, the Orioles immortals expressed their gratified emotions in distinctive ways. Bright, high-strung perfectionist Jim Palmer saluted sculptor Mendez, quipping, "There's a little bit of fear in that face, so you got it right." The always-gracious Brooks Robinson began by telling the huge crowd, "I just want to say to all of you fans here, I don't like to call you fans, I like to call you friends." Though he died in 1999, the spirit of Cal Ripken Sr. could be felt everywhere. "Old Man Rip. Special man," Eddie Murray said. "I think if he loved you, he liked you, that man would overwhelm you with knowledge of baseball."[43]

Another touching aspect about the 2012 ceremonies was that Earl Weaver lived to attend them all, to smell the roses and hear the applause for the last time. He died early in January 2013, just a few months after the Orioles 2012 season of rebirth. Many fans paid their respects by placing wreaths on his Camden Yards sculpture that depicted him with his hands in his back pockets and a furrowed brow, likely questioning an umpire's call. Throughout the 2013 season, the team paid homage to its departed former skipper by prominently featuring his number 4 on a uniform sleeve. It was a fitting gesture for what the stewardship of the Earl of Baltimore had meant to Orioles baseball, the city, and its many fans. It was a mutually shared affection because, as Weaver said at the end of his speech in 1996 upon his induction into the Baseball Hall of Fame: "I'm proud of the fact that I spent my whole major league career in one city, and for that I would like to thank the wonderful fans of Baltimore for letting me stay."[44]

16

A Missed Opportunity

Baltimore's Failed Stadium Project, 1969–1974

RICHARD HARDESTY

In 1971, Baltimore stood atop the sporting world. Several months earlier, in October 1970, the Orioles had made their second straight World Series appearance, defeating the Cincinnati Reds in five games. Three months later, it was the Colts' turn, appearing in their second Super Bowl in three years. In thrilling fashion, the Colts captured Super Bowl V on a last-second field goal by Jim O'Brien. The Bullets thrived, too. In 1971, Baltimore's sad sack professional sports team advanced to the NBA finals. Even though the Bullets would end up losing, the Orioles and Colts' success led *Baltimore Sun* columnist Bob Maisel to chortle, "if you want to call Baltimore the city of champions you've got my permission, because being on top of the heap in both baseball and football isn't something that happens often."[1]

The success of the Orioles, Colts, and Bullets masked a problem that threatened Baltimore's standing as a professional sports town. By 1971, the owners of all three teams had become disillusioned with the city. The Bullets suffered from public disinterest and ultimately moved to Washington, DC, in 1973. Both the Orioles and Colts were dissatisfied with Memorial Stadium and refused to commit to the city. More problematic, Colts owner Carroll Rosenbloom threatened to move his team elsewhere. Local and state officials responded by proposing the construction of a state-of-the-art sports complex in Camden Yards, near the harbor, just south of downtown. Designed not only to keep the Orioles and Colts but also to attract a new basketball team, the proposed complex sparked controversy. The fear was that public funds would be used. In 1974, Baltimoreans voted it down.

Without the complex, Baltimore's newfound reputation as a sports town was in jeopardy.

The Orioles and Colts linked their long-term profitability to a new stadium and the fan experience it facilitated. Memorial Stadium, the home venue of the Orioles and Colts, had problems—too few parking spaces, for example, and some obstructed-view seats. Proponents of the sports complex argued that the new venue would provide better views and increase the Orioles and Colts' profits. Not building the complex contributed to the Colts moving to Indianapolis in 1984. After the Colts left, it became apparent that a new stadium needed to be built if city leaders wanted to keep the Orioles and attract a new NFL franchise. The failed sports complex marked the beginning of the long, painful process that led to the development of Camden Yards, which is now widely considered to be a huge success.[2]

The failed sports complex told a larger story that extended beyond the issues of profits, loss, and sporting redemption. It was one tied to urban identity and redevelopment. Supporters viewed the sports complex as a "catalyst to rebuilding" downtown Baltimore, and argued that sport could play an influential role in the development of the Inner Harbor. The Orioles and Colts, supporters suggested, would provide the impetus to attract people

Home to the Colts and the Orioles, Memorial Stadium was razed in 2002.
Image by and courtesy of Scott Hubert.

and businesses back to the city. By tying sports to redevelopment, the complex linked Baltimore's identity to its professional sports teams. The city, for its part, played up the Orioles and Colts' championships, creating civic pride. But without a new sports complex, proponents argued, Baltimore would suffer a loss of stature. They were correct. In 1973, the Bullets left town, and soon word circulated that the Orioles and Colts might leave too. Without the sports complex, Baltimore would go from the city of champions to the graveyard of sports teams.[3]

The Orioles and Colts' main concern was the condition of Memorial Stadium. Part of the problem was the price of the venue. The main structure, which opened in 1950, cost Baltimore $6.5 million. However, as Frederic B. Hill of the *Baltimore Sun* reported in 1972, the design of "the 33d street structure . . . had a lot to do with its problems." Concrete supports, for instance, were cheaper than cantilevered decking. But the supports had their own issues: they created many obstructed-view seats, which the Orioles and Colts had a difficult time selling. Worse, the position of the supports prevented serious improvements to seating capacity. It was just too expensive. The seats themselves also had problems. They were uncomfortable. Many were benches. Maryland governor Marvin Mandel, a Colts ticket holder, had to pick out three splinters from his pants after one game in 1972.[4]

Seating represented only one problem. Memorial Stadium did not have enough concession stands, creating lines "slow as ever." The bathroom facilities were even worse. There were too few restrooms and the toilets lacked seats. Parking, however, represented the biggest problem. The stadium did not have enough spots, causing frustrating delays. The Orioles and Colts had their own gripes. There was not enough office space and locker room facilities to accommodate each franchise's players and executives. Memorial Stadium, as the *Baltimore Sun* editorialized, woefully lacked creature comforts. In 1969, Colts owner Carroll Rosenbloom offered a more direct assessment. "I can't allow my fans to . . . use those filthy facilities anymore," he stated.[5]

The city looked into plans to renovate Memorial Stadium. By mid-1969, a New York–based engineering and architectural firm had outlined plans. The cost was $20 million. The plan would remove the stadium's obstructed seating and expand spectator legroom. The plan would also raise and extend the upper deck, construct new end zone and outfield stands, and install a new spectator stand in the upper promenade. Memorial Stadium's capacity, according to the plan, would increase from 54,200 to 58,800 for baseball, and from 61,000 to 65,000 for football. In addition, the study called for the complete renovation of existing restrooms and construction of additional facilities, each "with new modern plumbing, tiled walls and floors, hung ceiling and fluorescent lighting." As many as 15,000 additional parking spaces would be added.[6]

The price, though, was too costly. Baltimore, by 1969, faced a financial crisis that stemmed from "not only conservative, but uninnovative [sic] and, at times, dangerously blind" fiscal policies. It was impossible for city officials to undertake a $20 million renovation project. However, officials did offer to pay for a new scoreboard, the installation of synthetic turf, and a new press box and locker room, among other things. The total cost was $6 million. In return, the Orioles and Colts were expected to extend their leases, both of which expired in 1973. Given Baltimore's financial situation, then-city council president William Donald Schaefer viewed the proposal as "especially ill-timed," arguing that the city should "consider 'only what is absolutely essential to keep the stadium in operation.'" The city, unable to follow through on its $6 million plan, instead offered a $2 million proposal, which included artificial turf, improved lighting, new folding seats, and doubling the number of restroom facilities.[7]

The Orioles and Colts did not view the renovations as a viable long-term solution. Both organizations worked closely with officials on the plans, but they would have preferred playing in a new stadium. The Orioles' owner Jarold C. Hoffberger criticized the proposed renovation as "imprudent expenditures." Three years later, he stated, "It would be a waste of the taxpayers' money to renovate Memorial Stadium." The Colts' owner Carroll Rosenbloom was harsher. In 1969, he threatened to build a new stadium in nearby Columbia, Maryland, and move the Colts. By 1972, Rosenbloom was openly toying with the idea of moving the team to Tampa Bay. Baltimoreans were aghast. "Don't Tampa with our Colts," went a popular rallying cry. Rosenbloom, regrettably, eventually swapped teams with the irascible Los Angeles Rams owner Robert Irsay.[8]

While the Orioles and Colts battled with the city over Memorial Stadium's condition, the Bullets were suffering from a lack of interest. The Bullets arrived from Chicago in 1963 (where they were called the Zephyrs), and, despite posting losing records, reached the postseason in their second and third seasons. Yet the Bullets were met with indifference. Mark Kram of *Sports Illustrated* observed in October 1966, "Nobody knows, or cares, that the Bullets are here." Even after the Bullets experienced greater success, most Baltimoreans still did not care. The Bullets occasionally attracted strong crowds. Usually, though, the team struggled. Attendance in Baltimore was described as "dreadful." By 1969–1970, the Bullets were averaging just 6,000 people per game. Part of the issue was that the Bullets had to compete with the Colts in November and December. As Bob Maisel explained, the

Baltimore working-class fan has "to pick his spots, take the top attractions and skip the others."[9]

Such disinterest pushed the Bullets closer to Washington, DC. By 1966, the Bullets were hardly receiving any television exposure in Baltimore. Although WJZ-TV in Baltimore carried thirteen games in 1963–1964, no games were televised in 1965–1966. Fortunately, the Bullets were able to negotiate with Washington-based WTTG-TV to broadcast twelve games, and as many as seven playoff games, for the next three seasons. Team officials also reached out to fans in Washington. In June 1966, the team's management estimated that 10 percent of home attendance consisted of people from the Washington area. By 1971, it was 12 percent. The Bullets owner Abe Pollin, a wealthy Washingtonian in the construction business, openly courted fellow Washingtonians. "In the not too distant future," he said in 1971, Baltimore and Washington "will become one. That's why I want people in Washington to say this is their home team."[10]

Meanwhile, the Bullets began playing the occasional game at the University of Maryland's Cole Field House. Games at College Park represented nothing new for the Bullets. The team played there during the 1960s. But, as home attendance in Baltimore continued to suffer, the Bullets scheduled four regular-season games at Cole for 1970–1971. The number doubled the next season. Even though the Bullets played only a handful of games at Cole, the club attracted large crowds, including a then franchise-best 14,239 for a game against the Los Angeles Lakers in early 1972. In contrast, only 8,468 people showed up at the Baltimore Civic Center two months earlier to watch the Lakers win their record-setting twenty-seventh consecutive game. The streak would end at thirty-three.[11]

The Bullets growing connection to Washington raised speculation that the team would eventually move. Initially, Pollin looked into building an arena in nearby Columbia, Maryland. The location made sense, given Pollin's views on the Baltimore and Washington area, and his ties to the District. However, Pollin also aspired to own a National Hockey League (NHL) franchise. But NHL officials had reservations with Pollin's plans. As the *Washington Post* reported, NHL president Clarence Campbell refused to endorse a town located between two major cities. Pollin was thus forced to choose. With the Washington area showing "absolutely unbelievable interest in hockey," Pollin staked his hockey hopes on moving the Bullets to the Washington suburbs. In May 1972, he announced his decision. The team moved after the 1972–1973 season.[12]

The loss of the Bullets hurt Baltimore. City officials soon began looking for other teams. Shortly after the Bullets announced their departure, the Civic Center Commission worked to stage an American Basketball

Association exhibition for October 1972, in hopes of luring a new franchise. The exhibition, however, never occurred. But the proposed exhibition raised questions over the suitability of the Civic Center for hosting sporting events. The arena was neither old nor dilapidated. Pollin was not dissatisfied with the venue, either. But Zanvyl Krieger, co-owner of the American Hockey League's Baltimore Clippers, argued that the Civic Center was "inadequate for anything from ice hockey to opera." For Baltimore to secure a major league team—basketball or hockey—Krieger believed the city needed "a new arena."[13]

Given the Orioles and Colts dissatisfaction with Memorial Stadium, the Bullets departure heightened the importance of the stadium issue. Maybe, people thought, the Orioles and Colts would leave too. In April 1973, the *New York Times* offered a sobering assessment: Other cities would gladly accept the Orioles and Colts. According to the paper, Washington and New Orleans represented two possible locations for the Orioles. In addition to Tampa Bay, the Colts had also received offers from Seattle, Phoenix, and Jacksonville. "Build new facilities or lose your teams," the *Times* ominously concluded.[14]

A year before the *New York Times* article, in May 1972, the Maryland General Assembly responded by establishing the Maryland Sports Complex Authority, a five-person commission headed by Maryland secretary of economic and community development Edmond F. Rovner. The General Assembly found "that professional sports add to the economy, the culture and the vitality of Baltimore City, the Greater Baltimore Region and the entire State of Maryland." Moreover, the General Assembly supported a policy designed to retain professional sports in the Baltimore metropolitan area, while simultaneously authorizing the operators, owners, or lessees of sporting venues financial benefits to offset the costs associated with constructing, operating, and maintaining the facilities. As the *Baltimore Sun* editorialized, the commission was responsible for addressing issues pertaining to a new sports complex, namely the location, the number of facilities, its cost, and its funding.[15]

The Authority examined several options. First, it proposed a complete renovation of Memorial Stadium, which would also increase parking by as many as 5,000 spaces. The Authority also examined remodeling Memorial Stadium and pairing the facility with an extended and renovated Civic Center to create an "an arena-convention-exhibition facility," costing over $91 million. Lastly, the Authority examined building a sports complex that included a 70,000-seat domed stadium with parking garages, a 600-room hotel, shops, and a convention center-arena addition to the Civic Center. The price was a whopping $114 million.[16]

The Authority recommended constructing a sports complex at Camden Yards. During the nineteenth century, Camden Yards had been tied to Baltimore's ambitions of commercial power. The site opened in 1857 and provided the headquarters and terminals for the Baltimore & Ohio Railroad, which city boosters hoped would solidify the city's status as a prominent commercial center. While being part of Abraham Lincoln's secretive entrance into Washington, DC, and the early Civil War clash between the Sixth Massachusetts regiment and Baltimore rioters, Camden Yards ultimately symbolized the city's decay and hope for redevelopment. The railroad vacated Camden Yards by 1971, thereby providing an ideal location for a sports complex. The Authority advised building a sports complex—not only because it would produce more revenue, but also because the Orioles and Colts were more likely to negotiate long-term leases with the city.[17]

Baltimore officials had previously examined the idea of a domed stadium. In 1944, after the International League Orioles stadium, Oriole Park, which was located at Twenty-Ninth Street and Greenmount Avenue, burned down, the City Council appointed a civic commission to look into stadium options for the team. A year later, the Baltimore War Memorial Stadium Committee submitted a $5 million plan for a domed stadium. Designed by airplane magnate Glenn L. Martin, the proposed stadium would have a one-eighth-inch-thick aluminum-alloy roof held up by air pressure. The stadium would host a variety of activities, from sporting events to political conventions. It would also have flexible seating and would seat as many as 100,000 people. In the end, the City Council nixed the idea, in part because of the price tag. Council members also feared that a domed stadium was impractical. Baltimoreans had similar concerns. As one letter to the editor huffed, "The Baltimore fine arts program is in danger of collapse. The Pratt Library was forced to suffer last year for the lack of a paltry $15,000. Away with this monstrosity! Let's show some sense."[18]

By the mid-1960s, Baltimore had renewed its interest in building a domed stadium, partly due to the success of the Houston Astrodome, which was then known as the Eighth Wonder of the World. Once viewed "as a sty [sic] in the eye of Texas," the Astrodome opened in April 1965. By the start of 1966, 3.8 million customers had walked through its gates. Such success attracted the attention of Colts owner Carroll Rosenbloom. Not long after the Astrodome opened, he visited the stadium, and came away so impressed that he brought the stadium's architect and engineer to Baltimore for further consultation (Orioles owner Jarold Hoffberger did not attend). The meeting again raised the prospects of a domed stadium in Baltimore, though some doubted the financial viability of such a plan. Bob Maisel wrote, "I really didn't think it was possible for private capital to finance a project of this magnitude, because it probably couldn't be made to pay for itself."[19]

Eight years later, the domed stadium became the centerpiece of a downtown sports complex, designed, in part, to help revive Baltimore's downtown business district. The proposed complex connected the Orioles and Colts to the redevelopment of the Inner Harbor. Beginning in 1959, Baltimore's Inner Harbor Program involved "the renewal of 240 acres surrounding the strategically located harbor basin where the City originated." Camden Yards resided on the western portion of the Inner Harbor. According to the Charles Center-Inner Harbor Management, Inc., the western portion of the Inner Harbor, which consisted of sixty-eight acres, would be targeted during the second stage of redevelopment. The sports complex would be nestled among high- and low-rise housing projects. The plan also called for the construction of major office and commercial buildings.[20]

The sports complex was viewed as an attraction that would draw people downtown. For years, downtown property owners and business leaders had struggled to attract people into the city. Historian Robert M. Fogelson recounted how Baltimore's Downtown Committee followed a plan of making downtown more accessible with improved roads and freeway development. The hope was that downtown businesses would increase revenues and their property values would rise. Instead, the plan backfired. More people now had better roads to leave the city, adding to the growth of the suburbs. The sports complex represented yet another attempt to bring people downtown. As Governor Mandel noted, "Downtown Baltimore would be changed overnight from a place that is vacant at night to an area to which people would realize they can come." Frank Novak, president of the Loch Raven Improvement Association, agreed. Writing to the *Baltimore Sun*, Novak believed, "If down town [sic] is to survive, it needs all the attraction it can get. The Stadium will be its biggest."[21]

Moreover, supporters argued that the sports complex would keep the Orioles and Colts in Baltimore. Both teams used this angle to show their support for the project, maintaining that Memorial Stadium did not offer a long-term solution. At a December 1973 press conference, Frank Cashen, Orioles executive vice president and general manager, noted, "It is our belief that the Stadium is incapable of being remodeled in such a way as to make it attractive for the fans over the long term as a modern, weather proof facility." Colts general manager Joe Thomas concurred, arguing that expenditures on Memorial Stadium would never reap long-term benefits. Consequently, both teams refused to commit to playing in Memorial Stadium. Bob Maisel described the press conference as "the kickoff of a public relations campaign to get everybody, especially the man in the street, to realize . . . that the complex should be built at the Camden Yards site downtown."[22]

But the sports complex did not meet with universal approval. Some downtown merchants expressed concern over placing the complex in Camden Yards, while neighborhood associations near Memorial Stadium believed that Camden Yards was a "poorly accessible downtown site." At the same time, though, many sought to protect Memorial Stadium, arguing that it maintained the stability of their communities. Howard Greenbaum, chairman of the Downtown Merchants Association, shared their concerns. In an April 1973 letter to Mayor Schaefer, Greenbaum indicated that the sports complex would make things worse. With a growing number of people working downtown, Greenbaum believed that the sports complex would further hamper traffic, thus harming downtown businesses. He wrote: "We feel that the 180,000 office workers plus our customers and businesses should not be severely inconvenienced by an additional 75,000 Colt fans!"[23]

Neighborhood associations near Memorial Stadium also offered opposition to the proposed sports complex. Ironically, people living near Memorial Stadium often expressed discontent with the facility, complaining about the noise, traffic, trash, and vermin produced by sporting events. But with the prospects of a new downtown sports complex, neighboring civic associations suddenly changed their tone. Though they acknowledged the problems Memorial Stadium brought to their neighborhoods, they also realized the stadium created economic benefits for the area. Without sporting events at Memorial Stadium, businesses and people would most likely leave the surrounding neighborhoods. As several members of the Ednor Gardens-Lakeside Civic Association told Mayor Schaefer, "We believe that the construction of a sports facility away from the 33rd Street site would seriously threaten the stability of the Waverly and Ednor Gardens-Lakeside communities." To them, Memorial Stadium still represented a "modern facility." It just needed some sprucing up.[24]

Opponents also had issues with the city and state's prioritization of funds. One letter to Mayor Schaefer questioned the decision of a sports complex, wondering, "With so much money needed for other ills of our city and all the politicians, including both you and the governor, trying to tell us this will help." Another offered a more specific complaint. With his daughter attending Northern Parkway Junior High School, the author noted that the city's "disgraceful" 1973 school budget allotted $5 per student. Such a view took on greater significance in February 1974 when city teachers, dissatisfied with their pay, went on strike. The month-long strike morphed into a larger one in June, as sanitary workers, police officers, and prison guards picketed over pay for roughly two weeks. With city leaders locked in a struggle with public workers, the sports complex seemed like an unnecessary problem.[25]

The concerns citizens had over government priorities raised a larger issue: funding. To be sure, Governor Mandel had specified, "We are not using any taxpayer's money for the development of a sports complex." Supporters also noted that the project could be funded through tax-exempt revenue bonds, money from sporting events, daytime parking fees, and private investments in the project. However, questions remained. The *Baltimore Sun* noted that recently built stadiums in Cincinnati, New Orleans, Philadelphia, and Pittsburgh incurred large deficits, ultimately requiring public funds. For Baltimore's sports complex, the General Assembly prohibited the use of state monies when establishing the Authority, and the municipal strikes of 1974 highlighted Baltimore's deep financial trouble. Baltimoreans believed that they would have to foot the bill. As one Baltimorean wrote to Mayor Schaefer, "The new stadium will not cost taxpayers money, but like many other projects, it undoubtedly will."[26]

Baltimore's taxpayers had a vocal friend inside City Hall: Hyman A. Pressman. Described as "the little man's hero," Pressman gained a reputation as the protector of taxpayer's money, having filed numerous taxpayer lawsuits against the municipal government prior to becoming city comptroller in 1963. He believed the Orioles and Colts represented civic treasures, and he wanted to keep them in Baltimore. In a book of published poetry, Pressman wrote of the Colts, "One thing will make us love you more—/ Just say you'll stay in Baltimore." But he opposed the sports complex, and he helped ensure it would never see the light of day. For example, he levied a complaint against the Baltimore Board of Estimates, accusing the board of illegally approving $150,000 for a feasibility study. Pressman believed that the sports complex would not guarantee the Orioles and Colts would stay in Baltimore. Instead, Pressman recommended that Maryland purchase the Orioles and Colts. By his count, it would only set the state back $30 million.[27]

Pressman wanted to have a citywide referendum regarding the sports complex. To do so, he sought to include the issue as an amendment to Baltimore's City Charter, which, if passed, could only be revoked by another referendum. Pressman and an opposition group, known as the Memorial Stadium Task Force, established a petition in June 1973, hoping to get 10,000 signatures, thus triggering a referendum in 1974. Pressman and the task force succeeded. However, William H. C. Wilson, a Roland Park real estate agent, tried to block the amendment by filing a lawsuit in the circuit court. He denied having any real estate interest in the sports complex, and instead portrayed himself as an avid sports fan who saw the plan as beneficial for downtown tourism and businesses. The court, though, rejected Wilson's lawsuit, ruling "voters should have a chance to vote on whether expenditures of city public funds should be limited to Memorial Stadium or used for a wider purpose."[28]

The proposed amendment, known as Question P, became a significant voter issue during the November 1974 elections. Using elements of patriotism, Question P proclaimed "that Memorial Stadium be a memorial in tribute to war veterans and prohibiting the construction of another stadium for professional sports with public funds." The amendment passed soundly by a vote of 50,916 to 39,527. By passing Question P, voters effectively ended any prospects of building the proposed sports complex. Pro-complex forces vowed to fight on, claiming that the vote merely represented "another fly in the ointment." Some even hoped to resubmit new plans to the General Assembly in 1975. But Governor Mandel remained firm. State funds would not be used to fund a downtown complex. As Authority member Robert C. Embry Jr. said, "The Governor has spoken. The authority will not resubmit the proposal. Referendum or no referendum there's not going to be a stadium."[29]

The failure to build the downtown sports complex intensified fears that Baltimore could lose the Orioles. A month before Question P passed, Frank Cashen noted, "If they don't build [a stadium], it may not be a wise business move to keep the team here." Fears increased when the *Washington Post* reported in January 1975 that local real estate developer Theodore N. Lerner had been negotiating with Hoffberger to purchase the Orioles. Invoking memories of Abe Pollin, Lerner suggested playing half of the Orioles home games in Washington's RFK Stadium. Baltimoreans erupted. City leaders formed a Committee to Save the Baltimore Orioles. Hoffberger, for his part, staunchly denied the report. However, with mounting family pressures and business concerns over the Orioles, in 1979 he sold the team to Washington lawyer Edward Bennett Williams, the former owner of the Washington Redskins, prompting continued concern about the Orioles future in Baltimore.[30]

The failed stadium complex posed a nastier situation for the Colts. In a statement loaded with hypocrisy, Irsay said: "I'm a patient man. I think the people of Baltimore are going to see those new stadiums [in New Orleans and Seattle] opening in a year or two around the country and they are going to realize they need a stadium . . . for conventions and other things besides football." Irsay's patience, though, wore thin, especially after plans for a Baltimore County stadium died in January 1976. Two months later, reports emerged that a Phoenix group presented Irsay with "an attractive offer" to move the Colts. That did not happen, primarily due to a bond issue that placed the burden of any unpaid stadium debts on the team. Irsay remained undeterred. In 1979, as he sought either a new stadium or major renovations to Memorial Stadium, Irsay met with the Los Angeles Coliseum Commission. Following the meeting, he declared, "I am 97 per cent sure the Colts will be playing in Los Angeles next season," that is, 1980. He eventually backed off, but not enough for him to keep the Colts in Baltimore.[31]

The Colts' eventual move to Indianapolis highlighted one major consequence of Baltimore's inability to build a sports complex. In a span of eleven years, Baltimore had lost its professional basketball and football franchises. The Colts' departure, moreover, heightened fears that the Orioles, too, would leave. While Williams indicated no intention of moving the team, the fear remained, especially when Mayor Schaefer received a report of T-shirts in Indianapolis that read, "Colts Today Orioles Tomorrow." City and state officials worked quickly to remedy the situation. By November 1984, city officials successfully placed a resolution on the ballot that would repeal Question P. The measure passed with approximately 62 percent of the vote. In 1986, the General Assembly established the Maryland Professional Sports Authority, and, a year later, the body passed a $200 million bill for the construction of Oriole Park at Camden Yards. The new stadium anchored the Orioles to Baltimore and, ironically, helped lure the Cleveland Browns in 1996, who became the Ravens, ending the long, painful battle over a new sports complex—a battle that began in the late 1960s when the city stood atop the sporting world.[32]

17

The Greatest High School Basketball Team Ever

The Dunbar Poets, 1981–1982 and 1982–1983

CHAD CARLSON

Their accomplishments seemed impossible and unattainable even as they occurred. However, the legacy of the 1981–1982 and 1982–1983 Paul Laurence Dunbar High School boy's basketball teams continued to grow after their incredible seasons. The 1981–1982 team finished its season undefeated. The 1982–1983 team followed with a 31-0 campaign and a number-one national ranking. This group of young men became widely known as the best high school basketball team of all time, and many of them went on to even greater basketball fame. Nineteen eighty-two Dunbar graduate Gary Graham played college basketball at the University of Nevada, Las Vegas (UNLV), which was then a powerhouse. David Wingate, another 1982 grad, won an NCAA championship with Georgetown University before embarking on a productive thirteen-year NBA career. Nineteen eighty-three graduates Tyrone "Muggsy" Bogues, Reggie Lewis, and Reggie Williams— the latter teamed with Wingate on Georgetown's 1984 national championship team—enjoyed lengthy and notable NBA careers. Tim Dawson, Keith James, and Mike Brown went on to star at the University of Miami, UNLV, and Syracuse University, respectively. The 1982–1983 team was so talented that Reggie Lewis, who became Northeastern University's fourth all-time leading scorer, a two-time conference player of the year, a first-round NBA draft pick, a NBA All-Star, and the captain of the Boston Celtics, could not even crack the Dunbar starting lineup.[1]

The 1982–1983 Paul Laurence Dunbar High School basketball team included Reggie Lewis (#31), Reggie Williams (*center rear*), and Tyrone Bogues (#14), all of whom had impressive college and NBA careers.
Courtesy of the Baltimore Sun.

Despite all of its accolades, awards, and honors, the undefeated 1982 Dunbar team may not have been Baltimore's best. The undefeated Calvert Hall Catholic School garnered that distinction, holding its number-one national ranking just out of Dunbar's reach in an environment that offers rich perspectives on Baltimore high school basketball, public education, race, and city politics. Dunbar, with a traditionally black student body, resides amid five housing projects in Baltimore's poor east side and remains central to the Baltimore City Public School system. Calvert Hall, an overwhelmingly white Catholic school located just outside of Baltimore's eastern city limits, represents the results of the "white flight" that affected Baltimore's demographics, which was true of many American cities in the middle of the twentieth century. Dunbar's incredible basketball success in the early 1980s— matched in Charm City perhaps only by Calvert Hall's success—and the juxtaposition of these two schools illustrates the complex social, athletic, educational, and political contexts in which Baltimore high school basketball at the time was embedded.

Paul Laurence Dunbar High School has a history that parallels the African American experience in Baltimore since the school opened its doors in 1918. The school's namesake, who led a brief but illustrious career as a poet and writer, garnered great fame among the African American and literary communities. The poet's legacy includes schools, parks, hotels, and libraries across the country named in his honor. Baltimore's Dunbar High School—nicknamed the Poets—started a basketball program not long after the school evolved into full K–12 service in 1940. Coach William "Sugar" Cain led early Poet teams to great success. Throughout the 1950s, Cain's teams were perennially among the best local high school basketball squads.[2]

In 1956, Dunbar joined the Maryland Scholastic Association (MSA) with three other historically black schools, integrating the organization. One year later, the Poets won their first MSA championship by defeating Loyola High School, a team that—like Calvert Hall—presented a number of contrasts from Dunbar. A Catholic school, Loyola and most of its student body migrated from inner-city Baltimore to neighboring Towson in 1941, taking its predominantly white student body away from the perils of the city. Dunbar, still a young and black school located in a troubled Baltimore neighborhood, faced Loyola in March of 1957 in an integrated game with an integrated crowd of spectators. The game was played without incident.[3]

The climate for this championship game marked progress from the tension that drove racially charged public policies in Charm City. Baltimore has a history of tension regarding race. Its geographic centrality along the Eastern seaboard led to a general lack of cohesiveness between the Northeast and

Deep South cultures that it dually—and often uncomfortably—embodied. Baltimore experienced heavy industrialization during the middle of the nineteenth century, like many northeastern conurbations. Its industrial basis made slaveholding inefficient, but the practice remained. Locals often had to contract their enslaved women and men out to work at hotels and shipyards to prevent financial losses. Outside of the small number of those enslaved, Baltimore was home to an extensive population of free African Americans, more than any other city in the antebellum period. The large and increasingly free black community in Baltimore created vast social networks in the post–Civil War years. Churches, schools, the print media, and civic associations became a source of pride for the black community, despite its second-class social status.[4]

A move toward segregated neighborhoods and housing also hindered Baltimore's African American community from gaining social equality. In 1880, African Americans comprised between one-tenth and one-third of the population in most of Baltimore's wards. However, because of the Camden Yards Railway Station expansion in 1885 that displaced an inordinate number of African Americans, Baltimore's black population became much more concentrated—the displaced residents joined other African Americans so that half of the city's black constituency lived in old west Baltimore. Between 1910 and 1913, the Baltimore City Council passed three ordinances that prevented black citizens from living in certain white neighborhoods.[5]

A number of segregated, large-scale housing projects cropped up three decades later to accommodate the influx of African Americans to Baltimore after World War II. While some of them joined the well-known black neighborhoods of west Baltimore, others fortified the black migration into east Baltimore. These communities fell into economic and social disrepair as the economy dwindled throughout the civil rights era and many African Americans lost the relatively well-paying industrial jobs that left the city. Five of these economically ravaged housing projects—Lafayette Courts, Somerset, Latrobe Courts, Lester Morton, and Douglas Holmes—surrounded Paul Laurence Dunbar High School, which naturally felt the effects, too, as drugs and violence became more commonplace along with the economic and social blight.[6]

Baltimore's increasing racial and socioeconomic segregation throughout the twentieth century evolved separately from the unusually peaceful progression of Charm City's high school basketball circuit. Throughout the civil rights era, Dunbar's squad of all-black players competed against many all-white opponents. However, many of these games were played without crowds. MSA authorities believed that interracial games would be acceptable but interracial crowds would not. The threat of incidents from nonparticipants ruining certain games may have been so great as to justify this policy.[7]

Dunbar's 1957 defeat of Loyola in front of a peaceful mixed crowd quelled many fears. The MSA consequently loosened its policies. Dunbar's victory also validated its prominence in Baltimore high school basketball. Poet dominance would continue and it shaped the local community's identity. Coach Cain had his team well disciplined, and the fans followed suit in support of their beloved Poets. By the early 1970s the Dunbar community expected basketball success every season. Catholic power Mount St. Joseph visited Dunbar in 1971 for a late season matchup with championship implications. The visitors led late in the game when a Dunbar fan smacked a visiting player as he was inbounding the ball. This set off a riot in the gymnasium. The game ended prematurely as Dunbar players had to fight their own fans to help their opponents get out of the gym safely. Authorities escorted the Mount St. Joe team out of the building and, once fighting had stopped, the police made nineteen arrests—including that of Baltimore Bullets star point guard Earl "the Pearl" Monroe, who had become a Dunbar fan.[8]

This game signified a defining moment in Baltimore high school basketball. Before the event, Catholic and public schools alike played together as one league. Afterward, the landscape changed. Six Catholic schools, fearing similar uprisings in the future from these racially and socioeconomically mixed contests, broke from the MSA and started the Baltimore Catholic League. Dunbar, for its part in hosting the fracas that set off the Catholic secession, was forced to play the 1971–1972 season with MSA sanctions that prohibited them from hosting any interscholastic games that season. Ironically, that Dunbar team rallied to an undefeated record despite the adversity it faced on the road every game.[9]

The infamous 1971 game marked just one basketball-related disaster that plagued Dunbar's poor, black, inner-city community. Tragedy struck again after the 1971–1972 season, as the team's star, Tony Brown, was murdered by his girlfriend less than a month after he played his last game. The rumor remains that on the day of his funeral, an official scholarship offer from UCLA's coach John Wooden arrived at Brown's home. Had Brown lived to accept the apparent offer, he would have been the first Baltimore prep hoopster to make a jump out of the perils of the city and into such a revered basketball program.[10]

After Brown's death, guard Allen "Skip" Wise became the new Poet star as a multitalented scoring threat. Wise and his teammates garnered widespread attention as they beat Washington, DC's DeMatha Catholic, which was coached by the legendary Morgan Wootten and featured future Notre Dame standout, Olympic gold medalist, and NBA All-Star Adrian Dantley.

Wise outplayed Dantley, scoring thirty-nine points to the DeMatha star's twelve.[11]

Inner-city Baltimore was not kind to young, talented hoopsters like Skip Wise in the 1970s. Despite a seemingly unmatched talent, "Baltimore's favorite son" succumbed to the streets. In fact, locals continue to affirm Wise as Baltimore's best basketball player ever—high praise considering all of the NBA stars that hail from Charm City. Unfortunately, his outstanding play against DeMatha may have been the highlight of his career. It certainly has a prominent place in Dunbar's basketball annals.[12]

The DeMatha game's legacy remains prominent for two reasons. First, it marked the end of an era. Coach Cain retired from coaching after the game but stayed on as athletic director—a decision he made at the beginning of the season. Archie Lewis, Cain's longtime assistant, coached for the next two seasons before Bob Wade, a Dunbar alum and former NFL safety, took over in 1975. Second, it influenced the Poet stars that took the team to national prestige over the next decade. Indeed, this game brought Dunbar theretofore unmatched regional attention, and it provided the next generation of Poets with new levels of possibility. In essence, they could dream bigger.[13]

In 1974, Dunbar's new $10.5 million building established it as a model community school that entertained visits from education specialists domestically and abroad. That same year, the Baltimore City Public School System's (BCPS) Board of Commissioners began classifying its high schools as either "citywide" or "zoned"—the latter's student population would depend on geography and the former would offer particular "magnet" areas of concentration to provide any student in the city who qualifies an extensive curriculum in that discipline.[14]

The Board of Commissioners' decision to classify Dunbar as one of only four citywide "magnet" schools, one that would emphasize health professions as its area of concentration, received mixed reviews from the Dunbar community. The board's decision coincided with Dunbar's new, state-of-the-art facility, and its designation as a health professions magnet may have been influenced by the fact that the new building was only two blocks away from the world-renowned Johns Hopkins University Medical Center. The backlash came from the tight-knit Dunbar residents who worked so hard to lobby for a new school building and appreciated the community-based traditions of Dunbar and its successful athletic teams. Further, citywide status would likely entail academic admissions standards that many of Dunbar's underperforming students would not meet.[15]

The Board of Commissioners held firm to its commitment to give Dunbar citywide status, but softened the change to appease local activists.

The board rescinded the admissions criteria that it established at other city-wide schools so that many students in Dunbar's local zone could continue to attend the school that was so central to its community identity. However, acceptance was not automatic. Students still had to complete and submit special applications indicating their interests in health-related professions to enroll at Dunbar, a process they would also have to complete to attend any of the other three magnet schools that maintained strict academic entrance requirements. This diplomatic move satisfied neighborhood activist groups, and its implications grew in ways that Dunbar's community would come to embrace.[16]

When Skip Wise played at Dunbar, he did so with teammates who all hailed from the decaying neighborhoods that comprised Dunbar's geographical zone. As Bob Wade took over in 1975, he inherited a team of local players steeped in the traditions of a community-based school. Yet that school could also now attract students from all over Baltimore who were interested in studying the health professions—or could at least claim to be. This opened doors previously unavailable.

Former Dunbar principal Elzee C. Gladden lamented that "team cohesiveness in terms of community support groups became more fragmented during the 1975 to 1980 era" because of the changed Dunbar culture. Gladden argued that Dunbar used to be a community school, and that its support came from local alums and other residents. Now that it was no longer a community-based school its community-based support diminished. Despite the increased regional prestige as a citywide school, Gladden worried about Dunbar losing its roots and diminished social capital that made it what it was—a community school supported by dedicated citizens. Yet its traditionally strong athletic teams suffered no long-term harms from the changes. In fact, Coach Wade's teams flourished because they could now attract players from a wider geographic swath—theoretically any student in Baltimore that claimed to have an interest in the health professions could attend Dunbar.[17]

By the 1980–1981 basketball season, Coach Wade had a power-house team that included players from outside Dunbar's district who took advantage of the school's citywide loophole of no entrance criteria. David Wingate, in particular, traveled from Baltimore's Northern district to play for the Poets during his junior season. The 6'5" guard/forward's transfer application—from basketball-poor Northern to traditionally top-tier Dunbar, because of his apparent interest in becoming a dental technician—was cosigned by his summer rec team coach. Already a star at Northern, Wingate further excelled at Dunbar, using his long arms and quickness to stymie opposing offenses and playing above the rim as a scorer in Dunbar's attack. He shared the wing with 6'7" Reggie Williams, a sophomore sensation who grew up in the nearby projects in Dunbar's district. That Poet squad, which also included star combo-guard Gary Graham, met Calvert Hall Catholic in a late-season game for the unofficial title of city's best.[18]

Dunbar entered the March 14, 1981, game with a 24-2 record led by Wingate and Williams. Throughout the season, Wingate's transfer received backlash from other Baltimore schools, some of which accused Wade of recruiting him away from Northern. *Sports Illustrated* proclaimed that "the Northern coach protested that Wingate had been enticed, but no collusion could be proved [sic]."[19] A local coach argued similarly, "When a kid is set on going to Dunbar that's the end of it. To try to stop him would be an exercise in futility." Wade responded to this accusation by arguing, "If we were 0-20, nobody would care what we did . . . but since we're winning, everybody is taking potshots at us."[20]

Not coincidentally, Dunbar's opponent in this "King of the Hill" matchup faced similar accusations. Calvert Hall coach Mark Amatucci took the reins at his alma mater a year after Wade began coaching at his. "The Hall's" student body was 99 percent white at that point and saw little increase in racial diversity in the following years. When Amatucci got the job, he made contacts at the inner-city Madison Square summer basketball league on Baltimore's east side. These contacts paid off, helping him to entice black sophomores Paul Kinney and Daryle Edwards to play for him in 1978. In the fall of 1979, two east Baltimore African American sophomores—best friends James "Pop" Tubman and Marc Wilson—joined them by choosing "The Hall" over Dunbar. Paul Edwards, Daryle's brother, also joined the team that season.[21]

Athletic scholarships, promises of varsity roster spots, and chances to start right away lured Tubman and Wilson—two standout guards—to the private, Catholic school east of Baltimore. Apparently, coach Wade had not offered such basketball-related promises to these Dunbar locals. In the fall of 1980, freshman Duane Ferrell, who went on to star at Georgia Tech before playing in the NBA, also chose to leave the city and play for Calvert Hall. This exodus worried Baltimore coaches, who charged "that the private schools string the inner-city recruits along academically just to enhance the school's athletic prestige."[22] Coach Wade became an especially vocal critic of this trend as he saw Tubman and Wilson flee from the projects at his doorstep. Calvert Hall principal Brother Ren Sterner called him out on this criticism, saying, "I think Bob Wade believes the blacks on our team have been stolen from him. That implies that the black inner-city schools own them, that they're betraying their race if they go to honky schools."[23] Despite the crossfire, Amatucci continues to absolve himself of guilt: "People say I buy players, but that's not true. I hustled. I outworked other coaches. And the results spoke for themselves."[24]

Thus, the backdrop for the 1981 unofficial title game provided a robust storyline. Dunbar entered the fray with a mostly local squad, with the exception of Wingate, whom they were accused of illegally enticing to become a Poet. "The Hall" had six black players regarded as traitors by their inner-city neighbors and a coach accused of paying and exploiting his inner-city stars. Amatucci would have had a seventh African American on his team were it not for the untimely death of Paul Kinney, one of his original recruits, in the preseason. "The Hall's" coach scheduled the Dunbar game in his honor. Amatucci made plain that his team was playing this game "for the [Paul Kinney Scholarship] fund. Not for No. 1. Not to beat Dunbar. But for Paul."[25]

Fans jammed into the Towson Center and witnessed a game for the ages. Dunbar led by nine points with 1:52 remaining when "The Hall" fought back to tie the game by the end of regulation. This brilliant comeback, however, came with controversy. Local Dunbar supporters, who admitted their partisanship, watched with skepticism as the final minutes of regulation unraveled. One alumnus noted, "There were some terrible calls down the stretch. There were some fouls that didn't get called and then we started fouling out like crazy." Another alum argued that, "The officiating was what changed the game, it wasn't the (players)." Nevertheless, "The Hall" carried its momentum into overtime, but it took three extra periods before they overcame the Poets, 94–91. The loss ended Dunbar's season. Calvert Hall, however, entered the prestigious Alhambra Catholic tournament a week later and, still emotionally exhausted from the Dunbar thriller, lost in the finals. Coach Amatucci blamed the loss on his team's emotional hangover from the Dunbar game.[26]

With such a young roster returning, Calvert Hall entered the 1981–1982 season ranked #1 in the country. Not surprisingly, then, local polls also had them pegged as the top team in the area. Dunbar's expectations were a bit more modest, holding the number-two spot locally. Three starters returned for Dunbar: Wingate and guard Gary Graham who would be seniors, and Williams was a junior. Coach Wade also had two stud newcomers to fill out his starting lineup. The 6'5" junior center Tim Dawson—a transfer from Towson Catholic—provided athleticism and a tireless work ethic that allowed him to beat much taller opposing pivot men. Additionally, 5'3" junior point guard Tyrone "Muggsy" Bogues was comfortable facing opponents of greater stature.[27]

Bogues spent his sophomore year at Baltimore's Southern High School. Because of Dunbar's citywide status, Bogues had to apply for admission.

However, between his freshman and sophomore years, he claimed that his paperwork somehow did not make its way to Dunbar or the BCPS central offices for review. So even though he grew up in the Lafayette Projects, a mere city block from Dunbar's campus, Bogues was forced to take two city buses across town to Southern for a year before he could reapply to Dunbar.[28]

Therefore, the diminutive point guard spent the 1980–1981 season at a school not known for basketball and away from those with whom he had grown up. This group included his best friend, fellow Lafayette Projects product, Reggie Williams, who quickly developed a reputation as a basketball sensation during his outstanding sophomore season at Dunbar. To make matters worse for Bogues, the coaches at his new school wrote him off because of his lack of height and lack of humility. The Southern coaches placed him on the junior varsity team, so he quit. Yet after a string of early losses, the coaching staff offered "Muggsy" a spot on the varsity.[29]

Bogues showed flashes of his unique skill set that season, but without much help his team struggled and received little attention. After Southern's season ended, Bogues followed his Dunbar friends through their postseason run that ended with the triple overtime loss to Calvert Hall. As the buzzer sounded to end that epic contest, Bogues remembered Coach Wade looking up at him in the stands with an expression that stated, "If we had you, we would have won."[30]

Bogues's matriculation to Dunbar in the fall of 1981 raised Wade's hopes for the season, but his undersized point guard and center were still unproven at high school basketball's top level. Calvert Hall, on the other hand, returned virtually everyone from its previous championship season. Amatucci hoped to play Dunbar in the upcoming season on terms that would not hurt his team's ability to win the Alhambra tournament. Dunbar's schedule was such that the MSA championship marked the end of its official competition. Since this contest usually occurred in early March, Dunbar had some flexibility to play Calvert Hall afterward. "The Hall," on the other hand, always set its sights on winning Alhambra, which generally took place a couple weeks after the Baltimore Catholic League championship that coincided with the MSAs.[31]

The season began with no Dunbar-Calvert Hall rematch scheduled. Dunbar rolled through its opening games, beating BCPS teams by 54, 38, 31, 30, and 43 points while also defeating McKinley Tech of Washington, DC, by 27 before Christmas. Most of this success came from Bogues's audacious play. The Harlem Holiday Classic in Manhattan, New York, subsequently proved what many people had already believed—that this was a truly special Dunbar team. In New York, the Poets thrashed local Rice

High School by 26 points before an 11-point win over East Orange, New Jersey, and a six-point victory over the tournament's defending champion, Hamilton High School of New York.[32]

Also over the holidays, Calvert Hall took an undefeated record across the country to convincingly win top honors in the Las Vegas Nike Holiday Classic. Amatucci's troops easily overcame some of the best teams out West despite a tough December schedule in which they also beat three top teams in DC. An early January championship in Philadelphia's Pepsi Challenge, in which "The Hall" beat Camden High School of New Jersey—the nation's second-ranked team—proved that "The Hall" also appeared to have a truly special team.[33]

Not to be outdone, after the holidays the Poets destroyed league opponents by 73, 20, 45, 11, 33, 45, 17, 73, and 38 points, and took down formidable Erie McDowell of Pennsylvania by 27 to set up its own showdown with #2 in the nation Camden of New Jersey. Calvert Hall beat the Garden Staters by five points in a battle that took everything they had. Dunbar knew this nonleague matchup with Camden on the road might be its toughest game of the season. Yet the Poets traveled to New Jersey with sizable chips on their shoulders since Calvert Hall and Camden received the national attention while they felt neglected.[34]

Those shoulder chips grew during warm-ups. The Camden crowd laughed at Bogues. The point guard's naturally competitive juices further boiled when Camden players, including future NBA small forward Billy Thompson and All-American Kevin Walls, commented on Bogues's height before tip-off. But "Muggsy" got the first, last, and only laughs in this game. After stripping Camden's point guard of the ball on the first possession and assisting on Dunbar's first four baskets—all in transition—the game was all but over. Dunbar coasted to an 84–59 blowout victory, greatly increasing its national acclaim. After the game, Camden's coach remarked, "Dunbar is the best team I've ever seen . . . They are better than Calvert Hall by 20 points."[35]

After the game, calls for a Dunbar-Calvert Hall showdown steadily increased. Local city officials and event promoters inundated Wade and Amatucci with offers to host and pay for the sought-after showdown. While both coaches felt overwhelmed by the requests, neither let it affect his team's focus. The Hall and the Poets continued to tear up the competition. Dunbar finished the season with wins of 30, 47, 35, and 16 points before beating Lake Clifton for the MSA title, 66–48. The team finished its season with a 33-point average margin of victory.[36]

Calvert Hall also finished the season undefeated. It had beaten five nationally ranked teams but won its games much less convincingly. Come-from-behind victories, including one game-winning tip-in at the buzzer, dotted the Hall's record. Dunbar did not experience any close-game scenarios. However, the Poets could not overcome Calvert Hall in local or national rankings due to the Catholic school's victory over Dunbar the previous year and its stronger national schedule this season. With the schools ranked No. 1 and No. 2 nationally, demands from Dunbar and high school basketball fans across the country increased. Local fans and national promoters realized this could be the game of the century.[37]

Unfortunately, scheduling became the unresolvable issue. After the MSA championship and the Catholic League championship, Calvert Hall had two weeks off before the Alhambra tournament. Dunbar, on the other hand, had nothing else scheduled. Coach Wade, therefore, wanted to play the game in the two weeks between his last game and Calvert Hall's entrance in the Alhambra tourney. Anything beyond that, he argued, and his team would be at a distinct disadvantage. Coach Amatucci, however, would not play in between the Catholic League title game and Alhambra. The coach argued that he had tried to set up this game for months but received no response from Dunbar until the middle of the season. At that point, he was not willing to cave in to Dunbar's newly increased demands that would hurt his team's chances of winning Alhambra.[38]

Without a head-to-head matchup, Calvert Hall finished the season ranked #1 in the country and Dunbar ended #2. While both sides believed they were the better team, the inability to schedule a game left the matter to speculation. Calvert Hall argued that it had the tougher schedule. Dunbar argued that it had a higher average margin of victory and defeated their only ranked common opponent by many more points. The veracity of each of these claims fueled debates and speculative theories.[39]

The following basketball season ensued without any doubt as to which school took the preseason top spot. Calvert Hall's 1982–1983 squad returned only one starter from the previous year; Dunbar only lost two. Wingate went to Georgetown and Gary Graham chose UNLV. Yet with Bogues, Williams, and Dawson still around—joined by junior starters Mike Brown and Keith James who would both go on to play major college basketball—the Poets' hopes for the season remained high. Further, this Dunbar squad, which included reserves Reggie Lewis, Derrick Lewis, and forward Herman Harried, who eventually starred at Syracuse University, had depth that the previous year's team lacked.[40]

The Poets opened the 1982–1983 season just as the previous one ended with four straight blowout victories—the first two by 63 and 64 points. The Poets then traveled to DC to face the capital's top two teams. DeMatha put up a fight in a 12-point loss, but Archbishop Carroll fell by twenty. Back in Baltimore, Dunbar took care of Poly 76–31 and then swept through a

Kentucky tournament the week before Christmas with win differentials of 28, 35, and 17 points. The following week, the Poets closed out the calendar year at the Johnstown, Pennsylvania, Holiday tournament by defeating Bay Village High School of Ohio before overcoming its closest challenge of the season, a five-point win over Martin Luther King High of New York City.[41]

That lone nail-biter served as a wake-up call, as the Poets entered the new calendar year winning sixteen straight games against local public schools. No team came within twenty points of coach Wade's troops until Lake Clifton played a slow-down pace and stayed within sixteen in the MSA Championship game at the end of February. Two days later, Dunbar squared off against Flint Hill of DC. The Poets regained their dominant ways with a 28-point win. Flint Hill's coach, a sixteen-year veteran, explained that this Poet squad was the best team he had ever seen—a meaningful comment coming from anyone privy to the talented DC rosters of the 1960s and 1970s. Further, when asked what he would do if he had to face this Dunbar team again, he replied that he would "cancel the game."[42]

On March 10, Dunbar concluded its season in the inaugural Metro Classic featuring the top public school team against the top Catholic league team that came about, in part, from Dunbar and Calvert Hall's inability to settle on a date the previous season. By virtue of beating Calvert Hall—which finished with a 19-12 record—for the Catholic league title, Cardinal Gibbons won the opportunity to face Dunbar. The *Baltimore Sun*'s pregame write-up concluded that Gibbons faced an "impossible" task. One local coach asserted, "they don't have a prayer." Another coach was slightly more helpful, saying, "you can't let them run and you can't let them steal the ball, because their transition game will kill you." However, this coach—whose team lost to Dunbar by 45, 33, and 48 points that season—also replied, "Don't ask me how you actually stop them. They are capable of doing anything they want."[43]

Dunbar finished its season true to form, crushing Cardinal Gibbons 82–53 for the Metro crown. Reggie Williams, the nation's most highly touted senior, scored thirty-seven points in his sendoff. Dunbar finished the season ranked as the #1 team in every national poll. After the game, Coach Wade offered extreme praise for his team, but did not say what every Baltimore high school basketball fan was thinking. "I know what you're looking for me to say," Wade uttered, "but I can't say this is the best team we've had. I don't want to slight players like Gary Graham or David Wingate, who played on last year's team."[44]

While the two undefeated seasons for the Poets could not have been any better, their stars were just heating up. Reggie Williams joined David Wingate at Georgetown after the season and helped the Hoyas to the 1984 national championship. Bogues attended Wake Forest, where he had a record-setting career. All three of these Dunbar alums enjoyed lengthy NBA careers. Yet the Poet who had the most NBA success did not even start for Dunbar. Reggie Lewis, the sixth man in 1982–1983, took a scholarship at Northeastern University with Coach Jim Calhoun. After the Boston Celtics drafted him in 1987, behind Bogues and Williams, he became an NBA All-Star and succeeded Larry Bird as the Celtics' captain. Unfortunately, he died of an undetectable heart condition in 1993, while in the prime of his career; he was twenty-seven.

Coach Wade became a hot commodity after his "national championship" team. The University of Maryland lured him away in 1986. Wade became the first black head basketball coach in ACC history, but his tenure was short lived. He led the Terrapins like he led the Poets, with a gruff demeanor and no-nonsense philosophy that did not endear him to the team's fan base. Further, his fatherly instincts to help the troubled young men on his team clashed with the rigid NCAA rulebook with which he was unaccustomed. Mild NCAA infractions along with middling on-court success led Maryland to fire him after three seasons. Consequently, Wade returned to Baltimore to direct the BCPS athletics programs.[45]

The 1981–1982 and 1982–1983 Dunbar basketball teams were obviously extraordinary. Their legacy is almost as remarkable. After all, consider how unlikely it is that another high school basketball squad will ever go undefeated for two seasons and produce four NBA players. And yet with all of the on-court success they had amid a culture that presented them with ever-present off-court challenges and dangers, it is difficult to overstate the accomplishments of this group of young men. They very well may have been the greatest high school basketball team of all time. Within Charm City, a metropolis as infamous for its urban decay and difficulties as much as anything else, these young men represented the ability to overcome life on the streets. They gave Baltimore residents a glimpse of what it could produce. Despite the drugs and violence on the street, and despite the white flight into suburbs and the recruitment of black, inner-city basketball talent to the suburban Catholic schools, the Baltimore City Public School system could produce something so remarkable that it had no peer anywhere in the nation.

18

Baltimore Baseball Icons

The Babe, Mr. Oriole, the Iron Man, and the Forgotten Day

DANIEL A. NATHAN

Extraordinary athletes and disparate men, Babe Ruth, Brooks Robinson, and Cal Ripken Jr. are Baltimore's most popular, historic, and iconic baseball players.

Obviously there have been other outstanding ballplayers in Baltimore. In addition to Robinson and Ripken, three of them are enshrined in bronze at Oriole Park at Camden Yards, in the picnic area beyond the bullpens in center field: Hall of Famers Eddie Murray, Jim Palmer, and Frank Robinson. (The late manager Earl Weaver is there, too.) Others such as nineteenth-century Orioles John McGraw and Willie Keeler, Negro leaguers Jud Wilson and Laymon Yokely, Gold Glovers Paul Blair and Mark Belanger, and contemporary stars Adam Jones and Manny Machado, among others, such as hometown boy Al Kaline, were (and are, in the case of Jones and Machado) also talented, accomplished, and widely admired.

Yet in terms of iconicity, as representative symbols of Baltimore and its people at specific historical moments, Ruth, Robinson, and Ripken are *sui generis*. In different ways, they express and can help us understand different cultural values and ways of thinking about the Monumental City.

Remembering and thinking about Ruth, Robinson, and Ripken are useful and fraught with at least one serious problem. Every remembrance is also an act of forgetting. We remember this and overlook or underappreciate that. Taken further, forgetting leads to and promotes ignorance. Forgetting is of course inevitable and natural. To function, we must forget things, all the time. According to sociologist Paul Connerton, "forgetting is not always a failure, and it is not always, and not always in the same way, something about which we should feel culpable."[1]

Still, to forget some things and people often seems and feels, well, wrong. At the very least, forgetting can be disappointing (once we are aware that we are doing it) and diminishes our sense of the past and our understanding of specific places and the present. To resist this phenomenon here, we need to add another ballplayer to this chapter: Baltimore's most underappreciated and least well remembered baseball great, Negro league pitcher Leon Day.

A Poor Kid from the Dock-Side Slums

"The Ruth is mighty and shall prevail."[2] Sportswriter Heywood Broun wrote this lyrical sentence after George Herman "Babe" Ruth Jr. of the New York Yankees hit two home runs in the second game of the 1923 World Series. At the time, the brash and charismatic twenty-eight-year-old Ruth was a remarkably accomplished and already historic ballplayer, who continued his on-field dominance for more than another decade. He was also a popular icon, a vibrant cultural symbol for his era, "the country's first modern superstar, the American dream of individual success personified."[3] Nonetheless, Broun could not have imagined how prescient his sentence was. All these years later, Ruth is still mighty. He has prevailed. His last game was more than eighty years ago. He died in 1948. And yet Babe Ruth endures, like a long-gone star whose light still shines bright.

Ruth endures in Baltimore, his hometown. He was born in the southwest Pigtown neighborhood, now called Ridgely's Delight, not far from downtown and the harbor. More specifically, George Jr. was born at 216 Emory Street (which was his maternal grandparents' rowhouse) in 1895. A rambunctious, mischievous boy, he had a "bleak but not crippling" childhood, writes one biographer.[4] Another asserts that Ruth "was the product of a childhood so bleak that it was almost no childhood at all."[5] Either way, it was bleak. In his autobiography, *The Babe Ruth Story* (1948), Ruth acknowledged that he "was a bad kid" and, due to neglect and his constant carousing in the streets, "hardly knew" his parents or "the difference between right and wrong."[6] Reminiscing without self-pity or contrition, Ruth explained:

> I spent most of the first seven years of my life living over my father's saloon at 426 West Camden Street in Baltimore. When I wasn't looking over it, I was living in it, studying the rough talk of the longshoreman, merchant sailors, roustabouts and water-front bums. When I wasn't living in it, I was living in the neighborhood streets. I had a rotten start and it took me a long time to get my bearings.[7]

By all accounts the "rotten start" part is true, even if the details are elusive.[8] And his transformation from a wild street urchin into a less unruly adolescent took time and the discipline and patience of the Xaverian Brothers at St. Mary's Industrial School, which was simultaneously "an orphanage, boarding school, detention home, reform school, and vocational school."[9] Ruth was not an orphan. His overwhelmed parents sent him to St. Mary's in 1902 (when he was just seven years old), where he was detained and reformed (for the time being), and he did learn a trade. He became a competent tailor and shirt maker. Most of this is well known, part of the carefully wrought and frequently repeated Ruth narrative of social mobility. His truly fantastic rags-to-riches story was far beyond anything Horatio Alger ever published or probably imagined.

Never before having traveled beyond Baltimore, the hard-throwing left-handed Ruth—svelte, strong, and socially naïve and inept—left St. Mary's in the spring of 1914 to play for the minor league Baltimore Orioles of the International League, where he picked up the "Babe" sobriquet.[10] By early July, his contract had been sold to the Boston Red Sox. A year later, the twenty-year-old Ruth was one of the best pitchers in the American League. With the Red Sox, he won eighty-nine games in six years, carried an impressive 2.19 earned run average, and helped Boston win three World Series. In December 1919, the financially strapped Red Sox owner Harry Frazee famously sold the pitcher-turned-slugging-outfielder to the New York Yankees for $100,000. With the Yankees, Ruth became the greatest power hitter in baseball history, wealthy beyond his dreams, and a media sensation, a folk hero, and a living legend. That, and his fun-loving, profligate lifestyle—he indulged himself with fast cars and women, stylish clothes, rich food and drink—and his genuine affection for and kindness to kids, is Babe Ruth in a nutshell. "No modern athletic hero exceeded Babe Ruth's capacity to project multiple images of the brute power, the natural, uninhibited man and the fulfillment of the American success dream," argues historian Benjamin G. Rader. "Ruth was living proof that the lone individual could still rise from mean, vulgar beginnings to fame and fortune, to a position of public recognition equaled by few men in American history."[11]

He was a Baltimore boy who made good, "a poor kid from the dockside slums" who had become one of the most famous and popular men in the country.[12] The city and many Baltimoreans loved him for it and have celebrated his successes and basked in his reflected glory for over a hundred years. During his lifetime, the local media, like the national media, followed his every triumph and foible. Whenever he visited or passed through Baltimore, during and after his playing days, it was newsworthy.[13] When he died, on August 16, 1948, of throat cancer at age fifty-three, it was front-page news and the Baltimore papers were replete with stories about Ruth. "The fabulous Babe Ruth, with his funny mincing walk, his barrel body, toothpick legs, flat nose, high cheeks and lusty laugh, has gone into the shadow of the dugout," mused Rodger H. Pippen of the *Baltimore News-Post*, who knew Ruth when he played for the Orioles in 1914. "Although asleep in a pine box, Babe never will vanish altogether from the scene."[14]

In Baltimore, one can find Babe Ruth many places. At the recently refurbished and reopened Babe Ruth Birthplace Museum, at 216 Emory Street, a few blocks west of Oriole Park at Camden Yards.[15] At the Sports Legends Museum (formerly Camden Station, a passenger terminal built in 1856 by the Baltimore & Ohio Railroad), with its 22,000 square feet dedicated to Baltimore and Maryland athletics, including a large, impressive section about Ruth. In front of Oriole Park's Eutaw Street entrance, where Susan Luery's sixteen-foot statue of Babe Ruth greets fans. Luery sculpted a young, trim Ruth, the one who played in Baltimore, not the rotund New York icon. He looks friendly, leaning on his bat, ankles crossed, his historically incorrect right-handed glove tucked in his back pocket.[16] Additionally, the Baltimore media never misses an opportunity to rekindle memories of and commemorate Ruth. Witness the outpouring of news stories on the hundredth anniversary of his birth in 1995, the fiftieth anniversary of his death in 1998, and the hundredth anniversary in 2014 of his four-month stint with the Orioles. Writing about the 1920s in *The Big Bam: The Life and Times of Babe Ruth* (2006), Leigh Montville declares, "The Babe sold papers. The papers sold him. It was a fine symbiotic relationship."[17] It still is. But retelling Babe Ruth narratives is more than just financially profitable. It also enables Baltimoreans to associate themselves and their city with transcendent greatness and an "odd, appealing, truly unique man."[18]

At the same time, Babe Ruth's Baltimore is either gone or has been transformed beyond recognition. In 1983, *Baltimore Sun* reporter David Simon noted that 216 Emory Street "is the only link to his childhood that is intact. The sandlot where he once played ball is now a Baltimore Gas and Electric Company power station, and his school, St. Mary's Industrial, as well as his father's tavern on Camden street, have long since been leveled."[19] These and other historical erasures make it all the more important for Baltimoreans to find or construct connections to the city's most famous and, yes, distinguished native son. As Joseph M. Burke of the *Baltimore News-American* put it in 1971, Babe Ruth "is an integral part of Baltimore, part of its heartbeat, part of its life's blood, part of its history and part of its fame. He ranks with Henry L. Mencken, James Cardinal Gibbons, Joe Gans, Betsy Patterson and Wallis Warfield and shares with them a common birthplace.

Along with them, in his own inimitable way, he has contributed to the fame of his native city."[20] Obviously he still does.

This does not mean Babe Ruth loved or had special affection for Baltimore. The hedonistic, live-in-the-moment Ruth was not romantic or nostalgic about his hometown, which is understandable. His youth in Baltimore was difficult and depressing. Thinking about it surely brought back melancholy memories. Nonetheless, after leaving town in 1914 to join the Red Sox, he returned to Baltimore in the offseason. But Ruth was no longer a St. Mary's ward; his mother had died in 1912; and he had a poor relationship with his father, who was killed in a bar fight in 1918. Coming back to Baltimore for his father's funeral, notes biographer Robert W. Creamer, was Ruth's "last extended visit to Baltimore, which he never again thought of as home. His father and mother were dead, his only sister was eighteen, a grown woman, and his stepmother had the bar. He was Babe Ruth of Boston now."[21] Ruth would occasionally play exhibitions in Baltimore, make public appearances, and pass through on his way to somewhere else. However, he "made no sentimental pilgrimages to his place of origin" and would sometimes go years without visiting Baltimore.[22] In the late twenties, when Ruth was at the zenith of his fame, a local reporter asked him, "Do you miss your native Baltimore and not living here?" Ruth replied, "Well, I always look out the window when our baseball club passes Baltimore."[23]

Leon Day Honored at Last

Like Babe Ruth a generation before him, Leon Day left Baltimore when he was a teenager and achieved baseball greatness—although not as much glory as he was due. Because of Jim Crow segregation most (white) people were unaware of Day's athletic achievements until he was elected to the National Baseball Hall of Fame in 1995, forty years after his long, remarkable baseball career was over. That Day was eventually enshrined in Cooperstown is a testament to his tremendous ability, persistence, and many accomplishments, and the doggedness of some of his advocates; that it took so long to happen tells us something meaningful about discrimination and commemoration, racism and remembrance.

Born in 1916 in Alexandria, Virginia, Leon Day was raised in Baltimore. "His father, Ellis Day, got a job at the Westport glass factory so that he and his wife, Hattie, could make enough to help raise their six children," writes Tom Kern of the Society for American Baseball Research (SABR). "They lived in nearby Mount Winans, then a poverty-stricken, all-black community in Southwest Baltimore in a house with no electricity or running water."[24] An athletic, baseball-loving young boy, Day told Negro league historian John B. Holway, "Ever since I can remember, I wanted to play ball. I started playing with the Mt. Winans AC, a team called the Silver Spoons [sic]. I was a second baseman, but if the pitcher got in trouble, I'd say, 'Give me the ball.'"[25]

In the mid-1930s, Day was scouted and recruited by the Baltimore Black Sox, a short-lived professional team in the Negro National League, based in Chester, Pennsylvania.[26] Day's mother disapproved of her son quitting high school to become a ballplayer.[27] However, the teenager had the following conversation with his father:

> "I asked my father if I could go," remembered Day. He asked, "Is that what you really want to do?" Leon Day thought a moment and said, "It's the only thing I want to do." "Well, if that's what you want go ahead."[28]

And so Day dropped out of Frederick Douglass High School, joined the Black Sox, and the next season played for the Brooklyn Eagles (soon to be the Newark Eagles).[29]

From 1936 through 1943, Day excelled with the Newark Eagles as a pitcher, but he also played second base, shortstop, and centerfield.[30] Some knowledgeable baseball people at the time thought "that Day, like Babe Ruth, was too valuable a hitter to be pitching," that he should be "a full-time outfielder to get his bat in the lineup every day."[31] Obviously multitalented and versatile, Day could do it all and well. "I would say he was the most complete ballplayer I've ever seen," attested Monte Irvin, a Hall of Fame outfielder who played with Day in Newark and later for eight seasons in the Major Leagues, mostly with the New York Giants. "I've never seen a better athlete, never seen a better baseball player all-around."[32] This is high praise from Willie Mays's former teammate.

Myriad sources suggest that Leon Day was the best pitcher in the Negro leagues during his career. This includes the more famous and self-promotional Satchel Paige, who towered over the relatively diminutive 5-foot 8-inch Day. Regrettably, as is the case with many Negro leaguers, Day's statistics are incomplete and inadequately measure his performance. Still, some numbers are useful and help us appreciate Day's baseball career.

In 1937, Day won thirteen games and lost none while batting .320 and eight home runs. He set a Negro league record in 1942 by striking out eighteen batters in a game, against the Baltimore Elite Giants (including the future Brooklyn Dodger and Hall of Fame catcher Roy Campanella three times).[33] That same year, Day bested Paige in their Negro League World Series pitching duel. It was one of the three times that Day beat Paige in their four recorded meetings. *The Pittsburgh Courier,* a widely respected and influential black newspaper, ranked Day ahead of Paige as the best Negro league pitcher in 1942 and 1943.[34] While in the army during World War II, Day served in the 818th Amphibian Battalion, drove a truck onto Normandy Beach six days after D-Day, and defeated a group of white Major Leaguers in a postwar exhibition game at Nuremberg Stadium.[35] On opening day in 1946, Day pitched a no-hitter against the Philadelphia Stars in his first game back from Europe.[36] He also played in a record seven East-West All-Star games. Some estimate that Day had a 70 percent winning average and approximately 300 wins in his twenty-two years as a pro, including the years he played in Mexico, Puerto Rico, and, in the 1950s when he was past his prime, in the minor leagues with the Toronto Maple Leafs, Scranton Miners, and Edmonton Eskimos.[37]

"It's a career," veteran Baltimore sportswriter John Steadman correctly asserted, "that when measured from any perspective deserves accreditation and applause."[38] Those who played in and followed the Negro leagues certainly knew all about and respected Day's accomplishments, his dignity and humility, and his "quiet, unassuming nature."[39] In the years after Day retired from baseball, when he worked as a bartender in Newark, and then as a security guard in Baltimore, many people in the black community knew and admired him. But public acts of approbation and commemoration were a long-time coming. Forced to play a separate and unequal version of the national pastime, talented, hard-working athletes such as Leon Day entertained and inspired countless fans, but most were quickly forgotten or ignored by those with the cultural authority to safeguard their memory and legacies.

Leon Day was finally elected to the Hall of Fame in 1995, only the twelfth Negro leaguer at the time. It was a hard-earned honor, the result of years of diligent advocacy on the part of former Negro leaguers like Monte Irvin and Buck O'Neil, both whom were on the Hall of Fame Veterans Committee that considered Day's candidacy, and others, such as Negro league historian Todd Bolton and members of the SABR Negro Leagues Committee and the black press. That is, a small, determined group of people who tried, successfully, to right an old wrong, to seek racial justice and historical commemoration.

For Day, as one can imagine, being a Hall of Famer was a long deferred dream come true. "I'm so happy, I don't know what to do," said Day after he was told the news, which was delivered by Max Manning, his former Newark Eagles teammate. The seventy-eight-year-old Day rejoiced, though he was confined to a St. Agnes Hospital bed with a heart condition and gout: "I never thought it would come."[40] He was not alone. In addition to his hopeful family, friends, and Negro league aficionados, the *Baltimore Sun* editorial page cheered: "Leon Day Honored at Last."[41] It was a good, redemptive day for black baseball and many Baltimoreans.

Six days later, Day died of heart failure, his wife, Geraldine Day, at his side.[42] "For most of his life," reported journalist Brad Snyder, "his country treated Day like a second-class citizen because of the color of his skin."[43] His education, baseball career, and military service were all segregated, less than they could and should have been. By contrast, Snyder noted that Day "received a first-class funeral yesterday [March 17, 1995] as more than 300 friends, family, former Negro leagues players and local dignitaries— including Sen. Paul S. Sarbanes and Mayor Kurt L. Schmoke—paid their last respects."[44] Most Baltimoreans, of course, had never seen Leon Day play or had probably heard of him until the recent Hall of Fame news. It was their loss and it impoverished their sense of baseball and Baltimore history. "In an age when baseball only seems to be about money and replacement players," Schmoke eulogized, in the midst of Major League Baseball's worst work stoppage, "Leon Day's life was about dignity, class and talent and so much more."[45] That so much more included a shameful history of racial segregation, the complicated politics of remembrance, and how the former impacts the latter.

No doubt writing on behalf of many people, *Baltimore Sun* columnist Michael Olesker responded to the sad news of Day's death with a sense of mournful frustration:

> Leon Day departs, six days after [his] election to baseball's Hall of Fame, and everyone must describe him with secondhand language and meager scraps of fact from a distinguished career: the 18 strikeouts over at old Bugle Field, the wins over the legendary Satchel Paige, the no-hitter he pitched after his return from World War II, but so little beyond that to flesh out the story.[46]

The humanity and depth that Olesker yearned for, the more complete portrait of Leon Day, is not accessible to most of us, in part because Day was modest and private. Unlike the extroverted Babe Ruth, who was loud and profane and whose every public act was well reported by the media and then repeated over and over again, Day played and lived in the shadows of white America. In addition, his early life and baseball career were not well documented. Much of it was forgotten—irretrievable and lost forever. The same is true of many Negro leaguers and other marginalized people. When

Ruth died, his legend was secure. When the Negro leagues died as a result of integration in the late 1940s and 1950s, "many of the old stars went into complete oblivion. Day was one of them," Olesker lamented.[47] Actually, Day was in Baltimore for the last fifteen years of his life, living quietly with his family, friends, and memories of games past.

Before Leon Day died, there were local efforts to celebrate his baseball career. Mayor Schmoke, for instance, declared January 31, 1992, Leon Day's Day in Baltimore.[48] In the spring of that same year, Governor William Donald Schaefer, the former mayor of Baltimore, did likewise at the State House in Annapolis when he proclaimed May 18 to be Leon Day Day in Maryland.[49] Also in 1992, on September 24, the Baltimore Orioles invited Day to throw the ceremonial first pitch at a home game.[50]

Similar efforts to memorialize Day have been undertaken since his death. The city renamed a west Baltimore park in Day's honor in 1997, near Gwynns Falls, on North Franklintown Road. The refurbished city park includes baseball fields, a basketball court, picnic and parking areas, and a large sign that welcomes visitors to "Negro League Hall-of-Famer Leon Day Park."[51] A few years later, in 2001, Day's widow established the Leon Day Foundation. Geraldine Day explains that the foundation promotes "self-awareness and lifelong learning for all ages through organized sports, resources, and educational programs; while preserving the legacies of Leon Day and the Negro League by giving recognition and exposure to a group of talented baseball players that were forgotten and never acknowledged."[52] More recently, the Hubert V. Simmons Museum of Negro Leagues Baseball, which is housed at the Owings Mills Branch of the Baltimore County Public Library, includes a small display about Leon Day.

Despite all of these efforts, and the hard, admirable work that went into creating these events, spaces, and institutions, one has to wonder about their efficacy at securing Leon Day's cultural memory in his hometown, the segregated city he had to leave to realize his baseball dreams. Under the best of circumstances, public memory is fragile, fragmented, and often ephemeral. Having a bronze plaque in Cooperstown helps to secure it. But that is no guarantee that Leon Day and his baseball achievements will be appreciated and remembered by many Baltimoreans, now and in the future. This is part of the high price of segregation.

Mr. Oriole

I do not know if the former Baltimore Orioles third baseman Brooks Robinson ever met Leon Day, his fellow Hall of Famer. Despite their dramatically different biographies and baseball odysseys, they would have gotten along well, I'm sure, as they shared a love of the game, were friendly and humble. They also experienced Baltimore much differently. It is true that Day earned some local (and national) recognition and respect late in his life for his baseball accomplishments and character. He deserved more, and earlier.

As for Brooks Robinson, Baltimore loved and loves him, deeply. For well over fifty years, Baltimoreans have cheered and embraced the genial Robinson, due to his on-field accomplishments, which were considerable, and for reasons that have nothing to do with them.

Certainly many athletes who were born or played in Baltimore, such as Babe Ruth and Leon Day, were more physically impressive than Robinson. He was not especially fast or strong, even in his youth. A few Baltimore athletes may be more venerated: John Unitas of the Colts, for example. None, however, are more genuinely beloved by generations of Baltimoreans than Brooks Robinson. Sportswriter Bob Maisel called it "unbridled love."[53]

Babe Ruth was and is mythic, larger than life, someone who was "transformed into something pretty close to a god," said one of his Boston Red Sox teammates.[54] Brooks Robinson was and is "just plain folks," a kind, warm man of human proportions, who had remarkable reflexes and hand-eye coordination, and equally impressive affability and graciousness.[55] "Of all the game's greats," sportswriter Thomas Boswell mused, "perhaps Robinson was least cursed by his own fame. He had great talent and never abused it. He received adulation and reciprocated with common decency. While other players dressed like kings and acted like royalty, Robinson arrived at the park dressed like a cabdriver. Other stars had fans. Robinson made friends."[56] More than he can count or know.

This is partly due to his impressive longevity as a ballplayer. Brooks Robinson debuted with the Orioles on September 17, 1955, at Memorial Stadium. Eisenhower was president and Robinson was eighteen years old, just months removed from graduating from Little Rock Central High School.[57] He was living his boyhood dream of being a major leaguer. After bouncing back and forth between the minor leagues and the Orioles for several years, Robinson made third base at Memorial Stadium his home in 1959—and remained there for close to a generation.

His last game was on August 13, 1977, post-Watergate and post-Vietnam. In all, he played twenty-three seasons and 2,896 games for the Orioles, setting the record for most consecutive seasons played for the same team (a record later tied by Carl Yastrzemski of the Boston Red Sox). In effect, "Baltimore saw Brooks grow up," wrote sportswriter Ed Linn in 1972. "During the long years when the club was developing, he was the franchise."[58]

As most Baltimoreans know, Robinson's genius was defense. He was an agile, brilliant fielding third baseman. From an early age, he saw and reacted to batted balls extremely well, hit to his left or right, on the ground or in the air. "If his feet were slow, his reflexes were the fastest," explained Boswell, who covered the Orioles for many years in the twilight of Robinson's career. "If his arm was average, his accuracy and quick release were the best. Somehow he always seemed languid, especially as he threw overhand toward first; yet the fastest runners were out by larger margins when Robinson made his syrupy perfectos than when the most kinetic jack-in-the-box third basemen made similar plays."[59] Hard working and well prepared, Robinson won sixteen consecutive Gold Gloves (1960–1975) for his defensive excellence and set Major League records at his position for putouts, assists, chances, double plays, and fielding percentage. All the Gold Glove awards did not "tell the half of it," Linn argued: "Brooks Robinson is undoubtedly the only player in history—choose your position—to whom the spectacular play is routine."[60] In the midst of the 1970 World Series, during which Robinson made myriad outstanding plays in the field, the loquacious Cincinnati Reds manager Sparky Anderson, frustrated by but impressed with Robinson's fielding, said: "I'm beginning to see Brooks in my sleep. If I dropped this paper plate, he'd pick it up on one hop and throw me out."[61]

Robinson was also a good, often clutch hitter, finishing his career with 2,848 hits, 268 home runs, and 1,357 runs batted in.[62] He was an eighteen-time All-Star, won the American League Most Valuable Player (MVP) award in 1964 and the All-Star Game MVP that same year. With Robinson at third, the Orioles won four American League pennants and two World Series—in 1966 and 1970—and he was World Series MVP in 1970, turning in a stellar, perhaps career-defining performance against the Reds on a national stage. "Suddenly," according to biographer Doug Wilson, "it seemed as though Brooks Robinson had just been discovered—a Rembrandt found under another painting, tucked away in an attic. He was the toast of the nation; everyone wanted a piece of him."[63] Seemingly indefatigable, he appeared on television talk shows, spoke at charitable fundraisers, visited people in hospitals, and was fêted at award banquets.

Seven years later, Robinson retired, his skills (especially his hitting) clearly in decline at age forty. Fittingly, the Orioles and the team's fans celebrated their longtime third baseman with Brooks Robinson Day at Memorial Stadium.[64] It was a festive event and the stadium was packed: a record regular-season crowd of 51,798 fans showed up to wish Robinson well in his retirement and to give him numerous gifts. They also wanted to thank him for the memories and "for being such an outstanding human being," wrote Bob Maisel.[65]

In 1983, Robinson was elected to the Baseball Hall of Fame in his first year of eligibility, earning 92 percent of the vote.[66] At his induction ceremony in Cooperstown, New York, "Robinson helped attract the largest crowd in Hall of Fame history," reported the *News American*, "a gathering twice as large as usual. Hall of Fame officials could not recall a more partisan gathering, nor one as intense."[67] It was the capstone to an excellent and much-appreciated career. To further affirm his playing excellence, Robinson was named to Major League Baseball's All-Century Team, one of just six third baseman.[68]

This brief rendition of Robinson's impressive career does not explain what he meant and means to Baltimoreans or why. To do that, we need to describe Brooks Robinson the man, his character, and put them in context.

Brooks Robinson never looked like an athlete: he was not especially tall, muscular, or fast. This made him seem like a kind of ball-playing Everyman, a regular guy, someone who had made it to and stayed in the big leagues largely due to his work ethic (it was often reported that he tirelessly practiced fielding groundballs in spring training and before games) and perseverance, not because of superior natural talent. As a result, many white, working- and middle-class Baltimoreans identified with him. He was a clean-cut, hard-working, middle-class white man with an easy smile and an endearing southern accent. His on-field performance, especially at third base, was consistently excellent, sometimes sublime, from the 1950s through the 1970s. Yet even when he dominated the competition—such as during the 1970 World Series—there was nothing Ruthian about Robinson.

This applied to Brooks Robinson's character, too. He was no late-night carouser. Ruth, by way of contrast, was extremely libidinous for most of his baseball career. Robinson was more of a superego family guy, sensitive to the needs and feelings of others, eager to please, inclusive and respectful. The fiery Frank Robinson, the former National League MVP who brought needed combativeness and leadership to the Orioles in 1966 when he was acquired in a trade with the Reds, said, "I suspect Brooks was a key reason why, for the first time in my 14 years in professional baseball, black players and white players had drinks together and meals together when we were on the road. Not every single night but two or three times on most road trips."[69] The team's interracial camaraderie contributed to its success. It also said something about Brooks Robinson's moral compass.

From early on, Robinson's character mattered to Baltimoreans. It still does. People appreciate his self-effacing manner, his graciousness, and the way he talks about his fans as friends and frequently praises his wife, Connie, for her years of support and devotion.[70] Likewise, people admire his consistency. "Brooks never changed, despite all the attention," said former

Orioles pitching coach George Bamberger. "He was always so humble, signing autographs with a smile."[71] Doug Wilson's biography *Brooks* (2014) is chockfull of testimony from childhood friends, former teammates, coaches, scouts, executives, sportswriters, and fans extolling Robinson's virtues. They include his work ethic, sense of responsibility, and willingness to follow the rules and respect authority, but just as important are his humility, integrity, loyalty, and warmth. Wilson asserts:

> Brooks Robinson remains an unquestioned icon in Baltimore. His genuine, humble demeanor, friendliness, and, above all, ability to remain a great role model have somehow grown in significance over the years as fans are continually disappointed by sports figures who are rude, selfish, and inaccessible. Brooks Robinson exhibits the exact opposite of all the traits that modern fans hate in their sports idols.[72]

Wilson is correct: when considering Robinson as a local icon, context matters. Obviously it is common for people to wax nostalgic about sports back in the day. Baltimoreans may be especially prone to do so, having lost their beloved Colts to Indianapolis in 1984 and suffered all kinds of decline and disappointment in the last forty years. Residents in troubled places regularly remember and dwell on the good old days.

Likewise, many people imagine that Major League Baseball was just a game (when they were kids, no matter when that was), not a highly commercialized and profitable business, which it has been since the late nineteenth century. "The changes in sports—moving of franchises, free agency—have made it impossible to count on a player, a team, an entire league still being around for next year's comeback," lamented sportswriter Robert Lipsyte in 1995, when Major League Baseball was in the midst of its most devastating work stoppage. "The connection between player and fan has been irrevocably destabilized, for love and loyalty demand a future. Along the way, those manly virtues of self-discipline, responsibility, altruism and dedication seem to have been deleted from the athletic contract with America."[73] Brooks Robinson, the ballplayer and the man, suggests that things were different in the past. He spent his whole career with one team. He could be counted on to be Brooks Robinson: that is, affable and altruistic, dedicated and decent.

To many fans, especially in Baltimore, Robinson seemed like one of the few athletes in the 1970s and beyond who honored the traditional, unwritten compact with them and their community. In 1971, Jim Murray of the *Los Angeles Times* wrote, "the best thing about Brooks Robinson is his lifestyle—which might be described as early Colonial Cheerful. For 25 years, he showed up for every game as if it were a privilege not a pain. He always looks like a little kid who just tasted his first ice cream cone. He's as eager to please as a Boy Scout. He's no trouble to the game, the law, the fans, the management. They just hand him a glove each year and say, 'Shut up and do miracles.'"[74] Robinson obliged, for as long as he could.

In addition to having soft hands and great reflexes, Robinson had and has terrific image management skills. He knows that people enjoy meeting him, and he genuinely likes meeting and engaging them. "I came here a couple years after the team moved from St. Louis and I kind of grew up with the Orioles—lived through the bad years and played in four World Series," he once explained. "I signed autographs and I went everywhere the people wanted me. I worked at being Brooks Robinson, but I loved it."[75] That work has yielded impressive results. In 1977, after Brooks Robinson Day at Memorial Stadium, Alan Goldstein of the *Baltimore Sun* declared that the third baseman "has meant more for Baltimore's image than anyone in memory. Yes, Babe Ruth started here, but he was only a transient on his way to New York. Brooks Robinson belonged to Baltimore and the city did its best yesterday to show its gratitude."[76]

It continues to do so. In 2011 and 2012, for instance, two larger-than-life bronze statues of Brooks Robinson were erected. The first, on a plaza at the intersection of Russell Street and Washington Boulevard across from Oriole Park, is nine feet tall and depicts Robinson wearing a gold glove, getting ready to throw a baseball. It was sculpted by Baltimore native Joseph Sheppard and cost $700,000, much of it contributed by local businessman Henry Rosenberg, Robinson's longtime friend. "Brooks is a superb individual who represents everything good, both on and off the field," Rosenberg said. "He was, and is, Mr. Oriole."[77] The second statue, as Lee Lowenfish mentions in this book, is one of six in Oriole Park. They were sculpted by Toby Mendez and were commissioned by the team to commemorate its Hall of Famers and the ballpark's twentieth anniversary. After the dedication, an upbeat Robinson declared that it was "wonderful for fans to have a look at the guys who really helped make this franchise and guys who are in the Baseball Hall of Fame. I couldn't be happier being out there as one of them."[78] That Robinson has been honored in bronze *twice* in the Monumental City reveals how much Baltimoreans cherish him and their memories of his play and the values he personified.

Ultimately, the best way to describe and understand the relationship between Brooks Robinson and Baltimore is to acknowledge that it was and is a love affair. Sometimes love is blind, mysterious, or irrational. This love story, however, is as understandable as it is enduring. For those who followed his career as it unfolded, Robinson was, as his former teammate and fellow Hall of Famer Jim Palmer put it, the "consummate pro. Everybody who saw him play knows how great a player he was."[79] That he was "gracious and humble" mattered, too.[80] Obviously there are thousands of people in Baltimore who are too young to have seen Robinson play. No matter. Thanks in part to baseball's ability to nurture intergenerational relationships and memories, some of them respect and feel affection for Robinson, too—and many of them proudly wear his No. 5 jersey at Orioles games and all over town, line up for and treasure his autograph, and take snapshots in front of his statues. This is not just nostalgia-driven commercialism or sentimentalism (although that is part of it). Brooks Robinson abides—because late twentieth- and early twenty-first-century Baltimoreans embrace the values and qualities that they think and feel he represents, and they would like to think the city does, too.

The Iron Man

The Orioles were Cal Ripken Jr.'s favorite team when he was growing up in Aberdeen, Maryland, in the 1960s and 1970s, and Brooks Robinson was his favorite player.[81] Makes sense. After all, his father, Cal Ripken Sr., had

On October 6, 1991, the last Orioles game played at Memorial Stadium, John Unitas shook Mayor Kurt Schmoke's hand, while Brooks Robinson and Cal Ripken Jr. enjoyed the moment. *Image by and courtesy of Scott Hubert.*

worked in the Orioles organization as a player, manager, coach, scout, and minor league instructor since 1957, joining the big league team in 1976 as its bullpen coach.[82] Further, during Cal Jr.'s youth thousands of base-ball-loving boys, especially in Maryland, adored Robinson and often imag-ined playing for the Orioles. Ripken realized that dream. Remarkably, like Brooks Robinson, Cal Ripken Jr. played his entire Hall-of-Fame career with the Orioles and in the process became a revered civic icon and nationally renowned.

Ripken's twenty-one-year Major League career was impressive. He was the American League Rookie of the Year in 1982, helped lead the Orioles to a World Series championship in 1983, was a two-time American League MVP, an All-Star nineteen consecutive times, and was named MVP of the All-Star game twice. He is the Orioles' all-time leader in virtually every offensive category, in addition to most games played (3,001).[83]

At 6'4" and 220 pounds, the sturdy, fundamentally sound Ripken chal-lenged traditional ideas about who could play shortstop. Moved from third base by manager Earl Weaver in 1982, Ripken ended up becoming the great-est power-hitting shortstop in Major League history, one of only seven play-ers with at least 400 home runs and 3,000 career hits. Ripken also won two Gold Gloves, and in 1990 he committed just three errors, setting a record for fielding percentage (.996) at his position. The combination of Ripken's slugging and sterling defense (which relied on preparation, positioning, and a strong, accurate arm) was unprecedented. He was the prototype for big, athletic shortstops such as Alex Rodriguez and Derek Jeter.

And there was also the Streak. In early September 1995, when Ripken played in his 2,131st consecutive game to break Lou Gehrig's fifty-six-year-old record, most of the sports world and much of the nation paid its respects and cheered. Fans and the media hailed Ripken—then thirty-five years old, a veteran of thirteen seasons with the Orioles—as an exemplar of all that was right and frequently absent in contemporary professional sports. He was often portrayed as a "throwback" ballplayer who evoked an earlier era of baseball history. "Ripken seems like some figure emerging from a time machine," quipped veteran sportswriter Heywood Hale Broun. "You half expect him to be wearing a baggy flannel uniform and using a skimpy glove."[84] Because Ripken bested a record that few thought was approach-able, observers lauded him for his work ethic and endurance and cast him as a symbol of reliability and consistency. Ripken's durability and determi-nation transformed him into the Iron Man.

Again, context matters. We need to remember that in 1994 Major League Baseball suffered its worst, most destructive work stoppage in history. After the final seven weeks of the regular season and the World Series were canceled, journalist Mark Maske offered the following analysis:

> An industry that had been projecting $1.8 billion in revenues in an uninterrupted season this year—and in which the average player's salary has soared to nearly $1.2 million per season—will not stage its crown jewel event, the World Series, for the first time in 90 years because management and labor cannot agree to a compensation system. Such squabbles are nothing new to baseball. This is the game's eighth work stoppage in 23 years, and labor-relations spats as far back as the 1800s have been chronicled. But never before did a shutdown do this kind of damage. The great strike of 1994 wiped out the final 52 days and 669 games of what had been shaping up as one of the most invigorating seasons in memory.[85]

Needless to say, many baseball fans were disappointed and frustrated with the work stoppage and the cancellations; some were furious and swore off the game forever.

The post-strike timing of the Streak's culmination was important. It contributed to the sense that Ripken was a living relic from a more innocent, less contentious bygone era. "At a time when the game is in serious rehab," wrote Curry Kirkpatrick in *Newsweek*, "Ripken stands out as the ideal role model—an anti-Mantle who, rather than abuse his family and body over the span of a distinguished career, has held them aloft as the twin citadels of his success."[86] Unlike many of his colleagues, Kirkpatrick added, Ripken is "a quiet, serene hero so gracious that he actually respects the integrity of the sport. He also signs autographs for hours for no charge, and drives and drinks what he endorses (Chevy Suburban, milk)."[87] To many fans and those in the media, Ripken was seen as a paragon of hard work, fortitude, and decency. He was transformed from an All-Star ballplayer into a symbol of All-American homespun masculine virtues.[88] Additionally, "for many fans alienated by baseball's bitter labor dispute, the Streak was an antidote to the Strike, the tonic that revived the national pastime."[89]

In Baltimore, the Streak was recognized "as a native son's defining glory," a joyous communal event worth celebrating.[90] Obviously most Orioles fans were jubilant. After the top of the fifth inning of game 2,131, when the contest against the California Angels became official, fireworks burst, orange and black balloons were released, the music on the public address system swelled, and the cheering at Camden Yards went on and on, as Ripken did an impromptu, ten-minute jog around the ballpark waving to and shaking hands with fans. After the game (which the Orioles won), Brooks Robinson

was among the dignitaries who praised Ripken. "I played baseball here
in Baltimore for over 20 years," he said, "and they called me Mr. Oriole,
but now, Cal Ripken, you're Mr. Oriole."[91] The next day, John Steadman
wrote, "What a compliment, especially coming from Robinson, who was so
gifted as well as inherently kind."[92] Thomas Boswell noted that after 2,131,
Ripken, "in a twist of fate that is beyond his ambitions or even his still-
modest sense of himself, the former clubhouse boy has become bigger than
Earl Weaver. Bigger than Jim Palmer. Bigger than Frank Robinson. Bigger
even than his childhood idol and adult role model—Brooks Robinson."[93]
The *Baltimore Evening Sun* headline declared: "CAL-LOSSAL!"[94] The newspaper's editorial page proudly asserted:

> He is as steady as a white, marble stoop.
> As feisty as a Chesapeake blue crab.
> As enduring as Fort McHenry.
> As graceful as a skipjack at sail.
> Cal Ripken Jr. doesn't just play for a team in Baltimore, he *is* Baltimore.[95]

Explaining the moment and enthusiastic local reactions to it, the *Sun*
continued: "It's about a place celebrating itself as it celebrates a native-son
hero. The Orioles shortstop values the things Baltimoreans like to think
they cherish, too: durability, dependability, family ties." All true. At the
same time, the *Sun* neglected to mention that over the years some people
questioned the Streak's effect on the team and Ripken's performance, as well
as his motives.[96]

Ripken kept playing and in 1997 moved to third base, his original position. The Streak continued for another 501 games, until Ripken voluntarily
ended it on September 20, 1998, the Orioles' last home game of the season.
"I've said it a thousand times, I never set out to break a record," Ripken
explained. "The significance in the streak isn't a number, but a sense of pride
in knowing this is how I approach my job."[97] Baseball fans and the media
once again extolled Ripken's professionalism, durability, and contributions
to the game. "No one ever will be able to quantify Ripken's immeasur-
able service to baseball in the aftermath of the strike," stated Bill Koenig in
Baseball Weekly. "He showed up for work on time, played hard all the time,
then signed autographs for hour upon hour. He was the beacon, guiding the
game back to some respectability."[98]

Other milestones lay ahead. Ripken notched his 400th home run in
1999 and his 3,000th hit in 2000. He homered in his final All-Star game in
2001. When Ripken retired that October, the Orioles retired his No. 8 and
unveiled a dugout plaque in memory of his father. During his last game,
more than 48,000 fans at Camden Yards stood and cheered in appreciation

for all that he had accomplished and meant to them.[99] "It's a proud and poignant night for Baltimore," said Mayor Martin O'Malley. "Cal really personified the greatest qualities about the people of this city, their work ethic and their perseverance."[100] Many people reiterated this theme; that is, Ripken represented Baltimore and "came to embody the city's dream of itself—its love of the simple, basic and humble," wrote journalist M. Dion Thompson. As a result, Baltimore "gave unconditional love to Ripken."[101]

It did so again in 2007 when Ripken was elected to the Baseball Hall of Fame with 98.5 percent of the vote, an all-time high for a position player. "Ripken not only played brilliantly, but he also always seemed to embody the very characteristics Baltimoreans use to describe their city," declared journalist Childs Walker after the election results were announced. "He was a small-town boy who spent his entire career with the franchise he grew up cheering. He didn't always have the game mastered, but he never stopped working to master it. He could be counted on."[102] Six months later, fans from Baltimore and nationwide converged on Cooperstown for Ripken's induction. My father and I were among the record-setting crowd of more than 70,000. The "sea of fans, with signs such as 'My Son is Named Cal Because of You,' came from distances and in numbers never before seen," reported Thomas Boswell.[103] Why? Because, in part, many people believed that Ripken (and his fellow inductee, Tony Gwynn) represented meaningful cultural values: dedication, excellence, hard work, integrity, loyalty, and respect for the game. The latter was especially important in the midst of the so-called steroids era, when artificially enhanced sluggers such as Mark McGwire and (allegedly) Barry Bonds were obliterating long-standing home run records. Self-effacing and grateful for all the support he received during his life and career, Ripken explained, "This [the massive crowd] was about the fans love of baseball, from generation to generation. The game continues long after any of us put away our glove." Ripken added, "This demonstrates that baseball is alive, popular and good."[104]

During his career (and now well beyond it), Cal Ripken Jr. was the pride of Baltimore. Over the years, despite the Orioles' chronic struggles, he became a civic institution, as much a part of the city's identity as rowhouses and Old Bay seasoning. His workmanlike style of play, reserved personality, and long tenure with the team resonated with many Baltimoreans—whom former Orioles executive Roland Hemond considered to be "hard-working, conscientious people who will always applaud those who give their best, who are there every day, and those who truly care for their city. That's why Cal is so special here."[105] It helped that, despite his wealth and fame, Ripken identified "with the dependability of the waitress in Dundalk and the sore feet of the cop in Crownsville."[106] Growing up in Cal Sr. and Vi Ripken's modest Aberdeen home surely contributed to this empathetic sensibility, the respect he has for working people. In this way Ripken was similar to Brooks Robinson and John Unitas. Historian David W. Zang makes the comparison between Ripken and Unitas explicit: "Unitas—quiet, strong, independent, a winner, a western-Pennsylvania boy who made himself a home in Charm City; Ripken—tough, resilient, a winner, a native of nearby Aberdeen, Maryland, who wandered the minor leagues with his dad before making himself a home in Baltimore. The public perception of both was and remains blue-collar."[107] In Baltimore—a tough, hardscrabble, idiosyncratic town—a blue-collar identity is important, probably imperative, for its enduring athletic icons.

Believe

Sometimes, a ballplayer is just a ballplayer. And sometimes a ballplayer signifies a great deal. Such is the case with Babe Ruth, Leon Day, Brooks Robinson, and Cal Ripken Jr. in Baltimore, a city that sometimes "defines itself by what's gone, what used to be," remarks mystery writer and Orioles fan Laura Lippman.[108] Ruth and Day died decades ago. Robinson and Ripken have been retired for many years. Yet in their glory days and for many years after these men reflected and helped define Baltimore.

For Ruth and Day, the burgeoning, segregated city was their childhood home. Talented, impoverished, and, in different ways, neglected, they left Baltimore as teenagers, taking baseball odysseys that yielded wildly dissimilar results, though both men ended up in Cooperstown. In Ruth, we see America's preeminent athletic hero, an uncouth man-child who was showered with accolades and fame, in which his hometown basked from afar. Modest and self-possessed, Day was not so fortunate, a victim of institutional racism that severely limited what he (and many others) could do and who he could become. Only late in his life did most Baltimoreans learn about and celebrate his baseball exploits. Unlike Day, who rarely expressed bitterness about what might have been, white ballplayers such as Ruth, Robinson, and Ripken did not have to wait forty years to have their accomplishments widely appreciated and glorified in Baltimore and beyond. This is of course shameful.

Robinson, whom sportswriter and native Baltimorean Frank Deford called the "noblest Oriole of all," played and lived in the city as it desegregated and slowly deindustrialized and declined. As Deford put it, Robinson "built his reputation largely with his glove—which is equivalent, say, of achieving grand stature in the music world as a yodeler. But Brooksie was our yodeler, the best there was at it, and the fancy-dan big cities could keep their sluggers and fireballers. Babe Ruth might have been born in Baltimore, but his bombast was too much for such a modest community."[109] Beloved by generations of Baltimoreans, the good-natured Robinson helped beget Ripken Jr., his Oriole heir on the left side of the infield. For twenty-plus years, Ripken doggedly continued the tradition that Robinson and Cal Ripken Sr. helped create, the Oriole Way. In the process he provided many people with a shining example and preferred vision of the blue-collar but noble Baltimore in which they wanted to believe. That was long before the hopeful word "Believe" became a civic rejuvenation campaign slogan painted on buildings, billboards, and bus benches.

19

The Ravens' Flight to Normalcy

How Winning Restored Baltimore's Football Culture

CHARLES KUPFER

Late December 2012. What mattered most was the storyline sportswriters ignored. A matchup in Baltimore between the Ravens and Indianapolis Colts usually mandated an editorial formula: fugitive franchise returns, local fans vent angst. The Ravens and Colts had played each other often; each game resurrected that story. But this time was different. This 2012 playoff tilt signaled not just a championship run for Baltimore, but the end of the old Baltimore/Indianapolis melodrama. The Ravens were about to give Baltimore fans something they needed—a return to football normalcy.

Chuck Pagano was the new focus. Indianapolis's coach was fresh off medical leave, battling leukemia. His return to the sidelines dominated pre-game press coverage. Pagano was a former Raven defensive coordinator. "He's like a dad to me," said veteran safety Ed Reed, whom Pagano coached at the University of Miami. "That's family, which is first before football." *Baltimore Sun* reporter Aaron Wilson noted that Pagano remained popular in the Baltimore locker room. "Chuck is a great coach, I'm sure the fans are going to welcome him," said safety Bernard Pollard. "We're going to love him, we're going to embrace him. At the same time, we've got to play him and we've got to beat him."[1]

Would rookie Colts quarterback Andrew Luck handle playoff pressure? Would Ravens quarterback Joe Flacco claim "elite" status? Would outgoing linebacker Ray Lewis inspire a Super Bowl run? These questions and stories dominated the media. There was no reopening the Baltimore Colt annals. Suddenly, the Mayflower vans were a hackneyed contrivance. Instead, the return of a beloved former coach prevailing over illness served everyone's needs. When the Ravens won 24–9, attention turned to the next round, a road game in Denver.

No other NFL franchise had such an ugly birth, due to intense labor pain stemming from Baltimore's nebulous thirteen-year exile and from the Colts' sad decline under renegade owner Robert Irsay. The quietus of Irsay's tenure was the March 28, 1984, nighttime exit, which abraded Baltimore's sense of itself. To locals, previous Colts' glories meant that NFL football was a deserved civic amenity justified by heritage. Hometown fan and poet Ogden Nash epitomized Baltimore's passion for the Colts. His adoring doggerel in *Life* celebrated:

> They've caught the disease fate
> holds in store
> For the population of Baltimore—
> A disease more virulent than rabies
> Felling men and women and even babies.
> The cynic becomes a true believer
> When caught in the grips of that
> old Colt fever.[2]

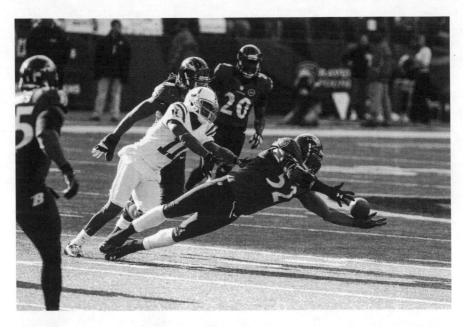

All-Pro linebacker Ray Lewis and the Ravens versus the Indianapolis Colts.
Image by and courtesy of Scott Hubert.

Once Irsay decamped, Baltimore's leadership was determined to get its city back into the league. Local lore credited the Colts with putting Baltimore on the sports map. What then did the loss of the team mean? That question nettled a middle-sized market wary of larger, prestigious neighbors like Washington, DC, Philadelphia, and New York. The insuperable Colts heist seemed to bear out Baltimore's insecurity. Maybe the city really was a pit stop on the East Coast highway. But that was anathema to the pugnacious city. Restoring professional football became a civic obsession.

First came the United States Football League (USFL), sort of. In 1984, the two-year-old spring league's marquee franchise, the Philadelphia Stars, nominally moved to Baltimore. Memorial Stadium was off-limits because of the Orioles, so the Stars played in College Park. "Baltimore" won the last USFL championship, in 1985. Positioning for an antitrust lawsuit against the NFL, or better yet, a settlement/merger, the USFL announced its plans to play in the fall. Baltimore fans hoped that a merger would provide a near-seamless transition from the Colts. But the USFL case went bust and the league folded.[3] There followed fruitless flirtations with the New Orleans Saints and St. Louis Cardinals, two bad NFL teams angling for richer stadium deals. In early 1987, "Baltimore Cardinals" shirts hit the shelves at Hutzler's, but team owner Bill Bidwill chose Phoenix instead.

Then came the agonizing NFL expansion derby, perhaps as radicalizing to Baltimoreans as the Irsay experience. Behind Governor William Donald Schaefer and Maryland Stadium Authority chief Herb Belgrad, Maryland political and business leaders backed legislation authorizing the Camden Yards stadium complex. Construction on the Orioles' ballpark began, but a team needed to be in place for the football stadium to be built. Baltimore attracted well-heeled would-be owners, including local hero Leonard "Boogie" Weinglass, Malcolm Glazer, and Al Lerner, a Cleveland billionaire with Baltimore roots who owned a piece of the Browns and was Art Modell's friend. Maryland's offer looked irresistible. Added to the rich package was a strong local sense that the image-conscious NFL wanted to rectify Irsay's midnight ride. But in 1993, the NFL chose Charlotte and Jacksonville. Commissioner Paul Tagliabue's insensitive press conference remarks made him the new focus of Baltimore's ire. Asked if another team might move to Baltimore, Tagliabue sneered, "I can't say that I've lost a lot of sleep over that," adding that Maryland might consider building a plant or a museum instead of a stadium. He noted that nobody forced the city into the expansion derby.[4] John Pica Jr., state senator and longtime expansion booster, tore into the commissioner. "One day we will have a football franchise in Baltimore," he vowed, warning Tagliabue to "Watch our games on television because if you show up at our beautiful new stadium, you will not be able to hide in the crowd."[5] At the time, nobody stressed that Tagliabue worked for the owners. His job description included protecting their financial interests, and securing new stadiums was a big part of that. Lerner retained his minority share of the Browns. He was well known in ownership circles, and now, so were the generous terms of Baltimore's stadium deal. Several NFL owners stood stymied in their efforts to secure new facilities. One was Lerner's friend in Cleveland, Art Modell.

After Tagliabue spoke, a galled Schaefer, his voice trembling, shook his head and murmured, "I've been hit twice—when the team left and now this."[6] In one afternoon, Tagliabue joined Irsay as Maryland's prime sports villain. It was in that press conference that the Ravens were born. Awareness dawned that Baltimore was a patsy. The *Baltimore Sun*'s John Eisenberg argued for a new, piratical approach. It was time, he wrote, to get a team by any means possible. Belgrad left his post. His replacement, named by incoming governor Parris Glendening, was John Moag Jr., a clear-eyed, tight-lipped, forceful attorney. Talented and disciplined, Moag was a graduate of Loyola High School, Washington College, and the University of Baltimore School of Law. A partner at Washington's white-shoe firm Patton, Boggs & Blow, Moag contacted every NFL owner with a potential yen to move.

Then came the Canadian Football League interlude. That league, reduced to eight teams in Canada, added teams in Sacramento, Las Vegas, San Antonio, Memphis, Birmingham, Shreveport, and Baltimore. The idea was to build a continental presence and land an American TV deal. Baltimore owner Jim Speros called his team the "CFL Colts," unveiling a blue-white-silver color scheme. Swift NFL trademark litigation banned that name, and for awhile the nameless team was simply the Baltimore Football Club, before settling on the "Stallions."

Sports Illustrated scribe Michael Farber covered the home opener. His July 25, 1995, article, "Don't Call them the Colts," had fun with the name. "A judge had ruled that, for the moment anyway, the team cannot call itself the C-word, but last Saturday, Baltimore's Memorial Stadium was the people's court," went Farber's lede. "Every time the public address announcer said, 'Your Baltimore CFL . . .' he paused to allow the crowd of 39,247 to bellow '*Colts!*'—and no judicial decree could stop it."[7] "Baltimore does not forget," Farber noted, adding that while "Irsay's midnight run was viewed as stabbing Baltimore in the back, the NFL's decision to snub the city and award expansion franchises to Charlotte and Jacksonville was viewed as twisting the knife. No NFL city, not even Green Bay, had experienced such a dizzying love affair with its team," Farber continued.[8] John Unitas and other old Colts visited the sidelines, giving the CFL team their imprimatur. Instantly a winner, the team made the Grey Cup in 1994, and won it in 1995. Baltimore led the league in attendance both seasons, the Colts Marching Band played at home games, and the Colt Corral fan clubs reactivated. The league announced plans to play a future Grey Cup in Baltimore.[9] The Stallions were such a hit that nationalistic Canadians worried about Baltimore's undue influence on "their" league. But to Baltimore fans, whose self-referential status as underdogs was intrinsic, the image of Baltimore as colossus was incomprehensible. To people in Baltimore, the CFL meant fun, but they still wanted back in to the NFL.

Some state legislators felt it was time to give up on the NFL chase. Glendening's power base was the Washington suburbs, where fans liked the Redskins. The Redskins themselves examined building a stadium in the Maryland suburbs. Moag reminded everyone that Baltimore's stadium offer would not last forever, also hinting at antitrust actions. Any NFL owner who wanted Baltimore's deal needed to make a choice. Art Modell's intention to move the Browns went public in October, so the 1995 Grey Cup was marked by speculation about where the Stallions would move once the Browns came.

Modell's Cleveland position was ambiguous. The Browns owner was a civic fixture, a philanthropist who owned the city's most beloved institution. Modell's wealth was tied up with his team. He was a respected figure in league circles during the Pete Rozelle years because he helped to sell "league-think," convincing owners to treat NFL television deals as collective, ensuring that franchises in smaller markets received equal payouts. That helped to generate the NFL-AFL merger.[10] But by the 1990s, the NFL ownership model was shifting. Dallas Cowboy impresario Jerry Jones epitomized the new breed: tycoons who wanted every dollar a team could earn. In Cleveland, the sixty-four-year-old Municipal Stadium was due for an overhaul or demolition. Modell wanted a football-only stadium with luxury suites and personal seat licenses. Cleveland had recently spent $650 million building a new Indians ballpark, Cavaliers arena, and the Rock-and-Roll Hall of Fame. Told to wait, Modell seethed. He dickered and bickered with Mayor Michael R. White. But local officials guessed that the Browns, with robust attendance and profound local attachments, would wait until the city was ready.[11]

Modell and Moag spent more and more time together, Lerner facilitating their relationship. Moag also talked with the owners of the Arizona Cardinals, Cincinnati Bengals, and Tampa Bay Buccaneers. Hastening, Modell reached out to Moag, hashing out the details of a Baltimore move aboard Lerner's private jet. By the time the deal was done, on October 27, 1995, Modell understood that moving the Browns would mean instant cash value. What the Browns owner also wanted, however, was secrecy. He understood how Irsay's getaway was smoothed over because it happened in the spring, not during football season.

Mayor White understood that the Browns represented one of pro football's proudest legacies. For all the fans' frustrations about not winning a title since Fran Ryan beat Unitas and Baltimore in 1964, they adored the Browns. The most visible fans, members of the Dawg Pound, embodied the self-image Cleveland prized, and which any Baltimorean recognized: tough, yet sentimental, unpolished but genuine. Hearing rumors of the move, fans' rage—and that of northern Ohio's political, business, and media apparatus—fixed on Modell for leaving and Baltimore for tempting him. Modell's intentions refracted massive focus on what an owner could do. Based upon recent NFL history, Modell had precedent on his side. But, as White knew, Cleveland fans were not without resources. Among their weapons was sympathetic press coverage.

The NFL detested bad public relations. The league counted on a servile press corps to avoid issues like illicit steroids or owner misbehavior. But now, in October 1995, Cleveland won the protagonist role. Media concern arose because of the subterfuge cloaking Modell's scheme, the allegiance of Cleveland fans, and the national regard for the Dawg Pounders and the Paul Brown roots of a great franchise. After somnolence regarding other franchise shifts and the expansion disgrace, the press at last noticed that the NFL was pitting markets against each other. All over the country, Modell's move to Baltimore was painted as a terrible injustice.[12]

In Baltimore, a welcome party went awkwardly. A rally at the Inner Harbor on November 6, 1995, saw Modell, Lerner, Moag, and Glendening on the dais. Schaefer sat in the crowd. Fans infiltrated the stage set, chanting Modell's name and cheering. The affair was covered live in Maryland and Ohio. Showing the effects of late-night negotiations and negative press attention, and realizing that after thirty years along Lake Erie, he was now cutting himself off from Cleveland forever, a weary Modell spoke hesitantly. His tone was level, his message more depressed than defiant. He acknowledged his welcome, thanked Lerner, and expressed disappointment over the way events played out in Ohio. Things had not gone according to plan, he explained. He had no choice but to move the team. Modell stressed that his pockets were nearly empty, that he had no external fortune on which to rely. A new stadium was all that stood between his team and ruin. Moag was also subdued. "Our elation is accompanied by pain that we know so well," he said, referring to Cleveland fans.[13] He suggested that Baltimore leaven its glee over getting football back with empathy for northern Ohio. Glendening rankled Clevelanders the most. On a good day, Maryland's Democratic governor came off as a bloodless technocrat. At worst, he was overconfident and obtuse. Purblind to the delicate situation, a laughing Glendening played up Browns history, waved a team mug over his head, and plainly enjoyed himself. Clevelanders and sympathizers across the country now had signature optics. Baltimore fans could barely conceptualize that they were now the bad guys, Clevelanders the victims.

Mayor Brown's campaign to slow or stop the Browns exit concentrated on the twenty-five-year stadium lease, which had four more seasons to run. White's actual strategy was to maintain the Browns name, colors, and heritage while gaining a replacement team. It took five months for that deal to come together. Every remaining Browns home game was a TV nightmare for the NFL. Fans stayed away or showed up to protest. It looked like a morality play: a blue-collar city, dowdy but proud, boasted a renewed waterfront with upgraded facilities for its home teams. The football team, with a championship history that shone through the ragged recent past, provided a touch point around which the diverse community rallied. A greedy owner who left his loyal fans behind to grab at dollars waved by a predatory wannabe market sundered that special relationship between town and team.

Baltimoreans recognized *that* story, but resented the media's comparative inattention during the Colts' move. The nadir, from a Baltimore perspective, came on December 4, 1995, when *Sports Illustrated* ran a cover cartoon of Art Modell sucker-punching a Dawg Pounder. "Battle for the Browns," the caption squealed. "Art Modell Sucker-Punched Cleveland, but the City Is Fighting Back." Inside, articles described the feelings of Cleveland fans, exposed Modell's bad business decisions, and lambasted the unfairness of fans in Ohio having to watch their favorite team play elsewhere. Oddly, Baltimore's status as a former NFL city went unmentioned. At Tagliabue's pre–Super Bowl "State of the NFL" talk, columnist Mike Lupica—heretofore not scandalized by moving teams—challenged the commissioner to protect deserving NFL cities like Cleveland from pirate markets. The parallel situation developing in Houston, where the Oilers owner Bud Adams was readying his team's exit to Tennessee, failed to generate commensurate attention. Baltimore fans decided that the media fuss was less a matter of principle than situation. It was the move of their favorites which Cleveland fans found unfair. Other franchise moves—Cardinals, Rams, Raiders, Colts, Oilers—were treated differently. To Cleveland supporters, this was because Browns fans were enthusiastic and the team's heritage a proud one. The Browns, they said, were different.

Modell backed off his insistence that the Browns name and legacy come with him. Cleveland would build a new stadium for an expansion team to inherit franchise records when the Browns reappeared three seasons later.

Baltimore would get Modell, his roster, and the chance to pick a new team name—as long as it was not the Colts. Baltimore consoled itself with a Ring of Honor in the new stadium dedicated to "Johnny Unitas and the Baltimore Colts" and a statue of Unitas in front of it. Across the nation lingered the pervasive sense that Baltimore's reentry into the NFL was underhanded, that Modell's franchise shift was uniquely wrong, that a coating of moral grime dimmed this new team. For several weeks after the move was approved, the team had no name or logo. When ESPN showed a graphic, it simply read "Baltimore." Fans in a *Sun* poll voted "Ravens" over "Marauders" and "Americans," and Modell liked the literary association with Edgar Allen Poe, so the franchise at least got a catchy moniker.[14] But former Browns tight end Bob Trumpy, a Hall of Famer who lent his name to one of the top-selling football annuals, captured what many felt about the Ravens when he wrote that he hated them and hoped they lost every game.[15]

What, exactly, came to Baltimore from Cleveland? Not the coach. Modell fired cranky gridiron theorist Bill Belichick, blaming him for the team's 5–11 fiasco in 1995. It might have been wiser to keep him, since Belichick grew up in Annapolis as a Colts fan. Not uniforms—those belonged to Cleveland. Not records. What came was a roster whose most illustrious player was quarterback Vinnie Testaverde, and the chance to build something fresh. The Ravens unveiled their logo: a shield with a winged "B" that included heraldic elements from the Maryland flag. It looked like a biker club insignia, which had outlaw appeal. However, because the original design was very close to one submitted by a fan, the trademark issue threatened yet again. The Ravens eventually adopted the angry bird logo, which they still retain. Their color scheme, purple-black-gold, evoked the sheen of Poe's ominous bird. Three team mascots were dubbed Edgar, Allen, and Poe.

With no coach and a new market to win over, Modell set his sights on landing Don Shula as head coach. To the rest of the United States, Shula epitomized the Miami Dolphins. But in Baltimore, Shula represented a living tie to the old Colts, which he coached during the 1960s. Shula stayed coy, so Modell turned instead to Ted Marchibroda, another former Baltimore Colts coach. "I think Ted is one of the most underrated coaches in league history," Modell opined.[16] "Uncle Ted" hired a staff that included Kirk Ferentz as offensive coordinator, Don Strock as quarterbacks coach, Ken Whisenhunt as tight ends coach, Marvin Lewis as defensive coordinator, Jim Schwartz as defensive assistant, Maxie Baughn as linebackers coach, and Earnest Byner as running backs coach. The most important figure was Ozzie Newsome, a former Browns tight end and Hall of Famer, now ensconced as vice president of player personnel. The presence of Bynum and Newsome showed that

Modell retained the loyalty of many former Browns. This left an opening for reconsidering Modell's reputation. If his former players remained friends, could he really be such a rat? If Modell, nearly alone among NFL owners, could place African Americans in positions of organizational power, perhaps he had some redeeming qualities.

Newsome built a new roster. His first order of business was the 1996 NFL Draft. His big target was a 6'9" UCLA offensive tackle Jonathan Ogden. "I was not ready to become a Raven," Ogden recalled. "I just had no knowledge about the Ravens—other than that they were the new team in town from Cleveland—and from the looks of it, neither did they. They had no logo, no jersey, no colors, no nothing . . . I was just, like, 'All right, we'll figure it out.'"[17] He certainly did. Ogden became a Hall of Fame anchor for the offensive line. Later in the first round, the team selected University of Miami linebacker Ray Lewis.

The team played in Memorial Stadium while new digs went up at Camden Yards. "We didn't have much in those early years," Ogden remembered. "We were all rookies in a sense, trying to find our way in a city where football hadn't been played in 13 years." *Sports Illustrated*, which warmed to Baltimore once the team started playing, dispatched a correspondent to see how old Colts fans coped with the adjustment. The local press did the best job of introducing the new team. The *Sun* had a first-class stable of football writers, including Jon Morgan, Vito Stellino, and the popular veteran John Steadman. Broadcasters like Nestor Aparcio, Scott Garceau, Tom Matte, and Gerry Sandusky took to the new team right away, providing wall-to-wall coverage. They also provided a robust defense of Baltimore's right to rejoin the NFL, arguing hotly against the perception that the Ravens were an NFL plague ship. The team's maiden appearance was a preseason game against the Giants. The Ravens beat the Raiders to win its first regular-season game, but finished the season 4-12. Testaverde had a top target in wide receiver Michael Jackson, and the offense could score. The trouble was a weak defense. "Who has the best offense in the NFL? The Ravens and whoever they're playing," went the predictable joke. But the first season was really about reintroducing the league to Baltimore fans, and vice-versa. Games sold out, fans threaded their way up Thirty-Third Street as in the Colts days. The record was tangential.

Season two, 1997, showed improvement, with a 6-9-1 mark. A fast 3-1 start raised fans' hopes, as did the play of linebackers Ray Lewis and NFL Defensive Rookie of the Year Peter Boulware. A highlight was beating the Redskins 20–17 at their new stadium in Landover, Maryland. The next season, 1998, brought a change at quarterback: the former Indianapolis Colt Jim Harbaugh replaced Testaverde. Other additions included cornerback

Rod Woodson and running back Priest Holmes. Players like Mike Flynn, Spencer Folau, Kim Herring, and Jermaine Lewis showed promise. The unquestioned high point of the season came when Harbaugh led the Ravens to a 38–31 home win over the Colts. But the 6-10 record cost Marchibroda his job. The Ravens hired Vikings offensive coordinator Brian Billick as their new head coach. The revived Browns had interviewed Billick, giving the coaching search the appearance of a duel, but they went with Paul Palmer. The new Browns owner was none other than Lerner, and Cleveland press accounts explained that Modell and his former banker were no longer friends. Browns fans could thus root for their new team without reflecting that the new owner helped drive away their old franchise.

Billick's 1999 team was slow out of the gate, 4-7, before going 4-1, for an 8-8 record. That kept the team in marginal contention for a wild card playoff berth. The team also saw change at the top, as Modell sold 49 percent of the team to local businessman Steve Bisciotti. A billionaire, who grew up in Severna Park, Bisciotti gained the option to buy remaining shares from Modell five years hence. Thus, the former Browns owner enjoyed a cash infusion, and Bisciotti guaranteed that he could own the Ravens soon.

The grimmest event occurred after the season. Star linebacker Ray Lewis was in Atlanta to watch Super Bowl XXXIV with people he called friends, reporters a posse, and a judge codefendants. A fight outside a nightclub resulted in two stabbing deaths. Lewis and two others were charged with homicide that February, and the image of the Ravens' best player in court, handcuffed in prison orange, was a national sensation. The team contemplated a future without their young star, but Lewis insisted to Billick and Newsome that he was innocent. The franchise decided to stand by Lewis and ride out the judicial process. In June 1999, murder charges were dropped, as Lewis plead guilty to a misdemeanor, obstruction of justice. Lewis served one year of probation, and did not miss training camp or any games. But the scandal contributed to the Ravens' renegade image. The controversy sharpened as Billick spoke up aggressively in support of Lewis. The criminal case shadowed Lewis's career. To Ravens haters, Lewis was a murderer who got off. To supporters in Baltimore, he was a celebrity targeted because of his fame and subjected to scrutiny by an unfriendly press corps, which relished trouble for Baltimore's football team.

The 2000 season was amazing. Even the most purple-hazed Ravens fan did not expect it. But in hindsight, the Ravens' Super Bowl XXXV victory made sense. Defensive coordinator Marvin Lewis's aggressive squad emerged as an all-time great defense. Ray Lewis became a superstar, Rod Woodson and Sam Adams were Pro Bowlers. Humongous defensive lineman Tony Siragusa, cornerback Duane Starks, and defensive end Michael

McCrary were equally effective. The defense allowed just 59 rushing first downs, 39 below the league average. Opponents averaged a mere 2.7 yards per rushing gain, 1.5 yards under the NFL average. Opponents had only five rushing touchdowns all season.[18]

Rookie running back Jamal Lewis rushed for 1,364 yards, veteran running back Priest Holmes added 588 yards. The top receiver was tight end Shannon Sharpe, with 67 catches for 810 yards. At quarterback, Tony Banks lost his job to the unspectacular but consistent Trent Dilfer, who wound up with 12 touchdown passes, 11 interceptions, and a knack for managing the offense with minimum risk. Despite Billick's pedigree as an offensive guru, the Ravens ground it out, depending on the run, possession passes to Sharpe, and an occasional downfield toss to wide receiver Brandon Stokley. The offense stalled during a midseason scoring drought, going a month without a touchdown, and had to depend on kicker Matt Stover. The low point came against the Tennessee Titans in game eight, a 14–6 loss. The defense kept the team intact, and the offense broke out in game 10, a 27–7 win over the Cincinnati Bengals. Baltimore then beat the Titans 24–23. A 44–7 laugher over the Browns and a 34–20 triumph over the New York Jets gave the Ravens a home wild-card berth.

The wild-card clash against the Denver Broncos treated Baltimore fans to their first playoff win in twenty-nine years, a 21–3 breeze. After watching Modell's team beat the Broncos, national reporters expected the owner to hold court, but the owner demurred. Days before the game, Modell's remarks showed that his reputation still bothered him. He wisecracked, "If they'd given me half of what they've given the new Cleveland Browns, I'd still be there. All I wanted was to make sure that the johns didn't leak, particularly the ones over my office."[19]

The divisional champion Titans were home favorites in the next round. In a pep talk, Billick disdained Tennessee. Some of his motivational speech was captured on film and displayed on Nashville's Adelphia Coliseum video screen before kickoff. "A Special Message from Brian Billick and the Baltimore Ravens," read the title. The capacity crowd saw Billick waving a *Sports Illustrated* with Titans running back Eddie George on the cover. According to the article, Tennessee was the NFL's best team. "Maybe that's true," Billick said to his team—and, thanks to the tape, to the stadium crowd. "But not today!" As his aghast players watched the video run above them, Billick called for a pregame huddle. He tore into the hosts and their film trick. "F— the Tennessee Titans," he said with lapidary profanity.[20] The game was tight, and the Titans opened with a touchdown. But Ray Lewis's fifty-yard interception return with six minutes left in the game proved decisive, netting Baltimore the 24–10 victory, and putting the Ravens into the

AFC championship game against the Oakland Raiders. Having upset the odds-on Super Bowl favorites, the Ravens did not seem like a long shot.

Besides having NFL teams, losing them, and getting them back, Oakland and Baltimore were old playoff rivals. In 1970's AFC Championship, Unitas outdueled George Blanda, sending the Colts to Super Bowl V with a 27–17 victory in a game remembered as the "Duel in the Dust." Nobody could have guessed then, but that was the last Colts' win in the playoffs in Baltimore. In 1977, Oakland tight end Dave Casper caught the famous "Ghost to the Post" pass from Ken Stabler, giving the Raiders a double-overtime 37–31 win. The 2000 contest, played in Oakland, was more one-sided. It featured the 340-pound Siragusa pancake tackling Oakland quarterback Rich Gannon, who left the game injured. Stover booted three field goals, and Dilfer managed the offense carefully, hitting Sharpe with a 96-yarder for the game's only touchdown. The 16–3 decision meant that the Ravens were headed to the Super Bowl, to face the New York Giants, Baltimore's original championship opponents in 1958 and 1959.

Throughout it all, the tall, black-clad Billick kept his cool. His style was cerebral, his tongue nimble, his tone ironic. Billick clearly enjoyed sparring with reporters, answering needling questions with barbed comments. He was cooperative, however, with the Baltimore media, including radio personalities like Aparacio, who was already leading the city's media into the digital age by targeting an Internet audience. Aparicio's WNST-AM station maintained a website replete with Baltimore-related blogs, paying special attention to the Ravens.[21] Billick appreciated the possibilities of the new communications age. He later wrote a WNST blog himself. Ravens players appreciated his style, but the national media saw Billick as arrogant. They had their chance to challenge him during pre–Super Bowl press conferences, taking umbrage when he censured their coverage of the Lewis case. To national reporters, Billick sounded like he was advising them on how to do their jobs. But to his own team and fans, Billick sounded like he was standing up for his player. The result was a bifurcated reputation. Across the country, Billick's demeanor became the latest in the litany of negative Ravens associations. In Baltimore, he emerged as a tough talker who would not let his team get pushed around.

Pregame coverage of Super Bowl XXXV in Tampa concentrated on whether the Ravens defense was the greatest ever. The 1985 Chicago Bears had their partisans, but all observers agreed that the conversation needed to include the current Ravens. The unit led the way to a 34–7 rout, with Ray Lewis the MVP, although Dilfer landed the "I'm going to Disney World!" television spot and the "Got Milk?" ad. Still, Lewis could see the first signs of his public rehabilitation. Assessing the linebacker on the eve of the game,

ESPN Magazine observed, "It was up to the leader of Baltimore's ravenous D to decide how people would see him. He could be bitter or get better. He could sue or pursue, choose as his image shackles or tackles. Each time, Lewis chose Door No. 2."[22] Art Modell finally hoisted the Vince Lombardi Trophy that eluded him in Cleveland for all those years. The fugitive owner and his problematic franchise were Super Bowl XXXV champions.

Billick did not rest on his championship laurels, and his decision to dump Dilfer in favor of free agent Elvis Grbac ushered in an era of instability at quarterback that eventually cost the coach his job. Billick also allowed ESPN into training camp for the debut of HBO's reality series *Hard Knocks*. In 2001, the team lost running back Jamal Lewis to injury in training camp. With their main offensive threat out for the season, the Ravens went 10-6, winning a playoff game against Miami before losing to the Pittsburgh Steelers, who were becoming the team's main rival.

Salary cap woes cut into Baltimore's roster in 2002; Ravens fell to 7-9. In 2003, after drafting University of California quarterback Kyle Boller, the 10-6 Ravens made the playoffs. A healthy Lewis rushed for over 2,000 yards, but the team lost to Tennessee in a home playoff game. The 2003 season saw another winning record, 9-7, but Boller's inconsistency was a prime topic as the team missed a postseason berth. As per his deal with Modell, Bisciotti took over as majority owner. The team struggled to 6-10 in 2005. Newsome brought in Titans veteran quarterback Steve McNair for 2006 and Baltimore cruised to 13-3. But the playoffs soured all pleasure when Peyton Manning's Colts shut down the Ravens 15–6 in a well-hyped playoff game. The hangover never dissipated, and 2007 saw a 5-11 record, which led to Billick's firing and the hiring of John Harbaugh, formerly the special teams coach for the Philadelphia Eagles.

Harbaugh's arrival—and the drafting of the 6'6" University of Delaware quarterback Joe Flacco—heralded a new era. A roster remade by Newsome featured few holdovers from Super Bowl XXXV. Ogden retired, Ray Lewis remained. In the wake of Orioles great Cal Ripken Jr.'s retirement, Ray Lewis was clearly Baltimore's number-one sports star. The embrace was fierce. The 2008 Ravens went 11-5. They made the AFC championship game, but winning on the road in Pittsburgh was too tall an order. Baltimore lost, 23–14. The 2009 season yielded another playoff berth. Once again, Indianapolis knocked them out. The result left Baltimore fans crestfallen. But demographics are irresistible. Careful observers noticed changes in the local sports culture. Younger fans, for whom the Colts' Baltimore years were purely reliquary, focused their animus on the Steelers, not Indianapolis. Moreover, since the Orioles were in the midst of a fourteen-season losing streak, the Ravens were celebrated as winners, and generated positive local vibes.

In the 2009 draft, the Ravens selected offensive tackle Michael Oher from the University of Mississippi. Oher's troubled childhood, adoption, and collegiate success sparked a best-selling 2006 book by journalist Michael Lewis, which was adapted into a hit movie, *The Blind Side* (2009). Sandra Bullock won a 2009 Best Actress Oscar for her role as Oher's adoptive mother. Oher's rookie season lent the team a touch of Hollywood gloss. It was a classic case of what postmodern author David Foster Wallace, in another context, identified as a beloved, if belabored, type of sports story: "inspirational . . . in its ad-cliché sense, one basically equivalent to *heartwarming* or *feel-good* or even (God forbid) *triumphant*."[23] Such adjectives were used aplenty when commentators talked up the real-life *Blind Side* story, giving the Ravens a rare touch of upbeat national coverage.

There was also the story of O. J. Brigance, the only pro football player ever to win the Grey Cup and Super Bowl playing in the same city. His championships came with the Stallions, for whom he was an all-CFL linebacker, and the Ravens, in Super Bowl XXXV. During his playing days, Brigance actively supported cystic fibrosis research, Habitat for Humanity, and local food banks and charities. In 2007, he was diagnosed with amyotrophic lateral sclerosis, commonly called ALS or Lou Gehrig's disease. By then a member of the Ravens front office, Brigance set up an ALS research foundation. In physical decline, he was a visible member of the franchise, meeting the team for motivational speeches, forging a relationship with current players, giving reporters a legitimate human-interest angle.

A 12-4 mark in 2010 kept the momentum going under Coach Harbaugh. Wide receiver Anquan Boldin proved to be a key pickup, proving a trustworthy pass-catcher. Pittsburgh also went 12-4, but a better divisional record gave the Steelers the AFC North crown. The Ravens beat Kansas City in the Wild Card game, 30–7. Ray Rice, a diminutive running back from Rutgers, was one of league's top rushers. At halftime of their playoff against the Steelers, the Ravens led 21–7 and looked set to exorcise recent Pittsburgh demons. But the Steelers rallied behind Ben Roethlisberger, winning 31–24. For the first time, whispers circulated among fans that Harbaugh and Flacco could not win the biggest games.

The 2011 season was capped by the most heartbreaking Ravens loss to date. Winning the AFC North at 12–4 was expected, as was a 20–13 win over the Houston Texans in the divisional playoff. That put the Ravens into the AFC Championship, against Bill Belichick's New England Patriots. The Ravens matched up well against the AFC's glamor team. The game was close all the way. During the fourth quarter, superstar quarterback Tom Brady dove in for a touchdown on fourth-and-one, giving New England a 23–20 lead. Flacco responded by engineering a drive to the red zone. With less than a minute to go, he nearly hit wide receiver Lee Evans for a TD. But cornerback Sterling Moore swatted the ball away. Evans then dropped what looked like a sure touchdown, and kicker Billy Cundiff ran in for a hasty thirty-two-yard field goal attempt, which he muffed. Baltimore fans never forgave Cundiff. The Patriots went to the Super Bowl, while the Ravens and their fans went home to argue about why their team did not win in the clutch.

Art Modell died four days before the 2012 season opener; he was eighty-seven. Although Bisciotti—who visited him during his final hours—owned the team outright, Modell kept up visiting training camp and practices since retiring, kibitzing with players and coaches. Bisciotti treated his predecessor with respect. Players liked him, and while his name remained a curse in Cleveland, Baltimore doggedly esteemed Modell. One subtext was that reporters, who controlled the voting, had long blocked Modell's entry into the Pro Football Hall of Fame. The case for enshrining Modell in Canton was easy to make, given his signature role in helping Rozelle craft the TV deals that included the hit show *Monday Night Football*. He helped to broker the NFL-AFL merger, taking the Browns (along with the Colts and the Steelers) into the AFC in 1970 to balance the two conferences. In Baltimore, WNST's irrepressible Nestor Aparacio crusaded for Modell's election. When Modell died unelected, bitterness ensued among Ravens players and boosters. To them, the shift from Cleveland did not negate Modell's accomplishments, and even the move deserved to be seen as restoring Baltimore while costing Cleveland. Ravens players—foremost among them, extroverted linebacker Terrell Suggs—wore Modell T-shirts and pledged to honor his memory. "Winning for Art" was a new theme in 2012. A 9-2 start lifted hopes, but in December, the Ravens fell apart. They lost three straight. Whereas redemption for Modell, and for the previous season's loss against New England, dominated the first three months of the season, the end saw making the playoffs no sure thing. On December 23, with offensive coordinator Cam Cameron recently fired, Flacco passed the team past the New York Giants. The win garnered a wild-card spot. Fans rationalized the regular-season-ending loss to the Bengals because Harbaugh rested his veterans, but going into the playoffs, Baltimore had lost four of its last five games.

After sitting out most of the season due to a torn triceps, the reactivated Ray Lewis announced that he would retire after the postseason. His return and looming retirement provided the dramatic context for the playoffs. Other trauma during the season included wide receiver Torrey Smith's brother dying in a traffic accident. A persistent line of media inquiry developed in Baltimore and on the national networks: was Joe Flacco an elite quarterback? Even social commentary was part of Ravens discourse. An intramural argument between special team ace Brandon Ayanbandejo, who blogged his support for gay marriage, and center Matt Birk, who posted his opposition, lent the Ravens a touch of political relevance beyond the sports section. But Lewis's imminent farewell dominated Ravens media coverage, and Chuck Pagano's return from leukemia inflected Colts reportage. In the game, Flacco played well and running back Bernard Pierce broke loose for 103 yards on the ground, setting up the next game, on the road in Denver. "I was hoping we'd get to play them," said receiver Boldin.[24] Lewis agreed, refusing to talk about the Colts after the game. "I've already turned to Denver film now," he said. "It's on to the next one."[25]

The game in Denver would be one of the franchise's most memorable victories, a 38–35 teeth-clencher featuring a late drive led by Flacco, who totaled 330 yards passing, outdueling Peyton Manning, tossing a late 70-yard touchdown to wide receiver Jacoby Jones, sending the game into overtime. Rookie kicker Justin Tucker nailed the game-winning 47-yard field goal, helping to ease the memory of Cundiff's 2011 miss. The Jones catch led national coverage all week, and the two salient questions—would Ray Lewis inspire the Ravens one last time? was Flacco elite?—were debated on every television sports show, in every article, at every sports bar, around every Baltimore kitchen table. The hype for the Patriots rematch was intense, providing more tension than the game itself. While the Ravens trailed 13–7 at the half, it was clear that their defense had the Pats' vaunted offense under control. Flacco hit three touchdown passes in the second half, netting 240 yards in a 28–13 romp. After the game, an ebullient Suggs badmouthed New England and dedicated the victory to Modell, affectionately referred to—at high volume—as "Art Modeezy!"

It was on to New Orleans for Super Bowl XLVII. The fact that the NFC champion San Francisco 49ers were coached by Jim Harbaugh, John's younger brother (and former Colts and Ravens quarterback) gave the Super Bowl hype mill plenty of grist. Inevitably, the game became the "Har-bowl," between the "Super Bro's." The lack of attention paid to two negative stories—Lewis's criminal past and Modell's move—was notable. The former theme was not entirely ignored. But so many other high-profile players had more recent stints on the "athletes behaving badly" roster, including quarterback Roethlisberger, twice accused of sexual assault; Green Bay defensive end Johnny Jolly, accused of cocaine possession; Tampa Bay cornerback Aqib Talib, accused of domestic assault; and, most recently and tragically, Kansas City linebacker Jevon Belcher, who murdered his wife and then shot himself in the team parking lot in December 2012.

Ray Lewis's Atlanta fracas could not be dismissed as old news, because two men were still dead. The younger brother of one victim had already expressed his hatred for Lewis. "Oh, Ray Lewis is going to get his one day. Just like he killed my brother," the distraught mourner said.[26] But the pre–Super Bowl stories concentrated on Lewis's redemption. For his part, Lewis—whose public religiosity had increased and who was by then well known for preaching on the sidelines, before the cameras, and in churches across Maryland and Florida—disavowed bitterness and blamed the media. "This is on TV, a 13-year-old child," he observed to a reporter when the younger brother's bitterness was made public in 2006. "All because of what y'all wanted to report that was dead-ass wrong!" Lewis added that, to him, "The saddest thing" was that "you got two young dead black kids on the street. The second sad part is, because of the court system and the prosecutor's lies, I got two families hating me for something I didn't have a hand in, and the people who killed their children are free."[27] To Lewis's detractors, this was self-serving double-talk. But these were fewer than before, since his on-field stardom and his multiple off-field good works, along with the passage of time and the ineptitude of Atlanta prosecutors, rehabilitated his public reputation to a degree. Lewis no longer represented the league's foremost image problem. Nor did the Ravens, when other teams like the Jaguars were losing games and making noises about moving elsewhere. As public memory grew hazy, Lewis's legal trouble came to be seen by sympathizers as a tribulation that Lewis endured, part of growing into an older, wiser man.

The Ravens beat the 49ers 34–31, grabbing a 28–6 lead and hanging on through a ferocious San Francisco comeback. Momentum shifted during a bizarre third-quarter blackout, when the Superdome lost power and went dark, offering the Niners a chance to regroup. A last-ditch pass from 49ers quarterback Colin Kaepernick to wide receiver Michael Crabtree sailed long, and the Ravens' second Super Bowl title—Baltimore's third—went into the record books. Flacco was the game's MVP, guaranteeing himself a major payout since his contract was up.

Ray Lewis hardly dominated play, but he retired on top. John Harbaugh earned plaudits for outcoaching his brother, and hundreds of thousands of Baltimore fans partied through the team's victory parade and rally. As they danced and shouted, they felt like fans do whenever their favorite team wins a Super Bowl: happy, excited, and relieved. What they did not feel, perhaps for the first time, was that the Ravens were a team with an asterisk, the "former Browns," a rebound franchise that could never be loved like the Colts. The joy Ravens fans felt was not lessened by historical tribulations. It was sincere and basic. The first Ravens' Super Bowl victory was a "so-there!" stunner. This one was simply Baltimore winning it all.

The off-season promised normal pleasures and pains: the rush to buy Super Bowl swag; the inevitable roster shifts, the draft, free agency. There was nothing different about the Ravens, or their fans anymore. Baltimore was purple now. Out came the car flags; on went the bumper stickers with the Super Bowl XLVII logo. As always, everywhere, fans projected the meanings they needed onto the team they supported. For a long time, in Baltimore, that mass psychological process involved asserting their city's worth, longing for old Colts glories, grumbling that Baltimore's best sports legacy was hijacked. But after Super Bowl XLVII, fans' projections were straightforward: Baltimore was number one! Joe Flacco was elite! Ray Lewis went out as a champ! The legitimacy of the Ravens was now a settled issue, their connection to Baltimore at last uncomplicated. The team was just the latest Super Bowl champion—paying or losing its stars, trying to retool, hoping to remain near the top before rebuilding. Ravens fans had seen it before. The second championship was fun. Its true legacy was that, when it came to football, Baltimore's long-tortuous path was finally straight. Baltimore was an NFL city with a winning team. To hundreds of thousands of cheering fans, it seemed like it had always been that way.

20

A Phelpsian Triptych

Mountain, Machine, and Man

DEAN BARTOLI SMITH

Mountain

In August of 2012, the Baltimore sports media—writers and radio commentators alike—debated a range of possibilities for a theoretical "Mount Rushmore of Baltimore Sports." Several names were tossed into the discussion, such as Brooks Robinson, Johnny Unitas, Cal Ripken Jr., Frank Robinson, Eddie Murray, Bert Jones, Ray Lewis, Jim Palmer, Babe Ruth, and Earl Weaver. Missing from the early discourse was the name of the most decorated Olympic athlete in the 116-year history of the games.

Comparing swimmer Michael Phelps to the likes of Unitas, the Robinsons, Ruth, Lewis, and Ripken at first blush may have seemed like a stretch—but similarities exist. In workman-like fashion, Phelps revolutionized competitive swimming in much the same way that Ruth transformed baseball with the home run and Unitas introduced the passing game and the two-minute offense to football. Ripken changed the position of shortstop with his range and power, and Phelps dominated the lanes with his long cobra-like torso and six-foot-seven wingspan—overpowering competitiors to the point where, ultimately, their bodies failed them. He has ruled the pool for more than a decade in much the same way that Lewis owned the middle line-backer position on the football field. Largely because of Lewis, opposing teams rarely ran sweeps or threw screen passes. Phelps brought the same physicality to the starting block that Ruth carried to the plate and to the pitching mound.

All of these athletes also shared the ability to grasp the moment in dramatic fashion. Babe Ruth (allegedly) pointed to the bleachers at Wrigley Field in 1932 and called his home run shot. Johnny Unitas led forty game-winning drives.[1] Cal Ripken Jr. mesmerized the nation with his lap around Oriole Park at Camden Yards after surpassing Lou Gehrig's string of consecutive games played. Ray Lewis came back from an injury to rally a struggling team to a Super Bowl victory—ending his seventeen-year career with a dramatic goal-line stand.

When Phelps touched the wall .01 seconds before Milorad Čavić in the butterfly event in the 2008 Beijing Olympics, he proved that he was capable of extraordinary athletic achievements. The finish was so controversial that the Serbian government demanded an investigation. Omega, the watch company whose devices timed the Olympic events and who claimed Phelps as a spokesperson, ruled that Phelps had touched first—10-thousandths of a second faster than Čavić—and had arrived "really pushing hard."[2]

The moment rivaled the concept of a Ruthian blast—a ball clobbered high into the air and nearly out of sight. It had been a "Phelpsian" finish. In that moment, Phelps earned the mystique of a champion in much the same way that the "dawn's early light" unveiled a flag that was still there.

As the debate simmered, Phelps had returned to his hometown and was basking in the spotlight of yet another magnificent performance—one that had been unexpected. He spoke of retirement and vowed that he would not return to a pool for a long time.

Starting at the age of fifteen, he'd appeared in four Olympics and had finished his run with twenty-two medals—eighteen of them gold. At that same age, he broke the world record in the 200 butterfly, and became "the youngest male ever to hold a world record in a stopwatch sport."[3] In Sydney, he became the youngest athlete to make the US Olympic team in sixty-eight years. He did not win a medal but finished fifth in the 200-meter butterfly. In Athens, he earned six gold medals and two bronze. He broke Mark Spitz's record of seven gold medals in Beijing in dramatic fashion. He'd won fifty-four gold medals in international competition.[4]

Heading into the London Olympics, Phelps was supposedly staring into the twilight of his career and would be relinquishing his position as the world's greatest swimmer to his USA teammate Ryan Lochte. In the weeks leading up to the games, his teammate Tyler Clary called him out for a lackluster training regimen.

Phelps used these doubts and jabs to sharpen his competitive edge along the Thames. The energetic kid who at age seven was afraid to put his head under water recovered from a rocky start and turned in a gutsy, grind-it-out performance. He won four gold medals and two silvers in London—and reinforced his continued dominance of the sport.

On "The Fan," a popular local sports radio station, the commentators settled on four visages that would be etched in the local sports version of Mount Rushmore: Johnny Unitas, Brooks Robinson, Cal Ripken Jr., and Ray Lewis. Babe Ruth was left out because he didn't play in Baltimore. Once this was decided, scores of callers and texts flooded in for Michael Phelps.

"Michael Phelps should definitely be there," said Ryan Sebring, a host at "The Fan." "He's the greatest athlete in the history of the state and he's from here. There is no question in my mind."[5]

Baltimore possesses a wealth of iconic sports heroes and, despite this rich tradition of athletic prowess, to be the hometown of the greatest swimmer in the history of the world seems as unlikely as the city having produced the national anthem—or is it? Perhaps more than any other athlete, Michael Phelps deserves a place in the pantheon of Baltimore's greatest athletes. His achievements and dedication to his sport align with the core values and working-class culture of the city. His love for the Ravens, Orioles, and a few "Natty Bohs" with his friends qualifies him as a "local" in more ways than his Rushmore brethren.

"Phelps definitely belongs on our Mount Rushmore of sports," wrote Peter Schmuck in the *Baltimore Sun*, "and since there's no way that we're going to remove one of the four Baltimore icons who are already up there, there's only one way to settle this. We're just going to need a bigger mountain."[6]

Michael Phelps needs his own mountain. He is both a local product and, as Paul McMullen, the first reporter to write about him in a book, *Amazing Pace* (2006), says, a "global citizen of the world."[7] Phelps follows the Orioles and the Ravens with passion and maintains close ties to the city. While his stature on the national stage includes such monikers as "the most decorated Olympic athlete in the history of the games," Phelps the Baltimorean reveals a more nuanced figure as he torpedoed a moribund sport into the prime-time living rooms of America—the networks and their checkbooks requiring the Chinese in Beijing to broadcast events in the morning so that Phelps could be seen in America winning his eight gold medals during the post-dinner hour. In London, the races were taped and then the narration rerecorded like the way Ronald Reagan read the plays amid phony applause after the baseball game had ended. McMullen referred to these moments as "plausibly live" events. "NBC wanted Michael to swim in primetime," he said. "That will never happen again."[8]

Machine

On June 30, 2011, I was enjoying a day at the Meadowbrook Aquatic and Fitness Center with my family. I went inside the main building to use the workout facilities on a catwalk above both the indoor and outdoor pools. I jogged slowly on the treadmill until my gaze drifted to a person by the diving board. His back was turned, and he was talking to a group of swimmers. The sun was out and shining on his massive elongated torso. His muscular back looked like it had been drawn by Da Vinci.

When he turned to the side, I recognized him. I remembered the passage in McMullen's *Amazing Pace* that talked about how "years of training had expanded Michael's lung capacity and widened his shoulders."[9] The book claims that "his most dominant feature was an abnormally long torso, which led the sailor who ran the club team to make the point that the boat with the largest wet surface moved the fastest."[10]

I thought of Jim Thorpe, Johnny Weissmuller (who grew up not far from Phelps's father), and Mark Spitz. Aquaman had arrived at the neighborhood pool. I knew that Michael Phelps had trained at the facility and had been enrolled in stroke clinics since the age of seven. Phelps was diagnosed with ADHD and expended his energy in the lanes, heading to the facility eleven times a week.

He was born in Towson, Maryland, in 1985 to Fred Phelps, a state trooper, and his wife, Debbie, a middle school principal, who would divorce when Michael was nine. His mother moved him closer to the Meadowbrook facility from their house in north Harford near the Pennsylvania line. He'd grown up a few miles away from the pool in a neighborhood called Rodgers Forge, named after a family of Irish blacksmiths who settled on four acres in 1800. It consists of more than 1,700 red-brick colonial homes with varied fronts. The neighborhood embodies the humble character, small-town feel, and work ethic of Baltimore. Debbie Phelps raised three kids; Michael's older sisters Hilary and Whitney also swam competitively. Michael and his father have never maintained a close relationship, but Fred is credited with teaching his son to look people in the eye and to adopt a "take no prisoners approach."

The pool, built in 1930 for residents of the Mount Washington neighborhood to escape the summer heat, has sent at least one swimmer to every Olympics since 1984. It is also the home of the North Baltimore Aquatic Club, a little known entity founded by Loyola High School swim team coach and former English teacher Murray Stephens more than forty years ago that has become an internationally known juggernaut on the swimming scene. During the summer, two weekends are set aside for swimming tournaments, and families from the Delmarva region make the pilgrimage to Meadowbrook, camping out for the weekend poolside with their cabanas and lawn chairs like it was a Bruce Springsteen concert in Central Park.

The perception around town a year before the London Games was that Phelps had been taking it easy and not training seriously. He had also developed a reputation for partying a little too hard after a 2004 DUI arrest. A photo that went viral in 2009 of Phelps wielding a bong helped further that perception. Looking back, these incidents appear to have served more as a wake-up call for someone whose transition into manhood was a very public one.

That June day in 2011, a cadre of young men and women swimmers gathered around Phelps but none came close to rivaling his physique. I stopped the treadmill and headed downstairs. I pulled up a chair close the pool and watched as he went through his workout. His longtime teacher and mentor, Bob Bowman, kept a watchful eye on his every move just as he had done when Michael was a boy.

Most of the capacity crowd didn't notice. He had slipped furtively in from the back of the facility and went quickly into his workout. He started using the kickboard and chopping his way back and forth as he had done for most of his life. He then used the hand paddles. He would stop and gaze from side to side like a periscope to see if anyone was watching.

He was going back to the basics, to the essence of the sport. I hadn't expected him to be using paddles and kickboards like the youngsters in the daily swim camp. I was mesmerized by his presence in the water. He swam laps slowly, focusing on the stroke and accentuating it. As he swam the butterfly, his rising torso encompassed the entire lane. I thought of the whale skeleton on display in the Nantucket museum and the notion of the leviathan as speedboat. The downward thrust of his body nearly emptied the fifty-meter lane. He plowed through the water effortlessly. He worked continuously for an hour and then left the facility in an Orioles cap and baggy shorts. It was his twenty-sixth birthday.

A few weeks after that session, he ended up winning six medals at the World Championships in Shanghai, including three gold medals, but he was not satisfied, calling it an "okay" performance. Ryan Lochte defeated him in the 200-meter free-style and in the 200-meter individual medley; this was either a potential changing of the guard in men's swimming or a motivational gift for Phelps prior to London.

His competitive drive and his "take no prisoners" attitude matched that of his idol Michael Jordan. Jordan focused his ferocious competitive spirit on destroying certain players such as Adrian Branch and Dan Majerle, who were receiving accolades he felt he deserved. Spanning two decades, Phelps focused intently on beating the likes of Ian Thorpe, Milorad Čavić, Yannick Agnel, and his teammate Ryan Lochte.

More than a year later on July 28, 2012, *NBC Evening News* anchor Brian Williams greeted the nation's viewers from the London Olympic Games with a lead story about a changing of the guard in swimming. "There is a new number one swimmer in the world and it's not Michael Phelps," Williams announced. Ryan Lochte had soundly beaten Phelps in the 400-meter individual medley. The *Los Angeles Times* headline read, "Ryan Lochte Whips Phelps."[11] Just the mere fact that swimming had become the lead story on the evening news is a credit to Phelps and his accomplishments. It was the first time he hadn't medaled in an Olympic race since 2000. As the games progressed, we learned that he wasn't ready to surrender his crown to anyone—not even a teammate.

The next night, he earned silver in the 4x100-meter freestyle relay. Phelps swam the fastest leg of the race but Team USA lost to the French as Yannick Agnel outswam Ryan Lochte.

On July 31, the changing of the guard in USA swimming changed back. Phelps finished second to Chad le Clos in the 200-meter butterfly by 5/100ths of a second. In an interview after the race with NBC, a steely-eyed Phelps implied that playing second fiddle on the podium as a silver medal winner wasn't good enough for him. He didn't like the national anthem being played second to last.

It would prove to be pivotal a night for the USA swim team and Phelps. The coaches had decided to restore Phelps back to the anchor leg of the relay team for the 4x200-meter freestyle relay. This was the defining moment of the games for the "Baltimore Bullet." He had been reinstated into a position of leadership while sending a message to the competitors that they had to face Phelps in the final leg of the relay. The French had withstood Phelps's contribution in the early part of the race and were able to catch Lochte. With Phelps in the anchor slot with his long body, their medal chances diminished. The move damaged opponents' psyches and elevated the level of Phelps's Olympic performance. His teammates handed him the lead, and he extended it to his fifteenth gold medal. With it, he passed the Soviet gymnast Larissa Latynina as the most decorated Olympian. Then he kicked into another gear.

He won his sixteenth gold medal by beating Lochte in the 200-meter medley and his seventeenth by besting Le Close in the 100-meter butterfly. His eighteenth came in the 4x100-meter medley relay.

Michael Phelps started slowly and finished strong. After his fourth Olympic stint, there remained no equals in the water. On August 16, after the games had ended, he tweeted, "I love being home."[12]

Man

The Baltimore Ravens opened their 2012 season against the Cincinnati Bengals and the offense was introduced first at M&T Bank Stadium that night. The Ravens original owner Art Modell had passed away a few days before, members of the Baltimore Orioles were in attendance, and Muhammad Ali was also there. The last offensive player to be introduced was Michael Phelps wearing number 12—perhaps a nod to the newest Ravens wide receiver and kick returner Jacoby Jones, who wore that number, or perhaps it was a reference to the number of years that Phelps had been swimming in Olympic competition. The crowd gave the local boy an ovation for his accomplishments and then settled in for football.

Phelps has stayed close to the Ravens and has often credited ex-linebacker Ray Lewis with advising him on his career. Football was in Phelps's blood. His father, Fred, had once tried out for the Redskins. Phelps would attend the Ravens Super Bowl in New Orleans and take part in the postgame victory celebration. When you catch glimpses of Phelps in these moments he is grinning like a little kid. He's not trying to be an actor like Mark Spitz. He's enjoying his post-Olympic life and has taken a much-needed vacation. He enjoys working with children. His foundation work and swimming schools keep him busy.

"He's been on a well-deserved vacation since London," said McMullen. "Michael's not a man-in-full yet. He's not even 30 years old. He's still learning about life beyond the pool."[13]

It's understandable that most of the pundits overlooked Phelps for the "Mount Rushmore of Baltimore Sports." Swimming rises to the national stage once every four years. Also, when he is in town, Phelps keeps a low profile as he enjoys time with friends, family, and a purple and black football team. He plays golf and raises horses with his coach Bob Bowman. Most of the time, he embraces the lifestyle of a typical twenty-eight-year-old (who happens to be a millionaire).

He is more of a Baltimorean than any other athlete etched in the mythical Rushmore granite. He frequents Pete's Grill in Waverly for breakfast, a small neighborhood restaurant that was once on the way to Memorial Stadium—a place where legends were born. Unlike basketball superstar LeBron James, Phelps is not looking for the first train out of Baltimore in a New York Yankees cap. His roots are here and will be for a long time. His love for his mother and sisters resides deep within his being.

"Baltimore was thrilled to see all the gold medals, yet for some reason, he was not embraced like Brooks, Cal or even Ray Lewis," said Fox45 Baltimore's sports personality Bruce Cunningham. "People like him here, but they don't seem to love him. He does prefer to lead a quiet life, and does not make the charity/benefit rounds so he's not as visible as he might be. Perhaps that's it."[14]

While he is a local boy who keeps to himself, he's also an international phenomenon. Phelps has one thing his Rushmore colleagues lack: a world-wide presence. He is a global ambassador for the Olympic Games and a key figure in its future. On the international stage, Phelps is more "Milano" than vintage Hampden, wearing Louis Vuitton threads and listening to the rap stylings of Lil' Wayne on his iPod. He has made swimming cool, sophisticated, and accessible to the scores of youth aspiring to swim for the North Baltimore Aquatic Club and their parents.

"Michael is a citizen of the world," said Paul McMullen. "You haven't seen anything yet. He will receive more television face time in Rio than any other USA athlete. They will also find a way to use him in the Winter Olympics."[15]

McMullen is worried about the future of the Olympics, that without Michael Phelps or sprinter Usain Bolt it will not attract a large viewing audience. "It's the only coverage of its kind on television," he said.[16] Sports like wrestling have been on the chopping block in favor of beach volleyball, and these trends are disturbing. The Olympics depend on personalities like Phelps and track star Carl Lewis.

Gold medal–winning Olympian Michael Phelps, longtime member of the North Baltimore Aquatic Club. *Courtesy of the Associated Press.*

In the weeks after London, slots in the Michael Phelps swim school in Baltimore filled beyond capacity. Names were put on a waiting list for the next session. New pictures of his latest triumphs were posted onto the walls, and shirts from the Olympics went on sale. The indoor pool became a non-stop waterway filled with North Baltimore Aquatic Club hopefuls "razoring" their bodies through water.

"What he's done is incredible, and it's helped people rethink the impossible," said Olympic gold medalist and phenom Missy Franklin in the *Baltimore Sun* in August 2012.[17]

In September 2013, Phelps started taking steps to return to competition. Meadowbrook sightings of Phelps in training led to the speculation that he might make one more Olympic run in Rio (2016). According to ESPN, Phelps is "occasionally training" with his former coach Bob Bowman. Fans were buoyed by a tweet on September 1, 2013, that read, "Tomorrow is a new start . . . can't wait."[18]

Phelps had returned to the pool—signifying a change in his mindset. He still had plenty of time to make his decision about the Rio Olympics.

A few weeks later, he showed up at Ravens' practice and tried fielding a few punts from the Jugs machine sixty-five yards away—according to Ravens senior vice president for public relations, Kevin Byrne.[19] Byrne had his doubts that Phelps would make the catch while Coach John Harbaugh expressed confidence in Phelps's ability to haul in the pigskin. He not only caught the ball—he did so on the run like Jacoby Jones who returns kickoffs for the Ravens.

As he expands his legacy in the coming years, he will remain a "Baltimore Boy" in ways that most other professional or Olympic athletes can't replicate. He never fails to honor his mother, and this plays well in a city known for its affectionate euphemism, "hon." He's not a showboat or flashy—something that wouldn't work well here. He may not be universally adored, but he is warmly received. After the 2008 Olympics, his old neighborhood Rodgers Forge held a parade for him. He remains an inspiration for Baltimore's youth and spends a lot of time with children. Generations of children believe they can also "be like Mike." Perhaps he will one day raise a family of his own as his journey into manhood continues to unfold.

He dominates the swim lanes with the same passion that Baltimoreans have for their city and his monumental accomplishments have helped to alleviate a long-standing municipal inferiority complex. Baltimore can be perceived as the pit-bull mix at the pound with the leopard spots and black eye patch that you have to take home. Those that have fallen in love with her will never leave her side. It's not a place that people consider in conversations about the great cities of the East Coast—but Michael Phelps changes that dynamic to a degree.

In the spring of 2008 I was taking the train back from New York and it was slowing into Baltimore's Penn Station. My train trip occurred during the last few weeks of HBO's acclaimed television series *The Wire*. The derelict rowhouses on the east side of town—all in the shadow of the great dome of Johns Hopkins Hospital—were burned out and boarded up. Once the residences of working people of all races, the slum properties were identical to the "vacants" referred to in season 4 of *The Wire* where "Snoop" and Chris hid their dead victims. The groundbreaking show was coming to a close with its final season depicting the dismantling of the city's newspaper, the *Baltimore Sun*. The woman seated in front of me said to her traveling companion, "This looks like a war zone." I was convinced that she had never experienced the city as I have. She'd never spent time on Federal Hill at dusk under a crystalline sky with the whole city laid bare before her. She'd never strolled along Eutaw Street looking north at the Bromo-Seltzer tower. She'd never seen the tin crosses of the churches on Orleans Street turn mother-of-pearl in the setting sun. She had never witnessed Michael Phelps—the "leviathan as speedboat" and the greatest swimmer in the history of the sport—train alongside the rushes of the Jones-Falls.

The city's sports tradition is a vast and bounteous one with world championships in football and baseball and now in Olympic swimming. Michael Phelps adds another dimension to the city that harkens back to its working-class roots. A gangly and awkward kid, he came from out of nowhere to dominate Olympic swimming and become the most-decorated Olympian of all time. And he's not yet finished.

His success makes us feel good about ourselves—just as the Ravens and Orioles do. We have unique and interesting things about us that other cities don't have, and he is one of our civic treasures. We have champions, like Unitas and Phelps, who have left indelible marks on us. We will continue to ponder their achievements for generations and relish those moments when they were in our presence, larger than life but quiet and humble as they went about their business—traits that we know are important to our own lives here.

Michael Phelps's mastery of swimming for more than a decade has equaled the reigns of the Colts (1958–1970), the Orioles (1966–1983), and now the Ravens (2008–2012). Like the city he resides in, Phelps is not infallible and has worked through the dalliances and missteps of his youth with resilience. When he climbed out of the pool after winning his twenty-second Olympic medal, his eighteenth gold, he helped repair the tattered ramparts of a city struggling to lift itself up—if need be on his shoulders.

In June of 2014, as I put the finishing touches on this chapter, Michael Phelps has ended his retirement and returned to competitive swimming. On April 14, 2014, the Associated Press reported on the *FoxNews* website that Phelps had returned to competitive swimming in a story titled: "Olympic Legend Michael Phelps Ending Retirement."[20] Ten days later, Phelps reportedly said, "I'm doing this for me . . . I enjoy being in the pool and [the] sport of swimming and having fun with what I'm doing."[21]

In his first few competitive meets, he has finished second to Ryan Lochte and Yannick Agnel. The cycle starts again. For Phelps, this becomes part of the same motivational process he's used in the past. He's not yet back in gold medal form—but he's making progress. He's just inside their heads enough, forcing his competitors to ask themselves whether they can finally surpass him.

At the age of twenty-nine, he's trying to see how far he can take the journey. He will be in Rio, not as a commentator but as an athlete capable of doing something that will electrify us again. He will drive us en masse to our televisions to watch his every stroke.

Notes

Introduction

1. Jessica I. Elfenbein, Thomas L. Hollowak, and Elizabeth M. Nix, eds., *Baltimore '68: Riots and Rebirth in an American City* (Philadelphia: Temple University Press, 2011). Elizabeth M. Nix, "Lessons for Baltimore from 1968," *Time*, April 29, 2015, http://time.com/author/elizabeth-m-nix/ (accessed July 22, 2015).

2. Randy Roberts, *Pittsburgh Sports: Stories from the Steel City* (Pittsburgh: University of Pittsburgh Press, 2000), 4.

3. Ibid.

4. Daniel Rosensweig, *Retro Ball Parks: Instant History, Baseball, and the New American City* (Knoxville: University of Tennessee Press, 2005), 1.

5. Jason Mittell, "*The Wire* in the Context of American Television," in The *Wire: Race, Class, and Genre*, ed. Liam Kennedy and Stephen Shapiro (Ann Arbor: University of Michigan Press, 2012), 30.

6. Quoted in Jess Blumberg Mayhugh, "What's the Biggest Misconception about Our City?" *Baltimore*, August 2014, 94.

7. Sarah Rose Attman, "When Did Baltimore Become So Chic?" *Baltimore Sun*, October 23, 2014, 21A.

8. Others agree with me. Rafael Alvarez explains, "A little bigger than a basketball court, the landmark assures the homesick they are near a place they love; the star by which intoxicated boaters navigate out of the Inner Harbor; the incandescent soul of a city built not on pleasure—as the modern waterfront's marinas might suggest—but the kind of hard work that takes place in the refinery whose product the sign represents." Gina Geppi ruminates, "Unparalleled in my mind by any other local structure including the Natty Boh Tower, the Bromo Seltzer Arts Tower, and yes, even Camden Yards, I repeatedly refer to this iconic symbol of the city as the Hollywood sign of Baltimore. I'm so absolutely enamored with it, I take longer driving routes home just to get a glimpse of that neon gem and its reflection on the water." Rafael Alvarez, *Hometown Boy: The Hoodle Patrol and Other Curiosities of Baltimore* (Baltimore: *Baltimore Sun*, 1999), 43–44; Gina Geppi, "My Way," *Baltimore*, August 2014, 100.

9. Quoted in R. W. Apple Jr., "In Bawlmer, Hon, Crab Is King," *New York Times*, February 19, 2003, F1.

10. Rafael Alvarez, "To Baltimore, My Beloved Crabtown," December 26, 2014, http://magazine.good.is/articles/love-letter-to-baltimore (accessed January 18, 2015).

11. Daniel A. Nathan, "The Baltimore Blues: The Colts and Civic Identity," in *Rooting for the Home Team: Sport, Community, and Identity*, ed. Daniel A. Nathan (Urbana: University of Illinois Press, 2013), 109.

12. Frank R. Shivers, *Walking in Baltimore: An Intimate Guide to the Old City* (Baltimore: Johns Hopkins University Press, 1995), xii.

293

13. Joanna Crosby, "This Ain't Aruba, Bitch," in The Wire *and Philosophy: This America, Man*, ed. David Bzdak, Joanna Crosby, and Seth Vannatta (Chicago: Open Court, 2013), 3.

14. "A Tour of Anne Tyler's Baltimore," March 29, 2012, http://www.npr.org/2012/03/29/149423103/a-tour-of-anne-tyler-s-baltimore (accessed December 17, 2014).

15. Daniel A. Nathan, "Introduction," in *Rooting for the Home Team*, 2.

16. Ibid.

17. Michael Olesker, *Michael Olesker's Baltimore: If You Live Here, You're Home* (Baltimore: Johns Hopkins University Press, 1995), 103.

18. *Gone But Not Forgotten II*, DVD, Dan Rodricks, Marilyn M. Phillips, and Jonathan F. Slade (Owings Mills, MD: Maryland Public Television, 1994).

19. See Roland Lazenby, *Johnny Unitas: The Best There Ever Was* (Chicago: Triumph Books, 2002); Frank Deford, "The Best There Ever Was," *Sports Illustrated*, September 23, 2002, 58–74; Lou Sahadi, *Johnny Unitas: America's Quarterback* (Chicago: Triumph Books, 2004); Tom Callahan, *Johnny U: The Life and Times of Johnny Unitas* (New York: Crown Publishers, 2006); Michael Olesker, *The Colts' Baltimore: A City and Its Love Affair in the 1950s* (Baltimore: Johns Hopkins University Press, 2008); and Mark Bowden, *The Best Game Ever: Giants vs. Colts, 1958, and the Birth of the Modern NFL* (New York: Atlantic Monthly Press, 2008).

20. Kevin Rector, Scott Dance, and Luke Broadwater, "Baltimore Descends into Chaos, Violence, Looting," *Baltimore Sun*, April 28, 2015, 1A.

21. See Amy Bass, "Can Baseball Still Bring a City Together?" April 29, 2015, http://www.cnn.com/2015/04/28/opinions/bass-baltimore-orioles/ (accessed April 30, 2015); Eyder Peralta, "In Baltimore, A Different Historic Moment: A Fan-less Baseball Game," April 29, 2015, http://www.npr.org/sections/thetwo-way/2015/04/29/403075695/in-baltimore-a-different-historic-moment-a-fan-less-baseball-game (accessed April 30, 2015).

22. *Time*, May 11, 2015, 11.

23. Eduardo A. Encina and Chris Kaltenbach, "Even with Camden Yards Closed to Public, Fans Found Way to Support O's," *Baltimore Sun*, April 29, 2015, 1D.

24. Kevin Van Valkenburg, "This Too Is Baltimore," April 30, 2015, http://espn.go.com/mlb/story/_/id/12792398/do-sports-matter-now-baltimore (accessed April 30, 2015).

25. Mark Kamine, "Walk This Way," *New York Times Book Review*, December 16, 2007, 34.

26. Stacy Spaulding, "'Love Letters to Baltimore': Civic Memory, Citizenship, and Urban Community Narrative," *Literary Journalism Studies* 4 (Fall 2012): 47.

1. Till Death Do Us Part: The Grand Tour of Baltimore's Graveyard Greats

The epigraph is from A. Bartlett Giamatti, *Take Time for Paradise: American and Their Games* (New York: Summit Books, 1989), 50.

1. The H. L. Mencken House is currently not open to the public.

2. "Maryland, My Maryland," http://msa.maryland.gov/msa/mdmanual/01glance/html/symbols/lyrics.html (accessed October 4, 2013).

3. John Eisenberg, *Native Dancer: The Grey Ghost Hero of a Golden Age* (New York: Warner Books, 2003), xi.

4. Burt Solomon, *Where They Ain't: The Fabled Life and Untimely Death of the Original Baltimore Orioles, the Team That Gave Birth to Modern Baseball* (New York: Free Press, 1999).

5. William Gildea, *The Longest Fight: In the Ring with Joe Gans, Boxing's First African American Champion* (New York: Farrar, Straus and Giroux, 2012).

6. Mark Chiarello and Jack Morelli, *Heroes of the Negro Leagues* (New York: Abrams, 2007), 56.

7. Van Smith, "Dead Zones," *City Paper*, May 25, 1994, 15; Carl Schoettler, "Cemeteries: Sinister Plots and Graceful Graves Tell Histories Befitting Halloween," *Baltimore Sun*, October 31, 1996, 31.

8. These quotes come from material in Princeton University's Seeley G. Mudd Manuscript Library. It was drawn from records made by members of the Princeton Class of 1897.

9. Quoted in Jacques Kelly, "The Garretts of Evergreen," *Baltimore News American*, January 1, 1984, 10A.

10. Barry Kessler and David Zang, *The Play Life of a City: Baltimore's Recreation and Parks, 1900–1955* (Baltimore: Baltimore City Life Museum, 1989).

11. Bill James, *Whatever Happened to the Hall of Fame?: Baseball, Cooperstown, and the Politics of Glory* (New York: Simon and Schuster, 1994), 170.

12. Larry Mansch, "Richard William 'Rube' Marquard," in *Deadball Stars of the National League*, ed. Tom Simon (Washington, DC: Potomac Books, 2004), 64.

13. "Jack I. Turnbull," http://apps.uslacrosse.org/museum/halloffame/view_profile.php?prof_id= 216 (accessed October 22, 2013).

14. See http://www.findagrave.com/cgi-bin/fg.cgi?page=dfl&GRid=9659 8399 (accessed January 17, 2014).

15. Jon Morgan, *Glory for Sale: Fans, Dollars, and the New NFL* (Baltimore: Bancroft Press, 1997); Mike Klingaman, Jon Morgan, and Ken Murray, "He Brought the NFL Back to Baltimore," *Baltimore Sun*, September 7, 2012, 12.

16. Brent Schrotenboer, "Not Forgotten, Not Forgiven," *USA Today*, June 18, 2013, 1C.

17. Mark Bowden, *The Best Game Ever: Giants vs. Colts, 1958, and the Birth of the Modern NFL* (New York: Atlantic Monthly Press, 2008).

2. Jockeying for Position: The Preakness Stakes, Pimlico, and Baltimore

1. On what some see as the decline of horse racing in North America, see Bennett Liebman, "Reasons for the Decline of Horse Racing," *New York Times*, June 6, 2010, http://therail.blogs.nytimes.com/2010/06/06/reasons-for-the-decline-of-horse-racing/ (accessed September 1, 2014). Baltimore's Preakness remains an international-caliber event. For example, in 2013 some of the celebrities attending the Preakness included Kevin Spacey, Gene Simons, Bela Karolyi, Governor Martin

O'Malley, Senator Ben Cardin, newscaster Harry Smith, Herman Edwards, and Baltimore Ravens Keleche Osemele, Arthur Jones, Justin Tucker, and Michael Oher. Julie Scharper, "Baltimore Insider: Celebrities at Preakness 2013" *Baltimore Sun*, http://www. baltimoresun.com/features/baltimore-insider-blog/bal-celebrities-at-preakness-2013-pictures-20130517,0,5827049.photo gallery (accessed February 10, 2014).

2. Kenneth Cohen, "'To Give Good Sport': The Economic Culture of Public Sporting Events in Early America, 1750–1850" (PhD diss., University of Delaware, 2008), 52.

3. Joseph J. Challmes, *The Preakness: A History* (Severna Park, MD: Anaconda Publications, 1975), 1–15.

4. On John W. Hunter, "The Turf: Further Review of Prominent Stables," *New York Times*, April 10, 1875, 8; "The Turf: Preparations for the Opening Day at Long Branch," *New York Times*, July 4, 1871, 1; *New York Times*, March 31, 1897, 7.

5. Challmes, *The Preakness*, 15.

6. "Local Matters: Baltimore Races," *Sun*, November 6, 1868, 1.

7. "The Pimlico Races," *Sun*, October 26, 1870, 1.

8. Challmes, *The Preakness*, 17; "Inaugural Meeting of the Maryland Jockey Club: Five Races Yesterday in Baltimore," *New York Times*, October 26, 1870, 1; D. Sterett Gittings, "Origin of Preakness: History of Its Sponsor, Maryland Jockey Club," *New York Times*, May 9, 1936, 21.

9. Challmes, *The Preakness*, 17.

10. Ibid., 1–20.

11. Ibid., 19.

12. See "Racing at Pimlico," *Indianapolis Journal*, May 29, 1882, 5; "The Lorillards' Flyers: Monitor Beats Parole and Eole," *New York Times*, August 12, 1883, 2.

13. "George Lorillard to Retire," *New York Times*, March 10, 1884, 5; "George Lorillard's Death: His Career as a Yachtsman and on the Turf," *New York Times*, February 5, 1886, 8. On Pimlico, see "No More Racing at Pimlico," *New York Times*, December 19, 1889, 1; "Ex-Gov. Oden Bowie: The Famous Railroader and Owner of the Famous Crickmore," *New York Times*, December 5, 1894, 5.

14. Challmes, *The Preakness*, 34.

15. On the National Jockey Club and the sale of the *American Stud Book*, see "National Jockey Club: The Scheme That Mr. Kirkman Has Been Laying," *New York Times*, December 19, 1893, 6; "Sale of the Stud Book," *New York Times*, May 19, 1897, 5; on the exclusion of blacks, see Sandra McKee, "Black Jockeys Glittered in Bygone Era," *St. Louis Post-Dispatch*, May 16, 1997, 3E.

16. Challmes, *The Preakness*, 18.

17. On the fire and Governor Bowie's death, see "Fire at Pimlico," *Sun*, September 3, 1894, 8; "Oden Bowie Stricken," *Sun*, November 28, 1894, 1. On the use of the track by Pimlico Country Club and Pimlico Drivers Club, see "Pimlico's Great Day," *Sun*, November 9, 1896, 6. On ownership of the track during the 1890s, see "For New Jockey Club," *Sun*, October 8, 1903, 9.

18. On the interest in and rise of the Maryland Jockey Club, see "A New Jockey Club," *Sun*, July 15, 1899, 6; "Old Maryland Jockey Club," *Sun*, June 20, 1901,

4; "Looking to Reorganization," *Sun*, September 24, 1904, 9; "Maryland Jockey Club: List of Proposed Members Grows," *Sun*, September 26, 1904, 9. "Changes at Pimlico: Maryland Jockey Club to Make Number of Improvements," *Sun*, October 4, 1904, 9.

19. On the restarting of racing at Pimlico and the Preakness, see "Pimlico Race Track Sold: Maryland Jockey Club Pays $70,000 for the Famous Course," *New York Times*, April 13, 1905, 1; "Horses and Horsemen," *New York Times*, April 10, 1909, 10.

20. Challmes, *The Preakness*, 49; "107,000 For Horsemen," *Sun*, January 27, 1918, 11.

21. "Sir Barton Wins Derby," *Sun*, May 11, 1919, C9.

22. "Sir Barton Wins Stake," *Sun*, May 15, 1919, 8.

23. Challmes, *The Preakness*, 51–53.

24. C. Edward Sparrow, "'Tis Preakness Day," *Sun*, May 18, 1920, 14.

25. Pimlico, "Maryland Becoming Recognized as Home for the Thoroughbred," *Sun*, April 11, 1920, 15.

26. "Record Throng Sees Preakness at Pimlico," *Sun*, May 19, 1920, 24.

27. "Rich Preakness Is Won by Broomspun," *New York Times*, May 17, 1921, 24.

28. "Preakness May Be Richest Turf Classic," *New York Times*, March 18, 1922, 16.

29. Challmes, *The Preakness*, 59.

30. "Horses, Jockeys and Odds in $50,000 Preakness Today," *New York Times*, May 13, 1922, 19. Benjamin G. Rader, "Compensatory Sport Heroes: Ruth, Grange, and Dempsey," *Journal of Popular Culture* 16, no. 4 (Spring 1983): 11; Warren I. Susman, *Culture as History: The Transformation of American Society in the Twentieth Century* (Washington, DC: Smithsonian Institution, [1984] 2003), 122–49.

31. "Winners of Preakness Stakes for the Last Twenty Years," *New York Times*, May 15, 1932, S9; Challmes, *The Preakness*, 76, 84–85, 89.

32. Challmes, *The Preakness*, 65.

33. Bryan Field, "Gallant Fox Ranks with a Kingly Host," *New York Times*, August 10, 1930, SM5.

34. Challmes, *The Preakness*, 67. On the use of Triple Crown, see Bryan Field, "Gallant Fox Beats Whichone 4 Lengths in $81,340 Belmont: Woodward's Preakness, Derby Winner Ties Sir Barton as Triple Crown Hero," *New York Times*, June 8, 1930, 147.

35. Bryan Field, "Omaha, 7–10, First Home in the $43,980 Belmont before 24,000 in the Rain," *New York Times*, June 9, 1935, S1.

36. On Triple Crown, see Challmes, *The Preakness*, 85. On war rationing and the Preakness, see ibid., 116.

37. "Black-eyed Susan Blanket," http://www.preakness-stakes.info/black-eyed-susan.php (accessed September 20, 2013); Bryan Field, "Mioland Is Second: Finish of the Preakness and Presentation of Trophy," *New York Times*, May 12, 1940, 81.

38. On Triple Crown winners of the 1940s, see John Kiernan, "Sports of the Times: Sights and Sounds at the Preakness," *New York Times*, May 11, 1941, S2; "Whirlaway Completes 'Triple Crown' Conquest by Easily Taking Belmont,"

Hartford Courant, June 8, 1941, C2; Bryan Field, "Closing Day at Belmont: A Juvenile Favorite Fails, a Champion Wins," *New York Times,* June 6, 1943, S1; "Assault Scores Triple by Capturing Belmont: Texas Horse Becomes Seventh Horse in History to Sweep," *Hartford Courant,* June 2, 1946, C2; "Citation, Turfdom's First Millionaire, to Be Retired Immediately by Owner," *Hartford Courant,* July 20, 1951, 18.

39. "Pimlico Sale Is Approved by Directors," *Baltimore Sun,* November 26, 1952, 34; "Pimlico Sale to Two Here Is Reported," *Baltimore Sun,* November 21, 1952, 38. On the potential move to Laurel in 1948, see "De Francis and Laurel," *Baltimore Sun,* December 7, 1984, 6G.

40. "Herman Cohen New Pimlico President; Boshamer Quits," *Baltimore Sun,* July 15, 1953, 15.

41. "Historic Clubhouse Burns at Pimlico," *Baltimore Sun,* June 17, 1966, A1.

42. Quoted in Frederick N. Rasmussen, "Much Was Lost in the Great Pimlico Fire of 1966," *Baltimore Sun,* July 20, 2002, 3D.

43. Challmes, *The Preakness,* 139; "Herman Cohen Heads Pimlico," *New York Times,* July 15, 1953, 31.

44. "Pimlico Names Lang General Manager," *Hartford Courant,* May 28, 1969, 48; Mike Klingaman and Kent Baker, "Former Pimlico General Manager Remade the Preakness," *Baltimore Sun,* March 19, 2010, 23.

45. From the horses to the jockeys and owners, men worked and ran the Preakness. Women were largely excluded. The 1973 victory of Secretariat, owned by Penny Chenery, helped to challenge this culture. While Secretariat subsequently won not only the Preakness, but also the Triple Crown and all three races in record time, the road to victory was marred in challenges. After Secretariat, Chenery went on to have a distinguished career as president of the Thoroughbred Owners and Breeders Association in the late 1970s and early 1980s. The Jockey Club, the national organization, had traditionally been all male. The club voted Chenery into its membership in 1983. However, horse ownership and jockeying continues to be dominated by men. See, for example, Steven Crist, "Matriarchs of the Meadow," *New York Times,* March 31, 1985, SMA38.

46. "Secretariat Enjoys Lazy Belmont Day Away from Cheers," *New York Times,* June 11, 1973, 1; Victor Mather, "For Secretariat, a Record 39 Years after a Victory," *New York Times,* June 22, 2012, B12.

47. A direct descendant of Man O' War and War Admiral, Affirmed was not the favorite, but edged out wins in all three Triple Crown races. There has not been a Triple Crown winner since 1978. While there have been twelve horses that won both the Derby and Preakness, racing has arguably become too intense for a horse to win the three crown jewels of the racing circuit. See "Undefeated Seattle Slew Wins Belmont and Captures Triple Crown," *New York Times,* June 12, 1977, 1; "Affirmed Noses Out Alydar for Triple," *Hartford Courant,* June 11, 1978, 1C.

48. "De Francis' Threat," *Baltimore Sun,* February 22, 1987, 6M.

49. "De Francis and Laurel," *Baltimore Sun,* December 7, 1984, 6G.

50. "Delayed Inaugural Ball," *Baltimore Sun,* December 31, 1986, 14A. Also, see "Herman Cohen, 95; Headed Pimlico Track," *New York Times,* May 18, 1990, D17; David Michael Ettlin, "Ben Cohen Dies, Co-owned Pimlico," *Baltimore Sun,* March 23, 1994, 2013, 1B.

51. "A New Preakness Era," *Baltimore Sun,* April 16, 1987, 1F.

52. "Frank J. De Francis Is Dead at 62; Lawyer and Horse-Racing Leader," *New York Times,* August 20, 1989, 38; John Scheinman, "De Francis Family Selling Its Remaining Stake in Maryland Tracks," *Washington Post,* September 25, 2007, E3.

53. "The Pimlico 13," *New York Times,* May 16, 2002, D8.

54. Dawn McCarty and Michael Bathon, "Magna Entertainment, Racetrack Company, in Bankruptcy," March 5, 2009, http://www.bloomberg.com/apps/news?pid=newsarchive&sid= alQ1UPVAN1AA (accessed September 20, 2013); Andrea K. Walker, "Preakness Key to Md. Racing, Track Owner Says," *Baltimore Sun,* July 30, 2011, 8.

55. According to the Jockey's Guild, in 2013 only around 50 of the close to 1,000 jockeys in the United States were black. See Mike Klingaman, "With the Weight of Racing History," *Baltimore Sun,* May 16, 2013, 1; on the legacy of African American jockeys and the Preakness, see McKee, "Black Jockeys Glittered in Bygone Era"; Sandra McKee, "Rich History in Recovery," *Baltimore Sun,* May 14, 1997, 1D.

56. Chris Korman, "Rising Star Napravnik Aims to Shine Here," *Baltimore Sun,* May 12, 2013, Sports, 1.

57. For an overview of the rise of sport and the American city, see Steven A. Riess, *City Games: The Evolution of American Urban Society and the Rise of Sports* (Urbana: University of Illinois Press, 1991), 1–93; On class struggles in Baltimore, see Seth Rockman, *Scraping By: Wage Labor, Slavery, and Survival in Early Baltimore* (Baltimore: Johns Hopkins University Press, 2009).

3. Black Knights and Engineers: The City-Poly Football Rivalry

1. Michael Olesker, "The Era Has Faded but the Cheers Still Echo," *Baltimore Sun,* January 7, 2003, 10B.

2. Ibid.

3. Ibid.

4. Interview with Michael Olesker, March 13, 2013.

5. Interview with Michael Olesker, July 10, 2014.

6. Ted Patterson and Dean Smith, *Football in Baltimore: History and Memorabilia from Colts to Ravens,* 2nd ed. (Baltimore: Johns Hopkins University Press, [2000] 2013), 7.

7. For more on City College, see http://baltimorecitycollege.us/apps/pages/index.jsp?uREC_ID= 52467&type=d (accessed November 16, 2014).

8. For more on Baltimore Polytechnic Institute, see http://www.bpi.edu/history.jsp (accessed November 16, 2014).

9. Patterson and Smith, *Football in Baltimore,* 7.

10. Ibid.

11. Ibid.

12. Mike Klingaman, "'The Biggest Thing Around': 125-Year City-Poly Rivalry Has Been Marked by Emotion and Mayhem," *Baltimore Sun,* November 9, 2013, 16.

13. Patterson and Smith, *Football in Baltimore,* 7.

14. Ibid.

15. City vs. Poly game program, November 25, 1948. Ted Patterson collection.

16. Patterson and Smith, *Football in Baltimore*, 8.

17. Quoted in ibid.

18. Ibid.

19. Interview with Vince Bagli, October 25, 2014.

20. Quoted in Dean Bartoli Smith, "At the Turkey Bowl, Loyola and Calvert Hall Meet to Revisit Ancient Rivalry," *Baltimore Brew*, November 24, 2009, https://www.baltimorebrew.com/2009/11/24/at-the-turkey-bowl-between-loyola-and-calvert-hall-an-ancient-rivalry-is-revisited/ (accessed September 1, 2014).

21. Smith, "At the Turkey Bowl, Loyola and Calvert Hall Meet to Revisit Ancient Rivalry."

22. Quoted in Patterson and Smith, *Football in Baltimore*, 11.

23. Quoted in ibid., 8.

24. Ibid.

25. Interview with Michael Olesker, March 12, 2013.

26. Interview with Ed Berlin, September 8, 2013.

27. Keith Mills, "When Stars Come Out," Pressbox, November 11, 2009, http://www.pressboxon line.com/story/5593/when-stars-come-out (accessed September 2, 2014); James H. Jackson, "Win Is 12th in Row for Collegians," *Baltimore Sun*, November 26, 1965, C1.

28. Mills, "When Stars Come Out."

29. Ibid.

30. Kent Baker, "Waibel Remembered as Man of Dedication," *Baltimore Sun*, January 12, 2001, 1E.

31. David C. Daneker, ed., *150 Years of the Baltimore City College* (Baltimore: Baltimore City College Alumni Association, 1988), 58.

32. Patterson and Smith, *Football in Baltimore*, 7.

33. Mills, "When Stars Come Out."

34. Ibid.

35. Klingaman, "'The Biggest Thing Around,'" 16.

36. Quoted in ibid.

37. Ibid.

38. Interview with Astrid Kamali, August 16, 2014.

39. Interview with Gregg Wilhelm, August 23, 2014.

4. "For a White Boy's Chance in the World": Joe Gans, Baltimore's Forgotten Fighter

1. William Gildea, *The Longest Fight: In the Ring with Joe Gans, Boxing's First African American Champion* (New York: Farrar, Straus and Giroux, 2012).

2. Mark Kram, "A Wink at a Homely Girl," *Sports Illustrated*, October 10, 1966, 86–103.

3. See David Remnick, *King of the World: Muhammad Ali and the Rise of an American Hero* (New York: Random House, 1998).

4. Gildea, *The Longest Fight*, 202.

5. See http://boxrec.com/list_bouts.php?human_id=9026&cat=boxer (accessed September 1, 2014).

6. Theresa Runstedtler, *Jack Johnson, Rebel Sojourner: Boxing in the Shadow of the Global Color Line* (Berkeley: University of California Press, 2012), 232.

5. On the Courts of Druid Hill: Lucy Diggs Slowe and the Rise of Organized

1. The organization of many black athletic clubs, leagues, and tournaments led to the crowning of many national champions. Slowe was the first woman in any black sporting league to earn that title.

2. For a compelling discussion of class terminology in the black community, see Michele Mitchell, *Righteous Propagation: African Americans and the Politics of Racial Destiny after Reconstruction* (Chapel Hill: University of North Carolina Press, 2004). Mitchell argues that using standard class terms to describe African Americans of this era obscures the specific circumstances of their lived experience, namely the fact that they were less than a generation removed from slavery, as well as to mark the gap between even elite blacks and their white middle-class contemporaries. Additionally, she notes that the term *elite* connotes a certain community standing that black leaders could occupy without being members of the elite class and all elite blacks were not, conversely, community leaders. Instead, Mitchell offers the term *aspiring class*. In this essay I use the term *aspiring class* as well as *middle class*. I use black middle class to point to a class ideology embraced by blacks who viewed themselves as part of the "better class" and asserted their class status through their education, group membership, clothing choices, recreational activities, and ability to uplift their community.

3. For examples of work that examines black sports institutions during the time of legal segregation, see Neil Lanctot, *Negro League Baseball: The Rise and Ruin of a Black Institution* (Philadelphia: University of Pennsylvania Press, 2004); Patrick Miller, "'To Bring the Race Along Rapidly': Sport, Student Culture and Educational Mission at Historically Black Colleges during the Interwar Years," *History of Education Quarterly* 35 (Summer 1995): 111–33; David K. Wiggins, "The Biggest 'Classic' of Them All: The Howard University and Lincoln University Thanksgiving Day Football Games, 1919–1929," in *Rooting for the Home Team: Sport, Community, and Identity*, ed. Daniel A. Nathan (Urbana: University of Illinois Press, 2013), 36–53; Gwendolyn Captain, "Enter Ladies and Gentlemen of Color: Gender, Sport, and the Ideal of African-American Manhood and Womanhood during the Late 19th and Early 20th Centuries," *Journal of Sport History* 18 (Spring 1991): 81–102; Theresa Runstedtler, "Visible Men: African American Boxers, the New Negro, and the Global Color Line," *Radical History Review* 103 (Winter 2009): 59–81.

4. Lucy Diggs Slowe Papers (LDSP), Box 90, Folder 1; Manuscript Division, Moorland-Spingarn Research Center (MSRC), Howard University. These papers were written as composition exercises for a class Slowe was in while obtaining her MA from Columbia University. Also see Carroll L. L. Miller and Anne S. Pruitt-Logan, *Faithful to the Task at Hand: The Life of Lucy Diggs Slowe* (Albany: State University of New York Press, 2012), 7–10.

5. Miller and Pruitt-Logan, *Faithful to the Task at Hand*, 7–10.

6. For more on the rural to urban migratory patterns of black Americans following the Civil War, see Steven Hahn, *A Nation Under Our Feet: Black Political*

Struggles in the Rural South, from Slavery to the Great Migration (Cambridge, MA: Harvard University Press, 2003); Tera W. Hunter, *To 'Joy My Freedom: Southern Black Women's Lives and Labors after the Civil War* (Cambridge, MA: Harvard University Press, 1997); Nell Irvin Painter, *Exodusters: Black Migration to Kansas after Reconstruction* (New York: W. W. Norton & Company, 1992); Ira Berlin, *The Making of African America: The Four Great Migrations* (New York: Penguin, 2010).

7. Population of Baltimore City, 1790–1990, Maryland State Archives.

8. The city's population had grown from 434,439 in 1890 to 508,957 in 1900. Richard L. Forstall, Populations of States and Counties of the United States, 1790–1990, US Bureau of the Census (Washington, DC, 1996). The immigrant population continued to rise as well and totaled 70,000 in 1900.

9. US Census Bureau, Population of the United States. Twelfth Census of the United States, Schedule No. 1 (1900), Stuart Household located at 1116 Division St., Baltimore, MD.

10. Miller and Pruitt-Logan, *Faithful to the Task at Hand*, 18.

11. Druid Hill as described by a *Baltimore Sun* journalist. "Druid Hill a Garden Spot," July 5, 1906, 12; Druid Hill benefited from Mayor Alcaeus Hooper's vision of a single, city-defining park that was "brought to perfection." While development slowed at Patterson, Clifton, and Carroll, Baltimore's other parks, Druid Hill flourished. For more, see James Edward Wells II, "The Historical Geography of Racial and Ethnic Access within Baltimore's Carroll Park: 1870–1954" (MA thesis, Ohio State University, 2006).

12. Frederick Law Olmsted Jr., "The Report upon the Development of Public Grounds for Baltimore," 1904, 52. Olmsted Associates Manuscripts, Library of Congress. For more on Olmsted and the 1904 report, see David Holden, "1904 Olmsted Bros. Report: The Advancement of City Planning in Baltimore," *Olmstedian* 15, no. 2 (Fall 2004): 1–3.

13. *Baltimore Sun*, July 5, 1906, 12.

14. Barry Kessler and David Zang, *The Play Life of a City: Baltimore's Recreation and Parks, 1900–1955* (Baltimore: Baltimore City Life Museums, Baltimore City Dept. of Recreation and Parks, 1989), 31, Homewood House Reference Collection (HHRC), Johns Hopkins University, Baltimore, MD.

15. *Baltimore Afro-American*, June 10, 1903, 4.

16. *Plessy v. Ferguson*, 163 US 537 Supreme Court Case (1896). Homer Plessey, a mixed-race citizen of Louisiana, attempted to challenge Louisiana law that mandated separate cars for "whites and coloreds." Arrested after trying to ride in the whites-only car on the East Louisiana Railroad, Plessey claimed the law violated his Thirteenth and Fourteenth Amendment. After losing in the Louisiana court system, the case was argued in front of the Supreme Court, which ruled against Plessey in a 7–1 decision. This case would set the precedent for state laws mandating segregation until the *Brown v. Board of Education* decision overturned it in 1954.

17. In 1902, Maryland passed laws that segregated railroads and steamships. Between 1898–1906 state Democrats introduced three state amendments to disenfranchise blacks. While these state amendments failed, the fear of growing black political power resulted in the legal segregation of the Republican Party of Maryland in 1907.

18. Gretchen Boger, "The Meaning of Neighborhood in the Modern City: Baltimore's Residential Segregation Ordinances, 1910–1913," *Journal of Urban History* 35 (January 2009): 236–58.

19. Although private residential segregation and the segregation of public places were parallel processes, historian Gretchen Boger reminds us that they were not identical ones. "Despite their surface similarities, Jim Crow segregation of public spaces and Jim Crow segregation of private residential neighborhoods had distinct geologies." Ibid., 238.

20. Kessler and Zang, *The Play Life of a City*, 3.

21. A.B.M., Letter the Editor, *Baltimore Sun,* June 15, 1903, 7.

22. Letters to the Editor, *Baltimore Sun*, March 27, 1903, 7; June 15, 1903, 7; September 8, 1903, 7; June 6, 1905, 7. Letters to the Park Board, Minutes to the Board of Park Commissioners, June 1905; Letters to the Park Board, Minutes to the Board of Park Commissioners, October 1905, Baltimore City Archives, Baltimore Record Group 51-5 (BCA BRG51-5).

23. *Baltimore Sun,* June 15, 1903, 7.

24. Letters to the Editor, *Baltimore Sun,* June 15, 1903, 7; September 8, 1903, 6; June 6, 1905, 7. Letters to the Park Board, Minutes to the Board of Park Commissioners, June 1905 (BCA BRG51-5).

25. Minutes to the Board of Park Commissioners, October 3, 1905 (BCA BRG51-5).

26. "Negroes Are Ruled Off," *Baltimore Sun,* October 4, 1905, 12.

27. "Jim-Crowin at Druid Hill Park," *Afro-American-Ledger,* June 10, 1905, 4.

28. Ibid.

29. For more on Rosenwald, see Mary S. Hoffschwelle, *The Rosenwald Schools of the American South* (Gainesville: University Press of Florida, 2006). Comprehensive examinations of northern philanthropy and southern black education include James D. Anderson, *The Education of Blacks in the South, 1860–1935* (Chapel Hill: University of North Carolina Press, 1988); Adam Fairclough, *A Class of Their Own: Black Teachers in the Segregated South* (Cambridge, MA: Harvard University Press, 2009); Eric Anderson and Alfred A. Moss Jr., *Dangerous Donations: Northern Philanthropy and Southern Black Education, 1902–1930* (Columbia: University of Missouri Press, 1999).

30. The debate over industrial vs. liberal arts curricula was the essential question surrounding the development of black education after the Civil War. From primary schools through colleges, educators, politicians, philanthropists, and journalists debated the merits and consequences of both types of schooling.

31. "Colored Training School," *Sun*, January 28, 1898, 8.

32. Observations from a white *Baltimore Sun* reporter. "Colored Society There," *Sun*, June 18, 1904, 6.

33. Untitled, LDSP, Box 90, Folder 1; MSRC.

34. See, for instance, the *Baltimore Afro-American*'s standing "High School Notes" section in its regular "About the City" column. While the paper would report news of interest, a great deal of its focus covered sporting engagements. For example, see "About the City," *Afro-American*, October 24, 1903, 8.

35. Susan K. Cahn, *Coming on Strong: Gender and Sexuality in Twentieth-Century Women's Sport* (New York: Free Press, 1994), 13–17.

36. "Baseball among the Fairer Sex Coming into Prominence," *Indianapolis Freeman*, December 26, 1908, in *The Unlevel Playing Field: A Documentary History of the African American Experience in Sport*, ed. Patrick B. Miller and David K. Wiggins (Urbana: University of Illinois Press, 2003), 55–57.

37. Ibid.

38. For more on progressive era reform and recreation, see Kathy Peiss, *Cheap Amusements: Working Women and Leisure in Turn-of-the-Century* (Philadelphia: Temple University Press, 1986); John F. Kasson, *Amusing the Million: Coney Island at the Turn of the Century* (New York: Hill and Wang, [1978] 2000); Elliott J. Gorn, *The Manly Art: Bare-Knuckle Prize Fighting in America* (Ithaca, NY: Cornell University Press [1986] 2012). For discussion of the "crisis of masculinity" and desire for the "strenuous life," see Gail Bederman, *Manliness and Civilization: A Cultural History of Gender and Race in the United States, 1880–1917* (Chicago: University of Chicago Press, [1995] 2008).

39. Kessler and Zang, *The Play Life of a City*, vii.

40. Baltimore CPA Development Report, 1909 in National Recreation Congress. *Collection of Selected Papers*, 1909.

41. Emmett J. Scott, "Leisure Time and the Colored Citizen," *Playground* 18 (January 1925). See also W. E. B. Du Bois, "The Problem of Amusement," *Southern Workman* 27 (September 1897): 181–84.

42. For more on this, see Davarian L. Baldwin, *Chicago's New Negroes: Modernity, the Great Migration, and Black Urban Life* (Chapel Hill: University of North Carolina Press, 2009), 204–9.

43. Marion Thompson Wright Papers, as cited in Miller and Pruitt-Logan, *Faithful to the Task at Hand*, 20.

44. Rolfe Cobleigh, "A New Day for Howard University: Progress and Needs of a Great University," *Congregationalist*, July 27, 1922, 108. For more on Howard, see Fairclough, *A Class of Their Own*, 232; Walter Dyson, *Howard University, The Capstone of Negro Education, A History: 1867–1940* (Washington, DC: The Graduate School, Howard University, 1941); Rayford W. Logan, *Howard University: The First Hundred Years, 1867–1967* (New York: New York University Press, 1969).

45. *Howard University Journal*, September 28, 1906, 21.

46. "Tennis Enthusiasts in a War to the Finish," *Baltimore Afro-American*, October 2, 1909, 4.

47. Wiggins, "The Biggest 'Classic' of Them All," 37.

48. "About the City-Tennis Tournament," *Afro-American*, September 17, 1910, 8; "Athletics in Baltimore," *Afro-American*, October 23, 1915, 7.

49. "Tennis—A Game for Women," *Afro-American*, September 18, 1915, 4.

50. "Baltimore Defeated in Tennis Tournament," *Afro-American*, August 7, 1915, 4; "Baltimore to Have Tennis Grounds," *Afro-American*, September 18, 1909, 6; *Afro-American*, June 17, 1916, 4; "More Interest in Athletic Field," *Afro-American*, September 9, 1911, 4.

51. "Sports and Athletics," *Afro-American*, June 24, 1916, 6; "Tennis Tourney," *Afro-American*, September 23, 1916, 1; "Miss Lucy Slowe Wins," *Afro-American*, August 26, 1916, 1.

52. "Miss Slowe for Women's Suffrage," *Afro-American*, October 23, 1915, 1.

53. *Afro-American*, October 24, 1915, 4; Miller and Pruitt-Logan, *Faithful*

for the Task at Hand, 37–45; Treva Lindsey, "Climbing the Hilltop: In Search of New Negro Womanhood at Howard University," in *Escape from New York: The New Negro Renaissance beyond Harlem,* ed. Davarian L. Baldwin and Minkah Makalani (Minneapolis: University of Minnesota Press, 2013), 271–91.

54. The *Afro* reported that Armstrong offered to double Slowe's salary. "Miss Slowe Resigns," *Afro-American,* November 6, 1915, 1.

55. Lucy Slowe, "Have You a Hobby," *Junior High School Review,* June 1921, 10.

56. Schlagball loosely translates into "hit the ball" and was a German-based ball game similar to cricket.

57. "Miss Lucy Slowe Again Champion," *Afro-American,* September 8, 1917, 4.

58. "Fighting for Tennis Honors," *Afro-American,* September 1, 1917, 1.

59. *Afro-American,* April 17, 1915, 7.

60. The Modern Women, *Afro-American,* August 12, 1916, 7.

61. LDSP, Box 90-4, Folder 102; MSRC.

62. Ibid.

63. *The Hilltop,* May 8, 1925, 16.

64. "Women Cannot Do Two Things Well," *Afro-American,* February 23, 1923, 1.

65. Slowe would refute this claim, noting that while she was "dissatisfied with her omission from the top-seeded players" she simply chose to stop playing because she "felt like withdrawing." Lucy Slowe, "Miss Slowe Did Not Quit Game," *Afro-American,* August 29, 1924, 15.

66. LDSP, Box 90-1, Folder 4; MSRC. For more on Slowe at Howard and as an educator, see Miller and Pruitt-Logan, *Faithful to the Task at Hand,* 79–207; Linda M. Perkins, "Lucy Diggs Slowe: Champion of the Self-Determination of African-American Women in Higher Education," *Journal of Negro History* 81, no. 1/4 (January 1996), and Lindsey, "Climbing the Hilltop," 272.

67. "Lucy Slowe Dies," *Chicago Defender,* October 30, 1937, 3.

68. Jason Lewis, "Lucy Diggs Slowe, the Mother of Black Tennis," *Sentinel,* April 31, 2011, B1-B2; "Lucy Diggs Slowe Inducted into Maryland Women's Hall of Fame," *Targeted News Service,* March 31, 2011, np.

69. *Afro-American,* August 27, 1938, clipping located in LDSP, Box 90-1, Folder 9; MSRC.

6. Sweat Equity: Physical Education at The Bryn Mawr School for Girls

1. See www.letsmove.gov (accessed August 23, 2014).

2. M. Carey Thomas, "The Future of Women's Higher Education," *Mount Holyoke College, Seventy-fifth Anniversary* (Springfield, MA: Springfield Printing and Binding Company, 1913), 101.

3. Title IX of the Education Amendments of 1972 states: "No person in the United States shall, on the basis of sex, be excluded from participation in, be denied the benefits of, or be subjected to discrimination under any education program or activity receiving Federal financial assistance." See http://www.justice.gov/crt/about/cor/coord/titleixstat.php (accessed July 12, 2013).

4. Elizabeth Nye Di Cataldo, *Ex Solo Ad Solem: A History of the Bryn Mawr School* (Baltimore: The Bryn Mawr School, 2011), 6. The committee members were M. Carey Thomas, Mary Elizabeth Garrett, Mamie Gwinn, Bessie King, and Julia Rogers.

5. M. Carey Thomas writing in her journal at age fourteen, quoted in Di Cataldo, *Ex Solo Ad Solem*, 2.

6. M. Carey Thomas, "Present Tendencies in Women's College and University Education," *Educational Review* 25 (1908), included as "Motives and Future of the Educated Woman," in *The Educated Woman in America: Selected Writings of Catharine Beecher, Margaret Fuller and M. Carey Thomas*, ed. Barbara M. Cross (New York: Columbia University Press, 1965), 160.

7. Edward H. Clarke, *Sex in Education: Or, A Fair Chance for the Girls* (1873; repr., New York: Arno Press and The New York Times, 1972), 18.

8. Thomas, "Present Tendencies in Women's College and University Education," 162.

9. Clarke, *Sex in Education*, 33; Susan Cahn, *Coming on Strong: Gender and Sexuality in Twentieth-Century Women's Sport* (New York: Free Press, 1994), 13.

10. Clarke, *Sex in Education*, 42.

11. Cahn paraphrases the logic: "An exercise regimen would theoretically return energy to the body and strike a proper balance between physical and mental activity." Cahn, *Coming on Strong*, 13.

12. Di Cataldo, *Ex Solo Ad Solem*, 9.

13. *Dr. Sargent's System of Developing Appliances and Gymnastic Apparatus*, 1883 pamphlet, 4. University of Rochester Medical Center, Atwater Collection of American Popular Medicine, Box 10/2.

14. Dr. A. Levertin, "Medico-Mechanical Gymnastics," *Scientific American Supplement*, December 5, 1896, 17447, Google Books (accessed June 26, 2013).

15. Andrea Hamilton, *A Vision for Girls: Gender, Education and the Bryn Mawr School* (Baltimore: Johns Hopkins University Press, 2004), 35.

16. Di Cataldo, *Ex Solo Ad Solem*, 141.

17. Lillian Welsh, *Reminiscences of Thirty Years in Baltimore* (Baltimore: The Norman, Remington Co., 1925), 4. The Women's College of Baltimore was later renamed Goucher College and is now coed.

18. Now the site of the Joseph Meyerhoff Symphony Hall.

19. Di Cataldo, *Ex Solo Ad Solem*, 9.

20. After her retirement Hamilton went on to write *The Greek Way* (1930) and *Mythology* (1942), texts that are still best sellers in the field.

21. Hamilton, *A Vision for Girls*, 57. Andrea Hamilton is no relation of Edith Hamilton or her sister Margaret, who was also a leader of the school.

22. Di Cataldo, *Ex Solo Ad Solem*, 142.

23. Ibid., 24.

24. Hamilton, *A Vision for Girls*, 102–3.

25. Judith Sealander, "'Shaped Up' by the State: Government Attempts to Improve Children's Diets, Exercise Regimes and Physical Fitness," in *The Failed Century of the Child: Governing America's Young in the 20th Century* (Cambridge: Cambridge University Press, 2003), 307.

26. Charles Tennyson, "They Taught the World to Play," *Victorian Studies* 2 (March 1959): 211–22.

27. Kathleen E. McCrone, *Playing the Game: Sport and the Physical Emancipation of English Women, 1870–1914* (Lexington: University Press of Kentucky, 1988), 12.

28. Tennyson, "They Taught the World to Play," 211–22.

29. See http://www.gilman.edu/about-us/history/index.aspx (accessed September 1, 2014).

30. In 1917 the Committee came to the school's aid once again in the form of fields at Montebello, the former estate of heiress Mary Garrett that M. Carey Thomas had inherited at Garrett's death. However, the estate lay beyond the end of the trolley line and demanded a half-mile walk after an hour-long ride. It simply wasn't practical for school-day practices. See Di Cataldo, *Ex Solo Ad Solem*, 143.

31. Ibid.

32. Hamilton, *A Vision for Girls*, 106–7.

33. "Dedicated to Interests of Women: Girls' Club Dedicated," *Baltimore Sun*, February 26, 1915, 7. This article details the opening of the girls' club, while "Thinks 'Jazz' Bound to Yield to Sports," *Baltimore Sun*, March 12, 1922, CA 12, provides evidence that a basketball team was functioning there in 1921.

34. S. R. Carter to Edith Hamilton, December 16, 1901, in the archives of The Bryn Mawr School for Girls, Baltimore, Maryland. This annual contest continues into the twenty-first century and is recognized as the longest-running girls' school basketball rivalry in the nation. Di Cataldo, *Ex Solo Ad Solem*, 143.

35. Millicent Carey McIntosh, November 4, 1960, in *The Bryn Mawr Bulletin*, 1960–1961. Quoted in Di Cataldo, *Ex Solo Ad Solem*, 142.

36. Senda Berenson, *Basketball for Women* (Park Place, NY: American Sports Publishing Company, 1903), excerpted in Jean O'Reilly and Susan K. Cahn, *Women in Sports in the United States, A Documentary Reader* (Boston: Northeastern University Press, 2007), 54.

37. Dr. Dudley A. Sargent, "Are Athletics Making Girls Masculine? A Practical Answer to a Question Every Girl Asks," *Ladies Home Journal*, March 1912, excerpted in O'Reilly and Cahn, *Women in Sports in the United States*, 56–59.

38. Lynn E. Couturier, "Considering *The Sportswoman*, 1924–1936: A Content Analysis," *Sport History Review* 41, no. 2 (November 2010): 111.

39. "Athletic 'Debs' Seek Basketball Honors: Gay Little Society Girls, Some Not So Little, Organize Team for Real Contests," *Baltimore Sun*, February 23, 1921, 16.

40. "Thinks 'Jazz' Bound to Yield to Sports," *Baltimore Sun*, March 12, 1922, CA 12.

41. Ibid.

42. James Rogers, "Athletics for Women," Department of the Interior, Bureau of Education, Physical Education Pamphlet Series, 4 (Washington, DC, 1924), 1. Quoted in Sealander, "'Shaped Up' by the State," 315.

43. Quoted in Di Cataldo, *Ex Solo Ad Solem*, 142.

44. McCrone, *Playing the Game*, 65–66.

45. Ibid., 73.

46. Ibid., 70–71.

47. Paul Atkinson, "The Feminist Physique: Physical Education and the Medicalization of Women's Education," in *From Fair Sex to Feminism: Sport and the Socialization of Women in the Industrial and Post-Industrial Eras*, ed. J. A. Mangan and Roberta Park (London: Frank Cass and Company, 1987), 49.

48. McCrone, *Playing the Game*, 72.
49. Donald M. Fisher, *Lacrosse: A History of the Game* (Baltimore: Johns Hopkins University Press, 2002), 150.
50. Ibid., 25–26.
51. Ibid., 66.
52. Ibid., 70.
53. Quoted in ibid., 28.
54. There is some confusion over Lumsden's first exposure to men's lacrosse. Fisher states that English women saw matches in one of the three exhibition tours the Canadian team made to Great Britain between 1867 and 1880. McCrone says Lumsden writes in her memoirs that she saw her first match in New Hampshire in 1884. Fisher, *Lacrosse*, 147; McCrone, *Playing the Game*, 72.
55. McCrone, *Playing the Game*, 72.
56. Jane Claydon, "Lacrosse Scotland Honors Pioneers and Legends," March 1, 2013, http://filacrosse.com/women/lacrosse-scotland-honors-pioneers-and-legends/ (accessed July 8, 2013).
57. Di Cataldo, *Ex Solo Ad Solem*, 145.
58. Constance Applebee, "The Story of Lacrosse and How We Came to Play It," *The Sportswoman*, November 1929, 13.
59. See Di Cataldo, *Ex Solo Ad Solem*, 144–45; Applebee, "The Story of Lacrosse and How We Came to Play It," 13.
60. Di Cataldo, *Ex Solo Ad Solem*, 145.
61. Joyce Cran and Joyce Riley, "An Ideal Game for Women and Girls," *Sportswoman*, October 1931, 14.
62. Sinclair, "Women's Lacrosse Rules," *Sportswoman*, January 1, 1925, 5.
63. Ibid., 7.
64. Cran and Riley, "An Ideal Game for Women and Girls," 14.
65. Sinclair, "Women's Lacrosse Rules," 6.
66. For more on the de-emphasis on competition during this period in women's sports, see Lynne E. Couturier, "Dissenting Voices: The Discourse of Competition in *The Sportswoman*," *Journal of Sport History* 39, no. 2 (Summer 2012): 265–82.
67. Cran and Riley, "An Ideal Game for Women and Girls," 14.
68. Ibid.
69. Quotation from Applebee, "The Story of Lacrosse and How We Came to Play It," 13. On USWLA, see *Women and Sports in the United States; A Documentary Reader*, xxv.
70. Susan Cahn, "Crushes, Competition and Closets: The Emergence of Homophobia in Women's Physical Education," in *Women Sport and Culture*, ed. Susan Birrell and Cheryl L. Cole (Champaign, IL: Human Kinetics, 1994), 332.
71. Ibid., 331, 333.
72. "Baltimore's Grand Dame of Lacrosse: At 67, Rosabelle Sinclair, Dean of American Women Players, Is Still Promoting the Game," *Baltimore Sun*, May 12, 1957, SM 18.
73. Martha Millspaugh, "Dancing across Europe at Bryn Mawr," *Baltimore Sun*, May 2, 1948, A5.
74. "'A joyous striving' Alumnae Remember Miss Sinclair," *Communique*, 1978, in the Archives of The Bryn Mawr School for Girls, Baltimore, Maryland.
75. Millspaugh, "Dancing across Europe at Bryn Mawr," A5.

76. "'A Joyous Striving' Alumnae Remember Miss Sinclair."

77. "Judy and Sue Devlin Return Home as World Champions."

78. "'A Joyous Striving' Alumnae Remember Miss Sinclair."

79. "US Lacrosse 2013 Participation Survey," US Lacrosse Headquarters, Baltimore, Maryland, 2014, 5.

80. Mike Tierney, "At a College, Dropping Sports in Favor of Fitness," *New York Times,* April 13, 2013, A4.

7. "More Than a Century of Champions": Johns Hopkins University Lacrosse

1. David G. Pietramala and Neil A. Grauer, *Lacrosse: Technique and Tradition: The Second Edition of the Bob Scott Classic* (Baltimore: Johns Hopkins University Press, 2006), 15.

2. Ibid.

3. Ibid.; Neil A. Grauer, "Baltimore's Game," *Style Magazine*, May/June 1998, 48.

4. Pietramala and Grauer, *Lacrosse*, 229.

5. Ernie Larossa, Sports Information Director, Johns Hopkins Department of Athletics.

6. Ibid.; US Lacrosse National Lacrosse Hall of Fame website (list of members by school), http://www.uslacrosse.org/TopNav/MuseumHallofFame/Visitthe Museum.aspx (accessed March 7, 2014).

7. Larossa, Hopkins Department of Athletics.

8. Pietramala and Grauer, *Lacrosse*, 13; William C. Schmeisser, *Lacrosse: From Candidate to Team* (New York: Spalding's Athletic Library, 1904); Kelso W. Morrill, *Lacrosse* (Baltimore: John Wiley & Sons, 1952); Bob Scott, *Lacrosse: Technique and Tradition* (Baltimore: Johns Hopkins University Press, 1976); Johns Hopkins University Press, royalty statement for David G. Pietramala and Neil A. Grauer, *Lacrosse: Technique and Tradition, The Second Edition of the Bob Scott Classic*, March 26, 2013.

9. Pietramala and Grauer, *Lacrosse*, 13; Wm. Ferguson, "Lacrosse Head," *New York Times Magazine*, June 7, 2013, http://www.nytimes.com/packages/html/magazine/2013/innovations-issue/#/?part=lacrossehead#/?part=lacrossehead& forceredirect=yes (accessed March 7, 2014).

10. Pietramala and Grauer, *Lacrosse*, 235, 230, 280.

11. Pietramala and Grauer, *Lacrosse*, 280–81; see http://www.lacrosse.gr.jp/eng_history/ (accessed March 7, 2014).

12. Pietramala and Grauer, *Lacrosse*, 280–81; Scott Soshnick, "Paul Rabil, Lacrosse's Million-Dollar Man," *Bloomberg Businessweek*, April 4, 2013, http://www.businessweek.com/articles/2013-04-04/paul-rabil-lacrosses-million-dollar-man (accessed March 7, 2014); Scott Soshnick, "Johns Hopkins Lacrosse Millionaire Hits Wall Street to Find Fame," *Bloomberg Businessweek*, March 27, 2013, http://www.bloomberg.com/news/2013-03-27/johns-hopkins-lacrosse-millionaire-hits-wall-street-to-find-fame.html (accessed March 7, 2014).

13. Neil A. Grauer, *Leading the Way: A History of Johns Hopkins Medicine* (Baltimore: Johns Hopkins Medicine in association with Johns Hopkins University

Press, 2012), 1, 3; John C. Schmidt, *Johns Hopkins: Portrait of a University* (Baltimore: Johns Hopkins University Press, 1986), 1–3.

14. Jim Stimbert, "Woodrow Wilson, JHU Alum & U.S. President," February 18, 2013, http://blogs.library.jhu.edu/wordpress/2013/02/woodrow-wilson-jhu-alum-u-s-president/ (accessed June 25, 2014).

15. Pietramala and Grauer, *Lacrosse*, 230.

16. Ibid.

17. Ibid.

18. Ibid.; US Lacrosse, Hall of Fame Website.

19. Pietramala and Grauer, *Lacrosse*, 231; Neil A. Grauer, "Five Flags over Hopkins," *Johns Hopkins Magazine*, October 1982, 39.

20. Pietramala and Grauer, *Lacrosse*, 231. In 1976, Maryland's Frank Urso became the second four-time, first-team All-American; in 1986, Hopkins' Del Dressel became the third four-time, first-team All-American; and in 2004, Syracuse's Mike Powell joined the exclusive club begun by Doug Turnbull.

21. Ibid.

22. Ibid.

23. Ibid., 231–32.

24. Ibid.

25. Ibid., 233.

26. "U.S. Team Victor at Lacrosse, 7 to 4," *New York Times*, August 13, 1932, 10.

27. Pietramala and Grauer, *Lacrosse*, 233.

28. Ibid.; *2012 Johns Hopkins Lacrosse Media Guide*, 60.

29. Pietramala and Grauer, *Lacrosse*, 234.

30. Ibid.

31. Ibid., 235.

32. Ibid.

33. Ibid. In 2016, US Lacrosse named the 1950 team as the first "Team of Distinction" for its impact on the sport.

34. Ibid., 236.

35. Ibid.

36. Ibid.

37. Ibid., 237. The backbone of Bob Scott's last three teams as Hopkins coach was the class of 1974, headed by future Hall of Famers Jack Thomas and Rich Kowalchuk.

38. Ibid.; *Sports Illustrated*, April 23, 1962; *Sports Illustrated*, April 25, 2005.

39. Pietramala and Grauer, *Lacrosse*, 240–43.

40. For more on the NCAA's attempt to rescind the waiver, see the report "It's not broken; why fix it?" available on http://www.rpi.edu/dept/NewsComm/sub/ncaaproposal65.pdf (September 6, 2014); "NCAA Division III Defeats Effort to Repeal Waiver," *Gazette*, January 20, 2004, http://www.jhu.edu/~gazette/2004/20jan04/20briefs.html (accessed September 6, 2014).

41. Pietramala and Grauer, *Lacrosse*, 19, 245–46.

42. Ibid., 251; US Lacrosse, Hall of Fame Website.

43. Pietramala and Grauer, *Lacrosse*. 250; US Lacrosse, Hall of Fame Website.

44. Pietramala and Grauer, *Lacrosse*, 249.

45. Ibid., 255.

46. Ibid.

47. US Lacrosse, Hall of Fame website.

48. Pietramala and Grauer, *Lacrosse*, 258; list of USILA Championships, http://en.wikipedia.org/wiki/United_States_Intercollegiate_Lacrosse_Association; list of NCAA Lacrosse Championships (accessed June 25, 2014), http://en.wikipedia.org/wiki/NCAA_Men's_Lacrosse_Championship#Team_Championship_records (accessed June 25, 2014).

49. Pietramala and Grauer, *Lacrosse*, 259.

50. Ibid., 261; *2012 Johns Hopkins Lacrosse Media Guide*, 35, 36.

51. Pietramala and Grauer, *Lacrosse*, 261.

52. Ibid., 261–62.

53. Ibid., 263, 27.

54. Ibid.

55. Ibid., 267.

56. Ibid., 271.

57. Ibid.

58. Ibid., 272.

59. Ibid., 273.

60. Ibid., 273–74.

61. Ibid., 278.

62. Ibid.

63. Ibid.

64. Ibid., 278.

65. Ibid., 279.

66. Ibid.

67. Ibid.

68. *2012 Johns Hopkins Lacrosse Media Guide*, 48.

69. Ibid.; Johns Hopkins Department of Athletics press release, May 28, 2007, "Johns Hopkins Captures Ninth Lacrosse National Championship," May 28, 2007, http://www.hopkinssports.com/sports/m-lacros/recaps/052807aac.html (accessed June 25, 2014).

70. Johns Hopkins Department of Athletics, press releases archives, 2008–2012, http://www. hopkinssports.com/sports/m-lacros/archive/jhop-m-lacros-archive.html (accessed June 25, 2014).

71. Eamonn Brennan, "FAQs for the Realignment Landscape," July 19, 2013, http://espn.go.com/mens-college-basketball/story/_/id/9462300/college-realignment-frequently-asked-questions-college-basketball (accessed March 7, 2014).

72. Brennan, "FAQs for the Realignment Landscape."

73. Johns Hopkins University press release, "Johns Hopkins, ESPNU Enter Exclusive National Broadcast Agreement," December 14, 2005, http://www.hopkinssports.com/sports/m-lacros/spec-rel/121405aaa.html (accessed June 25, 2014).

74. Greg Rienzi, "Game Changer," *Gazette*, July 2013, 9; Ronald J. Daniels, JHBroadcast e-mail, March 11, 2013, "From President Daniels: Study of Men's Lacrosse Conference Affiliation."

75. Ibid.; Jerome Schnydman and Christopher Watkins, JHBroadcast e-mail, March 19, 2013, "Request for Input from Blue Ribbon Lacrosse Committee."

76. *Report and Recommendations of The Blue Ribbon Committee to Study Conference Alignment for Men's Lacrosse Team*, submitted to President Ronald J. Daniels, May 10, 2013, 2.

77. *Report and Recommendations of The Blue Ribbon Committee to Study Conference Alignment for Men's Lacrosse Team*, 4; Ronald J. Daniels, JHBroadcast e-mail, "Johns Hopkins to Seek Conference Affiliation in Men's Lacrosse," May 17, 2013.

78. JHBroadcast e-mail, May 17, 2013.

79. Eddie Timanus, "Syracuse Nabs No. 1 Overall Seed in Lacrosse Tournament," *USA Today*, May 5, 2013, http://www.usatoday.com/story/sports/college/2013/05/05/syracuse-ncaa-menslacrosse-tournament/2137809/ (accessed March 7, 2014).

80. Ronald J. Daniels, JHBroadcast e-mail, "Johns Hopkins Joins the Big Ten," June 3, 2013; *Gazette*, July 2013; Author's interview with Ernest Larossa, October 9, 2013.

81. Author's interview with Jim Margraff, October 7, 2013.

82. Interview with Jim Margraff.

83. Interview with Ernest Larossa.

8. The Bears of Baltimore: Morgan State University Intercollegiate Athletics

1. Edward N. Wilson, *The History of Morgan State College: A Century of Purpose in Action, 1867–1967* (New York: Vantage Press, 1975), 148.

2. Ibid., 99.

3. Catherine E. Pugh and B. T. Bentley, "Morgan State: Urban College with a Special Role," *Baltimore Evening Sun*, February 4, 1992, 6.

4. "Famous Morgan Alumni," http://www.alumni.morgan.edu/s/1192/index.aspx?sid=119 2&gid=1&pgid=401 (accessed September 4, 2014).

5. See http://www.profootballhof.com/hof/colleges.aspx (accessed September 15, 2014).

6. Ocania Chalk, *Black College Sport* (New York: Dodd, Mead, 1976), 202.

7. See http://www.cdrewu.edu/about-cdu/DrCharlesRDrew (accessed September 4, 2014).

8. *2014 Football Media Guide*, 91.

9. "Hurt, Coach of Morgan Championship Teams, Dies at 89," *Baltimore Evening Sun*, March 29, 1989, E2.

10. See http://www.morganstatebears.com/hof.aspx?hof=23&path=&kiosk (accessed September 4, 2014). In 1950, the conference changed its name to the Central Intercollegiate Athletic Association.

11. *2014 Football Media Guide*, 91.

12. Ibid., 96.

13. Beatrice Hurt said of her husband, "He eats like a bird. He never was a heavy built man, always thin and never seemed to require food." Elizabeth M. Oliver, "'He'll Never Never Be Able to Give It Up,' Coach Hurt's Wife Says," *Baltimore Afro-American*, November 24, 1959, 20.

14. *2014 Football Media Guide*, 91.

15. Filip Bondy, "Before Jackie Robinson, Four Broke NFL Color Line," *New York Daily News*, September 16, 2014, 61.

16. Ford played his first two years at Morgan before transferring to the University of Michigan after a stint in the US Navy; http://www.profootballhof.com/hof/member.aspx?player_id=69 (accessed September 15, 2014).

17. See http://www.morganstatebears.com/hof.aspx?hof=28&path=&kiosk (accessed September 15, 2014).

18. See http://www.profootballhof.com/hof/member.aspx?PLAYER_ID=35 (accessed September 15, 2014).

19. See http://www.usatf.org/halloffame/TF/showBio.asp?HOFIDs=78 (accessed September 15, 2014).

20. Daraine Luton, "George Rhoden Relives Helsinki Games Glory," *Gleaner*, June 29, 2003, http://jamaica-gleaner.com/gleaner/20030629/sports/sports5.html (accessed September 15, 2014).

21. Quoted in "Edward P. Hurt, USTFCCCA Class of 2004," http://www.ustfccca.org/ustfccca-hall-of-fame/ustfccca-hall-of-fame-class-of-2004/edward-hurt-ustfccca-class-of-2004 (accessed September 4, 2014).

22. See http://www.morganstatebears.com/hof.aspx?hof=23&path=&kiosk (accessed September 15, 2014).

23. "Morgan's Hurt Gets Honor," *Baltimore Sun*, November 18, 2011, sports sec., 6.

24. Herman L. Wade, *Run from There: A Biography of Edward P. Hurt* (Tarentum, PA: Word Association Publishers, 2003), back cover.

25. See http://www.morganstatebears.com/hof.aspx?hof=80&path=&kiosk (September 15, 2014).

26. Rasheim T. Freeman, "Honoring 'Mama' Payne," *Morgan Magazine* 1 (January 2012): 20.

27. Quoted in ibid., 21.

28. See http://www.morganstatebears.com/hof.aspx?hof=171&path=&kiosk (accessed September 15, 2014).

29. See http://ivy50.com/blackHistory/story.aspx?sid=12/27/2006%20 12:00:00%20AM (accessed September 15, 2014).

30. See http://www.archives.upenn.edu/people/1800s/taylorjb.html (accessed September 15, 2014).

31. Allen Guttmann, *The Olympics: A History of the Modern Games* (Urbana: University of Illinois Press, 1992), 67–69.

32. See http://www.morganstatebears.com/index.aspx?path=mtrkout > Additional links > Morgan State Olympians (accessed September 4, 2014).

33. See http://www.thepennrelays.com/ViewArticle.dbml?DB_OEM_ID=1720& ATCLID=205112333 (accessed September 4, 2014). Spaulding would later earn a doctorate and chair the Department of Chemistry at Morgan. Also, the Penn Relays were often referred to as the "Negro Olympics," and were an important track and field meet that always allowed African Americans an opportunity to compete in an integrated setting at both the interscholastic and intercollegiate level of competition.

34. "Golden Mile Won by Morgan State," *Sunday Herald*, April 30, 1950, 56.

35. See http://news.pennrelaysonline.com/event-history/college-men-history/college-men-4x400/ (accessed September 18, 2014).

36. See http://www.morganstatebears.com/hof.aspx?hof=39&path=&kiosk (accessed September 18, 2014).

37. Quoted in Rick Kauffman, "Olympic Medalist and Norristown Native Joshua Culbreath Reflects on Life on Eve of Montco Hall of Fame Induction," *Times Herald Sports*, November 24, 2013, http://www.timesherald.com/sports/20131124/olympic-medalist-and-norristown-native-joshua-culbreath-reflects-on-life-on-eve-of-montco-hall-of-fame-induction (accessed September 27, 2014).

38. Doug Brown, "Jamaica's Morgan Ties to Olympics Run Deep," *Baltimore Sun*, July 23, 1991, http://articles.baltimoresun.com/1992-07-23/sports/1992205153_1_relay-morgan-la-beach (accessed July 29, 2015).

39. Ibid.

40. See http://www.sports-reference.com/olympics/athletes/rh/george-rhoden-1.html (accessed September 18, 2014).

41. Doug Brown, "Olympics Always Bring Sense of Sadness to ex-Bear Bragg," *Baltimore Sun*, July 23, 1992, http://articles.baltimoresun.com/1992-07-23/sports/1992205155_1_bragg-morgan-cry (accessed July 29, 2015).

42. "Art Bragg Breaks 23-Year-Old AAU Sprint Record," *Jet Magazine*, July 1, 1954, 51.

43. Quoted in Brown, "Olympics Always Bring Sense of Sadness to ex-Bear Bragg."

44. See http://www.morganstatebears.com/staff.aspx?staff=24 (accessed September 18, 2014).

45. See https://www.usatf.org/athletes/bios/TrackAndFieldArchive/2000/stevens.html (accessed September 18, 2014).

46. See http://www.morganstatebears.com/hof.aspx?hof=15&path=&kiosk (accessed September 15, 2014).

47. Quoted in Richard Goldstein, "Joe Black, Pitching Pioneer for the Dodgers, Dies at 78," *New York Times*, May 18, 2002, A13.

48. See http://www.baseball-reference.com/players/b/blackjo02.shtml (accessed August 8, 2015).

49. John Drebinger, "Three Dodger Homers Beat Yanks in Series Opener, 4–2," *New York Times*, October 2, 1952, 1.

50. J. Haywood Harrison, "A Salute to Joe Black," Official Program, The Annual Homecoming Game, Morgan State "Bears" vs. Hampton Institute "Pirates," November 15, 1952. Morgan State University, Beulah M. Davis Special Collections Department.

51. Wiley A. Hall III, "Return to Greatness," *Morgan Magazine* 2 (2014): 2.

52. Quoted in Mark Cheshire, "Earl Banks, Morgan Football Legend, Dies in Auto Accident," *Baltimore Afro-American*, October 30, 1993, A1.

53. Kent Baker, "'Papa Bear' Earl Banks Is Named to Hall of Fame," *Baltimore Sun*, January 17, 1992, 1A, 6A.

54. Ibid., 1A.

55. William N. Wallace, "60,811 See Morgan State Win Here, 9–7," *New York Times*, September 29, 1968, S1.

56. David Zurawik, "Film on Morgan's Game vs. Gambling in 1968 Goes Deep," *Baltimore Sun*, September 27, 2011, Sports, 1.

57. Quoted in ibid., 7.

58. Quoted in ibid.

59. Interview with Ronald Bethea, August 12, 2014.

60. See http://www.profootballhof.com/hof/member.aspx?PLAYER_ID=69 (accessed November 23, 2014).

61. See http://www.profootballhof.com/hof/member.aspx?PLAYER_ID=35 (accessed November 23, 2014).

62. See http://www.profootballhof.com/hof/member.aspx?PLAYER_ID=113 (accessed November 23, 2014).

63. David Whitely, "Whitley Writes: Historic Moment for Morgan State Highlights Orlando's HBCU History," November 21, 2013, http://www.florida citrussports.com/news/tabid/86/ID/ 365/Whitley-Writes-Historic-Moment-For-Morgan-State-Highlights-Orlandos-HBCU-History.aspx (accessed November 23, 2014).

64. *2014 Football Media Guide*, 87.

65. Ibid.

66. Ibid., 98; see http://www.sidearmdmg.com/morganstate/football/ (accessed September 15, 2014).

67. Hall, "Return to Greatness," 2.

68. John W. Stewart, "Bears Whip SW Missouri, 67 to 52, as Webster Stars," *Baltimore Sun*, March 16, 1974, B1.

69. See http://www.ncaa.com/history/basketball-men/d2 (accessed September 15, 2014).

70. Kent Hannon, "Cashing in on Marvin's Guardin'," *Sports Illustrated*, January 6, 1975, 68.

71. Interview with Joe McIver, February 9, 2011.

72. "Morgan State Hits Jackpot," *Reading Eagle*, March 16, 7.

73. Interview with Joe McIver.

74. *2013–14 Men's Basketball Media Guide*, 89.

75. *2008–09 Men's Basketball Media Guide*, 77.

76. "Butch Beard Goes to Morgan State," *New York Times*, January 13, 2001, D5.

77. Kent Baker, "After Five Seasons, Beard Resigns as Morgan Coach," *Baltimore Sun*, March 29, 2006, 5E.

78. See http://www.morganstatebears.com/coaches.aspx?rc=489 (accessed September 29, 2014).

79. Jeré Longman, "The Long Road to Coaching Redemption Winds Slowly," *New York Times,* December 28, 2007, D1.

80. *2013–14 Men's Basketball Media Guide*, 93.

81. Interview with Boubacar Coly, February 27, 2008.

82. Steve Yanda, "Morgan State Stuns Maryland, 66–65," *Washington Post*, January 8, 2009, E1.

83. "Holmes Leads Way with 20 Points as Morgan State Comes Away with Title," March 15, 2009, http://scores.espn.go.com/ncb/recap?gameId=290732415 (July 29, 2015).

84. See http://www.morganstatebears.com/coaches.aspx?rc=602 (accessed September 30, 2014).

85. Quoted in Mike Preston, "The No. 1 'Bear,'" *Baltimore Sun*, March 1, 2008, 10Z.

86. Miles Harrison Jr. and Chip Silverman, *Ten Bears* (U.S.: Positive Publications Books, 2001), 116.

87. Interview with Curt Anderson, August 10, 2014.

88. Ibid.

89. Quoted in "ESPN Feature on Morgan State Lacrosse," February 27, 2005, https:// www.youtube.com/watch?v=rOvkP_xUCj0 (accessed September 29, 2014).

90. Interview with Curt Anderson.

91. Phil Berger, "Honors for Offbeat Team That Shook Lacrosse," *New York Times*, February 27, 1990, B9.

92. Quoted in "Q&A with Ten Bears Author Dr. Miles Harrison," http:// www.laxpower.com/common/TenBears.php (accessed August 8, 2014). Many of those Morgan lacrosse players later became prominent community members. Curt Anderson, Clarence "Tiger" Davis, and Tony Fulton all became house delegates in the Maryland state legislature. Stan Cherry had a brief stint in the NFL with the New England Patriots and the Baltimore Colts. Wayne Jackson became the athletic director at Northwestern High School in Baltimore. Joe "Flaky" Fowlkes, who was a football star at Morgan while winning three MVPs on the lacrosse team, became a high school football and lacrosse coach and won four city championships. He was inducted into the Morgan State Athletic Hall of Fame for his accomplishments. And Miles Harrison Jr., after graduating from Morgan, went to the University of Pennsylvania School of Medicine and became a surgeon. John Eisenberg, "In Black and White, for the Silver Screen—A Lacrosse Story," *Baltimore Sun*, March 9, 2005, 9E.

93. "Morgan State Lacrosse Featured in Documentary," March 19, 2008, http:// fs.ncaa.org/Docs/NCAANewsArchive/2008/division+i/morgan+state+lacrosse+ featured+in+documentary+-+03-19-08+ncaa+news.html (September 29, 2014).

94. Interview with Curt Anderson.

95. Quoted in Berger, "Honors for Offbeat Team That Shook Lacrosse," B9.

96. "Morgan State University Moves to Return to Its Athletic Greatness," July 28, 2014, http://news.morgan.edu/morgan-state-university-moves-to-return-to-its-athletic-greatness/ (accessed September 29, 2014).

97. David Wilson, "President's Letter," *Morgan Magazine* 2 (2014): 1.

98. Hall, "Return to Greatness," 5.

99. See http://www.usatoday.com/sports/college/schools/finances/ (accessed September 29, 2014); Mark Schlabach, "HBCU Guarantee Money Could Dry Up," February 20, 2014, http://espn.go.com/college-football/story/_/id/10485669/ hbcus-heading-uncharted-waters (accessed September 29, 2014).

100. Wilson, "President's Letter," 1.

9. The Team That Made Baltimore Proud: The Baltimore Bullets and the 1947–1948 Championship Season

The author would like to thank Daniel A. Nathan for his comments on an earlier draft of this chapter.

1. *Baltimore Sun*, January 14, 1947, 18.

2. *Washington Times-Herald*, January 30, 1947, 28.

3. Team records in Robert W. Peterson, *Cages to Jump Shots: Pro Basketball's*

Early Years (Lincoln: University of Nebraska Press, [2002] 1990), 198, 200. For information on the Mets, see *Baltimore Afro-American,* January 10, 1942, 22; *Baltimore Afro-American,* February 14, 1942, 22; *Baltimore Afro-American,* February 28, 1942, 23; and *Chicago Defender* (national ed.), October 13, 1942, 23.

4. Between July 1942 and September 1945, Bethlehem Steel manufactured 518 ships, the equivalent of a ship every 2.18 days. See Gilbert Sandler, *Home Front Baltimore: An Album of Stories from World War II* (Baltimore: Johns Hopkins University Press, 2011), 55. For information on Glenn L. Martin, see Sherry H. Olson, *Baltimore: The Building of an American City, Revised and Expanded Edition* (Baltimore: Johns Hopkins University Press, [1997] 1980), 348–49, and Antero Pietila, *Not in My Neighborhood: How Bigotry Shaped a Great American City* (Chicago: Ivan R. Dee, 2010), 75–77.

5. *Baltimore Sun,* December 6, 1944, 18.

6. Ibid., July 8, 1945, 17. Information on Tinsley in *Baltimore Sun,* February 1, 1994, 5B. A good biography on Gottlieb is Rich Westcott, *The Mogul: Eddie Gottlieb, Philadelphia Sports Legend and Pro Basketball Pioneer* (Philadelphia: Temple University Press, 2008).

7. Embry biography in *Baltimore Sun,* May 27, 1980, 9A.

8. For more on Baltimore radio, see Lenora Heilig Nast, Laurence Krause, and R. C. Monk, eds., *Baltimore, a Living Renaissance* (Baltimore: Historic Baltimore Society, 1982), 141–45. Information on Dyer in 1947–1948 Bullets program, Paul Hoffman Scrapbook, Joseph M. O'Brien Historical Center, Naismith Memorial Basketball Hall of Fame, Springfield, Massachusetts.

9. Philip Sherman, "Baltimore's 104th Medical Regiment Armory," *Maryland Historical Magazine* 70 (Fall 1975): 275–78.

10. Paul M. Baker, *Moments in Time: A Broken Field Run through a Lifetime of Baltimore Based Sports Stories* (Baltimore: P. Baker, 1997), 71–76; John Grasso, *Historical Dictionary of Basketball* (Lanham, MD: Scarecrow Press, 2011), 178–79; and *Baltimore Sun,* September 15, 1946, 6SP. Author's interview with Seymour Smith, June 1, 2013. Mikan contract in *Chicago Daily Tribune,* March 16, 1946, 20.

11. Team record in 1948–1949 Bullets program, Maryland Department, Enoch Pratt Library, Central Library/State Library Research Center, Vertical File; Baltimore Bullets Basketball Club, Inc., Baltimore, Maryland.

12. *Baltimore Sun,* April 10, 1947, 25, and *Baltimore Evening Sun,* April 10, 1947, 39.

13. *Baltimore Sun,* June 13, 1947, 15.

14. *Newsweek,* October 18, 1943, 58, and *Life,* February 14, 1944, 13; *Baltimore Evening Sun,* October 4, 1943, 32. Frank Deford, "Bleeve It, Hon," *Smithsonian,* January 2007, 20.

15. *Baltimore Sun,* March 9, 1947, 6S.

16. Charley Rosen, *The First Tip-Off: The Incredible Story of the Birth of the NBA* (New York: McGraw Hill, 2009), 68, 83, 109, and Terry Pluto, *Tall Tales: The Glory Years of the NBA, in the Words of the Men Who Played, Coached, and Built Pro Basketball* (New York: Simon and Schuster, 1992), 18. Scoreboard in *Washington Evening Star,* February 3, 1980, 2D.

17. Backboard and cat in Rosen, *The First Tip-Off,* 39, 202. Dog in *Baltimore Sun,* January 31, 1948, 12. Gamblers in *Baltimore Sun,* April 21, 1998, 1D. Brawl

in Douglas Stark, *The SPHAS: The Life and Times of Basketball's Greatest Jewish Team* (Philadelphia: Temple University Press, 2011), 191–92.

18. For more on television in Baltimore, see Nast et al., *Baltimore: A Living Renaissance*, 138–41, and *Baltimore Sun*, April 22, 1997, 11A. Goss in 1947–1948 Bullets program, Paul Hoffman Scrapbook, Joseph M. O'Brien Historical Center, Naismith Memorial Basketball Hall of Fame, Springfield, Massachusetts.

19. For more on the Capitols, see Rosen, *The First Tip-Off*, 195–210.

20. *Baltimore News-Post*, November 12, 1947, 34, and *Washington Daily News*, November 11, 1947, 30.

21. *Washington Post*, November 13, 1947, 21.

22. *Baltimore News-Post*, December 4, 1947, 38.

23. *Baltimore Sun*, December 4, 6, 1947, 17, 3SP.

24. *Baltimore News-Post*, December 11, 1947, 38.

25. *Washington Evening Star*, December 11, 1947, 2C, and *Baltimore Sun*, December 12, 1947, 21.

26. *Washington Evening Star*, January 31, 1948, 8.

27. *Washington Daily News*, January 31, 1948, 16.

28. Ibid., February 3, 4, 1948, 35, 36.

29. B. Lewis Posen, "Baltimore for Your Plant, for Your Products!" *Baltimore* (November 1948): 41–45, Maryland Department, Enoch Pratt Library, Central Library/State Library Research Center, Vertical File: Baltimore, Envelope 5, Baltimore, Maryland. Labor and income figures based on metropolitan area data. See *Census of Population: 1950*, Volume II, Part 9, 20 (Washington, DC: US Government Printing Office, 1952), 9–25, 9–27, 20–42, 20–45. Russell Baker, *Growing Up* (New York: Congdon & Weed, 1982), 265.

30. *Washington Post*, February 5, 1948, 13, and *Washington Daily News*, February 5, 1948, 48.

31. *Washington Times-Herald*, February 22, 1948, 3(II).

32. Information on divisional playoff in *Baltimore Evening Sun*, March 22, 1948, 23, and *Washington Evening Star*, March 22, 13A.

33. For Washingtonians' perspective, see *Washington Daily News*, March 23, 1948, 44.

34. Area newspapers covered the early rounds. For the series against New York, see *Baltimore Sun*, March 28, 29, 1948, 31, 13, and *Baltimore Evening Sun*, April 2, 1948, 39, 42. For the Chicago series, see *Baltimore Sun*, April 8, 9, 1948, 17, 19, and *Washington Daily News*, April 9, 1948, 71. For the 1947–1948 BAA season, including information on the series against the Bullets, see Westcott, *The Mogul*, 154–58.

35. Information on Warriors in Rosen, *The First Tip-Off*, 179–93. For Fulks, see Grasso, *Historical Dictionary of Basketball*, 136–37.

36. *Philadelphia Inquirer*, April 11, 1948, 1S, 3S.

37. *Baltimore Sun*, April 14, 1948, 15S; interview with Seymour Smith; Hoffman quoted in *Baltimore Sun*, April 14, 1980, 7C. See also *Philadelphia Daily News*, April 14, 1948, 87.

38. *Baltimore Sun*, April 15, 1948, 24.

39. *Philadelphia Inquirer*, April 16, 1948, 37 and *Baltimore Sun*, April 16, 1948, 21.

40. Jeannette quoted in *Baltimore News-Post*, April 16, 1948, 38; *Philadelphia Inquirer*, April 16, 1948, 37; and *Philadelphia Daily News*, April 16, 1948, 23.

41. For game 4, *Philadelphia Inquirer*, April 18, 1948, S1; *Baltimore Sun*, April 18, 1948, S1; and *Philadelphia Daily News*, April 19, 1948, 41. For game 5, see *Philadelphia Inquirer*, April 21, 1948, 34; *Philadelphia Daily News*, April 21, 1948, 36; *Baltimore Sun*, April 21, 1948, 17; and *Baltimore Evening Sun*, April 21, 1948, 47.

42. *Philadelphia Inquirer*, April 22, 1948, 26.

43. *Baltimore Sun*, April 22, 1948, 21. See also *Philadelphia Daily News*, April 22, 1948, 48, 47.

44. *Baltimore News-Post*, April 23, 1948, 40, and *Baltimore Evening Sun*, April 24, 1948, 5.

45. Seymour Smith interview.

46. Embry quoted in *Baltimore Sun*, April 21, 1998, 1D.

47. *Baltimore News-Post* (night edition), April 12, 1948, 17.

10. Toots Barger: Queen of Duckpins

1. See http://www.ndbc.org/world_records_men.htm (accessed August 23, 2014).

2. See http://www.si.com/vault/1999/12/27/271866/the-master-list-the-50-greatest-sports-figures-of-the-century-from-each-of-the-50-states (accessed August 23, 2014).

3. The National Duckpin Bowling Congress in Linthicum, Maryland, is the sanctioning and governing body for adult duckpin bowlers. It compiles annual average rankings of the top twenty duckpin bowlers and has the lists for each year since it was established in 1927. It provided me with Toots's rankings and averages.

4. Stacy Karten, "Is Bowling Still Cool?" June 5, 2007, http://www.pressbox online.com/story/2075/is-bowling-still-cool (accessed August 23, 2014).

5. See http://wndatour.com/about-us/ (accessed September 6, 2014).

6. Frederick N. Rasmussen, "Elizabeth 'Toots' Barger, 'Queen of Duckpins,' Dies," *Baltimore Sun*, September 29, 1998, 6A.

7. Burt Solomon, *Where They Ain't: The Fabled Life and Untimely Death of the Original Baltimore Orioles, the Team That Gave Birth to Modern Baseball* (New York: Free Press, 1999).

8. Henry Fankhauser and Frank Micalizzi, *The Book of Duckpin Bowling* (South Brunswick, NJ: A. S. Barnes & Company, 1969), 18.

9. The Babe Ruth Birthplace Museum, Baltimore, Maryland.

10. J. E. Wild, "Duckpin Leagues Hold Own in Spite of Demands of War," *Baltimore Sun*, February 28, 1943, 5.

11. Ibid.

12. Stacy Karten, "A Baltimore Original?" *Baltimore Jewish Times*, September 23, 2005, 38.

13. Ralph Brackbill, "Uncle Robbie, Of Diamond Fame, Inaugurated Duckpin Bowling Fad Back in 1903," *Baltimore Evening Sun*, February 19, 1929, 28.

14. Fred Turbyville, "Wilbert Robinson Claims He Invented Duckpins," *Pittsburgh Press*, March 3, 1929, Sporting Section, 6.

15. Robert L. Naylor, "Duckpin Game Began in 1900," *Baltimore Sun*, December 24, 1965, B4.

16. Stacy Karten, "Duckpin Bowling Was Hatched in Baltimore," *Duckpin News*, Winter 1991, 8.

17. Ibid.

18. Marina Sarris, "Duckpin Enthusiasts Make Their Pitch," *Baltimore Sun*, February 6, 1992, 1B.

19. National Duckpin Bowling Congress.

20. Rasmussen, "Elizabeth 'Toots' Barger, 'Queen of Duckpins,' Dies," 6A.

21. See https://www.census.gov/population/www/documentation/twps0027/tab17.txt; https: //www.census.gov/population/www/documentation/twps0027/tab18.txt; https://www.census. gov/population/www/documentation/twps0027/tab19.txt (accessed August 23, 2014).

22. Michael Olesker, *The Colts' Baltimore: A City and Its Love Affair in the 1950s* (Baltimore: Johns Hopkins University Press, 2008), 79–80.

23. Robert L. Naylor, "Toots Barger Pin Ghost," *Baltimore Sun*, December 30, 1964, 16.

24. Mary Corey, "Mary Elizabeth 'Toots' Barger Bowler," *Baltimore Sun*, March 3, 1991, 1H.

25. Rasmussen, "Elizabeth 'Toots' Barger, 'Queen of Duckpins,' Dies," 6A.

26. Ibid.

27. Quoted in ibid.

28. Robert McG. Thomas Jr., "Toots Barger, 85, the Queen of Duckpins' Wobbly World," *New York Times*, October 2, 1998, C19.

29. Claudia Levy, "Elizabeth Barger, Duckpin Bowling Champion, Dies at 85," *Washington Post*, September 30, 1998, B6; "Champion Duckpin Bowler Dies," *All Things Considered*, National Public Radio (September 30, 1998).

30. Quoted in Ralph Brackbill, "Queen of Kingpins," *Baltimore Sun*, October 26, 1947, SM7.

31. Interview with Joan Corcoran, July 2014.

32. Interview with Joe Rineer, July 2014.

33. I worked for Fair Lanes, Inc. from 1979 to 1993 and became very knowledgeable about its history and had personal knowledge about how many duckpin centers and lanes it owned and operated.

34. Interview with Wally Hall, July 2014.

35. Interview with Ron Matz, July 2014.

36. See http://www.northamericanbowling.com/Articles/10-RINALDI1.HTML (accessed August 23, 2014).

37. Interview with Pat Rinaldi, July 2014.

38. "Baltimore's Toots," *Baltimore Sun*, October 1, 1998, A22.

39. Michael Olesker, "Heaven's Lanes Gain the Greatest in 'Toots,'" *Baltimore Sun*, October 1, 1998, 4B.

11. "The Best Ambassador Baltimore Ever Had": Art Donovan and the Colts

1. Quoted in Benjamin G. Rader, *In Its Own Image: How Television Has Transformed Sports* (New York: Free Press, 1984), 83–84.

12. Sam Lacy and John Steadman: Empathy and a Conscience on the Sports Pages

1. John Steadman, "A Tribute to Sam Lacy," *Baltimore Afro-American*, May 8, 1979, 3.

2. Bill Hughes, "Ode to John Steadman," *Baltimore Chronicle and Sentinel*, April 4, 2001, http://www.baltimorechronicle.com/sports_steadman.html (accessed January 16, 2014).

3. Sam Lacy with Moses J. Newson, *Fighting for Fairness: The Life Story of Hall of Fame Sportswriter Sam Lacy* (Centerville, MD: Tidewater, 1998), 14–15.

4. J. Douglas English, "Sam Lacy," entry in the *Dictionary of Literary Biography: Twentieth-Century American Sportswriters*, Vol. 171 (Detroit: Gale, 1996), 173. The best accounts of Lacy's early life are in Lacy and Newson, *Fighting for Fairness*; Daniel A. Nathan's entry in *African American Lives*, ed. Henry Louis Gates Jr. and Evelyn Brooks Higginbotham (New York: Oxford University Press, 2004), 507–8; Ron Fimrite, "Sam Lacy: Black Crusader," *Sports Illustrated*, October 29, 1990, 90–94; and Peter M. Sheingold, "In Black and White" (Bachelor's thesis, Hampshire College, 1992).

5. English, "Sam Lacy," 174.

6. Quoted in English, "Sam Lacy," 174.

7. English, "Sam Lacy," 174.

8. Quoted in Nathan, "Sam Lacy," 508.

9. Quoted in Mike Klingaman, "A Baltimore Legend, Champion of Underdogs," *Baltimore Sun*, January 2, 2001, 1A, 4A.

10. Quoted in Sandra McKee, "Steadman Worth 'All the Fuss,' Peers Say," *Baltimore Sun*, June 30, 2001, 3C.

11. Quoted in Klingaman, "A Baltimore Legend," 4A.

12. Quoted in ibid.

13. Quoted in ibid.

14. See http://hopclodgegolf.dealeron.com/site/TR/Golf/ GolfFY08SouthAtlantic67c5.html?sid= 35297&type=fr_informational&pg= informational&fr_id=11953 (accessed October 28, 2013).

15. Quoted in John Steadman, *Days in the Sun* (Baltimore: The Baltimore Sun, 2000), 200, 222.

16. English, "Sam Lacy," 178.

17. Lacy, "A to Z," *Baltimore Afro-American*, April 5, 1977, 13.

18. Ibid.

19. Quoted in Klingaman, "A Baltimore Legend," 4A.

20. Steadman's expertise as a storyteller is a point made in the "Introduction" to *Days in the Sun*, xi.

21. Michael Olesker, "Didn't We Have Some Great Times," *Baltimore Sun*, January 2, 2001, 1B.

22. Ibid., 2B.

23. Quoted in ibid.

24. "Baltimore's Best in Sports," *Baltimore Sun*, January 3, 2001, , http:// articles.baltimoresun.com/2001-01-03/news/0101030068_1_john-steadman-football-in-baltimore-writing-about-sports (accessed February 1, 2004).

25. Steadman, *Days in the Sun*, 212.

26. Klingaman, "A Baltimore Legend," 4A.

27. Steadman, *Days in the Sun*, 242.

28. Ibid., 238.

29. Ibid.

30. Quoted in ibid., 242.

31. Ibid.

32. Ibid., 153.

33. Ibid., 181.

34. Hughes, "Ode to John F. Steadman."

35. Quoted in Steadman, "A Tribute to Sam Lacy," 3.

36. Ibid.

37. Lacy and Newson, *Fighting for Fairness*, 45.

38. Ibid.

39. Ibid., 58.

40. Sean Yoes, "The Racist History of Sanford, Florida," *Baltimore Afro-American*, March 31–April 6, 2012, A1–A3.

41. Quoted in Steadman, "A Tribute to Sam Lacy," 3.

42. Lacy and Newson, *Fighting for Fairness*, 68.

43. Quoted in English, "Sam Lacy," 175.

44. Quoted in Lacy and Newson, *Fighting for Fairness*, 37.

45. See Jerome Holtzman, *No Cheering in the Press Box*, rev. ed. (New York: Henry Holt, [1973] 1995).

46. Quoted in Klingaman, "A Baltimore Legend," 4A.

47. John Steadman, "With Legendary Waibel, Wins Were Only Part of Success Story," *Baltimore Sun*, February 15, 1998; reprinted in *Days in the Sun*, 54–58.

48. Olesker, "Didn't We Have Some Great Times," 1B.

49. John Steadman, "Mary Dobkin's Way of Life," *Baltimore Sun*, August 24, 1987; reprinted in *Days in the Sun*, 40–43.

50. "John Steadman: Hall of Fame Sportswriter Reflected What Was Good in Local Athletics," *Baltimore Sun*, January 3, 2001, http://articles.baltimoresun.com/2001-01-03/news/0101030068_1_john-steadman-football-in-baltimore-writing-about-sports (accessed January 20, 2014).

51. Tim Lacy, "Why Was Sam Lacy Left Out of 42?" *Baltimore Afro-American*, April 26, 2013, https://www.afro.com/sections/sports/story.htm?storyid=78251 (accessed October 28, 2013).

52. Lacy and Newson, *Fighting for Fairness*, 172.

13. Baltimore's Bard of Baseball: Jim Bready Remembers the O's of Old

The epigraph is from James H. Bready, *The Home Team, A Full Century of Baseball in Baltimore, 1859–1959* (Baltimore: Moore & Co., 1958), 2.

1. James H. Bready, "Stealing Home," *Baltimore Sun*, April 1, 1996, 7A.

2. Baltimoreans of a certain age are inordinately passionate about the pile of bricks that was Memorial Stadium, the site of three Orioles' World Series flags and the 1959 NFL title game with Johnny Unitas leading the Baltimore Colts to their second consecutive championship over the New York Giants. Christina Smith, the largely unsentimental New Hampshire wife of the writer Dean Bartoli Smith—a Baltimore boy who bleeds orange—put it this way: "Three hundred murders in Baltimore every year and all you guys care about is Memorial Stadium being torn down."

3. Bready, *The Home Team*, 34, 43.

4. Interview with J. Hollis B Albert III, 2014.

5. Interview with Fred Koenig, October 7, 2013.

6. Mike Schofield quoted in John Steadman, "Old Oriole Park Fire Burns Imprint on Sports in City," *Baltimore Sun*, July 1, 1994, http://articles.baltimore sun.com/1994-07-01/sports/1994182219_1 _oriole-park-municipal-stadium-ball-of-fire (accessed December 4, 2014).

7. With 484 home runs, Héctor Espino, who played for twenty-five years, is considered the all-time minor league home run leader. See http://www.baseball-reference.com/bullpen/Hector_Espino (accessed August 23, 2014). In August 2015, first baseman and designated hitter Mike Hessman hit his 433rd minor league home run. Tyler Kepner, "A Home Run King Without Major Fanfare," *New York Times*, August 9, 2015, SP3.

8. Bready, "Stealing Home," 7A.

9. Interview with Chris Bready, June 12, 2014.

10. Interview with Raymond Daniel Burke, e-mail correspondence, October 2013.

11. Raymond Daniel Burke, "A Glimmer of the O's of Old," *Baltimore Sun*, April 6, 2010, 15.

12. Bready, "Stealing Home," 7A.

13. Ibid.

14. Ibid.

15. Frederick N. Rasmussen, "James Hall Bready," *Baltimore Sun*, November 1, 2011, 12.

16. See "SABR Salute: James Bready," http://sabr.org/content/sabr-salute-james-bready (accessed August 23, 2014).

17. Such ballplayers are a staple of the art of Baltimore painter Ron Russell, whose stool and shot glass at Roman's Place in southeast Baltimore await his arrival before the first pitch of every Orioles game.

18. Bready, *The Home Team*, 59.

19. Although Bready was never much of a drinker, he did belong to the Baltimore Antique Bottle Club and sipped politely on Hollins Street with Mencken while the old master quaffed, finding moments in the conversation to request Mencken's signature on a variety of items.

20. Interview with Pete Kerzel, e-mail correspondence, 2014.

21. Russell Baker, *The Good Times* (New York: Morrow, 1989), 104.

22. Ibid.

23. Jason Policastro, "James H. Bready, the Calvert Street Whirlwind," story was published on alvarezfiction.com in January 2011; the story is no longer on the website.

24. Rasmussen, "James Hall Bready," 12.

25. Harold A. Williams, *The Baltimore Sun, 1837–1987* (Baltimore: Johns Hopkins University Press, 1987).

14. Black Sport and Baltimore: Spats, the Judge, and the Pearl

1. Quoted in Jerry Milani, "Earl Monroe: Pearl of the Hardcourt . . . and the Diamond?" April 16, 2013, http://bleacherreport.com/articles/1606244-earl-the-pearl-of-the-hardcourt-and-the-diamond (accessed December 5, 2014).

2. See David K. Wiggins, *Glory Bound: Black Athletes in a White America* (Syracuse, NY: Syracuse University Press, 1997), 3–20.

3. Leslie A. Heaphy, *The Negro Leagues, 1869–1960* (Jefferson, NC: McFarland, 2003), 28.

4. Edward Hotaling, *The Great Black Jockeys: The Lives and Times of the Men Who Dominated America's First National Sport* (Rocklin, CA: Forum, 1999), 265.

5. Leroy Graham, *Baltimore: The Nineteenth-Century Black Capital* (Lanham, MD: University Press of America, 1982), 35–36.

6. James R. Coates Jr., "Recreation and Sport in the African-American Community of Baltimore, 1890–1920" (PhD dissertation, University of Maryland, 1991).

7. Jessie Carney Smith, *Black Firsts: 4,000 Ground-Breaking and Pioneering Historical Events*, 3rd ed. (Canton, MI: Visible Ink Press, 2013), 627.

8. James B. Henderson and W. A. Joiner, *Spalding's Official Handbook: Interscholastic Athletic Association of Middle Atlantic States* (Washington, DC: Spalding, 1910); Interview Sam Lacy, December 1992.

9. *Baltimore Afro-American*, March 15, 1927, 8; Interview Lacy; Interview Bernard Boyd, June 1988.

10. *Baltimore Afro-American*, January 15, 1927, 6.

11. Ibid.

12. Howell S. Baum, *Brown in Baltimore: School Desegregation and the Limits of Liberalism* (Ithaca, NY: Cornell University Press, 2010), 39.

13. Ibid., 41.

14. Ibid.

15. Ibid.

16. Eden Unger Bowditch, *Growing Up in Baltimore: A Photographic History* (Charleston: Arcadia Publishing, 2001), 35.

17. Daniel A. Nathan, "The Baltimore Blues: The Colts and Civic Identity," in *Rooting for the Home Team: Sport, Community, and Identity*, ed. Daniel A. Nathan (Urbana: University of Illinois Press, 2013).

18. William Gildea, *When the Colts Belonged to Baltimore: A Father and a Son, a Team and a Time* (New York: Ticknor & Fields, 1994), 50.

19. Quoted in Jason La Canfora, "For Some Longtime Residents, Seeing the Shoe on Another Foot Is Still Difficult to Grasp," *Washington Post*, January 13, 2007, E4.

20. Gildea, *When the Colts Belonged to Baltimore*, 5.

21. *Colts: The Complete History*, DVD, directed by Tom Brant, Chris Corbellini, and Dave Petrelius (Burbank, CA: Warner Home Video, 2006).

22. Quoted in Dave Klein, *The Game of Their Lives: The 1958 NFL Championship* (Lanham, MD: Taylor Trade Publishing, 2008), 182.

23. Lenny Moore, *All Things Being Equal* (Champaign, IL: Sports Publishing, 2005), 70.

24. Klein, *The Game of Their Lives*, 182.

25. Mary Jo Binker, "Lenny Moore," in *African Americans in Sports*, Vol. 2, ed. David K. Wiggins (New York: Sharpe Reference, 2004), 243.

26. Mark Bowden, *The Best Game Ever: Giants vs. Colts, 1958, and the Birth of the Modern NFL* (New York: Atlantic Monthly Press, 2008), 8.

27. Olesker, *The Colts' Baltimore*, 7.
28. *Colts: The Complete History*.
29. Quoted in *The Greatest Game Ever Played*, 2008.
30. Moore, *All Things Being Equal*, 92.
31. Ibid., 94.
32. Ibid.
33. Quoted in Gildea, *When the Colts Belonged to Baltimore*, 221.
34. Quoted in ibid.
35. Olesker, *The Colts' Baltimore*, 133.
36. Moore, *All Things Being Equal*, 97.
37. Quoted in Klein, *The Game of Their Lives*, 185.
38. Quoted in ibid.
39. Moore, *All Things Being Equal*, 79.
40. Ibid.
41. *Colts: The Complete History*.
42. Binker, "Lenny Moore," 243.
43. Quoted in *Colts: The Complete History*.
44. Julie Bykowicz, "Old Colt Is Still a Good Team Player," *Baltimore Sun*, July 30, 2008, 1B.
45. Sean Yoes, "Plans for Statue to Honor Lenny Moore," (Baltimore) *Afro-American*, December 3–11, 2011, A3.
46. Andrew Shinkle, "Revisiting the Frank Robinson Trade," November 23, 2013, http://www.redreporter.com/2013/11/23/5133726/revisiting-the-frank-robinson-trade (accessed June 23, 2015).
47. Leonard Shecter, "Frank Robinson's Cool Assault on the Black-Manager Barrier," *Look*, May 5, 1970, 83.
48. Quoted in William Gildea, "Ages of Defiance," *Washington Post*, August 31, 2005, E4.
49. Frank Robinson with Al Silverman, *My Life Is Baseball* (Garden City, NY: Doubleday & Company, [1968] 1975), 21.
50. Leonard Koppett, "Orioles Triumph Over Dodgers, 1–0, To Sweep Series," *New York Times*, October 10, 1966, 1.
51. Jack Mann, "Those Happy Birds!" *Sports Illustrated*, October 17, 1966, 33.
52. Gildea, "Ages of Defiance," E4.
53. Quoted in Cal Fussman, *After Jackie: Pride, Prejudice, and Baseball's Forgotten Heroes: An Oral History* (New York: ESPN Books, 2007), 204.
54. Don Baylor (with Claire Smith), *Don Baylor: Nothing But the Truth: A Baseball Life* (New York: St. Martin's Press, 1989), 50.
55. Shecter, "Frank Robinson's Cool Assault on the Black-Manager Barrier," 88.
56. John Eisenberg, *From 33rd Street to Camden Yards: An Oral History of the Baltimore Orioles* (New York: Contemporary Books, 2001), 165.
57. Dan Connolly, *100 Things Orioles Fans Should Know & Do Before They Die* (Chicago: Triumph Books, 2015), 21.
58. Tom Adelman, *Black and Blue: The Golden Arm, the Robinson Boys and the 1966 World Series That Stunned America* (New York: Little, Brown, and Co, 2006), 5.

59. Robinson, *My Life Is Baseball*, 71, 155.

60. Ibid., 27.

61. Interview Harvey Polston, June 23, 2015.

62. Interview Willard Wright, June 19, 2015.

63. Thomas Boswell, "After So Long, So Long," *Washington Post*, September 29, 2006, E10.

64. In 2006, when Robinson was the manager of the Washington Nationals, Carl Cannon wrote: "As for his obsession with winning, players smile whenever they hear someone say that Frank has mellowed." Carl Cannon, "Prime Time with the Nationals' Frank Robinson," *Washingtonian*, August 2006, 155.

65. Quoted in ibid.

66. Ryan Baillargeon, "Youngsters Get Support from Big-Time Crowd," *Baltimore Sun*, June 14, 2015, Sports, 3.

67. See "Earl Monroe, Basketball," http://www.baltimoresun.com/sports/bal-bs-bgc-411-bs_f20120427100458-photo.html (accessed February 8, 2015).

68. Robert B. Jackson, *Earl the Pearl: The Story of Earl Monroe* (New York: Henry Z. Walck, 1969), 63.

69. Quoted in Mike Klingaman, "Catching Up With . . . former Bullet Earl Monroe," *Baltimore Sun*, October 6, 2009, http://weblogs.baltimoresun.com/sports/thetoydepartment/2009/10/catching_up_with_former_bullet_1.html (accessed June 23, 2015).

70. Woody Allen, "A Fan's Notes on Earl Monroe," *Sport*, November 1977, 25.

71. Donald Hunt, *Great Names in Black College Sports* (Indianapolis, IN: Masters Press, 1996), 51.

72. Jackson, *The Story of Earl Monroe*, 15.

73. Ibid., 19.

74. John R. Schleppi, "Earl Monroe," in *African Americans in Sports*, Vol. 2, ed. David K. Wiggins (New York: Sharpe Reference, 2004), 239.

75. Hunt, *Great Names in Black College Sports*, 51.

76. Ibid.

77. Jackson, *The Story of Earl Monroe*, 26.

78. Ibid.

79. Hunt, *Great Names in Black College Sports*, 53.

80. Ibid., 27.

81. Ibid., 30.

82. Ibid.

83. Jackson, *The Story of Earl Monroe*, 32.

84. See "NBA.com: Earl Monroe Bio," http://www.nba.com/history/players/monroe_bio.html (accessed January 10, 2015).

85. Mike Wise, "The Pearl Changed the Culture of the Game," *Washington Post*, December 1, 2007, E9.

86. Jackson, *The Story of Earl Monroe*, 13.

87. Earl Monroe with Quincy Troupe, *Earl the Pearl: My Story* (New York: Rodale, 2013), 91.

88. *Black Magic*, DVD, directed by Dan Klores (ESPN Films in association with Shoot the Moon Productions, 2008).

89. Wil Haygood, "Pearl's Unfaded Luster," *Washington Post*, November 29, 2007, C1, C4.

90. Ibid., C4.

91. Ryan Hood, "Earl Monroe Celebrates Release of Autobiography," *Baltimore Sun*, June 24, 2013, http://articles.baltimoresun.com/2013-06-24/sports/bs-sp-earl-monroe-0622-20130621_1_earl-monroe-knicks-pearl (accessed February 8, 2015).

92. Harvey Araton, "The Parable of the Pearl," October 18, 2011, http://espn.go.com/nba/story/_/ page/nykbookexcerpt111018/nba-garden-was-eden (accessed February 8, 2015).

93. Ibid.

94. Ibid.

95. Ibid.

96. Ibid.

97. Ibid.

98. Quoted in ibid.

99. Quoted in ibid.

100. Quoted in Klingaman, "Catching Up With . . . former Bullet Earl Monroe."

101. Wise, "The Pearl Changed the Culture of the Game," E9.

102. Ibid.

103. Araton, "The Parable of the Pearl."

15. Orange and Black Forever: How a New Yorker Fell in Love with Earl Weaver's Baltimore Orioles

Epigraph. Anne Tyler, *Dinner at the Homesick Restaurant* (New York: Knopf, 1982), 269.

1. For more on the 1966 World Series, see Tom Adelman, *Black and Blue: The Golden Arm, the Robinson Boys and the 1966 World Series That Stunned America* (New York: Little, Brown, and Co., 2006).

2. Ibid., 2.

3. Gordon Beard, *Birds on the Wing: The Story of the Baltimore Orioles* (New York: Doubleday, 1967), 44.

4. John Eisenberg, *From 33rd Street to Camden Yards: An Oral History of the Baltimore Orioles* (New York: Contemporary Books, 2001), 9.

5. For more on Bauer, see Mike Gesker, *The Orioles Encyclopedia: A Half Century of History and Highlights* (Baltimore: Johns Hopkins University Press, 2009), 497–500.

6. Ibid., 506.

7. Quoted in Peter Schmuck and Mike Klingaman, "The Earl of Baltimore," *Baltimore Sun*, January 20, 2013, 21.

8. Peter Richmond, *Ballpark: Camden Yards and the Building of an American Dream* (New York: Doubleday, 1994), 25.

9. Ibid., 27.

10. Frank Deford, *Over Time: My Life as a Sportswriter* (New York: Atlantic Monthly Press, 2012), 91.

11. Eisenberg, *From 33rd Street to Camden Yards*, 13.

12. Gesker, *The Orioles Encyclopedia*, 258–59. For more on Criscione's brief career, see Jeff Seidel, *Baltimore Orioles: Where Have You Gone?* (Champaign, IL: Sports Publishing, 2006).

13. Thomas Rogers, "McBride Stars as Phils Top Reds, 3–0," *New York Times*, September 3, 1977, 28.

14. Gesker, *The Orioles Encyclopedia*, 502.

15. Robert W. Creamer, *Babe: The Legend Comes to Life* (New York: Simon and Schuster, [1974] 2005), 81–83.

16. Warren Corbett, *The Wizard of Waxahachie* (Dallas, TX: Southern Methodist University Press, 2007), 143.

17. Quoted in ibid., 316.

18. Ibid., 158.

19. Gesker, *The Orioles Encyclopedia*, 552–54.

20. Ibid., 429.

21. James Edward Miller, *The Baseball Business: Pursuing Pennants and Profits in Baltimore* (Chapel Hill: University of North Carolina Press, 1990), 75. For more on the Colts' early dominance in Baltimore, see Mark Bowden, *The Best Game Ever: Giants vs. Colts, 1958, and the Birth of the Modern NFL* (New York: Atlantic Monthly Press, 2008).

22. Miller, *The Baseball Business,* 88.

23. Ibid., 74.

24. Kevin Kerrane, *Dollar Sign on the Muscle: The World of Baseball Scouting* (New York: Beaufort Books, 1984), 114–21.

25. Miller, *The Baseball Business,* 74.

26. Donald Pries, phone interview, July 24, 2013. For more on Pries, see Lee Lowenfish, "Prospectus Q & A: Donald Pries," August 2, 2013, http://www.baseballprospectus.com/article.php?articleid=21417 (accessed February 17, 2014).

27. John Stokoe, phone interview, May 19, 2013.

28. Lou Gorman, *High and Inside: My Life in the Front Offices of Baseball* (Jefferson, NC: McFarland, 2008), 41.

29. Paul Hensler, *The American League in Transition: How Competition Thrived When the Yankees Didn't* (Jefferson, NC: McFarland, 2012), 97.

30. Warren Corbett, "Earl Weaver," in *Pitching, Defense, and Three-Run Homers*, ed. Mark Armour and Malcolm Allen (Lincoln: University of Nebraska Press, 2012), 5.

31. Ibid., 6.

32. Ray Poitevint, phone interview, November 1, 2012. Poitevint, who at the age of seventy-nine returned to the Orioles in 2012 as an international scout, emphasized the importance of the Oriole Way of playing defense: "We wouldn't promote a player one classification if he didn't always hit the cutoff man on throws from the outfield."

33. Benjamin G. Rader, *Baseball: A History of America's Game* (Urbana: University of Illinois Press, 1992), 193.

34. Don Baylor with Claire Smith, *Don Baylor: Nothing But the Truth: A Baseball Life* (New York: St. Martin's Press, 1989), 84; Don Baylor, phone interview, June 26, 2013.

35. Hank Peters, phone interview, October 29, 2012.

36. Eisenberg, *From 33rd Street to Camden Yards*, 359.

37. Ibid., 365.

38. Gesker, *The Orioles Encyclopedia*, 145.

39. Richmond, *Ballpark*, 144–48.

40. See http://www.tobymendezstudios.com/Asset.asp?AssetID=48617&
AKey=7C569C3T (accessed September 1, 2014).

41. Janet Marie Smith, phone interview, September 12, 2013.

42. Toby Mendez, phone interview, September 13, 2013.

43. Transcripts of statue ceremonies, Oriole Park at Camden Yards: Jim Palmer,
July 14; Eddie Murray, August 11; Cal Ripken Jr., September 6; Brooks Robinson,
September 29, 2013. Courtesy of Greg Bader, director of communications,
Baltimore Orioles.

44. Quoted in Jason LaCanfora, "Weaver Chalks Up Another Win at Hall,"
Baltimore Sun, August 5, 1996, 4A.

16. A Missed Opportunity: Baltimore's Failed Stadium Project, 1969–1974

The author would like to thank Chris Elzey for his support, encouragement, and
suggestions during the writing of this chapter.

1. Bob Maisel, "The Morning After," *Baltimore Sun*, January 18, 1971, C1.

2. See James Edward Miller, *The Baseball Business: Pursuing Pennants and
Profits in Baltimore* (Chapel Hill: University of North Carolina Press, 1990),
200–206; Peter Richmond, *Ballpark: Camden Yards and the Building of an
American Dream* (New York: Simon & Schuster, 1993); Thom Loverro, *Home of
the Game: The Story of Camden Yards* (Dallas: Taylor Publishing, 1999); Dennis
Purdy, *Kiss 'Em Goodbye: An ESPN Treasury of Failed, Forgotten, and Departed
Teams* (New York: Ballantine Books, 2010), 13–19; Jon Morgan, *Glory for Sale:
Fans, Dollars and the New NFL* (Baltimore: Bancroft Press, 1997), 97–130.

3. Miller, *The Baseball Business*, 149–50; Frederic B. Hill, "Stadium Drama
Arrives for a Long Baltimore Run," *Baltimore Sun*, November 23, 1972, E1–E2;
Frederic B. Hill, "Are the Big Leagues in Baltimore's Future?" *Baltimore Sun*,
February 1, 1981, K1–K2.

4. "The Demolition and Afterlife of Baltimore Memorial Stadium," *Design
Observer Group*, October 22, 2012, http://places.designobserver.com/feature/
demolition-and-afterlife-baltimore-memorial-stadium/36278/ (accessed October
2, 2013); Frederic B. Hill, "'Tin Cup' Moves Backfire: Economy Hurt Stadium,"
Baltimore Sun, November 24, 1972, C11, C20; "Uncomfortable Memorial Stadium,"
Baltimore Sun, November 28, 1972, A18; Miller, *The Baseball Business*, 201.

5. In 1969, the Metropolitan Baltimore Jaycee Coordinating Council and
the Towson Jaycees surveyed the public's views on the conditions surrounding
Memorial Stadium. The survey found that "more and cleaner rest room facilities
are favored more than anything else"; respondents also expressed a desire for
more back rests, an improved scoreboard, improved concession stands, increased
security around the stadium, satellite parking, and improved lighting in the parking
lots. "Fans' Views on Stadium Asked," *Baltimore Sun*, August 14, 1969, 29; "Rest
Rooms Get Priority in Poll on Stadium Needs," *Baltimore Sun*, August 22, 1969,
C10; Hill, "'Tin Cup' Moves Backfire," C11, C20; "Uncomfortable Memorial
Stadium"; "Baltimore Stadium 'Filthy,' Rosenbloom May Build Own," *Baltimore
Sun*, May 21, 1969, D4; Miller, *The Baseball Business*, 201.

6. Reports varied on the overall cost of the plan's proposed costs, which did
not include parking. For instance, the *Baltimore Sun* reported on the study in

February 1969, noting that the renovations would cost the city approximately $18.5 million. Praegen-Kavanagh-Waterbury published their report in June 1969, which included the $20 million price tag. The study also called for increased concession stands, the implementation of synthetic turf, and renovated press and front office facilities. In terms of satellite parking, the study suggested that the City of Baltimore look into purchasing property, whether by Lake Montebello, Montebello State Hospital, or Herring Run Park. John B. O'Donnell Jr., "A Feasibility Study for Baltimore Memorial Stadium Improvements" (New York: Praeger-Kavanagh-Waterbury, June 2, 1969), William Donald Schaefer Files, Inactive Administrative Files, Box 19, Baltimore City Archives, Baltimore; "$18.5 Million Plan Outlined for Stadium Modernization," *Baltimore Sun*, February 21, 1969, C28.

7. "City Bonds at Stake," *Baltimore Sun*, March 27, 1969, A18; "School Slowdown," *Baltimore Sun*, April 25, 1969, A14; Michael Parks, "Baltimore's Financial Troubles: Continued," *Baltimore Sun*, May 15, 1969, A20; "Bond Interest Increase Okayed by Voters," *Baltimore Sun*, May 18, 1969, SD17; Art Pine, "Modernized Stadium Plan Is Offered," *Baltimore Sun*, July 13, 1969, 20; Pine, "$5 Million Stadium Renovation Plan Proposed," *Baltimore Sun*, July 9, 1969, C1, C5; "$5 Million Stadium Renovation Plan," *Baltimore Sun*, July 13, 1969, SD17; "Stadium Plan Is Criticized," *Baltimore Sun*, July 15, 1969, C11; "Stadium, Renovation Plan," *Baltimore Sun*, July 20, 1969, ST16; Pine, "City Seeks Cheaper Stadium Plan," *Baltimore Sun*, August 5, 1969, C11, C22.

8. "Colts Threaten to Switch Parks," *New York Times*, May 21, 1969, 21; Pine, "Orioles Balk at City Plan for Stadium," *Baltimore Sun*, July 26, 1969, B10, B20; John B. O'Donnell Jr., "City, Colts, Orioles Move Closer on Stadium," *Baltimore Sun*, October 14, 1969, C8; "Moving Out Colts Are," *Chicago Daily Defender*, January 10, 1972, 24; Shirley Povich, "Colts Stir Baltimore Uproar," *Washington Post*, January 11, 1972, D1–D2; "The Week in Sports," *Baltimore Sun*, January 23, 1972, D19; Hill, "'Tin Cup' Moves Backfire," C11, C20; Alan Goldstein, "Colts Swap Roles, 'Tampa' with Fledgling Bucs," *Baltimore Sun*, October 4, 1976, C5, C7.

9. Mark Kram, "A Wink at a Homely Girl," *Sports Illustrated*, October 10, 1966, 93; Maisel, "The Morning After," *Baltimore Sun*, December 11, 1970, C1; Robert Fachet, "Dumdums Do It Dirty," *Washington Post*, February 14, 1972, D2.

10. William Hyder, "12 Bullets Games on Screen," *Baltimore Sun*, June 12, 1966, TV8; Goldstein, "Bullets Expand Ties to D.C.," *Baltimore Sun*, September 8, 1971, C1, C5; "Pioneer Moved Bullets: Wizards Owner Abe Pollin Dead at 85," *Baltimore Sun*, November 25, 2009, http://articles.baltimoresun.com/2009-11-25/sports/bal-sp.pollin25nov25_1_washington-sports-entertainment-abe-pollin-wizards (accessed July 7, 2014).

11. Mark Asher, "New Owners Keep Bullets in Baltimore: Shoot for Title," *Washington Post*, November 24, 1964, D2; "10,210 See Celtics Edge Bullets, 94–92, at College Park," *Baltimore Sun*, February 7, 1964, S17, 22; "Celtics Edge Bullets, 94–92," *Boston Globe*, February 7, 1964, 29; Ed Winsten, "Bullets Trounce Royals, 113–97," *Baltimore Sun*, October 5, 1969, A15; "Bullets Consider Playing Games at College Park," *Washington Post*, April 19, 1970, C17; Asher, "Bullets 'Represent' D.C. Area: Pollin Opens Door to More Dates," *Washington Post*, December 11, 1970, D8; "Wilt, Lakers Calmly Celebrate 27th Consecutive NBA Victory," *Baltimore Sun*, December 23, 1971, C4; "Lakers Set

Pro Record," *Chicago Tribune*, December 23, 1971, B1; "Lakers Run Streak to 27: Shatter Record, Beating Bullets by 127–120," *New York Times*, December 23, 1971, 31; Asher, "Bullets Can't Boost Dates at Maryland," *Washington Post*, January 25, 1972, D2; Fachet, "Dumdums Do It Dirty," *Washington Post*, February 14, 1972, D2; "McMillian Boosts L.A. over Bullets," *Boston Globe*, February 14, 1972, 24; "Lakers Turn It On in Final Period to Beat Bullets, 121–110," *Los Angeles Times*, February 14, 1972, D1, 4; Goldstein, "Lakers Thwart Bullets: McMillian and West Sparkle in 121–110 Game," *Baltimore Sun*, February 14, 1972, C1, C2.

12. Asher, "Bullets Can't Boost Dates at Maryland," *Washington Post*, January 25, 1972, D2; "Bullets Moving," *Chicago Daily Defender*, May 3, 1972, 28; "Bullets Are Said to Be Set for '74 Move to Suburbia," *New York Times*, May 3, 1972, 56; Goldstein, "Bullets' Fate on Line as Pollin Makes NHL Bid," *Baltimore Sun*, May 24, 1972, C4; Asher, "3 Factors Influence Switch by Pollin," *Washington Post*, June 6, 1972, D2; "Pollin Makes It Final—It's Largo for Bullets," *Baltimore Sun*, August 2, 1972, C6; "Remolding the Baltimore Bullets," *Newsweek*, March 5, 1973, 51.

13. Goldstein, "ABA Game Here Likely," *Baltimore Sun*, August 16, 1972, C1, C6.

14. The Orioles owner Jarold Hoffberger found the *New York Times* article of great importance; so much so, he included a clipping of the article in an April 9, 1973, letter to Mayor Schaefer. Hoffberger hoped to urge "you, the Governor and the Commission to announce in the very near future whatever plans you have to bring the matter of the stadium to a positive conclusion." "Civic Center Held Able to Offset Bullet Revenue Loss," *Baltimore Sun*, June 9, 1972; "3 Baltimore Teams on Way Out," *New York Times*, April 8, 1973, 258; Jarold Hoffberger to William Donald Schaefer, April 9, 1973, William Donald Schaefer Files, Inactive Administrative Files, Box 42, "Stadium Facility: Stadium Committee," Baltimore City Archives, Baltimore.

15. According to both the legislation establishing the Maryland Sports Complex Authority and the *Baltimore Sun*, the commission has the ability to float bonds in order to pay for the complex. The bonds would be paid for through the stadiums as well as the rent from commercial properties built on the selected land. Barry Rascovar, "Mandel Signs Bill for Sports-Complex Authority," *Baltimore Sun*, May 6, 1972, A12; "Sports and Airport Bills Signed," *Baltimore Sun*, May 14, 1972, D22; "The Sports Authority's First Tasks," *Baltimore Sun*, June 7, 1972, A14; "Report to the Governor of the State of Maryland and the Mayor of the City of Baltimore," May 15, 1973, William Donald Schaefer Files, Inactive Administrative Files, Box 42, "Stadium Facility: Preliminary Feasibility Study," Baltimore City Archives, Baltimore.

16. In the report given to Mayor Schaefer and Governor Marvin Mandel, the Authority noted that alternatives involving the complete renovation of Memorial Stadium with additions to parking would net the lowest return to the city, which ranged between $17.70 million to $18.68 million. The Memorial Stadium-Civic Center plan would generate $98.37 million for the city. However, the domed stadium-Civic Center plan would net the city $121.39 million. "Report to the Governor of the State of Maryland and the Mayor of the City of Baltimore," May 15, 1973,

William Donald Schaefer Files, Inactive Administrative Files, Box 42, "Stadium Facility: Preliminary Feasibility Study," Baltimore City Archives, Baltimore; "The Stadium Study," *Baltimore Sun*, March 25, 1973.

17. Earl Arnett, "Music Recalls the Past," *Baltimore Sun*, July 3, 1970, B1; "Report to the Governor of the State of Maryland and the Mayor of the City of Baltimore," May 15, 1973, William Donald Schaefer Files, Inactive Administrative Files, Box 42, "Stadium Facility: Preliminary Feasibility Study," Baltimore City Archives, Baltimore; "The Stadium Study," *Baltimore Sun*, March 25, 1973; Daniel A. Nathan, "Looking for the 'Marvellous' in Baltimore: A Sport History Sojourn," in *Representing the Sporting Past in Museums and Halls of Fame*, ed. Murray G. Phillips (New York: Routledge, 2013), 185.

18. Early reports of the committee's plan placed a $7 million price tag. However, by the fall of 1945, the price tag dropped to $5 million. "New Stadium May Have Roof Held Up by Air Pressure," *Christian Science Monitor* (Boston): May 2, 1945, 13; "Baltimore Plans Inclosed Stadium for Grid, Baseball," *Washington Post*, May 2, 1945, 10; "Air-Pressure Roof Support Involves No New Principle," *Baltimore Sun*, May 2, 1945, 14; "Stadium Put at $7,000,000," *Baltimore Sun*, May 3, 1945, 14; "Stadium Proposal to Go to Council," *Baltimore Sun*, July 24, 1945, 9, 22; "Council Gets Stadium Plan from War Memorial Group," *Baltimore Sun*, October 23, 1945, 14, 24; Mike Klingaman, "Baltimore First Put Lid on Dome Debate in 1945; Martin's Idea Predated Astrodome by 20 Years," *Baltimore Sun*, February 27, 1996, http://articles.baltimoresun.com/1996-02-27/sports/1996058051_1_dome-covered-stadium-baltimore (accessed July 7, 2014).

19. Of the 3.8 million people that visited the Astrodome, 2,539,470 people came to watch the ninth-place Astros. "Houston May Break Lease," *Baltimore Sun*, July 27, 1962, 23; Maisel, "The Morning After," *Baltimore Sun*, September 18, 1965, 13; Cameron C. Snyder, "Stadium Men in Baltimore," *Baltimore Sun*, November 24, 1965, C2; Robert Lipsyte, "The Astrodome Caps a Profitable Year," *New York Times*, December 31, 1965, 15.

20. Baltimore's Inner Harbor plan had been included in a letter to Richard A. Burnham from Mrs. Robert O. Bonnell Jr., director of information for the Charles Center-Inner Harbor Management, Inc. Mrs. Robert O. Bonnell Jr. to Richard A. Burnham, October 22, 1973, William Donald Schaefer Files, Inactive Administrative Files, Box 71, "Inner Harbor," Baltimore City Archives, Baltimore, "Baltimore's Inner Harbor Redevelopment Program," William Donald Schaefer Files, Inactive Administrative Files, Box 71, "Inner Harbor," Baltimore City Archives, Baltimore.

21. The letter Frank Novak wrote to the editor of the *Baltimore Sun* was undated. However, the letter had been stamped "Jan 30 Recd." Robert M. Fogelson, *Downtown: Its Rise and Fall, 1880–1950* (New Haven, CT: Yale University Press, 2003), 249, 314–16; Bready, "How a New Stadium Would Continue the City's Identity," *Baltimore Sun*, June 10, 1973, K3; Frank Novak to the Editor, *Baltimore Sun*, received January 30, William Donald Schaefer Files, Inactive Administrative Files, Box 42, "Stadium Facility: Stadium Committee," Baltimore City Archives, Baltimore.

22. Miller, *The Baseball Business*, 205; "Colts, Orioles Back Downtown

Stadium," *Baltimore Sun*, December 2, 1973, B1, B12; Maisel, "The Morning After," December 2, 1973, B1, B12; "Report to the Governor of the State of Maryland and the Mayor of the City of Baltimore," May 15, 1973, William Donald Schaefer Files, Inactive Administrative Files, Box 42, "Stadium Facility: Preliminary Feasibility Study," Baltimore City Archives, Baltimore.

23. At the time Greenbaum wrote his letter to Mayor Schaefer, the Baltimore Chamber of Commerce reported that the total employment downtown rested between 120,000 to 140,000 people. The Baltimore City Planning Department, however, projected that the figure would increase to 180,000 people within the next seventeen years. While employment downtown had not reached 180,000 at the time Greenbaum wrote the letter, he used the figure to accentuate his concern over building a downtown sports complex. "Release: Memorial Stadium vs. Sports Complex," February 2, 1973, William Donald Schaefer Files, Inactive Administrative Files, Box 42, "Stadium Facility: Stadium Committee," Baltimore City Archives, Baltimore; Howard Greenbaum to William Donald Schaefer, April 20, 1973, William Donald Schaefer Files, Inactive Administrative Files, Box 42, "Stadium Facility: Stadium Committee," Baltimore City Archives, Baltimore.

24. Mayor Schaefer knew of the concerns Baltimoreans had with Memorial Stadium. In a March 1973 letter to Betty Altshul, Mayor Schaefer indicated, "Many months ago, residents in the area called to my attention the problems caused by the Stadium, including noise, rats, inconvenience, etc. We have continually tried to correct these problems and will make every effort in the future." Betty Altshul to William Donald Schaefer, February 1973, , William Donald Schaefer Files, Inactive Administrative Files, Box 42, "Stadium Facility: Stadium Committee," Baltimore City Archives, Baltimore; William Donald Schaefer to Betty Altshul, March 1, 1973, William Donald Schaefer Files, Inactive Administrative Files, Box 42, "Stadium Facility: Stadium Committee," Baltimore City Archives, Baltimore; "Release: Memorial Stadium vs. Sports Complex," February 2, 1973, William Donald Schaefer Files, Inactive Administrative Files, Box 42, "Stadium Facility: Stadium Committee," Baltimore City Archives, Baltimore; Mary Pat Clarke to William Donald Schaefer, March 17, 1972, William Donald Schaefer Files, Inactive Administrative Files, Box 42, "Stadium Facility: Stadium Committee," Baltimore City Archives, Baltimore.

25. According to Louise Cook, "Labor unrest in scattered areas of the country is affecting a wide range of services—some of them vital. The most serious problems are in Baltimore, where police walked out Thursday night, joining 3,000 other city workers on picket lines." Ms. L. R. Warfield to William Donald Schaefer, March 9, 1973, William Donald Schaefer Files, Inactive Administrative Files, Box 42, "Stadium Facility: Stadium Committee," Baltimore City Archives, Baltimore; Joseph W. Spencer to William Donald Schaefer, April 8, 1973, William Donald Schaefer Files, Inactive Administrative Files, Box 42, "Stadium Facility: Stadium Committee," Baltimore City Archives, Baltimore; "Teachers Strike in Baltimore," *Washington Post*, February 4, 1974, A3; "Strike Settlement and What Is Left," *Baltimore Sun*, March 6, 1974, A14; Louise Cook, "Workers' Unrest Interrupts Municipal Service," *St. Petersburg Times*, July 15, 1974, 4-A.

26. Miller, *The Baseball Business*, 205; "Mandel Is Firm on Stadium," *Baltimore Sun*, November 22, 1972, C14, C24; Mark Reutter, "The Stadium: Who

Will Pay?" *Baltimore Sun*, August 13, 1972, D1, 3; Bill Richards, "Baltimore: A City in Deep Trouble," *Washington Post*, March 5, 1974, B1, B9; Elizabeth Gavis to William Donald Schaefer, July 4, 1973, William Donald Schaefer Files, Inactive Administrative Files, Box 42, "Stadium Facility: Stadium Committee," Baltimore City Archives, Baltimore.

27. "Use of Funds Opposed: Pressman's Complaint Threatens Stadium Study," *Baltimore Sun*, November 15, 1972, C7; "Pressman Wants Maryland to Purchase Colts, Orioles," *Washington Post*, June 4, 1973, D3; Carl Schoettler, Fred Rasmussen, and Scott Wilson et al., "Hyman Pressman, Colorful Booster of 'Little Guy,' Dies," *Baltimore Sun*, March 16, 1996, http://articles.baltimoresun.com/1996-03-16/news/1996076006_1_pressman-city-comptroller-william-donald-schaefer (accessed July 7, 2014); Joe Nawrozki, "Hyman Pressman Is Buried Amid Tributes," *Baltimore Sun*, March 18, 1996, http://articles.baltimoresun.com/1996-03-18/news/1996078028_1_pressman-pallbearer-patrick-day-parade (accessed July 7, 2014); Hyman A. Pressman, *Watchdog of Baltimore* (Baltimore: Urban Affairs Publishing Company, 1977), 126.

28. James D. Dilts, "Foes Seek Vote on New Stadium," *Baltimore Sun*, June 29, 1973, C12; Theodore W. Hendricks, "Stadium Legal Fight Thickens," *Baltimore Sun*, August 28, 1974, C6; Hendricks, "Move to Retain Present Stadium Going on Ballot," *Baltimore Sun*, October 1, 1974, C20.

29. "Voters Speak Out on City Questions," *Baltimore Sun*, November 7, 1974, C5; Richard Ben Cramer and James D. Dilts, "Stadium Backers Unfazed," *Baltimore Sun*, November 7, 1974, C1, C5.

30. Miller, *The Baseball Business*, 207, 214, 231–32; "Orioles for Sale, Hoffberger Says," *Washington Post*, October 11, 1974; Nancy Scannell and Shirley Povich, "Area Developer Bidding for Orioles Lerner Would Play Substantial Part of '75 Schedule in RFK," *Washington Post*, January 11, 1975, E1; "Hoffberger May Keep Orioles in Baltimore," *Washington Post*, March 2, 1975, C11; Scannell, "Family Wants Hoffberger to Sell Orioles: Hoffberger Family 'Wants to Get Out,'" *Washington Post*, August 2, 1979, C1, C3; "Fans Fear D.C. Buyer; Players Hail Hoffberger," *Baltimore Sun*, August 3, 1979, C5; Nigro, "Birds' Hoffberger Era Comes to an End Today," *Baltimore Sun*, November 1, 1979, D1, D5.

31. Miller, *The Baseball Business*, 293–96; "Colts Still Optimistic about New Stadium Complex," *Baltimore Sun*, March 1, 1974, C5; Tom Linthicum, "County Stadium for Colts Dies," *Baltimore Sun*, January 5, 1976, C14; Snyder, "Phoenix Approaches Irsay for Colt Franchise," *Baltimore Sun*, March 31, 1976, C5, C7; Snyder, "Stadium Terms Held Bar to Colts' Phoenix Move," *Baltimore Sun*, April 1, 1976, C7; "Phoenix Seeks Colt Franchise," *Los Angeles Times*, April 10, 1976, A4; Snyder, "L.A. Group Meets with Colts' Irsay," *Baltimore Sun*, January 28, 1979, C1, C15; "Irsay Vows to Move Colts," *Chicago Tribune*, June 12, 1979, C3; "Irsay Backs Off on Colts," *Washington Post*, November 1, 1979, F5.

32. Miller, *The Baseball Business*, 300–302; "Resolution No. 12," *Baltimore Sun*, November 1, 1984, D13; Sandy Banisky, "Voters Reject Changes in Council, School Panel," *Baltimore Sun*, November 7, 1984, 1A; Joe Nawrozki, "Hyman Pressman Is Buried Amid Tributes," *Baltimore Sun*, March 18, 1996, http://articles.baltimoresun.com/1996-03-18/news/1996078028_1_pressman-pallbearer-patrick-day-parade (accessed July 7, 2014).

17. The Greatest High School Basketball Team Ever: The Dunbar Poets, 1981–1982 and 1982–1983

1. Tom Dunkel, "Dunbar High: Brick House," *Slam*, September 21, 2007, http://www. slamonline.com (accessed September 10, 2012). Details vary regarding how many games the Dunbar team played in both seasons. In 1981–1982 that number is either 28 or 29 and in 1982–1983 it is either 30 or 31. Newspaper records for every game could not be found.

2. Elzee C. Gladden and Jessie B. Gladden, "The Dunbar Chronicle: A Case Study," *Journal of Negro Education* 57 (1988): 372; *Poet Pride: A Dunbar High School Documentary*, DVD, directed by David Manigault (Big Vision Films, 1990).

3. Baltimore's three historically black schools—Dunbar, Douglass, and Carver—all joined the MSA in 1956. Bill Free, "Around the MSA: Way Was Paved in '56 for Implementing Desegregation Order," *Baltimore Sun*, October 12, 1975, B5; *Poet Pride*.

4. Marion Orr, *Black Social Capital: The Politics of School Reform in Baltimore, 1986–1998* (Lawrence: University of Kansas Press, 1999), 19–29; Howell S. Baum, *Brown in Baltimore: School Desegregation and the Limits of Liberalism* (Ithaca, NY: Cornell University Press, 2010), 24.

5. Orr, *Black Social Capital*, 29–36.

6. Ibid.; W. Edward Orser, "Flight to the Suburbs: Suburbanization and Racial Change on Baltimore's West Side," in *The Baltimore Book: New Views of Local History*, ed. Elizabeth Fee, Linda Shopes, and Linda Zeidman (Philadelphia: Temple University Press, 1991), 204–5; *Poet Pride*; Preston Jay interview with the author, September 26, 2013.

7. *Poet Pride*.

8. Bill Free, "St. Joe Nips Dunbar, 69–67, for Title; Free-For-All Marks Overtime Game," *Baltimore Sun*, February 12, 1971, C1; "19 Arrested in Violence after Game," *Baltimore Sun*, February 12, 1971, C20.

9. *Poet Pride*.

10. "Dunbar Basketball Star Is Slain; Woman Charged," *Baltimore Sun*, March 29, 1972, C26; *Poet Pride*.

11. Kent Baker, "Dunbar Halts DeMatha Victory Streak, 85–71," *Baltimore Sun*, February 25, 1973, B1. Wise presents an acute example of the perils of living in east Baltimore. In the summer after he bested Dantley, he lost part of three toes in a freak accident attributed by his peers to life on the streets. Unaffected, he played well enough his senior season to garner a basketball scholarship to up-and-coming Clemson University. In the 1974–1975 season, the Atlantic Coast Conference recognized the former Poet as Freshman of the Year and the conference's first freshman to make all-league first team. That season, Wise led Clemson to a second-place finish in the conference—theretofore its best ever—and the school's first NIT bid. After the season and amid allegations that Clemson violated NCAA recruiting policies, Wise was granted a hardship waiver to leave school early and join the pro ranks. The American Basketball Association's Baltimore Claws signed him in the fall of 1975. Unfortunately, this team folded before the season even started, but not before they had suspended their local star for drug use. Thereafter, Wise had a tryout with the Golden State Warriors, but he was cut after a coach reportedly caught him using heroin in the team locker room. Wise played

two games with the San Antonio Spurs later that season in his only professional basketball experience before spending much of the 1970s and 1980s in prison for his involvement with drugs.

12. Ernest Graham, a 1977 Dunbar alum who set the University of Maryland's single-game scoring record in 1978, and Quintin Dailey, a Cardinal Gibbons Catholic graduate who brought the University of San Francisco to basketball fame in the early 1980s before also playing a prominent role in the basketball program's 1982 shutdown, both found a similar fate to that of Wise—allowing "the streets" to keep them from reaching their potentials. Michael Olesker, "Playground Dreams End in Shadow of Pros," *Baltimore Sun*, August 24, 1982, D1. NCAA and NBA stars Juan Dixon, Rudy Gay, and Carmelo Anthony all hail from Baltimore. *Poet Pride*.

13. Bill Free, "Edmondson Upsets Dunbar," *Baltimore Sun*, January 18, 1975, B7; Sam Lacy, "Each Day 'A Little Harder' for Coach," *Baltimore Afro-American*, February 24, 1973, 13; *Poet Pride*.

14. Gladden and Gladden, "The Dunbar Chronicle," 373.

15. Baltimore CORE, an activist group, had been lobbying since at least 1965. Howell S. Baum, *Brown in Baltimore: School Desegregation and the Limits of Liberalism* (Ithaca, NY: Cornell University Press, 2010), 122–23; Gladden and Gladden, "The Dunbar Chronicle," 374.

16. Gladden and Gladden, "The Dunbar Chronicle," 374.

17. Ibid.

18. Franz Lidz, "Two Kings of the Same Hill," *Sports Illustrated*, February 8, 1982, 72; Keith Mills, "Brother, Can You Spare a Rebound?" *Press Box*, September 23, 2009, http://www.pressboxonline.com/story/id/5272 (accessed February 28, 2013).

19. Lidz, "Two Kings," 74.

20. Ibid., 72.

21. Gregory Kane, "The Greatest Local Hoops Game That Never Was," *Baltimore Sun*, April 6, 2002, http://articles.baltimoresun.com/2002-04-06/news/0204060209_1_ hall-college-high-calvert-hall-amatucci (accessed February 28, 2012).

22. Lidz, "Two Kings," 74.

23. Quoted in ibid.

24. Interview with Mark Amatucci, June 4, 2013.

25. Kane, "The Greatest Local Hoops Game"; Susan Reimer, "The No. 1 Team Is the No. 1 Question," *Baltimore Sun*, December 6, 1981, C14; Susan Reimer, "Dunbar, Calvert Hall Cagers Meet Tonight," *Baltimore Sun*, March 14, 1981, B7.

26. Preston Jay interview; Greg Branch interview with author, February 25, 2013; Bill Glauber, "Calvert Hall Nips Dunbar in Third OT," *Baltimore Sun*, March 15, 1981, C1.

27. Kane, "The Greatest Local Hoops Game."

28. Tyrone "Muggsy" Bogues and David Levine, *In the Land of Giants: My Life in Basketball* (New York: Little Brown & Co., 1994), 47–49.

29. Bogues and Levine, *In the Land of Giants*, 47–49.

30. Ibid., 49.

31. Amatucci interview.

32. "Dunbar, Walbrook Triumph," *Baltimore Sun*, December 4, 1981, B4; Sam Davis, "Lakers, Dunbar Gain Tourney Final," *Baltimore Sun*, December 6, 1981,

C17; Sam Davis, "Williams Spurs Dunbar to Rout of Clifton and Tipoff Cage Title," *Baltimore Sun*, December 7, 1981, C3; "For the Record," *Baltimore Sun*, December 11, 1981, 34; "D.C. Carroll, Curley Score Tourney Wins," *Baltimore Sun*, December 19, 1981, B4; "Dunbar Overwhelms Mervo by 43," *Baltimore Sun*, December 23, 1981, C4; "Dunbar Wins Opener in New York Tourney," *Baltimore Sun*, December 27, 1981, C13; "Dunbar Trips East Orange to Advance to Harlem Final," *Baltimore Sun*, December 28, 1981, B3; "Dunbar Cagers Win Harlem City Tourney," *Baltimore Sun*, December 31, 1981, D4.

33. Lidz, "Two Kings," 72, 74.

34. "Prep Basketball Summaries," *Baltimore Sun*, January 7, 1982, C2; "Prep Basketball," *Baltimore Sun*, January 13, 1982, D6; "Prep Basketball Boxes," *Baltimore Sun*, January 21, 1982, B3; "Prep Basketball Boxes," *Baltimore Sun*, January 23, 1982, B2; Sam Davis, "Dunbar Smashes Lake Clifton, 75–42," *Baltimore Sun*, January 24, 1982, C14; "Prep Basketball Box Scores," *Baltimore Sun*, January 27, 1982, C3; "Dunbar, Lakers Triumph," *Baltimore Sun*, January 29, 1982, C2; "Dunbar Wins 19th in a Row," *Baltimore Sun*, February 1, 1982, C2; "Prep Basketball Results," *Baltimore Sun*, February 4, 1982, D5; "Unbeaten Dunbar Routs Carver for 21st Win," *Baltimore Sun*, February 6, 1982, B5.

35. Paul McMullen, "In a Class of Their Own, Poets Recall Glory Days," *Baltimore Sun*, July 19, 2002, http://articles.baltimoresun.com/2002-07-19/sports/02071 90019_1_dunbar-tommy-polley-michael-lloyd (accessed February 26, 2013); *Poet Pride*; Bill Glauber, "Dandy Dunbar Crushes Camden, 84–59," *Baltimore Sun*, February 14, 1982, C9.

36. Bill Glauber, "Basketball Kismet: Dunbar, Calvert Hall Can't Escape Their Links," *Baltimore Sun*, February 7, 1982, C1; "Prep Box Scores," *Baltimore Sun*, February 17, 1982, B2; Bill Glauber, "Lakers Roll On," *Baltimore Sun*, February 19, 1982, C1; Susan Reimer, "Poets, Lakers Reach Finals," *Baltimore Sun*, February 21, 1982, C4; Susan Reimer, "Dunbar Tops Lake Clifton," *Baltimore Sun*, February 22, 1982, C1; Alan Goldstein, "Play It Again, Poets, Cards," *Baltimore Sun*, February 28, 1982, C6; Susan Reimer, "Dunbar, Walbrook Add Boys', Girls' Titles," *Baltimore Sun*, February 28, 1982, C6; Kent Baker, "Local Cable Picture Scrambled," *Baltimore Sun*, March 23, 1982, C1.

37. Kane, "The Greatest Local Hoops Game."

38. Susan Reimer, "Cards Offer Poets 'Dream Game' Date, Place," *Baltimore Sun*, March 1, 1982, C1; Amatucci interview; "Game Talks Continue," *Baltimore Sun*, March 5, 1982, C5; Kane, "The Greatest Local Hoops Game."

39. Susan Reimer, "Promoters for 'The Game' Strike Out," *Baltimore Sun*, March 12, 1982, C1.

40. Bill Glauber, "Wingate Picks Hoyas," *Baltimore Sun*, April 16, 1982, B1; Bill Glauber, "Dunbar's Graham Picks Nev.-Las Vegas," *Baltimore Sun*, April 29, 1982, C6; Bill Glauber, "Beltway Classic Set in December," *Baltimore Sun*, August 13, 1982, C3; "Prep Basketball Pairings Made," *Baltimore Sun*, October 29, 1982, D3; "Sports Shorts," *Baltimore Sun*, December 2, 1982, AS8; "Baltimore Dunbar among All-Time Best," *National Federation of State High School Associations*, http://www.nfhs.org/content.aspx?id=6539 (accessed August 2, 2012).

41. Sam Davis, "Poets Roll in Tip Off Play," *Baltimore Sun*, December 3, 1982, D1; Sam Davis, "Dunbar Cruises into Semifinals," *Baltimore Sun*, December 4, 1982, B4; Gary Adornato and Mike Preston, "Call Dunbar the Best in Basketball,"

Baltimore Sun, December 5, 1982, 35; Sam Davis, "Dunbar Crushes Lake Clifton in Poet-Laker Final, 82–47," *Baltimore Sun*, December 6, 1982, D5; Bill Glauber, "Dunbar Rolls; Cards Upset by Carroll," *Baltimore Sun*, December 11, 1982, B1; Bill Glauber, "Dunbar Rips Carroll in Beltway Classic," *Baltimore Sun*, December 13, 1982, D1; "Prep Results," *Baltimore Sun*, December 17, 1982, C2; "Dunbar Routs Ocala in Ky. Tournament," *Baltimore Sun*, December 21, 1982, D2; Sam Davis, "Millers Help Murray Emulate Seidel," *Baltimore Sun*, December 22, 1982, F2; "Dunbar Romps to Kentucky Tourney Title," *Baltimore Sun*, December 23, 1982, C2; "Prep Statistics," *Baltimore Sun*, December 28, 1982, C2; Bill Glauber, "Loyola Sinks Southern for Capital Title," *Baltimore Sun*, December 31, 1982, B2.

42. Claire Abt, "McDonogh Nips Pats on Chisholm Shot," *Baltimore Sun*, January 6, 1983, C2; Bill Glauber, "Awesome Poets Rip Walbrook, 73–41," *Baltimore Sun*, January 8, 1983, B4; Bill Glauber, "Southwestern Upsets Lakers, 57–53," *Baltimore Sun*, January 12, 1983, B4; "Prep Statistics," *Baltimore Sun*, January 14, 1983, C2; "Southern Spills Lake Clifton," *Baltimore Sun*, January 19, 1983, B2; Bill Glauber, "Hammond Towers Over Oakland Mills," *Baltimore Sun*, January 22, 1983, B4; "Prep Scoreboard," *Baltimore Sun*, January 28, 1983, C3; "For the Record," *Baltimore Sun*, January 31, 1983, C7; "Prep Scoreboard," *Baltimore Sun*, February 3, 1983, C5; "For the Record," *Baltimore Sun*, February 6, 1983, 33; Bill Glauber, "Young Poly Team Wins, Continues to Surprise," *Baltimore Sun*, February 9, 1983, E2; "City Teams Begin Series," *Baltimore Sun*, February 18, 1983, D2; Bill Glauber, "Walbrook, Dunbar Advance to City Tournament Final," *Baltimore Sun*, February 20, 1983, C14; Bill Glauber, "Dunbar Overpowers Walbrook for Crown," *Baltimore Sun*, February 21, 1983, C1; Sam Davis, "Poets Stop Lakers," *Baltimore Sun*, February 28, 1983, D1; Sam Davis, "Dunbar Puts on a Show, Crushes Flint Hill, 87–59," *Baltimore Sun*, March 2, 1983, F5.

43. Bill Glauber, "Dunbar, Walbrook Favored Tonight," *Baltimore Sun*, March 10, 1983, F2.

44. Bill Glauber, "Dunbar Dumps Gibbons," *Baltimore Sun*, March 11, 1983, C1.

45. *Poet Pride.*

18. Baltimore Baseball Icons: The Babe, Mr. Oriole, the Iron Man, and the Forgotten Day

1. Paul Connerton, "Seven Types of Forgetting," *Memory Studies* 1, no. 1 (2008): 59.

2. Heywood Broun, "Ruth Comes into His Own with 2 Homers, Clinching Second for Yanks, 4 to 2," *New York World*, October 12, 1923, 1.

3. Kevin Cowherd, "Bigger Than Life," *Baltimore Sun*, October 19, 2003, 6F.

4. Marshall Smelser, *The Life That Ruth Built: A Biography* (New York: Quadrangle/New York Times Book Co., 1975), 3.

5. Roger Kahn, "The Real Babe Ruth," *Esquire*, August 1959, 28.

6. Babe Ruth (as told to Bob Considine), *The Babe Ruth Story* (New York: Pocket Books, 1948), 1, 2.

7. Ibid., 2.

8. Leigh Montville, *The Big Bam: The Life and Times of Babe Ruth* (New York: Broadway Books, 2006), 10.

9. Smelser, *The Life That Ruth Built*, 12.

10. Robert W. Creamer, *Babe: The Legend Comes to Life* (New York: Simon and Schuster, [1974] 2005), 65.

11. Benjamin G. Rader, "Compensatory Sport Heroes: Ruth, Grange, and Dempsey," *Journal of Popular Culture* 16 (Spring 1983): 12.

12. "Game Made Ruth—And He Remade Game," *Sporting News*, August 25, 1948, 10.

13. See, for example, "'The Babe' Returns Home Briefly, Greets Old Friends," *Baltimore Evening Sun*, July 14, 1948, Maryland Department V.F., Enoch Pratt Free Library, Baltimore, Maryland.

14. Rodger H. Pippen, "Pippen Tells Why Babe Ruth Was Baseball Legend," *Baltimore News-Post*, August 17, 1948, 1.

15. Connor Smolensky, "Babe Ruth Museum Reopens in Baltimore," June 12, 2015, http://m.orioles.mlb.com/news/article/130246954/babe-ruth-museum-reopens-in-baltimore (accessed June 12, 2015). The Babe Ruth Birthplace Museum has an interesting history. For years, *Baltimore Sun* writer James H. Bready published articles about 216 Emory Street, its sad condition and its need for refurbishing as "a Babe Ruth shrine." "In the fall of 1968," Ken Sobol explains, the City of Baltimore, like many municipalities in the midst of urban renewal, "decided to tear down the block of South Emory Street, which contained number 216. A group of prominent citizens immediately protested. Few of them had actually seen the street, which runs a few short blocks through the shabby old waterfront district south of the new University of Maryland Medical Center, but they all knew what was on it. Somewhere in that Catfish Row of tiny, ancient, brick row houses was Ruth's birthplace. And if that wasn't a Baltimore landmark worth saving, nothing was." Those fighting to preserve Ruth's birthplace won the day. But their struggle has been ongoing for almost fifty years. The venue is frequently cash strapped. In January 1983, David Simon wrote that "guardians of one of Baltimore's most ignored historical sites" were raising funds to "upgrade the birthplace of baseball great Babe Ruth to 'the quality of other Inner Harbor attractions.'" Thirty years later, that seems to have finally happened. James H. Bready, "Forgotten Shrine: Babe Ruth Birthplace," *Baltimore Sun Sunday Magazine*, September 17, 1961, 7; James H. Bready, "House That Built Ruth," *Baltimore Sun*, February 13, 1968, Maryland Department V.F., Enoch Pratt Free Library, Baltimore, Maryland; Ken Sobol, *Babe Ruth and the American Dream* (New York: Ballantine Books, 1974), 25; David Simon, "Ruth Fans Go to Bat for Museum Funds," *Baltimore Sun*, January 2, 1983, B8. For more on the Babe Ruth Birthplace Museum, see John Cahill, "The Babe Ruth Museum and Birthplace," *Journal of Sport History* 24 (Summer 1997): 203–5; John Bloom, "Sports Nostalgia and the Post Industrial City: The Babe Ruth Birthplace and Museum," *Journal of Sport History* 30 (Summer 2003): 265–70; and Daniel A. Nathan, "Looking for the 'Marvellous' in Baltimore: A Sport History Sojourn," in *Representing the Sporting Past in Museums and Halls of Fame*, ed. Murray G. Phillips (New York: Routledge, 2012), 176–203.

16. Jon Morgan, "'The Wrong Glove on the Right Man,'" *Baltimore Sun* June 12, 1995, 1A.

17. Montville, *The Big Bam*, 164.

18. Creamer, *Babe*, 21–22.

19. David Simon, "Ruth Fans Go to Bat for Museum Funds," *Baltimore Sun*, January 2, 1983, B8.

20. Joseph M. Burke, "Babe a Champ When the World Loved Heroes," *Baltimore News American*, January 31, 1971, 2B.

21. Creamer, *Babe*, 170.

22. Sobol, *Babe Ruth and the American Dream*, 25; "'The Babe' Returns Home Briefly, Greets Old Friends."

23. Quoted in Don Riley, "Riley Remembers," *Baltimore Sun*, April 1957, Maryland Department V.F., Enoch Pratt Free Library, Baltimore, Maryland.

24. Tom Kern, "Leon Day," June 17, 2011, http://sabr.org/bioproj/person/f6e24f41 (accessed July 17, 2015). Mount Winans remains mostly African American and impoverished.

25. Quoted in John B. Holway, *Blackball Stars: Negro League Pioneers* (New York: Carroll & Graf Publishers, [1988] 1992), 346. Other sources identify the team Day played for as the Silver Moons. See James A. Riley, *The Biographical Encyclopedia of the Negro Baseball Leagues* (New York: Carroll & Graf Publishers, [1994] 2002), 224; Donn Rogosin, *Invisible Men: Life in Baseball's Negro Leagues* (New York: Athenaeum, [1983] 1987), 56.

26. Riley, *The Biographical Encyclopedia of the Negro Baseball Leagues*, 49, 224.

27. Brad Snyder, "'You Made It, Man': Day Named to Hall of Fame," *Baltimore Sun*, March 8, 1995, 10A.

28. Rogosin, *Invisible Men*, 57.

29. Riley, *The Biographical Encyclopedia of the Negro Baseball Leagues*, 224.

30. The Eagles were owned and operated by Abe Manly, who was in the numbers business, and his wife, Effa Manley, who was elected to the National Baseball Hall of Fame in 2006 as a pioneer/executive. James Overmyer, *Queen of the Negro Leagues: Effa Manley and the Newark Eagles* (Lanham, MD: Scarecrow Press, 1998).

31. Holway, *Blackball Stars*, 349.

32. Quoted in Tom Keyser, "It's Day's Turn to Throw Again," *Baltimore Sun*, September 24, 1992, 6D.

33. Rick Hines, "Leon Day: The Man Cooperstown Forgot," *Sports Collector's Digest*, March 13, 1992, 70.

34. Kern, "Leon Day."

35. Holway, *Blackball Stars*, 350.

36. Hines, "Leon Day," 71.

37. John Steadman, "Integration Couldn't Catch Up with Day's Best Fastball, Either," *Baltimore Sun*, February 3, 1992, http://articles.baltimoresun.com/1992-02-03/sports/1992034186_1_leon-day-robinson-baltimore-black-sox (accessed August 4, 2015); John B. Holway, "Day Crossed a Road Less Traveled to Cooperstown," *Washington Post*, March 19, 1995, D5.

38. Steadman, "Integration Couldn't Catch Up with Day's Best Fastball, Either."

39. "Leon Day Honored at Last," *Baltimore Sun*, March 12, 1995, 2E.

40. Snyder, "'You Made It, Man,'" 1A.

41. "Leon Day Honored at Last," 2E.

42. Brad Snyder, "Day Dies a Week after Greatest Honor," *Baltimore Sun*, March 14, 1995, 1A. For more on Geraldine Day, see Ursula V. Battle, "Widow of Baseball Hall of Famer Needs Help," *Baltimore Afro-America*, February 1, 1997, A1, A11.

43. Brad Snyder, "300-Plus Pay Last Respects to Day," *Baltimore Sun*, March 18, 1995, 4C.

44. Ibid.

45. Ibid.

46. Michael Olesker, "At the Bottom of the Ninth, a Little Justice," *Baltimore Sun*, March 16, 1995, 2C.

47. Ibid.

48. Roch Eric Kubatko, "Maryland Honors Day, Star in Negro Leagues," *Baltimore Sun*, May 19, 1992, B5.

49. Ibid.

50. James A. Riley, *Of Monarchs and Black Barons: Essays on Baseball's Negro Leagues* (Jefferson, NC: McFarland, 2012), 156.

51. Jamie Smith, "Take Me Out to the Leon Day Park," *Baltimore Sun*, August 24, 1997, 3B.

52. See Leon Day Foundation, Inc., https://www.facebook.com/pages/The-Leon-Day-Foundation-Inc/576794845683514?sk=info&tab=page_info (accessed July 17, 2015).

53. Bob Maisel, "No Doubt about It Brooks Is the Star," *Baltimore Sun*, August 1, 1983, C1.

54. Harry Hooper, quoted in Lawrence S. Ritter, *The Glory of Their Times* (New York: William Morrow and Company, [1966] 1984), 222.

55. John Schulian, "Bawlmer Keeps Babbling about Brooks—Robinson," *Chicago Sun-Times*, July 31, 1983, 91.

56. Thomas Boswell, *The Heart of the Order* (New York: Penguin Books, 1989), 21.

57. Bob Maisel, "Orioles," *Baltimore Sun*, September 18, 1955, 1D; Doug Wilson, *Brooks: The Biography of Brooks Robinson* (New York: Thomas Dunne Books, 2014), 57–58.

58. Ed Linn, "Why Everyone Loves Brooks Robinson," *Sport*, June 1972, 80.

59. Boswell, *The Heart of the Order*, 22–23.

60. Linn, "Why Everyone Loves Brooks Robinson," 78.

61. Quoted in Wilson, *Brooks*, 207.

62. See http://www.baseball-reference.com/players/r/robinbr01.shtml (July 31, 2015).

63. Wilson, *Brooks*, 216.

64. Alan Goldstein, "Only Robinson's Eyes Remain Dry," *Baltimore Sun*, September 19, 1977, C5.

65. Bob Maisel, "The Morning After," *Baltimore Sun*, September 19, 1977, C5.

66. See http://www.baseball-reference.com/players/r/robinbr01.shtml (July 31, 2015).

67. Jeff Gordon, "He Shares Day with Adopted Hometown," (Baltimore) *News American*, August 1, 1983, 4A.

68. See http://mlb.mlb.com/mlb/history/mlb_history_moreinfo.jsp (August 4, 2015). The other third basemen are George Brett, Eddie Matthews, Paul Molitor, Mike Schmidt, and Pie Traynor.

69. Frank Robinson and Berry Stainback, *Extra Innings* (New York: McGraw-Hill, 1988), 63.

70. Wilson, *Brooks*, 285.

71. Quoted in Doug Brown, "In '77, Brooks Offered Final Thrill," *Baltimore Sun*, May 18, 1995, 7C.

72. Wilson, *Brooks*, 3.

73. Robert Lipsyte, "The Emasculation of Sports," *New York Times Magazine*, April 2, 1995, 52.

74. Jim Murray, "Baseball's Living Legend," *Los Angeles Times*, July 21, 1971, E1.

75. Quoted in Schulian, "Bawlmer Keeps Babbling about Brooks—Robinson," 91.

76. Goldstein, "Only Robinson's Eyes Remain Dry," C5.

77. Quoted in Mike Klingaman, "Rosenberg Man behind Statue of Brooks Robinson," *Baltimore Sun*, October 22, 2011, http://www.baltimoresun.com/sports/orioles/bs-sp-brooks-sculpture-20111021-story.html (accessed August 5, 2015).

78. Quoted in Jeff Seidel, "Brooks Honored with Statue at Camden Yard," September 29, 2012, http://mlb.mlb.com/news/print.jsp?ymd=20120929&content_id=39218330&c_id=mlb (accessed August 4, 2015).

79. Quoted in ibid.

80. Quoted in ibid.

81. Pete Caldera, "Why I Love . . . Baltimore," *Arrive*, March/April 2007, 68.

82. Mark Maske, "Ex-Manager Spent 36 Years with Team," *Washington Post*, March 26, 1999, D1, D3.

83. *Baltimore Sun*, October 10, 2001, 14S-15S.

84. Heywood Hale Broun, "The Twin Symbols of Baseball's Timeless Virtues," *New York Times*, September 3, 1995, sec. 8, p. 13.

85. Mark Maske, "The Evolution of a Major League Disaster," *Washington Post*, September 18, 1994, D1.

86. Curry Kirkpatrick, "The Pride of the Orioles," *Newsweek*, September 11, 1995, 79.

87. Ibid.

88. See Daniel A. Nathan and Mary G. McDonald, "Yearning for Yesteryear: Cal Ripken, Jr., the Streak, and the Politics of Nostalgia," *American Studies* 42, no. 1 (Spring 2001): 99–123.

89. "Cal Ripken Jr.," *People*, December 25, 1995, 107.

90. John Eisenberg, *From 33rd Street to Camden Yards: An Oral History of the Baltimore Orioles* (New York: Contemporary Books, 2001), 441.

91. Quoted in William Gildea, "Ripken, Gehrig Share a Numerical Bond," *Washington Post*, September 7, 1995, B6.

92. John Steadman, "This Sentimental Journey Is One for Ages 2,131," *Baltimore Sun*, September 7, 1995, 8C.

93. Thomas Boswell, "Nothing Streaky about Cal," *Washington Post*, September 6, 1995, B1.

94. *Baltimore Evening Sun*, September 7, 1995, 1.

95. "Aberdeen's best," *Baltimore Evening Sun*, September 7, 1995, 14A.

96. Years later, in John Eisenberg's oral history of the Orioles, Brooks Robinson said: "As Cal's streak unfolded, I thought it was unbelievable. I think he played a lot of times when he probably shouldn't have, and probably played a lot of times when it was detrimental to the club, but Cal's got that thing that clicks on and says, 'Hey, if there's a game, I have to be there.' I had it." Eisenberg, *From 33rd Street to Camden Yards*, 444.

97. Quoted in Bill Koenig, "The Iron Man Rests," *Baseball Weekly*, September 23–29, 1998, 3.

98. Ibid., 17.

99. "How Ripken's Night Unfolded," *Baltimore Sun*, October 7, 2001, 8D.

100. Quoted in M. Dion Thompson, "Fans Say City, Iron Man Were Perfect Fit," *Baltimore Sun*, October 7, 2001, 11D.

101. Ibid.

102. Childs Walker, "Ripken Ranks in Big 3," *Baltimore Sun*, 2007, 6E.

103. Thomas Boswell, "By Numbers Alone, Character Counts," *Washington Post*, July 30, 2007, E1.

104. Quoted in ibid.

105. Quoted in Harvey Rosenfeld, *Iron Man: The Cal Ripken, Jr. Story* (New York: St. Martin's Press, [1995] 1996), 280.

106. Thomas Boswell, "Quiet Cal Speaks Volumes," *Washington Post*, June 30, 1996, D9.

107. David W. Zang, *I Wore Babe Ruth's Hat: Field Notes from a Life in Sports* (Urbana: University of Illinois Press, 2015), 192.

108. Laura Lippman, *Baltimore Blues* (New York: Avon Books, 1997), 80.

109. Frank Deford, "From Baltimore, Another Working-Class Hero," *Washington Post*, September 6, 1995, F2.

19. The Ravens' Flight to Normalcy: How Winning Restored Baltimore's Football Culture

1. Aaron Wilson, "Ravens to Square off with Chuck Pagano, Colts in First-Round Playoff Game," *Baltimore Sun*, December 30, 2012, http://www.baltimoresun.com/sports/ravens/ravens-insider/bal-ravens-to-square-off-with-chuck-pagano-colts-in-firstround-playoff-game-20121230,0,6106229.story (accessed September 30, 2014).

2. Quoted in William Gildea, *When the Colts Belonged to Baltimore: A Father and a Son, a Team and a Time* (New York: Ticknor & Fields, 1994), 11. Ogden Nash, "Colts Is the Name, Football's the Game," *Life*, December 13, 1968, 75.

3. Michael MacCambridge, *America's Game: The Epic Story of How Pro Football Captured a Nation* (New York: Random House, 2004), 356–61.

4. Quoted in Jon Morgan, *Glory for Sale: Fans, Dollars, and the New NFL* (Baltimore: Bancroft Press, 1997), 195.

5. Quoted in ibid., 196.

6. Quoted in ibid., 195.

7. Michael Farber, "But Don't Call Them the Colts," *Sports Illustrated*, July 25, 1994, 57.

8. Ibid., 58.

9. Ted Patterson, *Football in Baltimore: History and Memorabilia* (Baltimore: Johns Hopkins University Press, 2000), 236–37.

10. David Harris, *The League: The Rise and Decline of the NFL* (New York: Bantam, 1986), 65–66.

11. Jon Morgan, "Inside the Browns Deal," *Baltimore Sun*, December 17, 1995, 12C.

12. Jon Morgan, *Gaining a Yard: The Building of Baltimore's Football Stadium* (Baltimore: Baltimore Sun 1998), 13.

13. Morgan, *Glory for* Sale, 5.

14. John Steadman, *From Colts to Ravens: A Behind-the-Scenes Look at Baltimore Professional Football* (Centreville, MD: Tidewater Publishers, 1997), 224.

15. See Milton Kent, "Trumpy: I Owe Fans No Apologies," *Baltimore Sun*, August 29, 1996, 1D.

16. *Preview: The Official Magazine of the Baltimore Ravens*, distributed by *Baltimore Sun*, 1998 Training Camp Issue, 8.

17. Jonathan Ogden and Andrew Lawrence, "The Way We Were: An Original Raven Reflects on the Early Years and the Foundation for Greatness," *Sports Illustrated Special Commemorative Issue: Super Bowl XLVII*, February 14, 2013, 80.

18. Larry Felser, "Baltimore Ravens: With All-World Defense and a Velvet Touch from Elvis, the Ravens Can't Help but Get Even Better," *Street & Smith's Pro Football 2001*, 83–85.

19. Quoted in Pete McEntegart, "This One's for You, Mr. Modell," *Sports Illustrated Presents: Champs! The Baltimore Ravens, Super Bowl Champions, 2001 Season*, 52.

20. Josh Elliot, "They Walked the Walk," *Sports Illustrated Presents: Champs!* 54–55.

21. See, for example, Nestor Aparicio, WNST-AM, *Purple Reign 2: Faith, Family, and Football in Baltimore, A Love Story*, http://www.wnst.net/author/nestoraparicio (accessed September 6, 2014).

22. "Staying Alive," *ESPN Magazine*, February 5, 2001, 67.

23. David Foster Wallace, *Consider the Lobster: And Other Essays* (New York: Back Bay Books/Little, Brown and Company, 2006), 150.

24. Don Banks, "Call of the Wild: AFC Wild-Card Round," *Sports Illustrated Special Commemorative Issue: Super Bowl XLVII*, 31.

25. Ibid.

26. Quoted in S. L. Price, "The Gospel according to Ray," *Sports Illustrated*, November 13, 2006, 80, reprinted as "The Book of Ray," in *Sports Illustrated Special Commemorative Issue: Super Bowl XLVII*, 73.

27. Ibid.

20. A Phelpsian Triptych: Mountain, Machine, and Man

1. See Pro-Football Reference.com http://www.pro-football-reference.com/play-index/comeback.cgi?player=UnitJo00 (accessed September 1, 2014).

2. "Omega releases official photos of 100-meter butterfly finish," August 23, 2008, http://sports.espn.go.com/oly/summer08/swimming/news/story?id=3550164 (accessed November 9, 2013).

3. Paul McMullen, "How They Got Started: First Impressions of Cal Ripken Jr., Michael Phelps and Others," October 15, 2013, http://www.pressboxonline.com/2013/10/11/how-they-got-started (accessed July 25, 2015).

4. See "Olympics 30: Great Olympic Stories," Michael Phelps, http://www.olympics30.com/30goldmedalists/michaelphelps.asp (accessed September 1, 2014).

5. Ryan Sebring, Sports Talk Show Host, 105.7 The Fan, Interview, March 20, 2013.

6. Peter Schmuck, "Make Room on Our Rushmore," *Baltimore Sun*, August 5, 2012, Sports, 7.

7. McMullen, interview, October 15, 2013.

8. Ibid.

9. Paul McMullen, *Amazing Pace: The Story of an Olympic Champion from Athens to Sydney to Beijing* (Emmaus, PA: Rodale Press, 2006), 2.

10. Ibid.

11. Lisa Dillman, "Ryan Lochte Whips Michael Phelps to Win 400-Meter Individual Medley," *Los Angeles Times*, July 28, 2012, http://articles.latimes.com/2012/jul/28/ sports/la-sp-on-ryan-lochte-20120728 (accessed June 5, 2014).

12. Michael Phelps, Twitter post, August 16, 2012, 7:42 a.m., https://twitter.com/MichaelPhelps/status/236110615758925825.

13. McMullen, interview, October 15, 2013.

14. Bruce Cunningham, interview, October 2, 2013.

15. McMullen, interview, October 15, 2013.

16. Ibid.

17. Quoted in Schmuck, "Make Room on Our Rushmore," 7.

18. Michael Phelps, Twitter post, September 1, 2013, https://twitter.com/MichaelPhelps/status/374333104887836672 (accessed September 1, 2014).

19. Kevin Byrne, "Olympian Michael Phelps as Kick Returner," *The Byrne Identity*, October 4, 2013, http://www.baltimoreravens.com/news/article-1/The-Byrne-Identity-Ozzie-Newsome-Explains-Decision-Behind-Trade/0e16104b-9966-43af-8650-ad579c999958 (accessed November 15, 2013).

20. Associated Press, "Olympic Legend Michael Phelps Ending Retirement," April 14, 2014, http://www.foxnews.com/sports/2014/04/14/olympic-legend-michael-phelps-ending-retirement/ (accessed June 26, 2014).

21. Jeff Metcalf, "Michael Phelps on Comeback: 'I'm Doing This for Me,'" *USA Today*, April 24, 2014, http://www.usatoday.com/story/sports/olympics/2014/04/23/michael-phelps-first-meet-london-olympics/8070765/ (accessed June 26, 2014).

Contributors

Daniel A. Nathan is a professor of American studies at Skidmore College. The author of *Saying It's So: A Cultural History of the Black Sox Scandal* (2003) and editor of *Rooting for the Home Team: Sport, Community, and Identity* (2013), he has published essays and book, film, and exhibition reviews for a variety of periodicals. Nathan has served as the film, media, and museum reviews editor for the *Journal of Sport History*, is on several editorial boards, and is past president of the North American Society for Sport History.

David K. Wiggins is professor and codirector of the Center for the Study of Sport and Leisure in Society at George Mason University. His primary research interest is issues of race and sport. He has published numerous essays and written or edited several books, including *Glory Bound: Black Athletes in a White America* and *Rivals: Legendary Matchups That Made Sport History*. He is the former editor of *Quest* and the *Journal of Sport History*.

A former *Baltimore Sun* reporter and staff writer for HBO's *The Wire*, **Rafael Alvarez** writes fiction and nonfiction. His books include *Hometown Boy: The Hoodle Patrol and Other Curiosities of Baltimore* (1999), *Storyteller* (2001), *The Wire: Truth Be Told* (2004), and *Tales from the Holy Land* (2014), among others. In 2014, *Baltimore* magazine's Best of Baltimore issue named him the city's Best Writer.

An Ohio Wesleyan University graduate, **Jerry Bembry** has written for the *Baltimore Sun*, ESPN.com, and *ESPN The Magazine* and taught journalism at Towson University and Morgan State University. He lives in Los Angeles and is a senior writer for a soon-to-be-launched ESPN website that will cover sports, race, and culture.

Chad Carlson is an assistant professor of kinesiology and an assistant men's basketball coach at Hope College. His research interests include the sociocultural aspects of sport and physical activity. Carlson has written on the metaphysics of play and games, sport ethics, race and sport, and the history of basketball. His work has been published in a variety of journals and edited collections. He is currently working on a book about the history of the NCAA and NIT basketball tournaments.

James Coates is a University of Maryland alumnus, a former University of Wisconsin-Green Bay education professor, and longtime member of the North American Society for Sport History. He specializes in American sports history, African American sports history, coaching, and multicultural education.

Amira Rose Davis is a PhD candidate in history at Johns Hopkins University where she studies twentieth-century US history with an emphasis on race, sports, and politics. She is completing her dissertation on the institutional, political, and ideological development of black women's athletics from the 1900s to the 1960s. Her article "No League of Their Own: Baseball, Black Women and the Politics of Representation" is in the *Radical History Review*.

Ari de Wilde is an assistant professor of kinesiology and physical education at Eastern Connecticut State University. His work has appeared in the *Journal of Macromarketing, Journal of Historical Research in Marketing, Journal of Sport History, Quest,* and *International Journal of Sport Management.*

Hannah Doban is a Skidmore College graduate, where she majored in American studies and psychology. She is interested in mass media and popular culture, specifically as it relates to television and film. She intends to be a television writer and critic.

Chris Elzey teaches in the history/art history department at George Mason University. He also oversees the sport and American culture minor and codirects the Center for the Study of Sport and Leisure in Society at George Mason. He has written on the Olympics and basketball, which he has played professionally abroad.

Dennis Gildea, a former sportswriter and sports editor, is a professor of communications at Springfield College (the birthplace of basketball). In addition to publishing numerous articles and book chapters, Gildea is the author of *Hoop Crazy: The Lives of Clair Bee and Chip Hilton* (2013).

A Baltimore native, **William Gildea** was a *Washington Post* staff writer from 1965 to 2005 and is the author of *When the Colts Belonged to Baltimore: A Father and a Son, A Team and a Time* (1994), *Where the Game Matters Most: A Last Championship Season in Indiana High School Basketball* (1997), and *The Longest Fight: In the Ring with Joe Gans, Boxing's First African American Champion* (2012), among other books.

A Johns Hopkins University alumnus, **Neil A. Grauer** is the creator of the cartoon Hopkins Blue Jay and the assistant director of editorial services for the Johns Hopkins Medicine Office of Marketing and Communications. He has written for *American Heritage*, *Smithsonian*, the *Baltimore Sun*, the *Washington Post*, and other publications. Among his books are *Remember Laughter: A Life of James Thurber* (1995), *Centuries of Caring: The Johns Hopkins Bayview Medical Center Story* (2004), and the coauthored second edition of *Lacrosse: Technique and Tradition* (2006).

Richard Hardesty is a PhD candidate in history at George Mason University. He is writing his dissertation about the Baltimore Orioles, urban development, and civil rights and is the author of "'[A] Veil of Voodoo': George P. Mahoney, Open Housing, and the 1966 Governor's Race" (2009), which explores white backlash in Maryland during the mid-1960s.

Stacy Karten grew up in the duckpin bowling hotbed of Baltimore. He worked in bowling center marketing for over thirty years. Karten was editor and publisher of the *Duckpin News* for twenty-seven years and still maintains a website and Facebook page for the *Duckpin News*. He has contributed a monthly marketing column to *Bowling Center Management* magazine for twenty years. A graduate of the University of Maryland, Karten served as contributing/sports editor for the *Baltimore Jewish Times* for eight years.

A Skidmore College graduate, **Nevon Kipperman** studies media culture and film. She was a student assistant for the American studies faculty at Skidmore, where she edited and conducted research for various projects, including a chapter on Los Angeles and sport films, the second edition of *Baseball without Borders: The International Pastime*, and a book about doomsday preppers.

Charles Kupfer, a former reporter, is an associate professor of American studies and history at Penn State Harrisburg and the author of *We Felt the Flames: Hitler's Blitzkrieg, America's Story* (2003) and *Indomitable Will: Turning Defeat into Victory from Pearl Harbor to Midway* (2012). He is past president of the Middle Atlantic American Studies Association.

Lee Lowenfish is the author of the baseball labor history *The Imperfect Diamond*, originally published in 1980 and updated in 1991 and 2010. He collaborated on Tom Seaver's *The Art of Pitching* (1984). His biography *Branch Rickey: Baseball's Ferocious Gentleman* (2009) won the Society for American Baseball Research's 2008 Seymour Medal for the best book published in baseball biography or history from the previous year and a Choice award from the American Library Association.

Elizabeth M. Nix is a professor of legal, ethical, and historical studies at the University of Baltimore, and coeditor with Jessica Elfenbein and Thomas Hollowak of *Baltimore '68: Riots and Rebirth in an American City* (2011).

Michael Olesker is the author of *The Colts' Baltimore: A City and Its Love Affair in the 1950s* (2008), *Front Stoops in the Fifties: Baltimore Legends Come of Age* (2013), and several other books. He spent twenty-five years as a metro columnist for the *Baltimore Sun* and twenty years as a nightly news commentator on WJZ-TV's *Eyewitness News*.

A graduate of Miami University, **Ted Patterson** had a forty-five-year career as a radio and television sportscaster. He was the sports director for WBAL, the nighttime sports anchor at WMAR-TV, and the sports director at WPOC radio. Patterson has been honored three times as Maryland Sportscaster of the Year and in 1979 won the Eclipse Award for his coverage of thoroughbred racing in Maryland. He is the author of *Baltimore Orioles: Four Decades of Magic from 33rd Street to Camden Yards* (1994) and *Football in Baltimore: History and Memorabilia* (2000), among other books.

Dean Bartoli Smith has covered the Baltimore Ravens and the Orioles for the *Baltimore Brew*. His sportswriting has appeared in *Press Box, Fan Magazine, Baltimore City Paper*, and on the websites Patch.com and the Midnight Mind Review. He is the director of the Cornell University Press and the author of *American Boy* (2000), a volume of poetry, and *Never Easy, Never Pretty: A Fan, a City, a Championship Season* (2013).

David W. Zang is the author of the award-winning *Fleet Walker's Divided Heart: The Life of Baseball's First Black Major Leaguer* (1995), *SportsWars: Athletes in the Age of Aquarius* (2001), and *I Wore Babe Ruth's Hat: Field Notes from a Life in Sports* (2015), and the producer of the documentary film *For the Love of Soul: A Story of Color, Music, and the Sixties* (2010)

Index

Note: Page number followed by and n and a number indicate endnotes. Page numbers in italic indicate an illustration.